Contents

Contributors

Colin Bamford is Professor and Head of the Department of Logistics and Hospitality Management at the University of Huddersfield. He has written various applied Economics textbooks and more specialist articles in his field of transport economics. Currently Chief Examiner in Economics with OCR, he has 30 years experience of examining at A Level.

Keith Brunskill was formerly Head of Economics at Greenhead College, Huddersfield. He is currently a part-time member of staff at Huddersfield University Business School. An experienced A Level examiner with various examination boards, including OCR, he has written a wide range of articles on topical areas of Economics.

Gordon Cain is a Sector Manager in Management, Leisure and Business at Bury College. He has taught A Level Economics in a range of schools and colleges. He is a Principal Examiner with CIE, with over 25 years experience of examining at A Level.

Richard Crum was a Lecturer in Economics at the University of East Anglia until his early retirement. He still teaches at the University, in particular on courses at all levels. He has had extensive A Level examining experience, including for many years Chief Examiner in Economics with the Oxford Delegacy.

Susan Grant is a Lecturer in Economics at West Oxfordshire College. She is an experienced examiner and written various text books and articles on Economics. She is a Principal Examiner with OCR and has a specialist area of interest in macroeconomic policies.

Stephen Munday is Principal of Comberton Village College in Cambridgeshire. He has produced recent textbooks on Markets and Market Failure. He is a Principal Examiner with OCR and has a specialism in market failure and government intervention.

Steve Tidball is Head of Economics and Business Studies and Housemaster at Ipswich School. He has written extensively for A Level students and is a regular contributor to *Economics Today*. A former Principal Examiner with OCR, he is a Principal Examiner with the Insitute of Export, a question setter and moderator with CIE and the IB Organisation.

Stephen Walton is Head of Economics at the Kings School Chester, having previously taught in Surrey. He is a Principal Examiner with OCR and has a specialism in aspects of the Economics of Europe.

Tony Westaway is a Senior Lecturer in Economics at Loughborough University. He is a Principal Examiner with OCR and has 25 years experience of examining at A Level. His specialist areas of interest are in welfare economics and the economics of sport and leisure.

Preface

A warm welcome to the second edition of *Economics for AS*.

This new edition has been specifically produced for OCR's revised AS/A Level specification in Economics for teaching from September 2003. It incorporates important changes to the methods of assessment and a few minor modifications to the specification content as approved by the Qualifications and Curriculum Authority (QCA).

The book contains certain new features including:

- a full set of specimen examination papers for each of OCR's AS Level units;
- new self-assessment tasks which have been adapted from various AS Level examination papers that have been set by OCR since January 2001;
- an update of statistical material in the Introduction and Unit 3 especially;
- a full real examination paper at the end of each of the three AS Level units; this is intended to be completed in $1\frac{1}{2}$ hours and is therefore $\frac{1}{2}$ hour longer than current AS Level examinations.

The authors have been very encouraged by the comments that have been received on the first edition from students and teachers. We have sought to include many of the suggestions that have been made in this new edition.

We have also been encouraged by the extent to which the first edition has been used by students taking AQA's and Edexcel's AS Level papers. Although aspects of the assessment arrangements are different, the content of Units 1, 2 and 3 is essentially the same for all awarding body specifications.

Finally, could I record my thanks to various people who have made this new edition possible. In particular to:

- Stephen Walton for updating sections 12 and 13 of the A2 synoptic unit.
- My fellow authors for entrusting me to make the remaining modifications, incorporating feedback that they have provided.
- Karen Brooke for assistance with word processing.
- Anne Rix for editing this new edition, building upon her management of the first edition.
- My wife Elisabeth and daughters Emily and Alice who have been very understanding and patient when I have been working to a deadline.

One of the most gratifying observations that can be made over the short life of the AS Level is that Economics as a subject appears ' to be on an upward trend'. Teachers should be encouraged and take much of the credit for this. Let us all hope that in the future, Economics will continue to interest and inspire those students who choose to study it. If this book has in any way contributed to this reversal of fortunes, the time and energy spent on its production will have been very worthwhile indeed.

Colin G Bamford
Head, Dept. of Logistics and Hospitality Management
University of Huddersfield
Chief Examiner, OCR Economics AS/A Level

February 2003

Introduction

The economist's 'tool kit' and the OCR examination

On completion of this unit you should:

➤ have a broad idea of what is meant by Economics
➤ know how economists seek to explain economic phenomena
➤ be aware of the 'tool kit' of skills required at AS level
➤ be aware of the structure of the OCR AS/A Level Economics specification

What is Economics?

There are almost as many definitions of Economics as there are economists! Although a definition of the subject is to be expected, it is probably more useful at this stage to set out a few examples of the sort of issues which concern professional economists. These topics occur in an introductory form in the OCR AS specification.

Let us take yourself first of all. Most teenagers find that they want to lead an exciting and full life but unfortunately do not always have the money necessary to do everything they would like to do. So, choices have to be made or, as an economist would say, individuals have to decide:

> How to allocate scarce resources in the most effective way?

A body of economic principles and concepts has been developed to explain how people and also businesses, react in this situation. This is a typical example of what an economist would refer to as 'microeconomics'.

It is not only individuals and firms who are faced with having to make choices. Governments face many such problems. For example, how does our government decide how much to spend on the National Health Service and how much should go into providing Social Security benefits? This is the same type of problem facing all of us in our daily lives but on a different scale.

The UK government also has extensive responsibilities in looking after the well-being of our national economy. The Chancellor of the Exchequer, for example, prepares an annual Budget for the economy, in which taxation and government expenditure plans are reviewed. It is also an opportunity to 'manage the economy', by seeking to ensure that policy objectives are being met. As the economist would say, the Chancellor has to decide:

> 'Which taxes to raise to fund a better health service' or, alternatively, 'how to reflate the economy to increase the number of jobs which are available'.

These are typical topics which come under the broad heading of 'macroeconomics' since they relate to the economy as a whole.

As you progress through this text you will come across many other economic problems and issues of both a micro and macro nature. You may now find it useful to complete the following self-assessment tasks.

Self-assessment tasks

1 Make a list, in your own words, of some of the economic decisions that:
     ◆ you are facing;
     ◆ your family has to take;
     ◆ the country has to take.
2 Pick up any quality newspaper. Look through it systematically and make a note of the various:
     ◆ microeconomic,
     ◆ macroeconomic
   problems and issues you find.
   Have you found it easy to classify problems in this way?

Source: Photo by Ann Doherty, *Sunday Times,* London.

The last part of the task is designed to get you to appreciate that many economic problems and issues cannot be satisfactorily classified as micro or macro. In other words, such problems encompass both of the main branches of Economics. For example, an increase in prescription charges may reduce the demand for prescriptions from patients – depending on the extent of this there is an effect on the income of individuals and the government and, in turn, this affects the economy as a whole. So, there can be complex inter-relationships coming into play. In many respects this makes Economics an interesting subject to study.

As you progress through this text, you will be introduced to concepts, theories and simple models which are used by economists to explain the many economic problems and issues which come within the scope of Economics. In time, you will build up a portfolio of such techniques, from a micro- and macroeconomic perspective. Virtually all have their origin in some sort of empirical investigation, that is a study of real economic phenomena. Some concepts

have their origin 200 years ago, others are much more contemporary or may have been refined and revised in the light of the growing complexity of the present-day global economy. Again, this serves to enhance the interesting nature of the subject.

Regardless of what you may think about Economics and economists at this stage of your AS studies, few would deny that Economics is a logical subject and that the advice provided by economists is derived from a set of well established principles relating to the operation of the market economy. Many of these are set out in unit 1 of this text. Figure 1 shows in simple terms how economists think and how they seek to explain real problems and issues like those you will have come across in the Self-assessment task above.

At this stage, bear the process shown in figure 1 in mind and return to it whenever you are learning new concepts as it will help you understand how economists think and operate.

To conclude, therefore, it is appropriate to give a clear definition of 'What is Economics?' For a start,

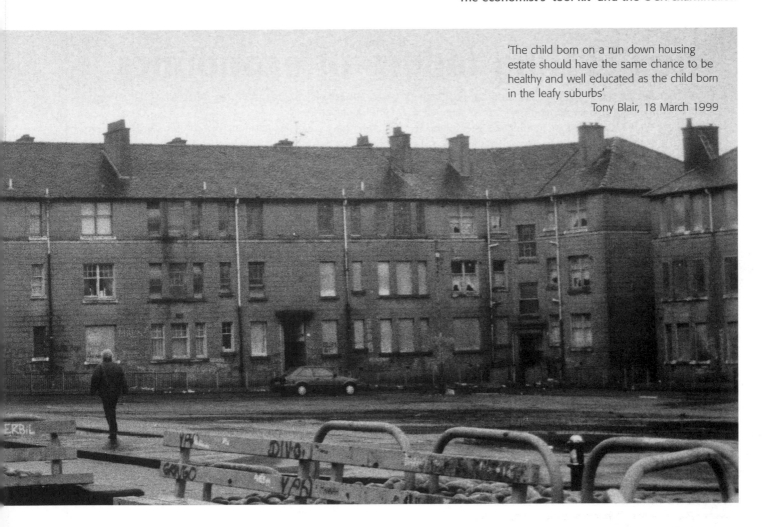

'The child born on a run down housing estate should have the same chance to be healthy and well educated as the child born in the leafy suburbs'

Tony Blair, 18 March 1999

Problem	Statement of a particular economic problem or issue.
Analysis	Application of concepts and techniques of Economics.
Outcome	The result of economic analysis.
Evaluation	An appraisal of the extent to which the outcome is acceptable for individuals or groups.

Figure 1 The road to economic explanation

Self-assessment task

Think again about what you have found out in completing the first Self-assessment task. Now read the article from *The Economist* on the so-called puzzling failure of Economics. Do you agree at this early stage of your studies with what the author is saying? Why might you not yet be in a position to make a proper evaluation?

The puzzling failure of economics

If the world were run by economists, would it be a better place? You might expect economists, not to mention a newspaper called *The Economist*, to think so. After all, many of the policies that people fight over have economics at their core – jobs, wages, investment, growth. Economists, professional and otherwise, are forever criticising those who do run the world for making such a mess of it, and are keen to change the way people think so that things will be run more to their liking. As one Nobel laureate put it, 'I don't care who writes a nation's laws ... if I can write its economics textbooks.'

Paul Samuelson, the author of that remark, has seen his wish fulfilled. His 'Economics', first published in 1948, has sold millions of copies and is still, with its 16th edition in preparation, doing well. Down the editions, the book's views on policy have changed, as have those of the profession at large. These shifting ideas have in turn influenced policy, and to a degree that would make other social scientists drool. Lately the results have been good. During the past decade, some of the worst economic incompetence has ended: central planning has given way to 'transition economics' in Eastern Europe and the former Soviet Union; many developing countries have opened their economies to the outside world; every week another state-run company is put up for sale. Textbook wisdom seems to prevail.

The message and the messenger

But don't praise the dismal scientists too much. Who designed those earlier policies, which failed so disastrously? Economists. Where were those theories of planning, of demand management, of industrial dirigisme and public ownership that did such harm in the third world so persuasively set out? In economics textbooks.

These days, it is true, the advice is better – but it often gets dangerously garbled in transmission. Trade is the best example. By pitting exporters against importers, successive rounds of trade negotiations have encouraged politicians in many countries to lower trade barriers. Yet this effort is based on a false premise: that freeing trade is good for you only if other countries do the same. This basic misunderstanding, left unattended, may one day lead governments to turn back the clock on liberal trade.

Other good policies have likewise been founded on bad economics. Privatisation, for instance, has more often been seen as a way to raise revenue than as a way to promote competition; and deregulation is often portrayed by governments as something that global markets have forced upon them, rather than as a way of raising living standards. As for bad policies based on bad economics, these remain too numerous to mention, despite Mr Samuelson's prodigious efforts.

Why has economics not done better? Economists tend to blame others for being too lazy or too stupid to understand their textbooks. There is doubtless something in this. Economics is hard to teach well. To the uninitiated, its basic principles often seem surprising or odd. And whereas most people will admit their ignorance of physics or biology, the armchair economist is convinced that he knows exactly what he is talking about.

But the economics profession itself also deserves much of the blame. Crucial ideas about the role of prices and markets, the basic principles of microeconomics, are uncontroversial among economists. These are the first ideas that politicians and the public need to grasp if they are to think intelligently about public policy, and the fact is that they are not widely understood. Yet because economists take these essential ideas for granted, they spend their time arguing about much more contentious notions, developed in one disputed way or another from those common underlying principles. The public and their politicians are treated to perpetual squabbles about the exact effects of raising interest rates or of cutting the capital-gains tax or whatever – and conclude that economists disagree about everything and understand nothing. As long as economists choose to talk loudest about the things they understand least well and to remain silent about the underlying ideas that unite them, this is unlikely to change.

And economists must shoulder a further portion of the blame for quite another reason. The biggest economic-policy mistake of the past 50 years, in rich and poor countries alike, has been and still is to expect too much of government. Statism has always found all the support it needs among mainstream economists. They are unfailingly quick to point out various species of market failure; they are usually much slower to ask whether the supposed remedy of government intervention might not, in practice, be worse.

This is not a failure of economics, in fact, but of modern (one might say Samuelsonian) economics. The classical economists viewed the market economy with a kind of awe. Amazing, it truly is, that all these workers, firms and households, acting without visible co-ordination and guided mainly by self-interest, manage to produce such extraordinarily beneficial results. Smith's 'Wealth of Nations' conveyed this sense that the market, for all its 'failures', is a marvel. Today precious few textbooks even try to guide their readers to any such inspiration. Implicitly, at least, their message is too often quite the opposite: that markets aren't perfect and governments (advised by economists) can be. Dismal is the word.

Source: The Economist, 23 August 1997.

Economics is a social science – it adopts a scientific framework but is particularly concerned with studying human behaviour, as consumers, in business or in taking decisions about the economy as a whole. More specifically:

Economics is the study of how scarce resources are or should be allocated.

All of the problems and issues you will come across fit into this broad definition.

The economist's 'tool kit'

The economist has a varied 'tool kit', the term that can be used to describe the skills and techniques available for the analysis of economic problems. Two that are introduced in the AS examinations are:

- the ability to interpret and use data;
- the ability to write in a clear and effective way.

Each of these will now be considered. *You may find it helpful to return to these parts intermittently when you are undertaking some of the Self-assessment tasks in the main units of the book. You should also refer back to this part before you take any of the OCR AS or A2 examinations.*

Data skills

Five main skills are required in the AS specification – they will be further examined at the A2 stage. These skills are:

- the ability to pick out the main trends and features in economic data;
- a knowledge of fractions, percentages, proportions and the rate of change in a set of time-series data;
- a working knowledge of index numbers;
- how to calculate a simple average and know what it means;
- how to understand economic information produced in visual form.

In addition, you will find it useful to know:

- how to plan an investigation into economic problems;
- what is meant by a forecast.

Each of the above will now be looked at. It is important that you feel confident in handling data – these simple skills will help you. You will also gain confidence as you become more familiar with economic data and complete the various self-assessment tasks in each section.

Economic data generally are of two main types. These are:

Time-series data – as the name suggests, the same information is recorded over a period of time, namely a period of years, for months in a year, days in a week and so on.

Cross-sectional data – the easiest way to imagine this type of data is in terms of a 'snapshot', that is a picture taken at a given time.

Another important introductory point concerns the nature of the data itself. Again two types can be recognised, namely:

Discrete data – the simplest way to imagine these is in terms of values which are shown as whole numbers, for example the number of people or number of cars.

Continuous data – such values can usually be measured in a precise way and are not confined to whole numbers, for example income, hours of work or economic growth.

So, when you are confronted with economic data for the first time, ask yourself:

- Is the data shown time-series or cross-sectional data?
- Are the values of the data discrete or continuous?

Data skill 1 – How to pick out the main trends and features in economic data

Look more carefully at the data in table 1. (You will find specific reference to unemployment statistics in section 7.)

Year	Number (in '000's)	Rate[2]	Annual charge
1992	2,769	9.7	+
1993	2,936	10.3	
1994	2,736	9.6	–
1995	2,454	8.6	–
1996	2,334	8.2	
1997	2,034	7.1	–
1998	1,766	6.1	
1999	1,710	5.8	–
2000	1,645	5.3	
2001	1,483	5.0	–

Table 1 UK Unemployment 1992–2001[1]
Notes
[1] ILO unemployment rate.
[2] Total unemployment as a percentage of all economically active persons.
Source: Regional Trends, 2002, Office for National Statistics.

The very first skill you need to develop is what is known as 'eyeballing'. All this means is looking down a column of data or going across rows of data very quickly. In examinations you should do this before you start answering the questions. For time-series data, like that in table 1, you might find it useful to very quickly write a '+' or a '–' between each year so you can see how the data changes over time. This is shown in the final column of the table. You can now tell from this that broadly speaking:

- unemployment increased between 1992 and 1993;
- it then fell consistently for the remaining years.

You can also get an overview of the data by comparing the end points in a time series, in this case 1992 and 2001. What is useful is to know how much the variable (in this case unemployment) fell over the period. To do this, you need to compare the total fall with the original level. The best way to do this is to calculate the *percentage change*. Using a calculator, this is

$$\frac{(2769 - 1483)}{2769} = 46.4\% \text{ (fall)}$$

In other words, there has been a substantial fall in unemployment of around 46 per cent over the period shown.

Looking at the cross-sectional data in table 2, you might find it useful to stand back and pick out the main patterns in these data. For example, you could look at the highest and lowest values and the difference between them. This is sometimes called the range. You could also see how each observation compares with the average. When you do this, you will find that:

- there is a difference of 5.8 per cent between the highest and the lowest;
- the average has relatively little regional significance – it is clear though that some regions, for example South East and South West, are doing better than others;
- the peripheral regions in the UK, for example Scotland and the North East, have the highest unemployment rates;
- the rate for London is very high, particularly when compared with the South East.

Both of these techniques are simple to apply – between them they give you a very useful insight into cross-sectional economic data.

Data skill 2 – Fractions, percentages, proportions and the rate of change

The simple calculations required to work with fractions, percentages and proportions should be well known to students with GCSE mathematics. (The use of percentage change over a period of time has already been referred to above.) Fractions, percentages and proportions are not far removed from each other – they are the same thing but with different names.

Let us stay with unemployment. Suppose a town has an economically active population of 50,000 and of these, 5,000 are unemployed. The unemployment rate is therefore 1 in 10 or 1/10 as a fraction, 0.10 as a proportion and 10 per cent as a percentage. The mathematical relationship is that a fraction can be converted into a proportion by dividing the bottom number or denominator into the upper number or numerator. By multiplying this by 100, a percentage can be obtained. Knowing these relatively straightforward links helps in understanding economic data.

The idea of *rate of change* is rather more difficult to grasp. It is a very relevant mathematical tool widely used and applied in Economics. Referring back to table 1, if we look at the period 1993–8, unemployment has fallen from 2.936m to 1.766m. In other words, it has fallen by 1.170m or 1,170,000 people over a period of five years. In turn, this represents a percentage fall of

Region	%	
North East	9.2	
North West	5.4	
Yorkshire and Humberside	6.1	
East Midlands	5.2	
West Midlands	6.3	UK average 5.3%
Eastern	3.6	
London	7.1	
South East	3.4	
South West	4.2	
Scotland	7.7	
Wales	6.2	
Northern Ireland	7.2	

Table 2 UK regional unemployment rates 2000[1]
Note: [1] Not seasonally adjusted.
Source: As table 1.

1.17/2.936 × 100%, that is approximately 40 per cent over this time. Averaged out, this is an 8 per cent fall per year or a rate of change of 8 per cent per annum.

Looking at table 1, we can also see that the rate of change varied over the years in question. For example, there was a particularly steep fall between 1996 and 1997 (12.9 per cent) and a modest fall from 1995 to 1996 (4.9 per cent). The figures in brackets, which are rates of change per annum, when looked at over a shorter period of time, do vary from the 8 per cent over a five year period. So, when using a rate of change, be very careful to always specify the time period you are working with.

A final word of warning. Often, with economic data, absolute totals for a particular variable might increase or decrease but the change could be at a slower or faster rate than in the past. Going back to table 1, unemployment fell consistently from 1993 to 2001. However, the rate of decrease varied quite dramatically from year to year. For example, it was just over 5 per cent from 1995 to 1996 yet almost 15 per cent between 1996 and 1997. Faced with these rates of change in isolation you might well conclude that unemployment increased between 1996 and 1997. This is clearly not true. Looking at the whole period, unemployment continued to fall but with the lowest rates of decrease towards the end of the period.

Data skill 3 – A working knowledge of index numbers

Table 3 contains a very familiar and useful set of data for economists (see section 7 for more details). Very simply the 'Index of Retail Prices' attempts to measure the underlying inflation rate, that is the annual price change for a wide basket of goods and services which are purchased by consumers. Not only is this series an index in itself, it is usual to represent it in terms of a *base year*. So, 1985 is the base year and it is given an index of 100. What this means is that the value for 1985 acts as the base value. Subsequent values are calculated in terms of the percentage change from this initial figure. For example, between 1985 and 1986, the 'Index of Retail Prices' rose 3.4 per cent. If the typical basket of shopping in 1985 had cost £20, in 1986, it would have cost £20.68. Although this is a gross simplification it illustrates how index numbers can be compiled.

So to construct an index number:

1986	103.4
⋮	⋮
1990	133.3
1991	141.8
1992	146.4
1993	148.7
1994	152.4
1995	157.1
1996	161.0
1997	165.9
1998	171.0
1999	174.9
2000	178.6
2001	182.4

Table 3 'Index of Retail Prices' in the UK, 1985–2001 (1985 = 100)
Source: *Economic Trends*, 2002, Office for National Statistics.

◆ choose a base value or a value for a base year and assign this an index of 100;
◆ divide it by 100;
◆ divide every subsequent value by this amount to calculate the index number for that value or year.

A crude 'eyeballing' of these data indicates that:
◆ retail prices have persistently increased on a year-on-year basis over the whole period;
◆ the annual rate of change has been more variable – it was particularly high between 1989 and 1990;
◆ there has been some relative slowing down in the rate of increase towards the end of the period.

Data skill 4 – How to calculate a simple average and know what it means

The *average* is a measure which is often used to summarise a particular set of data. Most of you will have come across it in GCSE mathematics, more specifically through being able to calculate various measures of average, such as the mean, median and mode. These different measures have their strengths and weaknesses from a mathematical standpoint. For the economist, usually through an arithmetic mean or weighted average, individual comparisons can be made in relation to the average for the population group as a whole. A good illustration of this is shown in table 4

Luxembourg	30,913
Denmark	22,646
Austria	18,392
Germany	18,212
Sweden	17,533
Belgium	17,397
Netherlands	16,984
Finland	16,642
France	16,596
UK	14,676
Italy	13,769
Ireland	12,824
Spain	9,665
Greece	8,047
Portugal	7,313

UK 14,676 ← EU average

Table 4 GDP per head in the EU in 2001 (£)

where the living standards of the 15 EU (European Union) member states are compared with the average for the EU as a whole.

Section 7 explains why the indicator shown in table 4, GDP per head, is a good measure of living standards. To see what is not so obvious is why the data in the table have to be looked at more critically.

Self-assessment task

Study the data in table 4.
(a) What can you deduce about relative living standards in the EU?
(b) What relevance might these data have for an economist employed by the European Commission?

Averages are also used by economists in the compilation of statistics. For example, the average weekly earnings of employed people in the UK would need to be calculated using a structured sample of all types of employee, that is male/female, professional/manual, salaried/hourly paid and so on. Its use is to give the economist a sound estimate in order to be able to make comparisons and possibly point to areas of potential poverty.

Data skills 5 – How to understand economic information produced in visual form

So far in this section all of the data used have been presented in tabular format. This might give a false impression because economists do use a much wider variety of visual means to present economic information. Charts of one form or another are a very good way of showing the main trends in data or emphasising a particular economic issue. Also, when economists produce business reports or write newspaper articles, various forms of data presentation are often used.

Figures 2 and 3 are typical examples of two such forms namely a *bar chart* and a *pie chart*. Both represent the rather tedious data of table 5 in a more effective manner. In particular it is relatively easy to see:
◆ the rank order of importance of government spending;
◆ how government expenditure in one area compares with that in another.

The basic principle behind the bar chart is that the particular economic variables (in this case social security, defence and so on) are represented by a series of bars or blocks, each of equal width. The bars though are of variable height, indicating their relative importance as measured on the vertical scale. In the pie chart, each slice of pie indicates the proportion or percentage of the total taken up by any one of the items. On figure 3, the respective percentages are indicated – this is not always the case. Students familiar with spreadsheets, such as Excel, will know that a very wide range of bar charts and pie charts can be easily produced from this software.

	% of Total
Defence	6
Health and social services	18
Transport	6
Debt interest	6
Social security	28
Education	13
Law and order	6
Other	17
	100

Table 5 Government spending in 2001/02

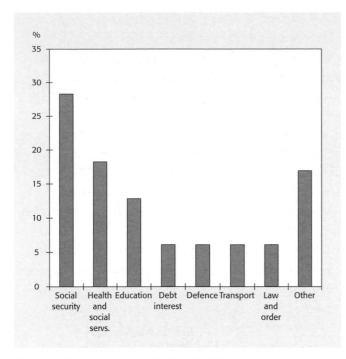

Figure 2 Government spending in 2001/02

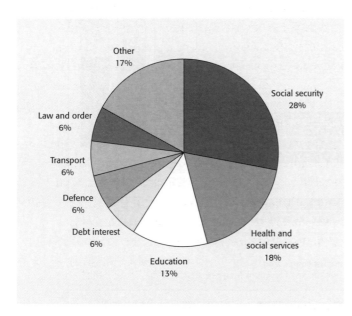

Figure 3 Government spending in 2001/02

When confronted with any chart, it is very important to look carefully at the vertical scale. In particular, see whether it has been modified to make small changes look bigger. You should also check to see if the section immediately above the origin is shown as a set of short straight cross lines. Again, this can indicate that the degree of change shown should be carefully considered.

Increasingly in newspapers, economic information is being represented in a highly attractive way in the form of inter-related graphs, charts, pictures and diagrams. A very good example of this is shown in figure 4, which contains a lot of economic information on many aspects of Premier League football including:

◆ sources of revenue for clubs;
◆ how clubs make profits or, in some cases, losses;
◆ the growing power of the Premier League clubs in football;
◆ the socio-economic profile of football spectators;
◆ the change in ticket prices and how this varies between the Premier League and other leagues.

All of the above concepts are covered in unit 1 of the book.

Self-assessment task

Study the information provided in figure 4. (You should be able to answer the following questions when you have completed unit 1.)

(a) Describe the cost structure and composition of revenue for a typical English professional football club. Why do many clubs run at a loss?

(b) Compare the revenue breakdown of Manchester United, Leeds United and Tottenham Hotspur. Do the variations shown have any economic implications for the respective clubs?

(c) In 1995/6 the rate of inflation was about 3 per cent. What might you deduce about the price elasticity of demand for football tickets?

(d) What might you deduce about the income elasticity of demand for watching football at Premier League clubs?

How economists investigate economic problems

So far in this introduction it has been assumed that the data being used by the economist are readily available and meet the particular need in hand. This is often the case – economists often use published data to support their views and theories. There are, though, many occasions where this is not possible and the economist has to carry out a specific investigation in order to obtain the data needed to make meaningful conclusions. This process in practice can be costly and time consuming.

A knowledge of how economists undertake an investigation into economic problems is very useful for

But clubs still lose out
Some clubs make big profits, but in total the 92 professional English clubs spent more than they made in 1995/96

Income £517m

million
- TV: £75
- Gate receipts/season ticket income: £218
- Commercial and other income: £224

Spending £578m

million
- Transfer fees to non-English clubs: £93
- Other operating costs: £187
- Wages and salaries: £298

How a typical Premier League club makes its money
These are estimates based on a model which takes 1995/96 as a total of 100. Gate receipts are rising – but proportionately other sources of income are rising more steeply, from a much lower base.

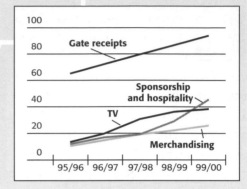

TV revenue is increasingly important

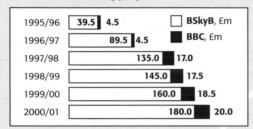

	BSkyB, £m	BBC, £m
1995/96	39.5	4.5
1996/97	89.5	4.5
1997/98	135.0	17.0
1998/99	145.0	17.5
1999/00	160.0	18.5
2000/01	180.0	20.0

How the Premier League cleans up
Percentage share of English football income

	95/96	94/95	93/94
Div 3	4.9	4.4	5.2
Div 2	8.1	8.9	7.7
Div 1	20.1	17.8	24.7
Prem	66.9	68.9	62.4

Key
- Prem
- Div 1
- Div 2
- Div 3

Earning power
Percentage of fans earning more than £30,000

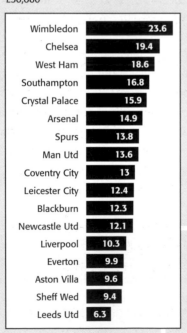

Wimbledon	23.6
Chelsea	19.4
West Ham	18.6
Southampton	16.8
Crystal Palace	15.9
Arsenal	14.9
Spurs	13.8
Man Utd	13.6
Coventry City	13
Leicester City	12.4
Blackburn	12.3
Newcastle Utd	12.1
Liverpool	10.3
Everton	9.9
Aston Villa	9.6
Sheff Wed	9.4
Leeds Utd	6.3

Going up
Average ticket prices

England	1996 (£)	1997 (£)	% increase
Premier	13.25	15.45	16.6
First	11.43	12.19	6.0
Second	10.25	10.60	3.4
Third	8.61	9.00	4.5

Scotland	1996 (£)	1997 (£)	% increase
Premier	10.56	11.78	11.5
First	9.63	10.25	6.4

Where the money comes from
Percentage breakdown of revenues for three Premier clubs

Manchester United: 35, 11, 19, 35
Leeds United: 46, 15, 29, 11
Tottenham Hotspur: 51, 10, 18, 15, 6

- Gate receipts
- TV income
- Sponsorship and hospitality
- Merchandising
- Other

Figure 4 The big match

students as it can enhance understanding of the concepts that are being measured. This involves

1 The design of an economic investigation, that is how it might be carried out and how the information might be collected.
2 The information to be collected in order to investigate a particular economic issue, that is what data are needed in order to be able to make some conclusions or calculations.

Understanding this is not easy for students of AS Economics. It does though fit more into place once the economic concepts involved have been studied and understood. Some typical examples are:

◆ how to plan an investigation into the price, income or cross elasticity of demand for the product or products of a business (see section 2);
◆ how to plan an investigation into the benefits of economies of scale for a particular firm (see section 3);
◆ how to plan an investigation into the respective costs and benefits of a particular project (see section 6).

There are others which can be added to this list, not least as most economic concepts have developed as a consequence of economists undertaking investigations.

In general, there are two main sources of original data. These are:

1 The internal information or records of a business or organisation. For example, data on fixed and variable costs could be compiled in this way as might information on the benefits gained from economies of scale. Often, though, in practice data are not always available in the specific form required by economists.
2 A particular investigation to obtain information. Often in such cases the data required are not available or have never been collected. For example, this is likely to be the case with most cost–benefit studies or for businesses looking to estimate their price elasticity of demand for a given product or service. Some sort of survey needs to be carried out to provide the first-hand data that are required.

Many investigations require a *sample survey* to be undertaken. This is intended to be representative of the population from which it is drawn and, if properly carried out, permits the economist to make statements about the population's characteristics. Various types of survey methodology (for example random, stratified or

quota) are used in practice to obtain the information that is required.

Each has their strengths and weaknesses:

1 A *simple random sample* is one where respondents have the same chance of being selected. To be able to achieve this it is usual for the population to be listed on some sort of sampling frame, such as a listing of customers or households.
2 A *stratified sample* can produce more accurate and robust estimates, mainly because the population to be sampled is split into strata on the basis of variables such as income level, sex or occupation.
3 A *quota sample* is widely used by commercial market research businesses. In such cases, a sampling frame is unlikely to be available. The quota is intended to be a 'footprint' of the population, normally in terms of some fundamental characteristic such as age, car availability and similar variables.

It is also interesting and relevant to note that most government statistics are obtained through sample surveys. A good example is the 'Index of Retail Prices' which was referred to earlier (see table 3). Other sample surveys are the *Family Expenditure Survey* and the *National Travel Survey*. All in all, these often provide valuable information – their accuracy, though, is not always understood by those using their results.

Self-assessment task

Your local 'take-away' has asked you to plan an investigation into how the sales of its products might change with variations in price. It is also considering whether to charge a discounted price on certain quiet mid-week evenings when demand is low. (You should be able to answer the following questions when you have completed unit 1.)
Explain:
(a) How you would collect the information required to investigate these two problems.
(b) What information you need to collect.

How and why economists make forecasts

One of the most important tasks of the professional economist, whether in government or private sector employment, is to be able to forecast future economic phenomena. For example, many economic variables are heavily dependent upon the state of the economy. Forecasts of economic growth in particular are widely used by economists for all sorts of reasons related to economic policy and business well-being.

For AS, no more than a general understanding of what is meant by a forecast is needed. For A2 modules though students should be familiar with the material which follows.

Economists use various types of forecasting method. The three main ones are:

◆ statistical forecasts based on simple or complex future extrapolation techniques;

◆ using models to produce a range of forecasts – this is particularly true of models of the economy such as the one developed by the Treasury;

◆ forecasts based on intuition, experience or even guesswork, that is not involving statistical methods.

Two examples of forecasts are:

Macroeconomic forecasts – the Chancellor of the Exchequer and other government departments find it essential to have estimates of projected variables, such as the unemployment rate, inflation rate, balance of payments position and economic growth rate (see figures 5 and 6 for a typical example). These are required on a short-term basis (1 year or less) or over a longer period of time. Take the case of the unemployment rate – the importance of forecasting is shown below in figure 7.

Figure 6 Current RPIX inflation projection based on constant nominal interest rates

This seems quite simple. In practice, though, the process is much more difficult to set out and at stages 3 and 4 requires further assumptions to be made with regard to other sources of revenue and taxation.

Microeconomic forecasts – these are not quite as obvious but one which develops out of section 7 is the need to be able to forecast tax revenue from wine consumption, which has a positive income elasticity of demand. This process is shown in a simplified way in figure 8.

How to write in a clear and effective way

It is really beyond the scope of this book to include a lot of material on this part of the 'tool kit'. But having said this, much of the work of economists is communicated in a written manner, in books and newspaper articles especially. For students, examinations in Economics (OCR included) require you to communicate your ideas in a written form. The section on Examination skills gives you very specific advice on how to impress examiners.

From a more general standpoint, you must always think about what you are writing and how you might improve your writing skills. You can enhance these skills by reading a good newspaper, particularly if you read material which supports your AS/A level studies.

For the time being, you might like to think about the following 'Ten tips for budding writers' (based on work by John Hart at the University of Huddersfield):

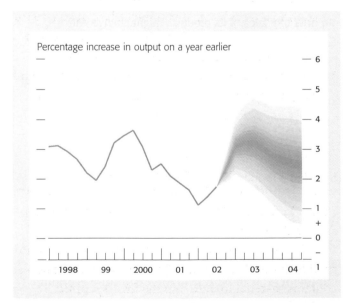

Figure 5 Current GDP projection based on constant nominal interest rates

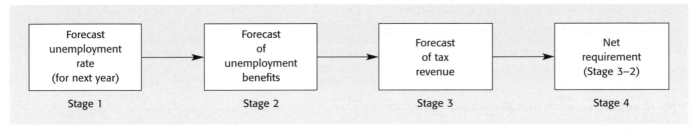

Figure 7 Use of unemployment forecasts

Figure 8 Use of income elasticity estimate

1 *Be clear and precise in your writing* – use words you understand and when using technical terms be specific, not least because Economics has many terms which are very similar.
2 *Remember to match your writing to your audience* – in most cases this will be your teacher or an OCR examiner. They are likely to be older than yourself and will be looking to read material from you which is written in a relevant way.
3 *Write impersonally* – in other words, do not use 'I' or 'we' in your written essays and examination answers. This particularly applies when you are asked to make an evaluation of an economic issue or argument.
4 *Think carefully about what tense you are writing in* – try and be consistent.
5 *Take care with sentences and punctuation* – in general, try to write short sentences, to the point and which contain words you understand and know how to use.
6 *Use one idea per paragraph and develop your ideas* – this makes it relatively easy for someone reading your work to know what your answer is about and to see how your idea has been developed.
7 *Support your arguments* – in other words, never make rash statements you cannot back up. Always try to

elaborate or develop your statements and arguments.
8 *Avoid humour* – if in any doubt, leave humour and wit out of your written answers. Many economists do have a sense of humour – examinations and essays are not the place for it to be demonstrated.
9 *Be professional* – do not insult or offend even if you do not agree with what you might have read or with the examination question. There are other ways in which you can make your opinions known.
10 *Keep working at your writing* – never be satisfied and keep thinking about how you can write in a clear, relevant, authoritative and positive way.

An outline of the OCR structure

It is useful from the outset for you to know the structure of the OCR Economics specification. This is shown in figure 9. The AS stage consists of three units, as does the A2 stage.

This book provides the subject content and skills you need to succeed at AS level. (The final unit of the book contains material to underpin the final 'synoptic' module if you go on to the A2 stage.)

AS

THE MARKET SYSTEM Unit 1	MARKET FAILURE AND GOVERNMENT INTERVENTION Unit 2	THE NATIONAL AND INTERNATIONAL ECONOMY Unit 3
Weight AS 30% A level 15%	30% 15%	40% 20%

Method of Assessment: Compulsory questions based on a particular theme or case study. See section on 'Preparing for examinations' for examples.

Time Allowed: All units – 1 hour

A2

OPTION 1 Unit 4 or Unit 5	OPTION 2 Unit 6 or Unit 7	ECONOMICS IN A EUROPEAN CONTEXT (SYNOPTIC) Unit 8
Weight A level 15%	15%	20%

Method of Assessment: Options: Data Response question | Pre-issued stimulus material

                             One structured essay from choice of three   Compulsory structured questions

Time Allowed: $1\frac{1}{2}$ hours $1\frac{3}{4}$ hours

Options:

Unit 4   Economics of Work and Leisure
Unit 5   Transport Economics
Unit 6   Economics of Development
Unit 7   The UK Economy

Figure 9 OCR's economics specification

Three important new terms are now introduced:
Module – this is the term used to denote a block of subject content from a teaching and learning standpoint.
Unit – this is the term used to describe the subject content of a module and its associated means of assessment; it is the smallest part of the qualification.
Stage – this is the term used to describe the two parts of the specification, that is the AS and the A2. The AS is in itself a recognised qualification and some students may decide to terminate their studies on completion of this stage. Others will use their AS studies as the basis for completion of the A2 stage and, if successful, obtain an A level award.

The OCR specification can be taken by you in a variety of ways to best suit your own needs and progress in studying Economics. (Don't worry too much about this as your teachers will know what is best for you.) The important thing to note is the *flexibility*. The following approaches are possible:

◆ *Staged assessment* – an arrangement whereby you can take the various units throughout your course. For example, you can take unit 1 in January of year 12, followed by units 2 and 3 in June. This cycle can be repeated in year 13 for the A2 units. Alternatively, you may prefer to take three units in June of year 12 (AS) and year 13 (A2).

◆ *Linear assessment* – this is the traditional way in which many students have taken A levels. It will involve you taking all six units in June of year 13.

You are allowed to re-sit any unit for one further time, the best mark being the one credited to you. This opportunity, though, can only really be realised if you study the specification in a staged manner by sitting units throughout the period of your course. Again, don't worry about this. The important things for you to be aware of are the flexible study and examination possibilities.

The section on 'Preparing for examinations' shows you some examples of specimen OCR AS examination papers. As you work through the units, and the content of this book, you will become increasingly familiar with the subject matter in these examination papers. You will also become familiar with the assessment methods which OCR use.

So, good luck and welcome to OCR Economics!

Summary

In this introduction we have established that:

- Economics is a social science concerned with how scarce resources are or should be allocated – it is often split into principles and concepts of microeconomics and macroeconomics.

- Economists have a varied 'tool-kit' to enable them to analyse economic problems and issues. Interpreting data and using data are particularly important – economists use many of the basic statistical skills for this purpose.

- It is also important that economists know what information they might need and how they can collect it. There are occasions when economists need to make forecasts.

- Economists must be able to express their ideas in a clear, relevant manner so that they can be easily understood.

- The above 'tool kit' will be assessed in OCR's Economics examinations at AS and at the A2 stage of the GCE A Level examination.

- OCR's examination consists of three AS and three A2 units which can be taken in various possible ways to best suit individual needs.

Unit 1

The market system

1 Managing scarce resources: the reasons for choice and its consequences

On completion of this section you should be able to:

➤ describe what economists mean by the 'economic problem'

➤ understand the factors of production as economic resources

➤ explain the concept of specialisation and the economic benefits it offers

➤ explain the concept of opportunity cost and the nature of trade-offs

➤ explain the principles underlying production possibility curves and how opportunity cost can be used to analyse production decisions which have to be taken in an economy

➤ understand the importance of money and exchange in an economy

➤ understand the role of markets

One economic problem or many?

Economists have to deal with a whole range of **economic problems**. You may have seen TV programmes about the misery of unemployment and poverty; you may have read about the difficulties caused by inflation or heard politicians discuss exchange rate crises on the evening news. You may also be aware of debates surrounding issues such as the United Kingdom's future relationship with the European Union, the problems of global warming and the population explosion in the Third World. Despite this extensive range of issues which economists are trained to consider, they often talk about *the* economic problem. This is the fundamental problem from which all others arise. This is the fact that we have scarce **resources** to satisfy our unlimited **wants**. As a result of this problem, which is sometimes called the problem of **scarcity**, we have to make **choices**, and it is the task of the economist to explain and analyse the nature of choice facing economic agents, such as consumers, producers and governments.

The economic problem is

SCARCE RESOURCES IN RELATION
TO UNLIMITED WANTS

Because the basic economic problem exists, societies need to confront three interrelated questions. These are:

1 *What to produce?*
   Because we cannot produce everything, we need to decide what to produce and in what quantities. We have to choose, for example, whether to produce lots of goods and services, such as food, clothing and leisure pursuits, to improve our standard of living, or whether we need to produce lots of military hardware to improve our defences.

2 *How to produce?*
   This question arises from the basic economic problem that, since resources are scarce in relation to unlimited wants, we need to consider how resources are used so that the best outcome arises. We need to consider how we can get the maximum use out of the resources available to us. It should be noted, however, that other issues besides purely economic concerns should be considered when deciding how to produce. It may be true, for example, that through slavery or forced labour we could produce more goods and services in an economy, but there is a moral objection to such arrangements. Similarly crop yields could well be increased through the introduction of genetically modified plants but this may lead to damage to the ecosystem. The decision to maximise output and satisfy more wants would need to consider the full impact on the environment and any potential long-term health risks.

3 *For whom to produce?*

Because we cannot satisfy all the wants of all the population, decisions have to be taken concerning how many of each person's wants are to be satisfied. On a broad level we need to decide whether everyone is going to have more or less an equal share of what is produced or whether some will have more than others. In some economies there are deliberate attempts to create a more egalitarian society through policies that re-distribute wealth and income from the rich to the poor. This could be through the adoption of progressive taxation systems. In other economies there are no such policies and inequalities of wealth and income, usually based upon inheritance, remain extreme. In answering this question, moral aspects of decision making again become important.

Self-assessment task

Read the article below and then answer the questions that follow.

Survey On The Economics of Ageing: The luxury of longer life

In the world's rich countries, when you retire at 65 you can expect to live, on average, for another 15 or 20 years. A hundred years ago you would, on average, have been already dead. The late 20th century has brought to many the ultimate gift: the luxury of ageing. But like any luxury, ageing is expensive. Governments are fretting about the cost already, but they also know that far worse is to come. Over the next 30 or 40 years, the demographic changes of longer lives and fewer births will force most countries to rethink in fundamental ways their arrangements for paying for and looking after older people.

In 1990 18% of people in OECD countries were aged over 60. By 2030 that figure will have risen to over 30%. The share of the 'oldest old' (those over 80), now around 3%, is set to double. The vast majority of these older people will be consumers, not producers. Thanks to state transfers, being old in developed countries mostly no longer means being poor. The old people will expect decent pensions to live on; they will make heavy demands on medical services; and some will need expensive nursing care. Yet while their numbers are expanding fast, numbers of people at work – who will have to foot the bill – will stay much the same, so each worker will have to carry a much heavier burden.

Mass survival to a ripe old age will not be confined to rich countries. Most developing countries, whose populations are now much younger than the developed world's, are starting to age fast. In Latin America and most of Asia, the share of over-60s is set to double between now and 2030, to 14%. In China, it will increase from less than 10% now to around 22% in 2030, thanks partly to the government's stringent population-control measures. Only Africa is likely to remain exuberantly young right through to the middle of the next century, though AIDS may reduce population growth in some countries.

Already the numbers of old people in poor countries are beginning to dwarf those in the rich world. By 2000, there will be 400m people over 60 in

Elderly people enjoy a supervised game of cards at Britain's first Granny Creche at Peugeot's car plant in Coventry
Source: Popperfoto Reuters.

developing countries, twice as many as in the developed. In many places, the ageing process is being compressed from the four or five generations that it took in rich countries to just one or two.

A new twist to getting old

This will produce a historical first: countries with big old populations that are also poor. All the other permutations are familiar: old and rich (most of the industrial world), young and poor (most of the developing world for now) and, less common, young and rich (Australia, New Zealand, Ireland; up to a point, America, though not for much longer). Eastern Europe is something of an odd case out, being old but, thanks to its communist past, not as rich as it should be; and in Russia life expectancy for men, against the trend elsewhere, is falling rather than rising.

The new combination of age and poverty in several countries in Latin America and Asia will create many problems that are already familiar to industrial countries, but with far fewer resources to tackle them. Ethical dilemmas over the use of scarce resources will be magnified. Financing of health care and pensions could be a nightmare.

When demographers first started drawing attention to the coming age bulge, the discovery was hailed as that rare thing in the affairs of nations, a foreseeable problem. Forewarned would, surely, mean forearmed. Even the tag invented for it, 'the demographic time-bomb', seemed to imply that the bomb could be defused. The demographic facts were inescapable because the people concerned had already been born. The same baby boomers who crowded the nurseries after 1945 would be packing the nursing homes of the 2030s. Yet so far there has been more talk than action.

The trouble has been that the demographic problems ahead, however predictable, are still not imminent enough to create any real sense of urgency. Modern democracies with electoral cycles of four or five years are not designed to solve problems that impose short-term costs to reap long-term benefits.

In many countries, older people are still too few in number, and for the most part too politically passive, to act as an effective pressure group for long-term policies to further their own interests (perhaps to the detriment of other groups). But that is changing as their numbers increase, and they learn to flex their political muscles. By 2030, it would be a bold politician who neglected one voter in three – especially as older people in general turn out to vote in much bigger numbers than others.

Source: Barbara Beck, *The Economist*, 27 January 1996.

(a) Summarise the trends in world population structure identified in the article.

(b) Discuss the significance of the changes for decisions concerning:
- ◆ what to produce;
- ◆ how to produce;
- ◆ for whom to produce.

Limited resources

In Economics we categorise the resources available to us into four types. These are known as **factors of production**:

1 **Land** This is the natural resource. It includes the surface of the earth, lakes, rivers and forests. It also includes mineral deposits below the earth and the climate above.

2 **Labour** This is the human resource, the basic determinant of which is the nation's population. Not all of the population are available to work however, because some are above or below the working population age and some choose not to work.

3 **Capital goods** These are any man-made aids to production. In this category we would include a simple spade and a complex car assembly plant. Capital goods help land and labour produce more units of output. They improve the output from land and labour.

These three factors are organised into units of production by firms.

4 **Enterprise** *(or entrepreneurship)* This factor carries out two functions. Firstly, the factor enterprise organises the other three factors of production. Secondly, enterprise involves taking the **risk** of production, which exists in a free enterprise economy. Some firms are small with few resources. The functions of enterprise are undertaken by a single individual. In larger, more complex firms the functions are divided, with salaried managers organising the other factors and shareholders taking the risk.

Some economies have a large quantity of high-quality factors at their disposal. They can create lots of goods and services to satisfy the wants of their population. They are said to have a good **factor endowment**. Some economies lack sufficient quantities of one or more of the factors. Developing countries, for example, might have large quantities of land and labour but lack sufficient capital and enterprise. The former economies of Eastern Europe, such as Poland, have found it difficult to develop because they have few people with entrepreneurial experience. As you may see in unit 4 these economies have to make some difficult choices if they are to develop.

Production and consumption

Resources are combined in the process of **production** to create goods and services. Goods and services have the capacity to satisfy wants. The process through which individuals use up goods and services to satisfy wants is known as **consumption**. Some goods, such as a chocolate bar, are quickly used up to satisfy our wants. Others satisfy wants over a longer period of time. These are called consumer durables. Examples of consumer durables include television sets and washing machines.

Unlimited wants

If we were asked we could all identify certain basic wants which must be satisfied if we are to stay alive. These include the obvious essentials of food, shelter and clothing. We might also identify those wants which are clearly less essential but which we think improve our quality of life. Some might include television sets, cars, trips to the cinema and so on. These are sometimes called luxuries but it is important to remember that what might be a luxury for one individual may be considered an essential for others. This is because we all have a **scale of preference** with our more urgent wants at the top and the less urgent ones at the bottom. Each individual's scale of preference is a product of a complex set of influences, involving our culture, upbringing and life experiences. These together influence our likes and dislikes. Unsurprisingly, since we all have different experiences, there is bound to be great variation between any two individuals' scales of preferences. You may find it interesting to conduct a class exercise in which everyone makes a list of ten wants in descending order of priority. When you compare results you may be surprised to find that, although there may be broad agreement on the first few choices, there is likely to be considerable variation as you compare people's choices over the full list. You may also consider how your list would compare with lists compiled by others with very different life experiences, such as your teacher, your grandparents or even a student of Economics in another country, such as in Africa. A further point to consider is whether you could imagine any end to your list if you were not limited to ten choices. It is important to remember that our wants are continually expanding, developing and changing. Some wants expand as we grow up, marry and raise a family. Imagine how our housing needs change as we

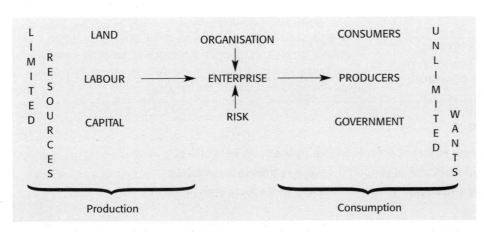

Figure 1.1 Elements of the economic problem

go through this process or how we change from wanting a small car with two doors to wanting a large family saloon with four doors. Some of our wants develop and expand when we see others enjoying goods and services around us and we feel the need to keep up. Sometimes our wants change as we have new experiences, for example we might become vegetarian because we have seen a TV programme on the health risks of eating meat.

All of this points to the fact that we can never imagine a time when all our wants are satisfied. Our wants are continually expanding and changing. Despite the fact that we are continually finding new, more efficient ways to produce more and more goods and services with the resources available to us, we are still faced with the basic economic problem that we have limited resources and unlimited wants. This is sometimes called the problem of scarcity. As a result we have to make choices.

Self-assessment task

Read the article below and answer the questions that follow.

Rich and miserable … or poor and happy?

It's often said that those who say that money can't buy you happiness simply don't know where to shop. So when you've finished leafing through the Guardian, the odds are that you'll be off to the mall, armed with your plastic for a bit of conspicuous consumption.

After all, Christmas is only five weeks away and spending money makes you happy, right? Wrong. According to economists it's a myth that the more we spend, the better we feel.

The evidence – to be published in this month's edition of The Economic Journal – that the link between happiness and income/consumption is tenuous – is quite compelling.

The West is much richer than it was 50 years ago but:
- in the USA, reported 'happiness' has gone up only fractionally over this period;
- in Europe, 'satisfaction with life' is actually lower than it was 20 years ago.

This is evidenced in a number of ways. For example:
- in rich countries, male suicide rates have gone up;
- unemployment rates have increased – unhappiness is far more prevalent amongst the jobless.

According to Professor Andrew Oswald of Warwick University, money is to blame for this state of affairs. He argues that it buys very little well-being, yet everyone wants more of it. He says it is akin to the spectator who stands up at a football match to get a better view; by the time all of his neighbours are standing up, everybody is no better off than before.

Other economists agree:
- Yew Kwang Ng, a Chinese economist, has argued that production and consumption, 'to keep up with the Joneses', continue to impose substantial environmental costs, making economic growth happiness decreasing.
- Robert Frank, an American economist, argues that we would be better off if we all agreed to consume less. We could work less, meet other people more regularly and cut down on workplace commuting.

But what can we do to change?
Frank's solution is a progressive consumption tax, levied on a family's income minus its savings. A large standard deduction would ease the burden on poor families with low levels of consumption. For everyone else, the resulting real increase in consumption would encourage greater savings and permit a transfer of resources into the things that really make us happy – better education, good health and a decent environment.

Source: *The Guardian*, 22 November 1997 (adapted).

This article expresses the view that, through economic growth, people may actually be worse off.

(a) What other examples can you think of which might support the views of these economists?

(b) Do you see any conflict between these views and your understanding of the 'economic problem'?

Specialisation and exchange

One of the ways in which more goods and services can be produced in the economy is through the process of **specialisation**. This refers to a situation where individuals and firms, regions and nations concentrate upon producing some goods and services rather than others. This can be clearly illustrated at the individual level. Within the family there may be some specialisation in the performance of household tasks, with one person doing the ironing and gardening while another does the shopping and cooking. At the workplace, of course, the fact that some people are computer programmers while others are accountants is also a reflection of specialisation. At this level, specialisation allows individuals to concentrate upon what they are best at and thus more goods and services will be produced. With such specialisation, however, although more is produced no-one is self-sufficient. It becomes necessary to exchange goods and services. As an individual specialises they will produce a surplus beyond their needs, which they can exchange for the surpluses of others.

In very early economies, exchange took place through a barter system in which goods were exchanged for others. This was very inefficient, however, and inhibited trade. As a result **money** arose as a **medium of exchange**. This had several advantages and allowed for expansion in specialisation, exchange and trade. Markets developed in which buyers and sellers came together to exchange surpluses using the medium of money.

With the expansion of the use of money and the development of markets, the benefits of regional and national specialisation became apparent. Surpluses produced by regions and countries were bought and sold, allowing world living standards to rise. Just as individuals concentrated on what they were best at, so did regions and countries.

Specialisation has clearly resulted in a massive expansion in world living standards, but there are dangers in specialisation. Given the pace of technological change in modern society, there is always the possibility that the specialist skills and accumulated experience, which any individual has acquired, may become redundant as the economy develops. Individuals need to be flexible and multi-skilled and be able to move between occupations. At regional and national levels, changes in consumers' wants can sometimes mean that the goods and services produced in a region or country are no longer required in the same quantity and unemployment can result. Policies then have to be adopted to deal with the economic and social problems that will arise. This issue will be looked at in depth in section 9 of unit 3.

The division of labour

With the technical advances of the last few hundred years, production of goods and services has taken place on a much bigger scale. The concentration of large numbers of workers within very large production units allowed the process of production to be broken down into a series of tasks. This is called the **division of labour**. For example, Adam Smith, writing at the end of the eighteenth century, showed how the production of pins would benefit from the application of the division of labour in a factory. He suggested that pin-making could be divided into 18 distinct operations and that, if each employee undertook only one of the operations, production would rise to 5,000 pins per employee per day. This was compared with his estimate that each employee would be able to produce only a few dozen each day if they produced pins individually.

Although the division of labour raised output, it often created dissatisfaction in the workforce, who became bored with the monotonous nature of their task. The process was taken a stage further in the 1920s when conveyor belt production was introduced in the United States car industry by Henry Ford. Ford's method of car production provided the model for much of manufacturing production in the twentieth century. In more recent times the de-humanising impact of production techniques, such as those using a conveyor belt, have been recognised and alternative methods of production have been introduced.

Choice and opportunity cost

Given limited resources and unlimited wants we have to choose which wants to satisfy. The true cost of any choice we make between alternatives is expressed by economists through the notion of **opportunity cost**. This looks at the cost of our choice in terms of the next best alternative foregone. For example, suppose you were given a £15.00 gift voucher for your birthday. You could either buy a new compact disc which cost £15.00

or two paperback books for £7.50 each. It is clear that you could not have the CD *and* the books. The opportunity cost of the CD, therefore, is the two paperback books. The value of the concept of opportunity cost is that it brings home to us the real cost of our choices. It can be applied in a variety of contexts in Economics and is helpful for economic decision makers, such as households, firms and governments.

Production possibility curves

How many goods and services an economy is capable of producing is determined by the quantity and quality of resources available to it, together with the state of technical knowledge. These factors determine an economy's production possibilities.

Example: An imaginary economy, given its available resources, can either produce military goods or consumer goods or a combination of each. The various possibilities are shown on the following production possibility schedule.

Military goods	Consumer goods
10,000	0
8,000	4,000
6,000	8,000
4,000	12,000
2,000	16,000
0	20,000

It is sometimes useful to illustrate the choices open to an economy by considering the **production possibility curve**. From the above schedule we can produce a production possibility curve with military goods plotted on the vertical axis and consumer goods on the horizontal axis.

Figure 1.2 shows all possible combinations of military goods and consumer goods which could be produced given the existing quantity and quality of resources in our imaginary economy and the existing state of technical knowledge. At point a, only military goods are produced, and, at point d, only consumer goods are produced, but between these two extremes lie all the other possibilities. The term production possibility curve emphasises that this shows what levels of output an economy can achieve with its existing resources. It

Figure 1.2 A production possibility curve

can also be used to show what the economy is *not* able to achieve. Point Y on the graph represents a combination of military and consumer goods which it is not possible to achieve. It is beyond our production possibilities. Sometimes the curve is called a **production frontier** because it draws the boundary between what can and cannot be achieved.

This diagram is also useful in illustrating the real cost to society of unemployed resources. The point *X* on the diagram represents a production of 4,000 military goods and 2,500 consumer goods. This is possible to achieve because it is within the production frontier, but it represents a point where some resources are unemployed or not employed effectively. The economy is capable of moving to point b with more military goods and the same number of consumer goods or to point c, which would bring more consumer goods and the same quantity of military goods. Alternatively at point e the economy can have more of both types of goods. Looking at the diagram in this way illustrates the waste from unemployed resources. We are not satisfying as many of our wants as possible.

A further alternative name for the production possibility curve is the **product transformation curve**. This emphasises a further use for the concept in introductory Economics. As the economy moves along the curve from point a through to point d then a different combination of goods is being chosen. More consumer goods are being produced and fewer military goods. This emphasises that the cost of producing more consumer goods is the military goods which have to be sacrificed. Given the figures, we can calculate the opportunity cost of consumer goods in terms of military goods. A move from b to e on the graph leads to a gain of 4,000 consumer goods but we sacrifice 2,000 military goods. The opportunity cost of one consumer good is therefore half of a military good. This is equivalent to one military good having an opportunity cost of two consumer goods. As we move along the curve the composition of our output is being transformed. We should also note that for this to happen we need to switch our resources from one use to another. Resources have to be switched from producing military goods to producing consumer goods and vice versa. This is known as the **reallocation of resources** and in the real world, as we decide to change the composition of our output, we need to consider the costs of reallocating resources between uses. These include the costs of re-training our workforce in the skills required to produce different types of goods and services. This might take a considerable period of time and might only be possible as new entrants to the labour force are trained in new skills. The extent to which resources can be reallocated from one line of production to another is known as **factor mobility** and, if we want resources to be swiftly allocated to the use we choose, we have to ensure that factors are as mobile as possible.

It should be noted that, in our example, the opportunity cost of military goods in terms of consumer goods has not changed as we have chosen different combinations of the two goods. This is in fact quite unrealistic. A more likely outcome is that the production possibility curve will illustrate increasing costs. Consider the production possibility schedule in table 1.1, which shows the quantities of agricultural goods and manufactured goods that can be produced in an economy given existing resources and state of technology.

Agricultural products	Manufactured products
700	0
660	100
600	200
500	300
300	400
0	500

Table 1.1 A production possibility schedule

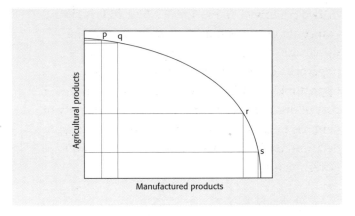

Figure 1.3 A production possibility curve with increasing costs

Assume that initially the economy is producing at point p with 660 agricultural products and 100 manufactured products (figure 1.3). Then assume that it is decided to move to point q to gain an extra 100 units of manufactured products. Clearly resources need to be reallocated from agricultural use to manufacturing. At first the least fertile land will be reallocated and only 60 units of agricultural produce will be sacrificed. This means that each extra consumer good has cost 0.6 of an agricultural good. Now compare this with a movement from r to s, to gain an extra 100 manufactured goods we have to sacrifice 200 agricultural goods. This means that one extra manufactured good has cost 2 agricultural goods. The cost has increased as we have reallocated our resources. This is because at this stage we are switching the more fertile land into manufactured good production so that agricultural output is going to be affected to a much greater extent. This diagram illustrates a production possibility curve with increasing costs.

Shifts in production possibility curve

A production possibility curve is drawn on the assumption that the quantity and quality of resources and the state of technology are fixed. Through time, of course, economies can gain or lose resources, the quality of resources and the state of technical knowledge can change. Such changes will shift the production possibility curve to a new position. Figure 1.4 illustrates the outcomes of changes in the quantity and quality of resources and changes in technology.

Figure 1.4(a) shows a situation in which the production possibilities available to an economy have expanded. This is known as **economic growth**. This

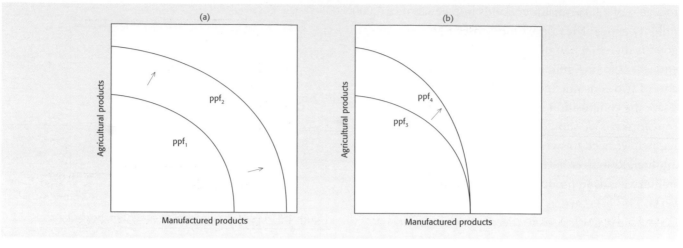

Figure 1.4 Shifts in production possibility curves

could be due to an increase in the quantity and/or the quality of resources available to the economy or an improvement in the state of technology. Here the changes have improved the economy's ability to produce both agricultural and manufactured products. In Figure 1.4 (b) however only our ability to produce agricultural products has been improved. This could perhaps be because there has been a technological breakthrough in producing agricultural products, which does not apply to the production of manufactured products. Nevertheless, this economy's production possibilities have improved and the curve has pivotted outwards.

The production possibilities could also have declined. This could be because in some way the resources available to the economy have declined. Perhaps some of the economy's natural resources have become exhausted or the working population is falling. It might also be because the technology available to us has changed. An example might be the impact of controls on global emissions, which will affect our production possibilities as controls become more rigorous.

Applications of production possibility curves

We can use production possibility curves to illustrate some of the issues facing economic decision makers in the real world.

Jam today or more jam tomorrow? As stated previously, the production possibilities open to an economy are determined by the quantity and quality of resources available. In the process of production, resources are used up and they need to be replaced if production possibilities are to be maintained. The term **capital consumption** or **depreciation** describes the using up of capital goods during the process of production. Some resources need to be devoted to the production of capital goods if production possibilities are to be maintained. The creation of capital goods in the process of production is known as **investment**. This can be defined as *any production not for current consumption*. A choice has to be made therefore between producing consumer goods and services or producing capital goods through the process of investment. The more consumer goods and services produced, the higher the standard of living in the current time period, but the standard of living might fall in the future if there is a failure to produce enough capital goods to replace those worn out in the process of production. In addition, the quality of an economy's capital goods will not be improved and the full benefits of new technology will not be enjoyed if there is a failure to devote sufficient resources to investment.

Figure 1.5 shows the production possibilities between capital goods and consumer goods. These possibilities are determined by the quantity and quality of resources in the economy, which include the capital goods that have been produced in the past. If we assume that the quantity of capital goods which are wearing out in each time period is shown at a, then we can see the consequences of our choices. If we fail to produce the quantity at a then our capital stock will decline. Our production possibilities will diminish and the curve will shift to the left.

We use the term gross investment to describe the total quantity of capital goods produced. If we deduct

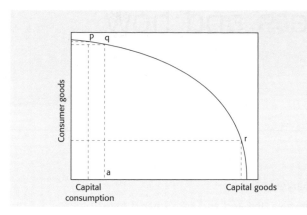

Figure 1.5 The choice between consumer goods and capital goods

Figure 1.6 Capital consumption in a developing economy

from this the capital consumption allowance then we are left with net investment:

Gross investment minus capital consumption = Net investment

Self-assessment task

Use the terms gross investment, capital consumption and net investment to analyse the effect of economic decision makers choosing each of points p, q and r in figure 1.5. Explain the choices in terms of the present and future standard of living in the economy.

Hard choices for developing economies Developing economies are characterised by low standards of living. If they are to grow then they need to increase their capital stock. Like all economies they need to divert resources from current consumption to investment. Some resources must be devoted to consumption, however, to keep their expanding populations alive. We refer to this as the subsistence level of consumption. The difficulty they face is that in the poorest developing economies almost all their production possibilities need to be devoted to subsistence.

In figure 1.6 0a represents the capital consumption in a developing economy and 0b represents the consumer goods required for the subsistence of the population.

Self-assessment task

Explain the choices facing decision makers in this developing economy. Discuss the difficulties they face and suggest any solutions to their problems.

Summary

In this section we have recognised that:

● All economies face the so-called economic problem of limited resources and unlimited wants.

● Choice is necessary in order to decide what to produce, how to produce and for whom to produce.

● Factors of production (land, labour, capital and enterprise) are essential for the production process.

● Specialisation allows more goods and services to be produced.

● The true cost of choices we have to make is known as opportunity cost.

● A production possibility curve is a representation of what can be produced in an economy and the trade-offs involved in making choices.

Key words

Definitions of Key words can be found in the Glossary on page 240.

capital consumption	money
capital goods	opportunity cost
choice	production
consumption	production frontier
developing economy	production possibility
division of labour	curve
economic growth	product transformation
economic problem	curve
enterprise	resources
factor endowment	reallocation of resources
factor mobility	risk
investment	scale of preference
labour	scarcity
land	specialisation
medium of exchange	wants

27

2 Competitive markets and how they work

On completion of this section you should be able to:

➤ understand what is meant by a competitive market

➤ explain the role of markets in allocating resources

➤ understand the different objectives of consumers and producers in markets

➤ understand what is meant by individual demand, market demand, effective demand and consumer surplus

➤ explain how demand is influenced by price, income, the prices of other goods and taste

➤ analyse the difference between shifts in demand and movements along a demand curve

➤ explain what is meant by the concepts of price, income and cross elasticity of demand and how they can be calculated

➤ evaluate the business relevance of these elasticity estimates

➤ explain what is meant by individual supply, market supply and producer surplus

➤ understand the range of factors influencing supply

➤ analyse the difference between shifts in supply and movement along a supply curve

➤ explain the concept of elasticity of supply, how it can be calculated and its economic relevance

➤ analyse how equilibrium price and quantity are determined

➤ analyse how and why the equilibrium position changes

➤ apply the analysis of demand and supply to the labour market and to the money market

Markets

'Oil prices fall to $10 per barrel – consumers everywhere will rejoice at the prospect of cheap, plentiful oil for the foreseeable future' *Economist*, 6 March 1999

'Cheap mortgages fuel boom in house prices' *Sunday Times*, 28 March 1999

'Personal computers are now more affordable than ever bringing the power and convenience of modern technology within the reach of most people' *Daily Mail*, 25 March 1999

'Rent one of our new widescreen TVs and you can get a Nicam stereo video for only £5 per month extra' Advert in *East Anglian Daily Times*, 11 March 1999

'Fly with us to Singapore for £355 return and get quality accommodation from only £20 per night' Advert in *Independent on Sunday*, 28 March 1999

To many people a market is something that happens in the town or city centre once or twice a week. It is characterised by a large number of traders setting up stalls that sell a whole range of products: food – such as fruit, vegetables, fish – clothes and a wide selection of other items. Economists, however, take a broader view of the world market. The essence of any market is trade – somebody has something to sell and somebody else wants to buy the product that is being offered. So, whenever people come together for the purposes of exchange or trade, we have a market.

For example, economists talk about the housing market, where people buy and sell houses; look in the newspapers or estate agents and you will see evidence of this market. They also refer to the labour market, where individuals' labour power is 'bought and sold' – if any of you have jobs part time or full time, then you have participated in the labour market as a seller of labour.

The television news often makes reference to the stock market, where shares are bought and sold, and the foreign exchange market, where currencies are bought and sold. Think about what happened when you last went on holiday overseas – if you at any time bought foreign currency you influenced the foreign exchange market in a small way, although you probably didn't realise it!

These examples indicate that to an economist a market does not have to have a clearly defined physical presence as the typical town or street market might have. It is simply a term used to describe the process through which products that are fairly similar are bought and sold.

Self-assessment task

How do you participate in the following markets:

- the personal computer market?
- the fast food market?
- the telecommunications market?
- the transport market?

Sub-markets

You might, however, begin to feel a bit uneasy at this point. Whilst it is clear that houses, labour, personal computers (PCs) and fast food may be fairly similar, it is also clear that there are significant differences within each market – the types of houses, PCs and transport services that are traded are not identical. So a good question to ask is: 'How valid is it to lump all the different types of computer together into one single market?'

Whenever we break an investigation down into smaller sections of the overall market, we are looking at sub-markets. So, if we want to look at the sub-markets of the computer industry, we might want to look at the various types of computer: memory, speed, features, PCs and laptops, the various brands and so on. We may need to consult (or become!) specialists in the economics of particular industries.

Demand

Let us first of all look at the buying side of the market – this is referred to as the demand side of the market. To an economist:

demand refers to the *quantities* of a *product* that *purchasers* are *willing and able* to buy at *various prices* per *period of time, other things remaining the same.*

Self-assessment tasks

1 What are the various sub-markets that we could identify if we wanted to look in more detail at the following products:
- alcoholic drinks?
- leisure equipment?
- holidays?
- personal computers?

2 Why do you think it is often important for companies to look more at sub-market issues? How could we break the market down even further to find out about an individual consumer's demand for a particular product?

3 Find out about the last big equipment order placed by your school or college – see if you can find out what factors influenced the decisions of the person who made the choices.

Definitions are of critical importance in Economics, so let us break this definition down to understand in some depth what this means.

- *Quantities* – economists often deal with numerical values and very often try to represent information in a quantitative way. This point is reinforced by the use of the term 'prices'.
- *Product* – this is a general term that simply refers to the item that is being traded. It can be used for goods or services. We could also stretch this to include tradable items like money or other financial assets such as shares.
- *Purchasers* – these are the buyers of the product and are often referred to as 'consumers', although they may simply be intermediaries in the production–consumption chain, for example Nestlé purchasing large amounts of cocoa to be used in the production of chocolate for sale to the final consumer. We could look at an individual purchaser's demand for a product or, more usefully, we can aggregate this to look at the demand of an overall market or sub-market.
- *Willing to buy* – clearly purchasers must want a product if they are going to enter into the market to buy it. Economists use the terms 'satisfaction' or 'utility' to describe the benefit or pleasure that the final consumer derives from the product.

◆ *Able to buy* – to an economist, the notional demand for a product, which emerges from wanting it, must be backed by purchasing power if the demand is to become effective. Companies are only willing to sell a product if the purchaser has monetary ability to pay for the product – the world is full of wishful thinkers who would love to own a Ferrari sports car or the most sophisticated music or computer system. It is, however, effective demand that is of real importance for economists.

◆ *Various prices* – prices are crucial to the functioning of a market. Although demand for a product is influenced by many things, it is at the moment of purchase, when we have to hand over our money and pay the price, that we really judge whether the product is value for money, that is, whether we really are willing and able to buy it. As the price goes up, and provided no other changes have occurred, more and more people will judge the product to be less worthwhile.

◆ *Per period of time* – demand must be time related. It is of no use to say that the local McDonalds sold 20 Big Macs to consumers unless you specify the time period over which the sales occurred. If that was per minute then demand is probably quite high, but if that was per week then clearly there is little demand for Big Macs in this sub-market.

◆ *Other things being equal* – we will see shortly that there are numerous potential influences on the demand for a product. Analysing the connections between the various elements is very difficult if lots of these elements are changing simultaneously. The process is similar to that of a scientist who, when conducting an experiment, will control the general conditions except for the two elements that he/she wishes to investigate. So, for simplicity, we start with the assumption that all the other factors are constant and analyse the response of purchasers on the basis that price alone changes. We will relax this assumption as we progress. Economists often use a Latin phrase, ceteris paribus, to indicate this assumption – this simply means '*other things being equal*'.

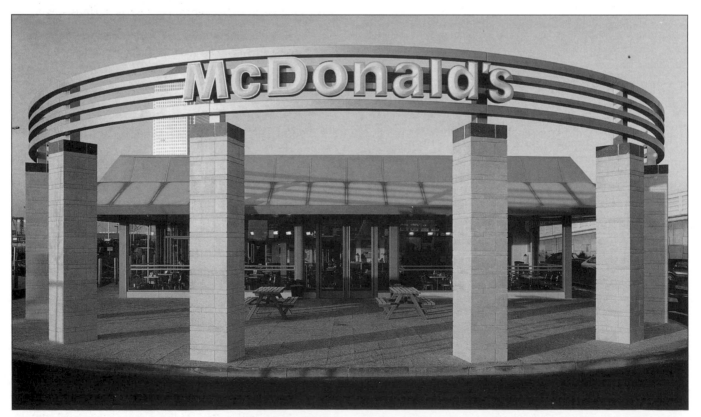

The innovative quick service restaurant concept pioneered by Dick and Mac McDonald in California has grown into the world's largest food service organisation, serving millions of customers every day
Source: McDonald's Corporation.

The demand curve

Let us now take this definition and represent it diagrammatically to construct what is known as a demand curve. We will make up an example based on the overall market demand for personal computers to illustrate the point. Let us make an assumption that we can identify and therefore analyse a typical personal computer, that is one with a set of standard specifications. Remember we can break the analysis into sub-markets later if we want to become more detailed. Let us also assume that we have collected statistical data about people's preferences and that the quantity of PCs that people are willing and able to buy at various prices per period of time, ceteris paribus, can be represented by table 2.1. This is known as a demand schedule. We can now plot the market demand schedule on a graph to see how the quantity demanded of PCs relates to variations in price. Figure 2.1 shows the demand curve for the data in table 2.1.

Price of a 'standard' PC (£)	Quantity demanded per week – demand curve D_0
2,000	1,000
1,800	2,000
1,600	3,000
1,400	4,000
1,200	5,000
1,000	6,000
800	7,000

Table 2.1 Market demand schedule

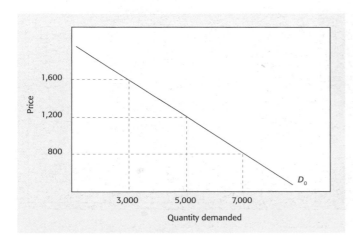

Figure 2.1 The market demand curve for PCs

Points to note:

♦ An inverse or negative quantitative relationship between price and quantity demanded. When price goes up, there is a **decrease** in **quantity demanded**. When price goes down, there is an **increase** in **quantity demanded**. Notice the language that is being used here – changes in price cause changes in quantity demanded and we can illustrate this by movements up and down the demand curve.

♦ A causal relationship – we are saying that changes in price cause changes in quantity demanded.

♦ A linear relationship – this demand curve has been drawn again for simplicity as a straight line. However, it is perfectly acceptable for price and quantity demanded to be related in a non-linear manner such as a curve.

♦ A continuous relationship – we could look at the diagram and find out at what price consumers would be willing and able to buy 1,259 PCs.

♦ A time-based relationship – the time period here is weekly.

Note that we are also assuming ceteris paribus – you should briefly review what this means.

Notice how important it is to label diagrams – the price axis, the quantity demanded axis, the demand curve and the P and Q_D reference points on each axis.

Self-assessment tasks

1 How many PCs per week are people willing and able to buy if the price is £1,100?
2 What price will persuade people to buy 1,350 PCs per week?
3 What assumptions are you making when you answer these questions?

Figure 2.1 is a very useful diagram since it allows us to visualise a quite complex relationship – simple pictures are usually easier to understand and remember than a large number of words. It also allows us to estimate how much consumers may spend when buying PCs, or conversely how much revenue companies may receive from selling PCs. If the price of PCs is £1,800 and the above information is accurate then consumers will buy 2,000 units and their total spending will be equal to £3,600,000, which, of course, will be the revenue that companies receive from selling this quantity of the product. (Note that, since we do not know the firm's production and distribution costs, we are as yet unable to say anything about profit.)

Self-assessment task

Explain how the area under the demand curve could be used to illustrate total consumer expenditure/total revenue of the firms selling PCs.

Consumer surplus

The underlying principles behind the demand curve are relatively simple to understand. They are also ones which many of us follow in our daily lives. For instance, when a product is on 'special offer' in a local shop, and its price has been reduced, more will be demanded and purchased.

For any good or service, though, there are always some people who are prepared to pay above the given price to obtain it. Two of the best examples where this happens are in the cases of tickets to popular rock concerts or to watch premier league football clubs, such as Manchester United or Newcastle United or even tennis at Wimbledon. The stated price of tickets may well be £20 per ticket, but there will always be some

people who are willing to pay over £20 to obtain a ticket. Another example might be the case of a chocoholic who is prepared to pay over the odds to get a bar of his or her favourite chocolate. To the economist, such situations introduce the concept of consumer surplus.

Consumer surplus arises because consumers would be willing to pay more than the given price for all but the last unit they buy. This can be illustrated in figure 2.2(a) where consumer surplus is the shaded area under the demand curve and above the price line. More specifically, it is the difference between the total value consumers place on all the units consumed and the payments they need to make in order to actually purchase that commodity.

If the market price changes then so does consumer surplus. For example, if the price increases then consumer surplus is reduced as some consumers are unwilling to pay the higher price. This reduction is shown in figure 2.2(b). The loss of consumer surplus is shown by the area $P_1P_2E'E$.

Manchester United's Ryan Giggs (2R) celebrates with team mates David Beckham (2L) Nicky Butt (L) John O'Shea (R) and Roy Keane (C) after scoring in their Champions League phase two group D match against Juventus
Source: Popperfoto/Reuters.

Figure 2.2 Consumer surplus

Shifts in the demand curve

Whilst the above analysis is useful, it is clearly limited because the price of a PC is not the only, or in many cases not the most important, factor influencing demand for it – other things play a part and are not always constant. Changes in these 'ceteris paribus' factors can be illustrated by shifts in the demand curve. A rightward shift indicates an increase in demand; a leftward shift indicates a decrease in demand. Notice how the language changes here when we are talking about a shift in the whole curve rather than simply a movement along it – a change in demand rather than quantity demanded (see table 2.2 and figure 2.3).

Price of a 'standard' PC (£)	Quantity demanded per week – demand curve D_2
2,000	2,000
1,800	3,000
1,600	4,000
1,400	5,000
1,200	6,000
1,000	7,000
800	8,000

Table 2.2 Shifts in the demand curve

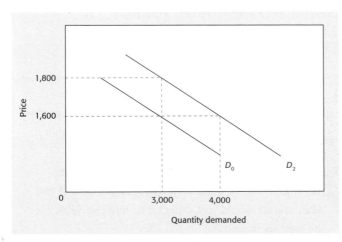

Figure 2.3 A shift to the right in the market demand curve for PCs

Points to note:
- *Explanation in terms of the horizontal shift* – consumers are now willing and able to buy more PCs at each and every price. So, whereas previously they were only prepared to buy 3,000 units per week

at £1,600, now they are prepared to buy 4,000.
- *Explanation in terms of the vertical shift* – consumers previously were prepared to pay £1,600 for 3,000 PCs, now they are prepared to pay £1,800 for that quantity.

Self-assessment task

Use the information below to draw a demand curve and explain what has happened to that demand curve – remember you are showing a decrease in demand. Draw in the demand curve D_0 as well so that you can use it as the basis for your comparison.

Price of a 'standard' PC (£)	Quantity demanded per week – demand curve D_1
2,000	0
1,800	1,000
1,600	2,000
1,400	3,000
1,200	4,000
1,000	5,000
800	6,000

Causes of shifts in the demand curve

Individuals may differ widely in their attitudes towards products. We could therefore spend a lot of time constructing a very long list of non-price influences. This might be useful in certain circumstances but not in all cases; remember the ideas of simplification and generalisation. Fortunately, economists have identified that there are three key non-price categories that can be used to describe and analyse the factors that influence the demand for most products. They are:
(a) the financial ability to pay for the product;
(b) our attitudes towards the product itself;
(c) the price, availability and attractiveness of related products.
Let us look at each in turn.

The financial ability to pay

We have already noted the importance of effective demand. So what influences someone's ability to pay for a product? This includes
- the purchasing power of their income after taxation;

◆ the availability of loans/credit and the interest rate that must be paid on loans or credit card balances.
In general we would expect a positive relationship between the financial ability to pay and the demand for a product. So an increase in purchasers' financial ability to pay generally leads to an increase in demand, and this would be represented by a rightward shift in the demand curve from D_0 to D_2 in figure 2.3. A decrease in the ability to pay would lead to a decrease in demand, and this would be represented by a leftward shift in the demand curve from D_2 to D_0.

Self-assessment task

Draw diagrams and briefly explain how you expect changes in the following to influence the position of the demand curve for PCs:

◆ an increase in interest rates;
◆ a large increase in unemployment;
◆ a sustained rise in earnings from work;
◆ a reduction in income tax.

There is an important qualification to this general rule. The single most important influence on people's financial ability to pay for goods and services is generally considered to be income. In most cases there is a positive relationship between income and product demand, that is, as income rises, the demand for the majority of goods and services also increases; as income falls, so does the demand for most products. Such products that are characterised by such a relationship are labelled normal goods.

However, there are some products that are characterised by a negative relationship between income and demand. As income rises the demand for dated types of PC, such as 366 and 486MHz speed PCs, will fall; as income rises people tend to choose UK-based holidays less often. Products that are characterised by such a relationship are referred to as inferior goods.

Attitudes towards the products

We all buy products for a reason, that is our behaviour is purposefully motivated, at least at the time of purchase! Economists usually consider our behaviour to be a reflection of our tastes and preferences towards different types of goods and services. For example, you may buy a PC to play computer games or to help with

Self-assessment task

Would you classify the following products as normal goods or inferior goods? In each case draw a diagram to explain how a decrease in income will shift the demand curve. Explain your reasoning. What difficulties did you have in deciding? What information would you need to resolve these difficulties?

◆ Premium brand lager beers — Supermarket own label beers
◆ Holidays in Malaysia — Holidays in Blackpool
◆ Black and white TV sets — Nicam stereo, digital TVs

school work or to get access to the internet. You may buy a particular type or brand of PC because of its reputation for reliability. You may buy a pair of branded name trainers because you want to play sport and you genuinely believe them to be of better quality or you may buy them simply because they are fashionable and you want to look cool.

Detailed understanding of the psychological motives that determine our behaviour are beyond our scope here, but clearly we are influenced by our own individual likes and dislikes, by peer pressure and by advertising and the marketing images that surround us. Nowhere of course is this more evident than in markets for clothing and recorded music, where tastes and preferences can be extremely volatile.

Self-assessment tasks

1 What, at present, is the dominant brand of sports clothing? Why do you think it is dominant? Is it because it is of genuinely superior quality or is there another explanation?
2 Think of a successful advertising campaign that is running on the TV at present. Why is it successful and what impact would you expect it to have on sales over the next six months?

The price, availability and attractiveness of related products

Economists classify types of related products into two categories: substitutes and complements.

◆ Substitute products are alternatives – products that satisfy essentially the same wants or needs. The range of substitutability can be fairly narrow, for example in terms of different product brands: IBM and Dell computers, Casio and Accurist watches and Ford and Vauxhall cars. Or the range of substitutability can be broad, in terms of product groups, for example different types of transport – rail, buses and cars; different types of alcoholic drinks – beer, wine, spirits, alcopops. Changes in the price or attractiveness of one of these products will have an impact on the demand for all substitutes.

◆ *Complements* are products that enhance the satisfaction we derive from another product. Common examples are fish and chips, TVs and video recorders, airline flights and hotel accommodation, PCs and modems or software. In some cases, without the complement the main product would be useless. Examples here include: cars and fuel; video recorders and video tapes. Once again changes in price or the attractiveness of one of these products will have an impact on the demand for the complementary product.

Self-assessment tasks

1 What would you expect to happen to the demand for Dell PCs if IBM cut their prices?
2 What would you expect to happen to the demand for all PCs if the price of software and printers came down sharply?
Use a diagram to help explain your answers.

Other demand-influencing factors

Clearly this is not an exhaustive list of the factors that influence demand. Each product will have some factors that are peculiar to it, for example the weather may influence the demand for ice cream. Expectations of the future can be important in determining the demand for certain products. If house prices or share prices are expected to rise, this can be a major influence in boosting demand. If unemployment or interest rates are expected to go up, this can have a dampening effect on the demand for some products. The skill of the economist is to use the categories above and knowledge or intuition to identify the key influences on demand, in any particular market, to explain past behaviour or to try to predict future behaviour.

Supply

We must now turn our attention to the other side of the market and consider the meaning of and influences on supply. To an economist:

supply refers to the *quantities* of a *product* that *suppliers* are *willing and able* to sell at *various prices* per *period of time, other things remaining the same.*

Note the similarities below with the definition of demand:
◆ *'Quantities'* – once again we must emphasise that economists often deal with numerical values and very often try to represent information in a quantitative way.
◆ *Product* – as with demand we are using the term to refer to any item that is being traded. It can be used for goods or services. We could also stretch this to include tradable items like money or other financial assets such as shares.
◆ *Suppliers* – these are the sellers of the product and are often referred to as 'producers', although they may not be manufacturers of the product but again may simply be an intermediary in the production–consumption chain or they may be selling services. We could look at an individual company's supply of a product or, more usefully, we can aggregate this to look at the supply for an overall market or sub-market.
◆ *Willing and able to sell at various prices* – clearly, in a market economy, companies must gain from selling their products. The ability to earn profits is likely to be a major (but probably not the only) influence on company behaviour – the higher the price, ceteris paribus, the more profit companies are likely to make. However, as companies produce more, they may find that costs start to go up (because of something called diminishing returns or capacity constraints), so they may need to sell at higher prices to convince them to produce more of the product.
◆ *Per period of time* – supply must also be time related. It is of no use to say that IBM supplied 200 computers unless you specify the relevant time period. Clearly this needs to be consistent with the time period being used for demand.
◆ *Other things being equal* (ceteris paribus) – we will see shortly that there are numerous potential influences on the supply of a product. Analysing

the connections between the various elements is very difficult if lots of these elements are changing simultaneously.

The supply curve

We need to take this definition and represent it diagrammatically to construct what is known as a supply curve. We could do this for an individual firm selling PCs or, by aggregating each separate company's supply curve, we could get the industry or market supply curve for PCs. Assume again that we have collected statistical data about companies' selling intentions and that these plans can be represented by table 2.3 (this is known as a supply schedule). We can now plot this supply schedule to see how the quantity of PCs supplied relates to variations in price. Figure 2.4 shows the supply curve (S_0) for the data in the table.

Price of a 'standard' PC (£)	Quantity supplied per week – supply curve S_0
800	1,000
1,000	2,000
1,200	3,000
1,400	4,000
1,600	5,000
1,800	6,000
2,000	7,000

Table 2.3 Market supply schedule

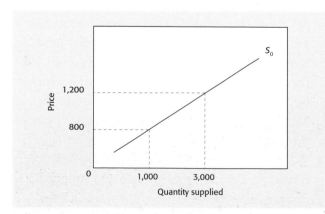

Figure 2.4 The market supply curve for PCs

Points to note:
- A positive or direct relationship between price and quantity supplied.

When price goes up there is an **increase** in **quantity supplied**.
When price goes down there is a **decrease** in **quantity supplied**.

- Again notice the language that is being used – changes in price cause changes in quantity supplied and we illustrate this by movements up and down the supply curve (again some economists prefer to use the terms extension of supply for a movement up the supply curve and a contraction of supply for a movement down the curve).
- A causal relationship – we are saying that price changes cause the change in quantity supplied.
- A linear relationship – the supply curve has been drawn for simplicity as a straight line, but of course there is no reason why the supply curve should not be represented in a non-linear way.
- A continuous relationship – we could look at the curve to find out how many PCs companies would plan to supply at a price of £1,150.
- A time-based relationship – the time period again is weekly.

Note we are also assuming ceteris paribus – any other supply influencing factor is assumed to be unchanged.

Self-assessment tasks

1 How many PCs per week are companies planning to supply if the price is £1,100?
2 What price would persuade companies to supply 1,350 PCs?
3 What assumptions are you making when you answer these questions?
4 What might be the advantages and disadvantages of using a diagrammatic form such as in figure 2.4 to represent supply?

Producer surplus

This is a similar concept to that of consumer surplus introduced above, but, as its name indicates, it is looked at from the perspective of the supply of a product. A very brief outline of the concept follows.

Looking at figure 2.5, the total value of the output supplied can be represented by the area $0P_1EQ_1$, that is the market price multiplied by the quantity supplied. Below this price, producers are still willing to supply the market but not at the same quantity as when price is P_1.

Figure 2.5 Producer surplus

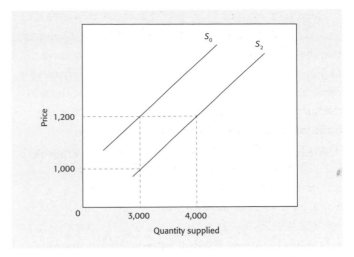

Figure 2.6 A shift to the right in the market supply curve for PCs

So as price falls towards P_0, where no units will be supplied, producers are less and less willing to supply.

Producer surplus is the shaded area above the supply curve and below the price line. It occurs because units of a firm's output are sold at the same market price P_1 – all except for the last unit are produced at less than the market price. The area P_0P_1E, therefore, are 'surplus earnings' for the firm.

Shifts in the market supply curve

Whilst the above is useful, one of the limitations is that companies' supply intentions are influenced by factors other than the price of the product (which, if you think about it, is the most tangible expression of consumers' buying intentions). Other things are most certainly not always equal. Changes in these 'ceteris paribus' factors can be illustrated by shifts in the supply curve. A rightward shift indicates an increase in supply;

a leftward shift indicates a decrease in supply. Notice again how the language changes when we are talking about a shift in the whole curve rather than simply a movement along it – a change in supply rather than quantity supplied (see table 2.4 and figure 2.6).

Points to note:

◆ *Explanation of horizontal shift* – companies are now more willing and/or more able to supply PCs at each and every price. Whereas previously they had only been prepared to supply 3,000 units per week at £1,200, now they are prepared to supply 4,000.

◆ *Explanation of vertical shift* – companies previously wanted £1,200 per unit to persuade them to supply 3,000 units per week, now they are prepared to accept £1,000.

Price of a 'standard' PC (£)	Quantity supplied per week – supply curve S_2
800	2,000
1,000	3,000
1,200	4,000
1,400	5,000
1,600	6,000
1,800	7,000
2,000	8,000

Table 2.4 An increase in supply

Although this PC superstore is called Office World, many homes now have a computer

Self-assessment task

Use the information below to draw a new supply curve (S_1) and explain what has happened to that supply curve – remember you are showing a decrease in supply. Draw in the supply curve S_0 as well so that you can use it as the basis for your comparison.

Price of a 'standard' PC (£)	Quantity supplied per week – supply curve S_1
1,000	1,000
1,200	2,000
1,400	3,000
1,600	4,000
1,800	5,000
2,000	6,000

Causes of shifts in the supply curve

Companies clearly differ in their willingness and ability to supply products and, as with demand, we could spend a long time building a list of possible factors other than price that will affect supply. If we were required (and paid!) to conduct a detailed analysis of supply conditions in a particular industry, that might be justified. For our purposes we need to simplify and generalise about the factors that can influence supply in most industries. As with demand, we can focus on three main influences:

◆ the costs associated with supplying the product;
◆ the size, structure and nature of the industry;
◆ government policy.

Let us discuss each in turn.

Costs

Since in a market-based economy, no firm (in the absence of government support) can exist indefinitely if it makes losses, companies will make supply decisions on the basis of the price they can get for selling the product in relation to the cost of supplying it. You will see in the next section how costs may rise as a firm increases production with a given capacity – this will influence the shape of the supply curve. What we are interested in here, however, is what factors can influence the position of the supply curve – in other words, what factors can cause an increase or a decrease in the costs of supplying each and every unit, since it is likely that this will impact on the price that companies charge for each and every unit. Below are listed some potentially

influential factors – if the factor pushes up costs, there is likely to be a leftward shift in the supply curve or decrease in supply; if the factor lowers costs, there is likely to be an increase in supply:

◆ wage rates;
◆ worker productivity (output per worker);
◆ raw material and component prices;
◆ energy costs;
◆ equipment maintenance costs;
◆ transport costs;
◆ the state of technology.

Self-assessment task

Go through each of the above factors in turn and work out what sort of change in that factor will cause:

◆ an increase in supply,
◆ a decrease in supply.

The size and nature of the industry

If it is clear that there is substantial profit to be made by selling a product, firms inside and outside the industry are likely to react. Firms currently in the industry may invest in capital equipment in an attempt to grow bigger and take advantage of the situation. Firms outside the industry may try to enter this market and of course new firms may set up in business. The ease with which they can do so will depend on whether there are any barriers to entry into the industry and, if there are, how easy it is to overcome them (see section 3). Nonetheless if the size of the industry increases, because there are more firms or bigger firms, then it is likely that the supply of the industry will increase. Equally, if firms in the industry start to compete more intensively on price, it is likely that the supply curve will shift to the right as the effects of this price competition start to affect the price that all companies are willing to accept for their products. Of course if a fierce price war does break out, then consumers, at least temporarily, may enjoy very much lower prices for any given level of supply.

Self-assessment tasks

1 Why might firms choose to leave an industry?
2 What is likely to happen to the industry supply if the size of the industry shrinks?
3 What might happen to supply if all firms decide to try and increase the amount of profit they make on each unit they sell?

Government policy

Governments influence company decisions in many ways. Legislation designed to protect consumers or workers may impose additional costs on companies and this may affect the supply curve. Governments may also impose indirect taxes (excise duties or value added tax) on companies. These taxes can act like a cost increase as companies may seek to pass the tax on to the consumer in the form of higher prices. As such, indirect taxes often result in a decrease in supply. On the other hand, a relaxation of certain types of legislation or government subsidies can increase supply by encouraging firms to lower prices for any given level of output.

Price of a 'standard' PC (£)	Quantity supplied per week	Quantity demanded per week
800	1,000	7,000
1,000	2,000	6,000
1,200	3,000	5,000
1,400	4,000	4,000
1,600	5,000	3,000
1,800	6,000	2,000
2,000	7,000	1,000

Table 2.5 Market supply and demand schedules for PCs

Self-assessment task

Refer to the supply curve S_0 in figure 2.6. What would happen to this curve if the government introduced a tax of:

♦ £100 per computer?

♦ 10% on the pre-tax selling price?

♦ legislation that raised companies' costs by about 20 per cent on average?

Other supply-influencing factors

As with our treatment of demand, this is not intended to be a complete list of the factors that influence supply. Each industry will have some features that are relevant to it. For example, the supply of agricultural produce is particularly influenced by weather conditions. Some industries may be able to switch production from one product to another fairly easily and so the relative profitability of alternative product areas may be important. In financial markets, like the stock market or the foreign exchange market, supply may be significantly influenced by expectations of future prices. Once again the skill of the economist is to use theory, insight and observation to identify the key influences on supply in any situation to explain the past or to try to predict the future.

Putting supply and demand all together – markets in equilibrium and disequilibrium

We have now analysed each side of the market separately and it is time to put it all together. At any

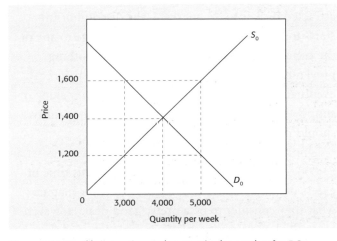

Figure 2.7 Equilibrium price and output in the market for PCs

point in time, there will be a given set of conditions influencing demand and a given set of conditions influencing supply (see table 2.5). Let us say that those conditions are reflected in demand curve D_0 and supply curve S_0 from earlier on – these relationships have been drawn for you in figure 2.7.

The term **equilibrium** refers to a situation of balance where at least under present circumstances there is no tendency for change to occur. In this particular situation, equilibrium will exist when the plans of consumers (as represented by the demand curve) match the plans of suppliers (as represented by the supply curve).

The market equilibrium in this case will, therefore, be at a price of £1,400 with 4,000 units bought and sold. Total consumer expenditure (and therefore industry revenue) will be £560,000 per week. Just think about what would happen if for some reason companies thought that consumers were prepared to pay £1,600 and supplied 5,000 units to the market. In this case the market would be in a disequilibrium (an imbalance where change will happen). At a price of £1,600, under present circumstances, consumers are only planning to buy 3,000 units. As such companies will build up excess stocks at the rate of 2,000 PCs per week. There is a **disequilibrium** of excess supply. Companies would be irrational to carry on with this unplanned stockbuilding. How might they react? Well for a start they could cut price; they would also probably start to reduce the quantity they supply to the market. Of course, as they cut price, some consumers who would not have been prepared to pay the higher price are now attracted back into the market – the disequilibrium starts to narrow. Provided there is no change to any of the conditions of supply or demand, and nothing prevented companies adjusting in this way, then eventually, perhaps through expert decision making or simply trial and error, the market price and quantity should move back to equilibrium.

Think now what would happen if the price was set at £1,000. Again we have a disequilibrium – this time of excess demand. Consumers are now keen to snap up what they consider to be a pretty good deal. However, given the low prices, supplies are fairly low and there are not enough PCs to meet demand – they run out of stocks far quicker than they had expected, so there are unmet orders. Profit-orientated companies, if they are reasonably sharp, will recognise this and will start to raise price and increase the number of PCs available for sale. However, as prices rise, some consumers will decide that PCs are a bit too expensive at the moment and the quantity demanded will fall. Once again, as a result of trial and error and good management on the part of businesses, the market will adjust back to the equilibrium.

Of course, this process of market adjustment may not happen instantly, there will be time lags, perhaps quite lengthy ones if companies are managed badly. The point, however, is that there will always be a tendency for the market to move back to its equilibrium because that is where the underlying motives and plans of consumers and suppliers are driving it.

Self-assessment task

In the figure 2.8 below symbols, instead of numbers, are used to represent the same situation.

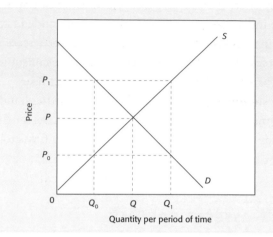

Figure 2.8 Typical supply and demand diagram

(a) What is the market equilibrium price and quantity?

(b) What area will show the total expenditure by consumers? This will be the same as the total revenue earned by companies.

(c) What is the state of the market if the price is at P_1?

(d) What is the state of the market if the price is at P_0?

(e) Explain what will happen if the market is in a disequilibrium of:
   ◆ excess demand;
   ◆ excess supply.

(f) What advantages/disadvantages are there in using symbols, such as P_s and Q_s, to analyse markets rather than actual numbers?

Changes in the equilibrium

The equilibrium will change if there is a disturbance to the present market conditions – this could come about through a change in the conditions of supply (the supply curve shifts) or a change in the conditions of demand (the demand curve shifts).

Self-assessment tasks

1 Review the factors that can cause the demand curve to shift.

2 Review the factors that can cause the supply curve to shift.

3 Review how disequilibrium positions are eliminated in a market.

A change in demand

Look at figure 2.9 – notice we are using P and Q symbols again instead of actual numbers – if there is an increase in demand (D_0 to D_2), then, at the original price, there is now a disequilibrium of excess demand equal to $Q_1 - Q_0$. As suppliers begin to recognise this they will start to raise price and increase quantity supplied. The rise in price will lead some consumers to decide they do not want to buy the product at the higher price. Although the process may take some time, the market will move back towards the new equilibrium at $P^* Q^*$, where the market is once more in balance. Note that the new equilibrium is at a higher price with a larger quantity traded than in the original situation.

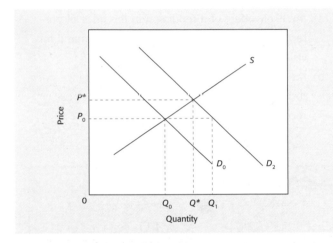

Figure 2.9 The effect of a shift of the demand curve on the equilibrium price and quantity

Self-assessment task

What will happen if there is a decrease in demand? Use a properly labelled diagram to explain clearly how both the market equilibrium price and quantity traded will fall.

A change in supply

Look at figure 2.10 – if there is an increase in supply (from S_0 to S_2) then, at the original price (P_0), there is now a disequilibrium of excess supply ($Q_1 - Q_0$). This would of course eventually be eliminated as price falls towards its new equilibrium level and the quantity traded in equilibrium rises from Q_0 to Q^* where the plans of consumers and companies once more coincide.

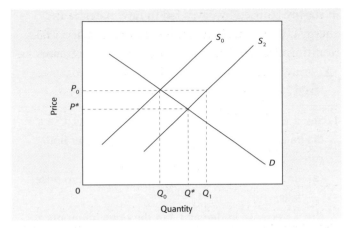

Figure 2.10 The effect of a shift in the supply curve on equilibrium price and quantity

Self-assessment task

What would happen if there was a decrease in supply? Use a properly labelled diagram to explain clearly how the market equilibrium price would rise but the equilibrium amount traded would fall.

A change in supply and demand

The above analysis is useful to deal with simple situations. However, in many situations the conditions of both supply and demand may change simultaneously. Look at figure 2.11. The initial equilibrium is at P and Q with the demand curve D_0 and the supply curve S_0. The increase in demand for the product (caused by, say, the increase in the price of a substitute) puts upward pressure on price. However, the simultaneous increase

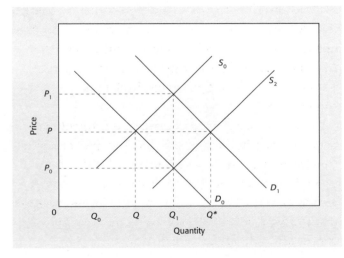

Figure 2.11 An unchanged equilibrium price and a changed equilibrium quantity

in supply (caused by, say, a fall in raw material and energy costs) puts downward pressure on price. The resulting effect is that the equilibrium price remains unchanged, although of course there is a fairly significant increase in the quantity traded (from Q to Q^*).

Self-assessment tasks

1 See if you can explain the following situations. Use a diagram to help you in each case – remember both curves are shifting now:
   (a) an increase in demand, but the equilibrium price falls;
   (b) a decrease in demand, but the equilibrium price goes up;
   (c) a decrease in supply, but the equilibrium quantity remains unchanged;
   (d) an increase in supply, but the equilibrium price increases.

2 (a) Explain the factors which might determine the demand for foreign holidays by households in the UK.
   (b) Discuss the impact of a reduction in air fares on the demand for holidays abroad and in the UK.

3 The opening of the Channel Tunnel increased the supply in the market for cross-Channel trips. With the aid of a diagram explain how this affected the market for cross-Channel trips.

4 Do some research, perhaps using the World-Wide Web (www), to find out what has happened:
   (a) to the numbers of people attending the cinema in the last ten years;
   (b) to house prices, nationally and in your area, in the last year.
   Use supply and demand analysis to explain why the changes may have occurred.

5 Analyse with the aid of diagrams:
   (a) the likely effect of a reduction in the price of pre-recorded compact discs (CDs) on the demand for visits to live music concerts;
   (b) the likely effect of a reduction in the entrance price to live music concerts on the demand for pre-recorded compact discs.

The Channel tunnel shuttle train emerges from the tunnel opening on the French side at Sangatte on 28 April as tests continued prior to the official opening ceremony on 6 May 1993
Source: Popperfoto Reuters.

The importance of elasticity

So far our analysis of markets and sub-markets has concentrated on understanding the direction of any change in supply, demand, prices or output and sales. For example, we have looked at what can cause an increase or decrease in demand and whether this change will raise or lower prices or output. We now want to add more depth to our understanding by looking at the extent of demand changes and whether there is likely to be a large or a small impact on the equilibrium. In some cases a small increase in income, for example, may have a really big impact on demand and this in turn may have a really significant impact on the equilibrium price. In other cases, the same increase in income may have little impact on demand and the market equilibrium. We need some tools or concepts to help us understand these changes more precisely. The concept that allows us to move forward in this way is elasticity.

Elasticity is simply a way of quantifying cause and effect relationships. It is defined generally as a numerical measure of *the responsiveness of one economic variable (the dependent variable) following a change in another influencing variable (the independent variable), ceteris paribus!* Where relationships are elastic (responsive), a small change in the cause or the independent variable has a big effect on the other dependent variable. Where relationships are inelastic, a large change in the cause has limited effects on the dependent variable. This might seem a bit confusing, so let us look at specific examples of elasticity – this general definition will then start to become clearer.

Price elasticity of demand (PED)

Price elasticity of demand is a numerical measure of the responsiveness of demand for one product following a change in the price of that product alone. If demand is elastic, then a small change in price will result in a relatively large change in quantity demanded. On the other hand, if price goes up by a lot and quantity demanded only falls slightly, then demand would be price inelastic. A numerical example will help clarify this. First, however, we need a way of expressing PED in a numerical form – the formula we will use at this stage is:

$$PED = \frac{\% \text{ change in quantity demanded of a product}}{\% \text{ change in price of that product}}$$

Let us take two specific examples of price changes for two general products that we will call product A and product B (see figure 2.12). Assume that both of these unrelated products currently are priced at £100 and demand for them is 1,000 units per month. Consider what is expected to happen to the demand for A and B if the price rises to £105. The quantity demanded of product A only falls from 1,000 to 990, whereas the quantity demanded of product B falls from 1,000 to 900. Now let us put these values into the PED equation to calculate the elasticity.

Figure 2.12 Elastic and inelastic demand curves

Product A $\dfrac{\% \text{ change in quantity demanded of A}}{\% \text{ change in price of A}} =$

$\dfrac{1\% \text{ fall}}{5\% \text{ increase}} = (-)0.2$

Product B $\dfrac{\% \text{ change in quantity demanded of B}}{\% \text{ change in price of B}} =$

$\dfrac{10\% \text{ fall}}{5\% \text{ increase}} = (-)2.0$

Notice that in both cases a negative figure is given, this is because of the negative (or inverse) relationship between price and quantity demanded, that is, as the price goes up, the quantity demanded goes down. Conventionally economists refer to PED in absolute terms either by ignoring the negative sign or by multiplying the PED value by −1.

Product A – because the numerical value (0.2) is less than one we say that the demand for this product is relatively inelastic or unresponsive to price changes. Over this particular range of prices, the 5 per cent increase has resulted in a much smaller change in quantity demanded.

Product B – because the numerical value (2.0) is greater than one, we say that the demand for this product is relatively elastic or responsive to price changes. Over this particular range of prices, the same 5 per cent price change has caused a much bigger change in quantity demanded.

Self-assessment tasks

1 Calculate the PEDs in each of the following cases and explain whether demand would be considered price elastic or price inelastic.

Original price	New price	Original quantity demanded	New quantity demanded
(a) £100	£102	2,000 units per week	1,950 units per week
(b) £55.50	£54.95	5,000 units per week	6,000 units per week

2 With the aid of a numerical example of your choice explain the meaning of these PED values:
   (a) PED = (–)1.5,   (b) PED = (–)0.6.

Some special PED values

It is important to realise that mathematically PED values can range from 0 to infinity. These values need explanation. Consider, for example, the demand curve shown below in figure 2.13. Irrespective of the price charged, consumers are willing and able to buy the same amount – in this case demand would be said to be **perfectly inelastic**. Let us just look at the PED calculation for an increase in price from £10 to £11

$$PED = \frac{\% \text{ change in quantity demanded}}{\% \text{ change in price}} = \frac{0\%}{+10\%} = 0$$

Hence, when the PED = 0, demand is perfectly inelastic, perfectly unresponsive to price changes.

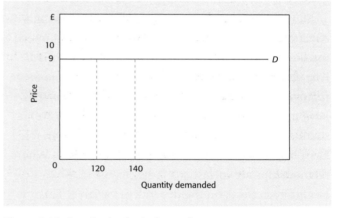

Figure 2.14 A perfectly elastic demand curve

Consider the demand curve above in figure 2.14. At a price of £10 per unit consumers are not prepared to buy any of this product; however, if price falls to £9, they will buy all that is available. The relative change in quantity demanded here, of course, is infinite, since the original demand was zero

$$PED = \frac{\% \text{ change in quantity demanded}}{\% \text{ change in price}} = \frac{\infty}{-10\%} = (-)\infty$$

Unitary elasticity

If the relative increase in price is exactly matched by the relative fall in quantity demanded, then the PED value will equal (–)1 and demand will be said to have **unitary elasticity** over that particular price range. So, for

Figure 2.13 A perfectly inelastic demand curve

example, if the price of the product goes from £1,000 to £1,050 and quantity demanded decreases from 10,000 to 9,500, then the PED will equal (−)1 over this particular range of prices.

Factors that influence price elasticity of demand
There are three key factors that influence whether, over a particular price range, demand for a product is likely to be price elastic or inelastic.

◆ *The range and attractiveness of substitutes* – the greater the number of substitute (alternative) products and the more closely substitutable those products are, the more we would expect consumers to switch away from a particular product when its price goes up (or towards that product if its price falls).

It is important, however, to distinguish between the substitutability of products within the same group of products and substitutability with goods from other product groupings. For example, different types of wine are a group of products in their own right; they are also part of a larger group of alcoholic drinks and part of the even bigger category of products that we could label as 'drinks'. If we are concerned with the price elasticity of demand for a particular type of wine produced by a specific wine maker, then it will have a fairly high PED (probably) because of the range of substitutes. As we aggregate products into groupings, such as 'white wine',

or 'all wines' or 'all alcoholic drinks', demand will start to become more price inelastic.

Other substitutability issues to consider include:
– the quality and accessibility of information that consumers have about products that are available to satisfy particular wants and needs;
– the degree to which people consider the product to be a necessity;
– the addictive properties of the product, that is, whether the product is habit forming;
– the brand image of the product.

◆ *The relative expense of the product* – a rise in price will reduce the purchasing power of a person's income (real income). The larger the proportion of income that the price represents, the larger will be the impact on the consumer's real income level of a change in the product's price. For example, a 10 per cent increase in the price of a flight to Malaysia will have a bigger impact than a 10 per cent rise in the price of a bus trip into town. The greater the relative proportion of income accounted for by the product, the higher the PED, ceteris paribus!

◆ *Time* – in the short term, perhaps weeks or months, people may find it hard to change their spending patterns. However, if the price of a product goes up and stays up, then over time people will find ways of adapting and adjusting, so the PED is likely to increase over time.

Self-assessment tasks

1 Classify the following products into whether, in your opinion, the PED is likely to be relatively high (elastic) or relatively low (inelastic):
◆ Coca Cola
◆ Pepsi Cola
◆ soft drinks in general
◆ Nike trainers
◆ Marlboro cigarettes
◆ all tobacco products
◆ Shell unleaded petrol
◆ all forms of car fuel

Justify your classification.

2 A tie manufacturer has received a market research estimate of PED values for their ties that are currently sold in three markets: to independent retailers, to prestige fashion stores and via mail order, mainly to sports clubs

Market	Current price	Current sales	PED value
Independent retailers	£8	40,000 p.a.	−1.0
Fashion stores	£15	10,000 p.a.	−0.2
Mail order	£10	3,000 p.a.	−3.0

Explain and comment upon the PED values shown above.
Source: UCLES, Paper 4381, March 1995 (adapted).

PED and a downward-sloping linear demand curve

So far the impression may have been created that PED and the slope of a demand curve are the same – this, however, is incorrect. Table 2.6 and the associated Self-assessment task will help you see the difference.

Self-assessment task

Use the information in table 2.6 to calculate the PED values as price falls from £10 to £9, from £9 to £8, from £8 to £7 and so on. You should see that the PED value falls as you move down the demand curve in figure 2.15. In the top half of the demand curve, PED > 1; in the bottom half of the demand curve, PED < 1. We could show that for very small changes in price PED = 1 at the mid point of the demand curve. That is why, in theory, a demand curve with unitary price elasticity throughout can be drawn – it is called a rectangular hyperbola. Total expenditure (the area beneath this curve) for any price quantity combination is constant.

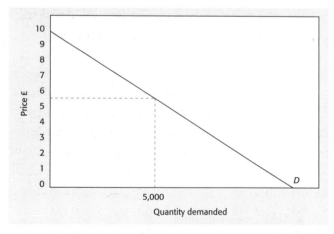

Figure 2.15 The demand curve for product R

Price of product R (£/unit)	Quantity demanded of product R (units per week)
10	0
9	1,000
8	2,000
7	3,000
6	4,000
5	5,000
4	6,000
3	7,000
2	8,000
1	9,000
0	10,000

Table 2.6 Demand schedule for product R

It is important to recognise that the relationship between income and demand changes may not always be positive. If an increase in income leads to an increase in demand (or a decrease in income leads to a decrease in demand), then there is a positive relationship and the product is classified as **normal**, and the YED has a positive value. However, there are some products (**inferior goods**) that exhibit a negative relationship between income and demand. Here an increase in income would cause a decrease in demand (a decrease in income would cause an increase in demand) and the YED has a negative value. So the sign that precedes the YED tells you the nature of the relationship between income and demand; the numerical value tells you the strength of that relationship.

Suppose that there has been a 2 per cent increase in consumer income and that has led to the following changes in demand:

Income elasticity of demand

Income elasticity of demand (YED) is defined as a numerical measure of the responsiveness of demand following a change in income alone. Once again if demand is responsive, then it is classified as elastic; if unresponsive, it is inelastic.

The formula used in this case is

$$\text{YED} = \frac{\%\ \text{change in quantity demanded}}{\%\ \text{change in income}}$$

	Original demand (per period of time)	New demand
Product A	100 units at the current price (£10)	103 units at the same price (£10)
Product B	100 units at the current price (£10)	99 units at the same price (£10)
Product C	100 units at the current price (£10)	101 units at the same price (£10)

The YED of A = $\dfrac{\text{3\% increase in demand}}{\text{2\% increase in income}}$

= +1.5 (normal good – elastic response)

The YED of B = $\dfrac{\text{1\% decrease in demand}}{\text{2\% increase in income}}$

= –0.5 (inferior good – inelastic response)

The YED of C = $\dfrac{\text{1\% increase in demand}}{\text{2\% increase in income}}$

= +0.5 (normal good – inelastic response)

Self-assessment task

Use figure 2.16 to explain the YED calculations for each of these three products. Note: the sign indicates the direction in which the demand curve shifts, the numerical value indicates how far the curve shifts at the original price.

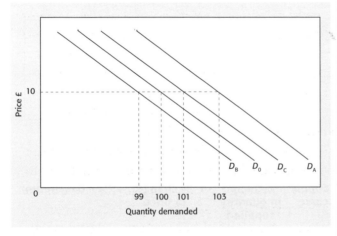

Figure 2.16 The effect of alternative income changes on the demand curve

Cross elasticity of demand

Cross elasticity of demand (XED) is a numerical measure of the responsiveness of demand for one product following a change in the price of a related product alone. Note the causal relationship that is being measured, and, since this has altered the conditions of demand, we would illustrate the impact of this change in the price of a related product by a shift in the demand curve (similar to YED above).

The formula used is

$$\text{XED} = \dfrac{\text{\% change in quantity demanded of product A}}{\text{\% change in the price of product B}}$$

One of many laptop computers on the market – a normal good but with a positive cross elasticity of demand

Products that are substitutes for each other (e.g. different types of laptop computer) will have positive values for the XED. If the price of B goes up, then people will begin to turn to product A because of its more favourable relative price. If the price of B falls, then consumers will start to buy B instead of A. Products that are complements (e.g., computers and printers or software) will have negative values of XED. If the price of B goes up, the quantity demanded of B will drop and so will the complementary demand for A.

A numerical and diagrammatic illustration

Assume the current average market price of a standard type of personal computer is £1,000 and current sales are 100 units per day (figure 2.17). Consider what might happen if, following a 2 per cent decrease in the price of laptop computers (a substitute product), demand for PCs falls from 100 units to 98 units per day at the original price (D_0 to D_1). Our calculation becomes

$$\text{XED} = \dfrac{\text{2\% fall in demand for PCs}}{\text{2\% decrease in price of laptops}}$$

= +1

The positive sign indicates that the products are substitutes.

Self-assessment task

What would have happened to the demand for PCs if, following the same change in the price of laptops, the XED had been +2. Redraw figure 2.17 to illustrate this.

Figure 2.17 A change in the demand for PCs

Now consider that the average price of software (a complement) falls by 5% – this encourages extra sales of PCs so that demand for PCs rises to 101 per day at the original price and the demand curve shifts from D_0 to D_2.

The elasticity calculation is

$$\text{XED} = \frac{1\% \text{ increase in sales of PCs}}{5\% \text{ fall in price of software}} = -0.2$$

Note again the sign indicates the nature of the relationship (a negative one between complements), the numerical value indicates the strength of that relationship.

Self-assessment tasks

1 What would happen if demand for PCs had risen to 110 units per day? Calculate the XED and redraw the diagram to illustrate what has happened.

2 The owner of a local golf course loans out equipment to non-members who want to play occasional rounds. She estimates that in June and July, if she lowers the hire price of clubs by 10 per cent, the number of non-members playing will increase by 25 per cent. Calculate and comment on the XED. What other factors should the owner consider?

Price elasticity of supply

Price elasticity of supply (PES) is a numerical measure of the responsiveness of supply to a change in the price of the product alone. The supply could be that of an individual firm or group of firms; it could of course refer to the supply of the overall industry. It is expressed as

$$\text{PES} = \frac{\% \text{ change in quantity supplied}}{\% \text{ change in price}}$$

Since the relationship between the price and quantity supplied is normally a direct one, the PES will tend to take on a positive value. If the numerical value of PES > 1, then we say that supply is relatively price elastic, that is supply is responsive. If the numerical value of PES < 1, then supply is relatively price inelastic, that is supply is unresponsive.

Figure 2.18 shows five supply curves each with different PES values.

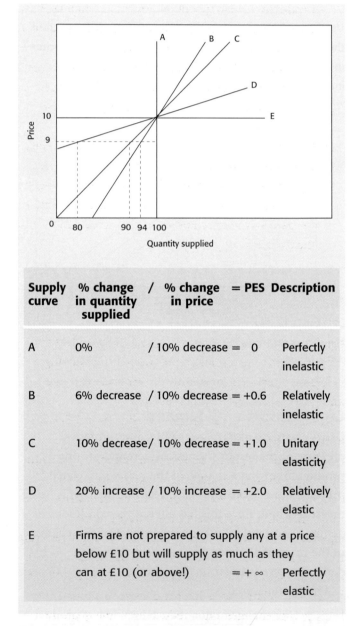

Supply curve	% change in quantity supplied	/ % change in price	= PES	Description
A	0%	/ 10% decrease	= 0	Perfectly inelastic
B	6% decrease	/ 10% decrease	= +0.6	Relatively inelastic
C	10% decrease	/ 10% decrease	= +1.0	Unitary elasticity
D	20% increase	/ 10% increase	= +2.0	Relatively elastic
E	Firms are not prepared to supply any at a price below £10 but will supply as much as they can at £10 (or above!)		= + ∞	Perfectly elastic

Figure 2.18 Five different supply curves

Factors influencing PES

The key words in understanding PES are supply flexibility – if firms and industries are more flexible in the way they behave, then supply tends to be more elastic. The main influences on PES are:

- *The ease with which firms can accumulate or reduce stocks of goods.* Stocks allow companies to meet variations in demand through output changes rather than price changes – so the more easily manufacturing firms can do this, the higher the PES. Companies that provide services are, of course, unable to build up stocks.

- *The ease with which they can increase production.* In the short run firms and industries with spare productive capacity will tend to have a higher PES. However, shortages of critical factor inputs (skilled workers, components, fuel) or transport difficulties will often lead to inelastic PES. In recent years use of better management techniques and improved relations between firms and their suppliers has probably increased the PES in many industries.

- Over time, of course, companies can increase their productive capacity by investing in more capital equipment, often taking advantage of technological advances. Equally, over time, more firms can enter or leave an industry and this will increase the flexibility of supply.

Business relevance of elasticity

Price elasticity of demand

An understanding of PED is useful to help understand price variations in a market, the impact of changing prices on consumer expenditure, corporate revenues and government indirect tax receipts.

In figure 2.19 you can see how variations in PED can lead to price volatility following a change in the conditions of supply. D_e represents a demand curve with PED > 1 over the relevant price range. D_i represents a demand curve with PED < 1 over the relevant price range. In both cases, however, the current market equilibrium is at $P_e Q_e$. Now a decrease in supply resulting from an increase in, say, production costs would result in a leftward shift in the supply curve, from S_0 to S_1. Whilst we can see in both cases that the change in equilibrium leads to higher prices and a reduction in the quantity traded, the extent of the changes varies according to the

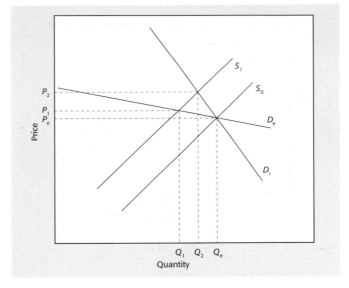

Figure 2.19 Price volatility following a change in supply

PED. For D_e, as producers try to raise prices (to pass on the higher costs to their customers), consumers reaction is to stop buying this product in their droves. This reaction constrains the extent to which prices rise only from P_e to P_1 – quantity, therefore, takes the strain here and falls considerably from Q_e to Q_1. On the other hand, when demand is relatively price inelastic, producers have the scope to raise prices considerably (P_e to P_2) without suffering from a significant drop in sales (Q_e to Q_2).

PED and total expenditure/total revenue

PED can help us understand how total spending by consumers will change as price rises or falls assuming the price change is caused by a shift in the supply curve.

$$\text{Total expenditure} = P \times Q = \text{Total revenue of a firm or industry}$$

In figure 2.20, assume there are two products each with the same equilibrium price (£10) and quantity traded (100 units per day). Total expenditure by consumers per day = £10 × 100 = £1,000 – this is of course equal to the revenue received by companies. Now, if the price rises to £11, the differences in PED indicate that consumers respond in different ways, and the total expenditure will change:

- D_e is relatively price elastic over the relevant price range, and quantity falls considerably to 80 units (PED = −2). Total expenditure is now down to £880 per day – the reason, of course, is that the relative fall in sales is greater than the relative increase in price.

- D_i is relatively price inelastic over the relevant price range and the quantity traded only falls slightly to

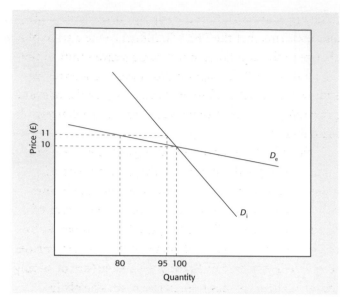

Figure 2.20 Demand curves of varying elasticities over the price range illustrated

95 units (PED = –0.5). Total expenditure actually rises even though less is traded! The reason is that the increase in price exerts a more powerful influence in this case.

Income elasticity of demand

Since YED provides information about how demand varies as income changes, the concept is potentially of great importance to planners both in business organisations and government.

If the YED for a normal good exceeds unity, then demand for that product will grow more rapidly than consumer incomes during normal periods of economic growth – hence considerably greater productive capacity may be required. However, during a recession, when incomes fall, firms producing this sort of product will be extremely vulnerable, given the large reduction in demand that might be expected.

Self-assessment tasks

1 You used this demand schedule when we looked at PED on a linear demand curve at the beginning of this section. Figure 2.21 shows the resulting demand curve.

　　Refer back to how PED varies along a linear demand curve – note, in the top half of the demand curve PED > 1 whereas in the lower half PED < 1.

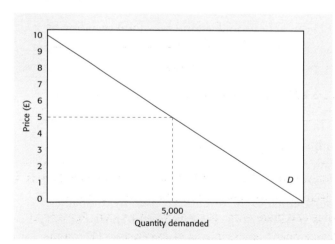

Figure 2.21 The demand curve for product R

　　Calculate the total expenditure (TE)/total revenue (TR) figures and graph the resulting values underneath the demand curve in figure 2.21 (put TE on the vertical axis and quantity on the horizontal axis – it will help if you use the same scale on the horizontal axis).

Price of product R (£/unit)	Quantity demanded of product R (units per week)	Total expenditure £ per week
10	0	
9	1,000	
8	2,000	
7	3,000	
6	4,000	
5	5,000	
4	6,000	
3	7,000	
2	8,000	
1	9,000	
0	10,000	

- ◆ What do you notice about TE/TR figures as price is cut from £10 towards £5 per unit?
- ◆ Why does this happen?
- ◆ What do you notice about the TE/TR figures as price is raised from £0 to £5?
- ◆ Why does this happen?
- ◆ Where is TE/TR maximised?

2 If a government is interested in raising more revenue from indirect taxes, such as VAT or excise duties, should it tax products that are price elastic or price inelastic? Explain and illustrate your answer with diagrams and examples.

If the YED is negative then firms producing such inferior goods will see their sales decline steadily over time as the economy grows – however, they may be the sort of business to benefit from the hard times of recession.

Self-assessment tasks

1 What will happen to sales of a product whose YED = + 0.6?
2 How could you use YED values to advise a company on how to produce a mix of goods and services that would reduce the risk often associated with only producing a very narrow range of products?
3 Why might government planners be interested in the YED values of different products?

Cross elasticity of demand

Many companies are concerned with the impact that rival pricing strategies will have, ceteris paribus, on the demand for their own product. Remember that substitutes are characterised by a positive XED: the higher the numerical value, the greater the degree of substitutability between these alternatives in the eyes of the consumer. In such cases there is a high degree of interdependence between suppliers, and the dangers of a rival cutting price are likely to be very significant indeed.

Companies are increasingly concerned with trying to tie consumers to buy not just one of their products but a whole range of complementary ones, for example computer printers and print cartridges. XED will identify those products that are most complementary and help a company introduce a pricing structure that generates more revenue. For instance, market research may indicate that families spend most money at the cinema when special deals are offered on ticket prices, even though the PED for ticket prices is low. In this case, for example, the high negative cross elasticity between ticket prices and the demand for food, such as ice cream and popcorn, means that, although the revenue from ticket sales may fall, this may be compensated for by increased sales of food. This points to the need for a more sophisticated pricing structure within the cinema looking at the relationships between the demand for all products and services offered, including other merchandise such as T-shirts and posters.

Price elasticity of supply

You have already seen how variations in PED will influence the nature of a change in the equilibrium following a given shift in the supply curve. Figure 2.22 also confirms that the PES will influence the nature of a change in the equilibrium following a given shift in the demand curve. The diagram illustrates two alternative supply curves with different elasticities over the relevant price range. S_e is relatively price elastic, S_i is relatively price inelastic.

If the initial equilibrium is at PQ and then demand for a normal good increases, perhaps because of an increase in income, in both cases the new equilibrium price and quantity are higher. However, in the case of S_e, the greater flexibility in supply allows companies to respond to this increased demand without raising prices so much. In the case of S_i, the inflexible nature of supply means that companies raise prices more sharply in response to the surge in demand.

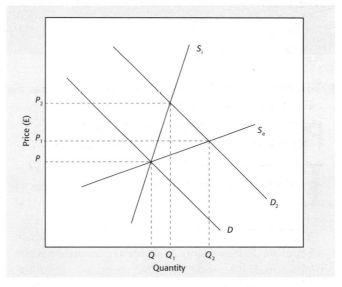

Figure 2.22 Supply curves of varying elasticities over the price range illustrated

Self-assessment task

Redraw figure 2.22 to consider what will happen if there is a decrease in demand, perhaps because of a change in tastes and preferences away from this product. Remember you are analysing the impact of variations in PES on the new equilibrium.

◆ Under what conditions will prices fall most? Why is this?
◆ Under what conditions will there be the greatest decrease in sales? Why is this?

You will note that as with PED, prices tend to be more volatile when supply is inelastic, and quantity is more changeable when supply is price elastic.

Self-assessment task

Source: Still Pictures.

Read the case study below and then tackle the exercises that follow.

Package Holidays

Last year, 18 million Britons went on package holidays. Most of these were low to mid-priced 'sun and sand' packages to the Mediterranean and to Florida with one of the big operators.

The package holiday business is a complex one, which requires the tour operators to secure accommodation and flights often 12 to 18 months ahead of departure. Thereafter, matching this supply with demand from holiday makers takes place via the market mechanism. Peak period prices, usually during school holidays, are much higher than the equivalent off-peak package. Equally, if customers want choice then they must book early, otherwise they take a risk that the holiday of their

dreams will not be available at the last minute at a reduced price. The table below shows some estimated elasticities of demand for three typical package holidays.

Package holiday type	Price elasticity of demand		Income elasticity of demand
	Peak	Off-peak	
Self-catering to Ibiza	(–)0.6	(–)1.2	–1.0
Fly drive to Florida	(–)0.8	(–)1.4	1.6
Villa holiday to Portugal	(–)0.4	(–)0.8	2.4

(a) State and give examples of **three** different factors of production needed to produce a package holiday.

(b) ◆ Define elasticity of supply.
   ◆ Using the information above, would you expect the elasticity of supply for package holidays to be elastic or inelastic? Justify your answer.

(c) With reference to the table, use diagrams to analyse how an increase in the incomes of package holiday makers might affect their demand for:
   ◆ self-catering holidays in Ibiza,
   ◆ villa holidays in Portugal.

(d) Discuss how the information in table 2 could be used by a tour operator.

Source: OCR, Paper 2881, June 2001 (adapted).

Cautionary note

We have assumed that calculating elasticity values is straightforward. In fact there are enormous statistical problems. As an example consider the difficulties of calculating PED values from historical data. Have the price changes only been caused by supply variations? Have there been any non-price demand influences at work? Remember, if we are to calculate the PED value accurately, we need to separate out all the other influences and just measure the impact of the price change alone on quantity demanded – the difficulty encountered here is referred to as the identification problem. Collecting data from other sources, such as market testing, or surveys (using questionnaires and/or interviews), is costly in terms of time and money and may not be particularly valid or reliable. As such, many companies may prefer to make rough 'guestimates' of elasticity values or to work with incomplete data, particularly if they are operating in markets where rapid change means past data cease to be a good indicator of the future.

Factor markets and how they work

The previous section provided an introduction to the nature of factors of production. Like the product market, there is also a market in operation for land, labour, capital and enterprise. In particular, the case of the labour market will be described here, not least because its operation is something which affects all of us at some stage in our lives. The general principles which operate are the same as those described earlier in this section.

Labour earns an income in the form of hourly paid wages, monthly salaries or, in some cases, bonuses on top of such regular payments. It is a well-known fact, though, that in the labour market some people earn more than others. For example, if you have a part-time job, then you are likely to be paid £3 per hour or possibly £4. At the other extreme, a top Premier League footballer earns say £20,000 per week – he probably earns as much for a few minutes warm up before a game as you might earn for a whole day's work filling shelves in a supermarket. Why is this? In simple terms it is due to market conditions of demand and supply, which operate in the labour market.

The economic principles which apply are no different from those analysed earlier but with one important difference. This is that in factor markets it is firms that

demand labour and it is households that supply them with labour. In other words, the positions are the reverse of those which have applied throughout the rest of this section. To provide a service or to produce goods firms need to employ factors of production, such as labour. For this reason the demand for labour is referred to by economists as a **derived demand**. Take the case of a sixth former working at the local supermarket. The reason for this is that the supermarket needs goods to be stacked onto shelves so that customers can buy them. If there were no goods on the shelves, then the supermarket's tills would be standing idle! Similarly, for someone employed in a car assembly plant or making CD players, that worker is employed as a consequence of the demand from consumers for new cars and CD equipment. The demand for labour is, therefore, derived from the demand for the final product.

In general the demand and supply curves for labour are the same as those illustrated earlier for goods and services. Figure 2.23 shows a typical example of the market supply and demand curves for hotel workers in London. Take the supply curve first:

- the higher the wages paid, the more people will want to work in hotels;
- consequently, the supply curve for hotel workers is upwards sloping.

For the demand curve:

- the higher the wages that hotel companies have to pay, the fewer workers they will want to employ;

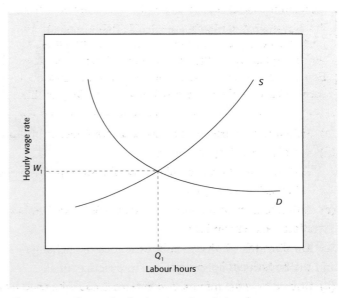

Figure 2.23 The market for hotel workers in London

♦ consequently, the demand curve for hotel workers is downward sloping.

Equilibrium in the market is determined by the intersection of the demand and supply curves for labour. The wage paid, W_1, is the price at which the particular market clears.

The above is a very simplified representation of the way labour markets actually operate. In practice they are much more complex than this and influenced by many things. The market supply curve for labour is very dependent on the elasticity of supply of labour. If wages change, only a few (or possibly a lot more workers) may join the labour market. A whole host of factors relating to labour immobility could explain this (see unit 2, section 5). Equally, the elasticity of demand for labour with respect to changes in wages depends on the ease of substitution of labour by other factors of production, the proportion of wage costs in total costs and the response time involved.

In conclusion, figure 2.23 assumes we are dealing unrealistically with a labour market which operates as a perfect market. In practice very few labour markets are perfect, although some do generally operate in this way, particularly where there are many buyers and sellers and the labour concerned has no particular skills and qualities.

Self-assessment tasks

Refer back to figure 2.23

1 Explain, with the aid of a diagram, how the equilibrium wage rate would change if:
   ♦ a major sporting event such as the European Football Championships or the Olympic Games were being held in London;
   ♦ hotels in London did not recruit migrant workers from the rest of the EU.

2 From your own experience what determines how much you might be paid for a part-time job? How does this relate to the simple theory of wages described above?

The money market

Section 1 of this unit introduced the idea of exchange and the benefits of specialisation. In practice, in all except for the most primitive economies, these fundamental processes are facilitated by means of

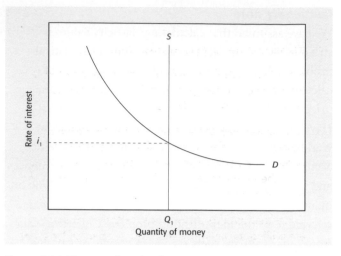

Figure 2.24 The overall market for money

money. Just think about how tedious our daily lives would be if we had to physically exchange one good we might have for others we might require. This is where money comes in, for it is money which facilitates the free flow of goods in an economy. But what is money? This may seem an obvious question, with Bank of England notes and coins being an obvious answer. To the economist, though, money is rather more than this. For the time being money can be regarded as anything which is readily acceptable as a means of settling debt. Money need not be coins and notes – it could be something more tangible like precious stones, goats or salt (a very valuable resource a few hundred years ago). The item classed as money, though, must be acceptable to all concerned as a means of exchange. This overriding definition therefore covers the supply of money. At this stage, it is necessary to see the demand for money as the desire to hold money; in other words, to keep one's wealth or assets in the form of money to give immediate access to its purchasing power.

The operation of the **money market** in practice is dealt with in detail in unit 7 of OCR's specification. At a simple level this market operates in the same way as all other markets analysed so far in this section. This is shown in figure 2.24. The supply curve of money is assumed to be perfectly inelastic with respect to the rate of interest, whilst the demand curve is downward sloping like other demand curves. Where they intersect is the **rate of interest**. To the borrower, this is the payment that has to be paid in order to obtain money; to the lender it is the reward received for parting with the money. In simple terms, it acts as a price in the money market.

Summary

In this section we have recognised that:

- A market exists whenever people come together for the trade or exchange of goods and services; it is also possible to identify sub-markets.

- The buying side of the market is referred to by economists as the demand side. It is possible to derive a demand curve for any market – this shows how the quantity which is demanded varies with the price of a product.

- Consumer surplus arises because some consumers are willing to pay more than the given price for what they buy.

- The demand curve shifts to the left or right when, 'other things being equal', the assumption is changed. Three important causes of this are a change in income, a change in consumer tastes or attitudes and a change in the price of related products.

- The selling side of the market is known as the supply side. It is possible to derive a supply curve for any market – this shows how the quantity which is supplied varies with the price of the product.

- Producer surplus can arise when firms produce below the market price.

- The supply curve shifts to the left or right when, 'other things being equal', the assumption is changed. Three important causes of this are a change in the costs of supply, a change in the characteristics of the industry and changes in government policy.

- Equilibrium occurs in the market where there is no tendency for change, when the plans of consumers match the plans of suppliers. A change to the equilibrium position will produce a new equilibrium price and quantity.

- Elasticity is a very important concept in markets; it is the responsiveness of one economic variable following a change in another variable.

- Price, income and cross elasticity of demand are relevant numerical measures which have considerable value and use in enhancing our understanding of how markets operate. The price elasticity of supply is relevant in understanding how producers can react in markets.

- The labour and money markets operate in the same way as any other market. Wages are the price of labour and the rate of interest is the price for obtaining or lending money.

Key words

Definitions of Key words can be found in the Glossary on page 240.

ceteris paribus	market
complements	market demand
consumer surplus	money market
costs	normal goods
cross elasticity of demand	notional demand
demand	perfectly elastic
demand curve	perfectly inelastic
demand schedule	price elasticity of demand
derived demand	price elasticity of supply
disequilibrium	producer surplus
effective demand	rate of interest
elasticity	sub-market
equilibrium	substitutes
income elasticity of	supply
demand	supply curve
inferior goods	supply schedule
labour market	unitary elasticity

3 Firms and how they operate

The firm's costs of production

An entrepreneur must consider all the costs of the factors of production involved in the final output. These are the **private costs** directly incurred by the owners. Production may create costs for other people but these are not necessarily taken into account by the **firm**. In order to understand cost structures in business economists split costs into different categories and use specific cost concepts.

Fixed costs

These are the costs which are completely independent of output. Total **fixed cost** data when drawn on a graph would appear as a horizontal straight line. At zero output, any costs that a firm has must be fixed. Some firms operate in a situation where the fixed cost represents a large proportion of the total. In this case it would be wise to produce a large output in order to reduce unit costs.

Variable costs

Variable costs include all the costs which are directly related to the level of output, the usual ones being labour and raw material or component costs. Sometimes a cost has elements of both; for example a firm's electricity bill may consist of the heating and lighting cost of the premises and the power to operate production machinery. Electricity, therefore, could be considered to be a **semi-fixed** and semi-variable cost.

Total cost (TC) equals fixed cost (FC) plus variable cost (VC).

From this information all the relevant cost concepts can be derived.

Average fixed cost (AFC)

$$\text{equals} \quad \frac{\text{total fixed cost}}{\text{output}}$$

Average variable cost (AVC)

$$\text{equals} \quad \frac{\text{total variable cost}}{\text{output}}$$

Average total cost (ATC)

$$\text{equals} \quad \frac{\text{total cost}}{\text{output}}$$

Marginal cost (MC) is the addition to the total cost when making one extra unit and is, therefore, a variable cost.

The most important cost curve for the firm will be the ATC. If it is U shaped, the most efficient output for the firm will be where the unit cost is lowest. If the firm chose to produce in the downward-sloping part of the average cost curve it would be experiencing **increasing returns** to the variable factors. The unit cost is falling because the fixed cost is being spread over an increasing output. The firm will be most efficient if it produces at the minimum point of the average total cost curve. This is known as the **optimum output** and the marginal cost always cuts the ATC at this point. The most efficient output is not necessarily the most profitable. For a firm wishing to maximise its profits, its chosen output will depend on the relationship between its revenue and its costs.

Costs in the short run and the long run

The **short run** for the firm is a period of time when it cannot alter its fixed inputs. The level of production can only be changed by altering its variable inputs such as labour. The time taken to alter fixed factors differs, depending on how easy it is to get new capital installed.

In the **long run**, the firm can alter *all* of its inputs, so that they become variable in nature.

In the very long run, technological change can alter the way the whole production process is organised, even the nature of the products themselves. In a society with rapid technological progress this will be shrinking the time period. There are now examples in consumer electronics where whole processes and products have become obsolete in a matter of months.

Short-run costs

When a firm working with fixed factors increases the variable ones, there will come a point where the returns to the variable units begin to fall. This is the principle of **diminishing returns**. It will be reflected in an increase in the firm's marginal and, eventually, its average total costs. The firm will be at its most efficient in the short run if it can operate at the optimum or the lowest point on the average total cost curve (see figure 3.1(a)).

Figure 3.1(a) Costs in the short run

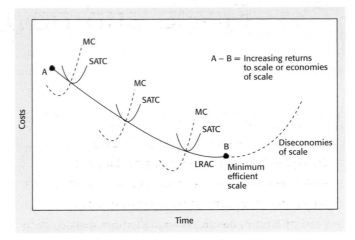

Figure 3.1(b) Costs in the long run

Costs in the long run

It is possible that a firm can find a way of lowering its cost structure over time. One way might be by increasing the amount of capital used relative to labour in the production process, with a consequent increase in factor productivity.

The long-run average cost curve (LRAC) shows the least cost combination of producing any particular quantity. Figure 3.1(b) shows a firm experiencing falling ATC over time. This would enable it to lower the price without sacrificing profit. Products such as Walkmans, personal organisers and games consoles are examples where prices have fallen through competition and changing technology.

Economies of scale

Where an expansion of output leads to a reduction in the unit costs, the benefits are referred to as **economies of scale**. They occur because the firm's output is rising proportionally faster than the inputs; hence the firm is getting increasing returns to scale.

What kind of economies of scale can be identified?

Internal economies are those benefits which only affect an individual firm, whereas external economies will benefit all the firms in a locality or in the market.

Technical economies refer to the advantages gained directly in the production process. Some production techniques only become economic beyond a certain level of output. The economy of increased dimensions occurs in a number of business applications.

If one takes the production of a box structure, and doubles the scale, its production costs will double. If it is being used to carry something, then the operating costs may not increase in proportion. The capacity of the box will have increased eightfold, generating a much larger potential revenue. The trick is to make sure that the extra capacity is fully used. Making full use of capacity is also important on a production line. Car production is the result of various assembly lines. The number of finished vehicles per hour is limited by the pace of the slowest sub-process. Firms producing on a big scale can increase the number of slow-moving lines to keep pace with the fastest, so that no resources are standing idle and the flow of finished products is higher. One of the problems of the British motor industry was its small-scale output limited by low sales. Some firms produced at higher unit cost than competitors and this is one of the motives behind takeovers and mergers over the years, to get a bigger market share and benefit from economies of scale.

In addition to technical economies, economists have identified:

- *Marketing economies.* This is where large firms can achieve savings in unit cost from advertising or packaging. The usual one is the benefit of lower prices by buying in bulk from suppliers.
- *Financial economies.* Large firms will find both the access to borrowed funds easier, and the cost lower, than smaller firms will. This is because the perceived risk of lending to large-scale operators is lower.
- *Managerial economies.* Firms producing on a large scale may be able to re-organise the structure in order to get a more efficient management of resources. They may also attract the best management talent through higher salaries.
- *Risk-bearing economies.* These might explain why, as firms get larger, they become more diversified. It is a way of spreading business risks. A diversified conglomerate can cover any losses on one activity with the profits from another, an option not open to smaller firms. Risks can be further reduced by co-operating with rivals on large capital projects.

The last example above may be an illustration of an *external* economy since all firms will benefit from savings in research and development costs. Large firms may also benefit from locating close to others in the same market. The advantages may include a pool of skilled labour or a convenient supply of components. This may explain the trend for firms to cluster in business and science parks in certain parts of the country. The better transport infrastructure will be another advantage to all the firms.

It must be recognised that there are limits to economies of scale. A firm can expand its output too much with the result that unit costs start to rise. This may be the beginning of **diseconomies of scale**. The most likely source of these lies in the problems of co-ordinating large organisations and the effect size has on morale and motivation. A firm that is producing at its optimum output in the short run and at the lowest unit cost in the long run (sometimes called the minimum efficient scale [MES]) has maximised its efficiency (see section 4). Industries where the MES is low will have a big population of firms. Where it is high, competition will tend to be between a few large players.

The firm's revenue

In looking at the revenue of a firm, economists are dealing with the receipts the firm receives from the sale of the various products it produces. In general terms the total sales revenue will be influenced by the selling price of the product and the number of units bought by consumers at that price. The following general definitions apply:

Total revenue (TR) equals price (P) multiplied by quantity (Q);

Average revenue (AR) equals total revenue divided by quantity and is the same thing as the price;

Marginal revenue (MR) is the addition to the total revenue resulting from the sale of one extra unit of output.

A firm that accepts the ruling market price will get the same price whenever it increases its output. Therefore the marginal revenue will be constant and equal to average revenue. If, however, the market price falls as output increases, the firm will be facing a downward-sloping demand curve and its marginal revenue will be less than the average revenue. Any firm must look carefully at potential revenue together with its cost structure when determining its output. It is only possible to predict what this output will be if one has this data and the objectives of the firm are clearly understood.

The objectives of firms

The standard assumption made by economists is that firms will seek to maximise their profits. **Profit**, in economic terms, is simply the difference between the firm's total revenue and its total costs. There will be a minimum level of profit necessary for the entrepreneur to stay in business. This is the concept of **normal profit**. It reflects the opportunity cost of the business capital used by the firm in the production process, that is what it could earn in its next most desired economic activity. This element of total profit can be considered as an essential cost of production and as such it is included in the firm's average costs. A firm making the minimum level of profit is said to be producing the break-even output. In most situations the firm could be expected to increase its profit by raising output. Any extra profit is termed **abnormal** or **supernormal** and it is assumed that this is the motive for firms to supply to the market. It is the reward for risk taking and managing resources.

If the firm produces up to the point where the cost of making the last unit is just covered by the revenue from selling it, then the profit margin will have fallen to zero and total profits will be greatest.

The rule for **profit maximisation** is therefore that the firm should produce where

MC equals MR

and the distance between TR and TC is greatest.

At any output below this, the firm is sacrificing potential profit, whilst any output above it is being sold at a loss, reducing the firm's total profit. Profit maximisation therefore is an ideal for firms to work to.

From a business standpoint, there may be several reasons why firms do not operate at the profit maximisation output:

- In practice it may be difficult to identify this output. It is also likely to be very difficult for firms to be able to calculate their marginal cost and their marginal revenue. Instead the firms may simply work out the cost per unit and add on a profit margin in order to determine the selling price. This cost plus pricing technique is unlikely to result in maximum profit, although it could produce a high level of profit.
- Short-term profit maximising may not be in the long-term interest of the company. Firms with large market shares may wish to avoid the attention of the Competition Commission.

- Large abnormal profit may attract new entrants into the industry and make existing firms vulnerable.
- High profits may damage the relationship between the firm and its stakeholders, such as the consumers and the company workforce. Profit maximisation may not appeal to the management, who may have different objectives.
- High profits might trigger action by the firm's rivals and it could become a target for a takeover.

Alternative objectives

Because of the problems of applying the profit maximisation objective, economists have recognised other objectives of firms. These are of particular significance from a practical standpoint. Some of the most important ones are described below.

Sales revenue maximisation

This is where a firm may be willing to accept lower short-run profit in order to increase its share of the market. A firm choosing this option would raise output beyond MC = MR until MR had fallen to zero. Extra sales after this would contribute nothing to total revenue; therefore it is the sales revenue maximisation output. There may still be abnormal profit if total revenue is higher than total cost.

Sales maximisation

This option maximises the volume of sales rather than the sales revenue. In this option the firm would increase output up to the break-even output where the total revenue just covered the total cost. A higher output implies loss-making behaviour. The only situation where this would be possible is where the firm could use the profit from some other activities to cover these losses, using the principle of cross subsidisation. The most likely motive for loss-making behaviour is to gain a toehold in a new market or to deter new entrants into an existing one. Short-term profit is therefore the opportunity cost of raising the level of sales.

Satisficing

This behaviour would occur when a firm is determined to make a reasonable level of profits to satisfy the shareholders but also to keep the other stakeholding groups happy. It may choose to sacrifice profit in order to improve the workforce's pay and conditions or to keep prices down for the benefit of consumers. Firms may have charitable or environmental objectives, which must be financed at the cost of profit. Satisficing can also be a feature of firms that have enjoyed a high market share over a long period of time. Complacency can lead to firms losing their focus on the cost structure or failing to devote resources to either product or process innovation. Either situation can lead to a loss of profits.

Where the ownership is divorced from the control in a company, the managerial motives may differ from those of the shareholders. If management salaries are linked to output, the management will prefer rapid growth and sales revenue maximisation. If the firm has close rivals and the growth strategy entails taking big risks, it can lead to a more cautious managerial approach because job security and career advancement prospects will influence their decisions. Also, time and money may be used in improving the non-monetary rewards, such as company cars, private health insurance and company pension rights. In some firms a desire for greater prestige leads to the construction of expensive head offices and greater emphasis on corporate entertaining.

One must be careful of sweeping statements concerning firms' short-run behaviour. Extra long-run profits may follow from short-term sacrifices. As a working assumption, it is though still valid to see profit maximisation as the major long-term objective influencing firms' competitive behaviour.

Self-assessment tasks

1 The following items are a selection of business costs. Indicate whether each one is fixed, variable or a mixture of both:

the rent of a factory	business rates
workers' pay	electricity costs
raw materials	advertising expenditure
interest on loans	management salaries
transport costs	depreciation on fixed capital

2 Calculate the firm's costs and revenue from the following information. The firm is operating at a uniform price of £60 per unit sold.

Output	FC	VC	TC	AFC	AVC	ATC	MC	TR	AR	MR
0	60									
1		50							60	
2		80								
3		105								
4		152								
5		225								
6		330								

(a) What is the profit-maximising output?

(b) What is the TR at this output?

(c) What is the TC at this output?

(d) How much abnormal profit is made?

(e) What output would maximise sales revenue?

3 Study the case study below and then answer the questions that follow.

Big business in coffee retailing

Coffee retailing is big business. The best city-centre sites command rents of more than £100,000 a year and when a site becomes vacant there is often intense competition from the major coffee retailers to obtain it. Before a new outlet can open for business, up to £300,000 has to be spent on equipping it with attractive furnishings and catering equipment. The figure shows a typical cost structure for producing a cup of cappuccino by a high street coffee retailer.

Price of a cup of coffee – where your money goes

(a) Using the figure give **one** example of a fixed cost and **one** example of a variable cost to a coffee retailer. Justify your answers.

(b) Discuss the likely effects on this retail market for coffee of a large increase in city-centre rents.

Source: OCR, Paper 2881, January 2003 (adapted).

4 Study the information provided below on the operating costs of heavy goods vehicles and then answer the questions that follow.

Steady Haul Logistics is a small road transport company. Its owner, Eddie Shifter, is becoming increasingly concerned about rising fuel prices. A typical annual cost structure for operating one of his goods vehicles is shown in the table opposite.

Annual vehicle operating cost structure (% total costs)		
Fixed Costs	Rent	10%
	Other	20%
Variable Costs	Fuel	35%
	Labour	25%
	Maintenance costs	10%

(a) What is the difference between fixed costs and variable costs.

(b) Explain **one** fixed cost item that might have been included in the 'Other' category of the table.

(c) Using the information in the table discuss whether Eddie is right to be 'increasingly concerned about rising fuel prices'.

Source: OCR, Paper 2881, January 2001 (adapted).

5 The following case study looks at some of the objectives of the firm. Read it and answer the questions which follow:

Chefaid plc

A row has broken out in the boardroom of Chefaid plc, the kitchenware company, over the firm's prospects and future direction. The marketing director announced a record level of sales for the last quarter and suggested that there should be a 10 per cent target for the growth of sales revenue over the coming year. It was suggested to him that this was unwise. The firm's latest product, an exclusive set of kitchen tools, has yet to break even. The sales record owes a lot to the current popularity of cookery programmes on TV; there is a danger that the sales boom is a flash in the pan.

The managing director was more interested in the firm's profitability. He was under pressure to declare higher future dividends and to get the funds to finance the planned new factory. He believed that a profit-maximisation strategy was the best way forward. The production director warned the meeting that cost pressures were building up and that industrial relations with the workforce were fragile because of the beginning of talks about wages and new working conditions. Management in general had been delighted with the new share option scheme and the bonus linked to sales performance.

It was suggested that the prospects for growth in general were good, because of the increase in consumer confidence, and the firm's market share had benefited from the closure of two large rivals during the recession. It was argued that the market structure was becoming less competitive and this might give an opportunity for price rises. The company must not lose sight of its long-term drive to raise profitability by reducing unit costs. This sparked further disagreement over the firm's sponsorship commitments, its promotions budget and its charitable contributions.

(a) What do economists understand by the phrase 'the market structure is becoming less competitive'?

(b) What will be the best output for the firm if the profit-maximising strategy wins the day?

(c) What are the risks associated with this strategy?

(d) What output would maximise turnover?

(e) What does the phrase 'fail to break even' mean? What advice would you give to improve the performance of the new product?

(f) Explain why the management may not favour profit maximisation.

(g) To what extent does the case show that businesses have a range of objectives?

(h) Discuss the idea that each business decision to reach an objective has risks attached to it.

The market operations of firms

Firms operate in markets; in any particular market, though, there may be just one or many firms competing for business. The term **market structure** is used by economists to describe the context in which firms compete with each other and refers to the number of firms and their relative size in the market. Firms' behaviour from a business standpoint is influenced by the characteristics of particular market structures. The safest and potentially most profitable situation is that of a **monopoly**, a single seller without close rivals, whilst at the other end of the spectrum lies a theoretical structure economists have called **perfect competition**. The purpose of studying extreme models such as these is to provide benchmarks, against which real markets can be judged. **Monopolistic competition** has features of both the extreme cases, but is closest to perfect competition. **Oligopoly**, on the other hand, is closer to a monopoly situation. The important thing to understand is that the boundaries between these market structures can become blurred – this is particularly the case as an oligopoly moves towards a monopoly. One of the key economic concepts in explaining how firms come to be operating in a particular market structure is that of **barriers to**

Concorde is the only operational supersonic transport aircraft. It was developed as a joint Anglo-French venture when it was realised that neither country alone could fund the project. The Concorde project would probably have never been started had it not been for hopelessly optimistic initial estimates of development cost. As the true costs escalated, and the British economy faltered, the British Government attempted to pull out, but this was implacably resisted by France. Initial entry of Concorde into service was hampered by American resistance on the pretext of the high noise levels. As a consequence it was some time before flights to New York were permitted. The aircraft now returns an operating profit, but the development costs will never be recovered. Subsequent studies for a replacement have so far always floundered on the inability of manufacturers to demonstrate a positive return on investment. Sadly, Concorde will cease to operate from Autumn 2003.
Source: This photo appears with kind permission of Dick Barnard.

entry. The more difficult it is for new firms to compete, the closer the industry will be to a monopoly.

Barriers to entry

These consist of a mixture of obstacles, which either deter or prevent new firms from competing with the established players in a market. The construction and maintenance of these barriers can become part of a firm's competitive behaviour. Below are some of the main barriers that can be identified:

◆ Some industries such as car manufacturing and aircraft production have huge set up costs. The barrier to new firms is really the access to capital. Fixed capital represents a high proportion of total cost in these activities. In addition, the research and development cost necessary to compete effectively will put a strain on the resources of all but the largest firms. Where the new entrants would have to spend a huge amount on fixed capital and it would simply duplicate existing capital, for example railway infrastructure and electricity networks, this is sometimes referred to as a natural monopoly. It might therefore not make economic sense to have more than one producer

◆ The risk attached to entering such industries is increased if the capital cannot be recovered in the event of business failure. It will happen whenever the firm uses specialist capital that is not easily transferable to other economic uses. This is the concept of sunk cost and it acts as a barrier to exit from as well as entry into an industry.

◆ Advertising and brand names with a high degree

of customer loyalty may prove to be a difficult obstacle to overcome. This explains why firms regard their marketing expenditure as an act of investment. Existing firms can make entry more difficult through brand proliferation, giving the customers an apparent abundance of choice and closing any market niches that new entrants could exploit.

◆ In a market dominated by firms with a large output, economies of scale can create an effective barrier. New entrants will naturally be at a cost disadvantage because the large ones can produce at lower average cost. This also gives them an opportunity to consider price cutting as a way of eliminating any high-cost producers. This is the concept of predatory or destroyer pricing.

◆ Some existing firms may have a monopoly access to either raw materials, components or retail outlets, which will make it difficult for new firms to break into the market. Vertically integrated manufacturing businesses are protected by the fact that rivals' costs will be higher. The firms may have also acquired specific technical knowledge through experience of production, which newcomers find difficult to match.

◆ The production process or the products themselves may be protected by patents. This is an example of a legal barrier to entry. In the past, when industries have been nationalised this has created state-owned legal monopolies. Some activities, such as the sale of alcohol and medicines, are still controlled by licensing, which limits access to approved suppliers. In the case of retail development, the refusal of planning permission for new outlets can create a legal protection for existing suppliers.

◆ In activities such as computer manufacturing and consumer electronics, the pace of product innovation is so rapid that the existing firms will be working on the next generation products whilst launching the current range. Unless the new entrants have new ideas or can exploit a new market segment, they are destined to fail.

◆ It may be possible for existing firms to hide the existence of abnormal profit by what is called entry limit pricing. This involves deliberately setting low prices to deter potential rivals. It may be in the interest of all the firms to do this, in which case a kind of restrictive practice might be the barrier to entry.

◆ Collaboration or co-operation between big firms to develop new products, though not a restrictive practice, may mean that the resources necessary to compete in such markets are beyond the means of any single firm, so deterring new entrants.

◆ Market conditions such as a fall in demand resulting from economic recession can leave firms with excess production capacity and this will deter entry.

Some of the barriers to entry are easier to overcome than others. New firms will only enter a market when they think that the economic returns will be greater than the cost of breaking the barriers. Where the barriers to entry and exit are low, the market is sometimes described as being contestable. In these market situations there are potential competitors, even if few actually appear.

Strong barriers to entry are associated with oligopoly and monopoly, but there are very good particular examples of monopoly power being eroded by new competitors. The Virgin Group for example has achieved this in the airline industry and the soft drinks market. Even firms with a domestic monopoly are likely to be challenged by imported goods, especially if large profits are possible. In a world where the financial resources of international firms are large, they may be prepared to break into markets by using cross subsidisation to cover initial losses.

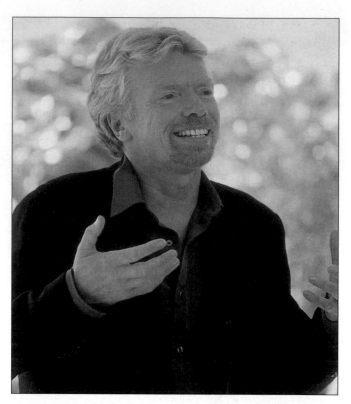

Richard Branson, chairman of Virgin Atlantic Airways, addresses a gathering of US airline executives in Washington. Branson called upon the US Congress to allow him to own and operate a US airline.
Source: Popperfoto Reuters.

Self-assessment task

For each of the following business activities, consider what barriers to entry there might be for a new firm wishing to enter this particular market:

◆ a local newsagent's shop
◆ a town centre travel agency
◆ beer production
◆ car manufacturing

Characteristics of market structures

This unit will now be completed with a brief description of the main types of market structures identified and used by economists. (Models of these structures will be developed in the A2 stage of OCR's syllabus.)

One of the quickest ways of determining what kind of market structure exists in a particular industry is to use concentration ratios. Data on the sales revenue of the biggest three or five firms, relative to the total sales revenue of the industry, will show the market power of the big firms. A high sales concentration ratio is associated with oligopoly and monopoly whilst a low one would be a feature of monopolistic competition. This is a very useful starting point for the analysis of any market – unfortunately data are not always readily available to allow this calculation to be made.

Figure 3.2 shows the main characteristics of each of the recognised market structures. The significance of barriers to entry, discussed earlier, is clearly shown in the competition roadmap in figure 3.3.

Perfect competition

In this market structure, although there would be a large number of competing firms, the individual firm

Monopoly

Market dominated by single firm.
In theory the monopoly firm is the industry.
Barriers to entry.
Abnormal profit is possible in short and long run.
Monopolist is a profit maximiser.
Monopolist is a price maker.

Oligopoly

Market dominated by handful of big firms.
Barriers to entry and exit.
Firms may or may not be profit maximisers.
Firms are price makers.
There is product differentiation.

Monopolistic competition

Market consists of large number of firms.
Products are differentiated.
There are no or few barriers to entry and exit.
Firms are profit maximisers.
Abnormal profit is only a feature of short run.

Perfect competition

Very large number of buyers and sellers with perfect knowledge.
Each firm is a price taker.
Firms are profit maximisers.
The products are homogeneous.
There is complete freedom of entry.

Figure 3.2 Economic models of competition

has little scope for competitive behaviour. This is because the products are all of the same quality, the firm has no power to alter the price it could charge and there are no barriers to entry. The firm is a **price taker** and its revenue depends on the output it chooses. The only way that firms will end up with different profits is if some of them have lower production costs than others. If any firms do make abnormal profit, it will only be temporary because in the long run new firms will be attracted into the industry and the abnormal profit will be competed away. From this description it is unlikely that there will be any markets that match this description. The nearest economic activity might be parts of the agricultural industry where large numbers of small producers supply a homogeneous product, such as milk or grain.

Monopolistic competition

The main feature which distinguishes this market structure from a perfect market is product differentiation. Each of the suppliers also has a degree of control over the price that is charged. Firms can therefore indulge in both price and **non-price competition**. The large number of substitute products makes this a very competitive market structure. Firms will only be successful in making abnormal profit in the short run because there are no or few barriers to entry. However a successful advertising policy to promote the brand, combined with product innovation, could shift the firm's demand curve to the right and at the same time reduce its price elasticity of demand if consumers no longer see rivals' products as close substitutes. The market power of firms is constrained by the ease of entry and the behaviour of rival firms. This is a very relevant type of market structure and includes hairdressers' shops, video rental outlets and driving schools.

Oligopoly

When an industry is dominated by a handful of big firms, action taken by one will have a big impact on the others. It becomes risky for a firm to alter its price because the reaction of the others is uncertain. Firms in this market structure may prefer to use non-price competition, such as product innovation, advertising and brand proliferation. The risks associated with competitive behaviour may become so great that firms

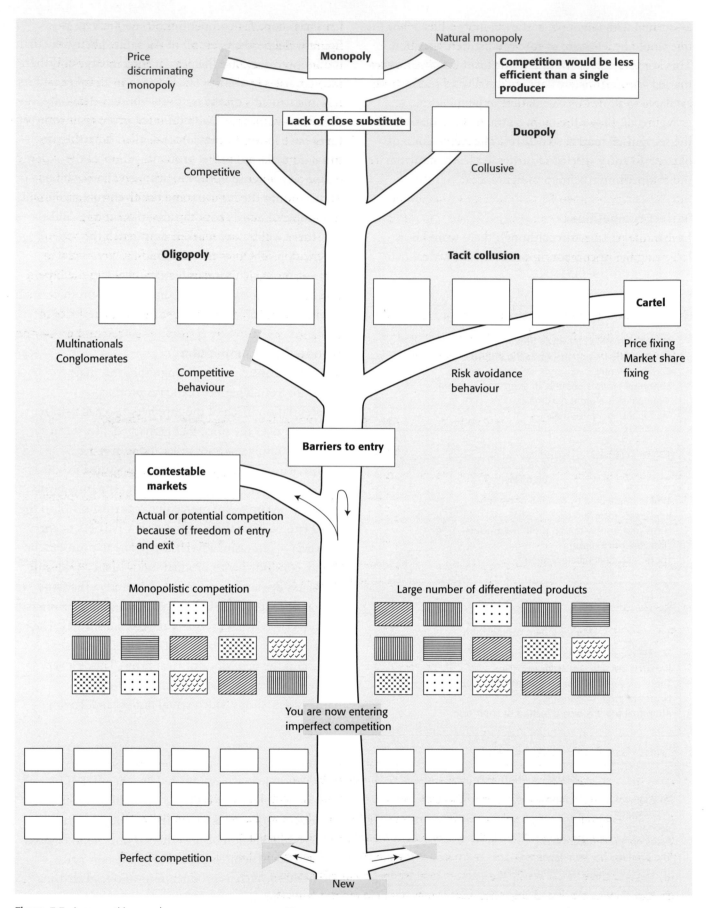

Figure 3.3 A competition road map

are tempted to collude or settle for a quiet life; hence the relevance of the satisficing objective. There may be takeover and merger activity, which can take the market towards duopoly or monopoly. The difficulty of getting extra sales may lead to firms diversifying in order to grow in a different direction. In the real world, firms' behaviour in oligopoly is difficult to predict. Some oligopolies are highly competitive even though there are not many rivals. The example often quoted is the intense rivalry between Pepsi and Coca Cola. On the other hand, the giant petrol companies and breweries have in the past been accused of collusion and following the price leadership of a main player.

Monopoly

There are few situations where one firm has nearly all of the industry sales. The definition of monopoly used by the Competition Commission is where the dominant firm has more than 25 per cent of the market. This figure is deliberately set low to allow any potential monopoly situation to be investigated in the public interest. Sales concentration ratios show that a large number of firms operate in industries close to a monopoly structure. The reason for this is mainly to be found in barriers to entry. Monopolists have the power to raise prices and make abnormal profits at the expense of the consumer in both the short run and the long run, but monopoly does have some positive benefits. Some monopolies such as passenger train operating companies are a consequence of government action; others are not. Other monopolies have been created through a patent, for example cats' eyes and the Dyson vacuum cleaner.

Finally, table 3.1 summarises the characteristics of competitive markets in terms of their relevant economic characteristics.

	Perfect competition	Monopolistic competition	Oligopoly	Monopoly
Number of firms	Many	Many	Few	One or two
Entry into the industry	Easy, perfectly contestable	Easy	Barriers	High barriers
Products	Homogeneous	Differentiated	Varied	Lack of close substitutes
Pricing policy	Price taker	Price maker	Price maker	Price maker
Profit maximisers	Yes	Yes	Not necessarily	Yes
Profits	Abnormal profit only in short run	Abnormal profit competed away in the long run	Yes	Both short and long run
Non price competition	No	Yes	Yes	Yes
Choice for consumers	Yes	Yes	Yes	No

Table 3.1 Features of competitive market structures: a snapshot

Self-assessment tasks

1 Read the case study on page 68 and then answer the questions below.
   (a) Explain using examples relevant to this case, what is meant by the term low overheads.
   (b) Using economic theory, explain why price rises will not make a fish and chip shop owner better off.
   (c) How would behaviour differ, if the owner was in a local monopoly situation?
   (d) Discuss the non-price methods of boosting revenue. What will determine their success in this case?
   (e) Suggest three reasons why the barriers to entry are low in this example.
   (f) Explain why a fish and chip shop owner may not be a profit maximiser.

Fish and chip sales take a battering

Over the past few years, fish and chip shops have been doing a roaring trade especially in the North. The typical shop is family run, has low overheads, and the owners have a pride in supplying traditional food to local people. Many of them look at their costs, add on a profit margin and hope that sales will be high enough to give them a reasonable income. Prices range from as low as £1.60 to £2.80, but there are significant regional variations and local prices are influenced by the number of direct competitors. Sales are sensitive to price changes, but the suppliers think that the quality of the product is most important. Reputation is everything in maintaining sales in an increasingly competitive market.

The short-term problems that have hit the suppliers are a rise in fish prices reflecting the growing scarcity of high-quality white fish and the weather conditions that have increased potato prices. A spokesman for the Fish Fryers Association was recently reported as saying:

Things are getting so bad that some of our members are barely covering their wages and the cost of materials. Normally, businesses would react to this by raising prices. Our members are reluctant to do this because of the economic circumstances of their customers. Price rises and cutting the size of portions will not make us better off. The take-away food business is easy to start and is getting more diverse all the time. Our members are trying to increase the range of food served and must have an eye on long-term business rather than short-run difficulties.

Trends and fashions in food consumption may be starting to affect the most loyal of fish and chip consumers. The demand for low fat foods is increasing and survey data show that, as they get better off, consumers are widening the range of take-away food they eat. Even in the world of fish and chips the market is changing. Although there are a huge number of shops, a growing proportion are franchise outlets of large businesses, such as Harry Ramsden's. This business grew rapidly from a single shop near Leeds to a multinational operation in only a few years. All in all, the traditional chippy may be a disappearing feature of urban life. Will only grandparents remember fish and chips with salt, vinegar and bits wrapped in newspaper? Is the future trend towards up-market fish restaurants serving fish in sauces rather than batter and chips that are low fat and from organically grown potatoes?

Harry Ramsden's in Bournemouth. Harry Ramsden's has broken the world record on four occasions for selling the most portions of fish and chips in a day. The current record being 12,105 in Melbourne.
Source: Harry Ramsden's.

2 Study the information below and then answer the questions that follow.

Increasing concentration in the UK brewing industry

In 1989, the former Monopolies and Mergers Commission (MMC) published an extensive and controversial report on 'The Supply of Beer'. This report followed a three-year investigation into the business practices of the UK's large brewing companies. Its impact has seen a fundamental change in the organisation, structure and operations of these companies.

The MMC were concerned about the so-called public interest. Their report drew attention to 'a complex monopoly that exists in favour of the brewers with tied estates and loan ties'. These practices, whereby brewers owned public houses and gave cheap loans in exchange for being the sole supplier of beer, were seen to be restrictive to consumer choice and value. The government subsequently ordered brewers to own no more than 2,000 public houses plus 50 per cent of their original holdings, to eliminate loan tie arrangements and to permit at least one brand of beer from a brewer other than its normal supplier. It forced brewers to decide between brewing and retailing activates.

As a consequence, there is now increased competition in the market, downward pressure on prices, a reduction in retail capacity and, interestingly, further consolidation of brewing activity. The retail sale of beer is now largely in the hands of new owners – most outlets are not owned by the brewing companies.

The table below shows how the market has changed since 1989.

UK beer market in 1989, 1996 and 2001 (% share)

1989	1996	2001
Bass 22%	Scottish Courage 31%	Scottish Courage 26%
Allied-Lyons 14%	Bass 23%	Cors 23%
Whitbread 13%	Carlsberg Tetley 16%	Interbrew 17%
Grand Met 13%	Whitbread 14%	Carlsberg Tetley 14%
Scottish & Newcastle 11%	Others 16%	Others 20%
Courage 10%		
Others 17%		

(a) Calculate appropriate concentration ratios from the above data. What might you conclude from them?

(b) Use the information provided to compare the business practices of the UK brewers before and after the MMC's report and subsequent government action.

(c) Discuss:
  ◆ how brewers and public houses now compete,
  ◆ whether consumers are now getting a better deal.

(d) What evidence is there that the brewing industry has once again become a monopoly?

3 On completion of this unit, you should be able to answer all questions in the examination paper below.

The price of petrol

In September 2000, farmers and road hauliers in the UK, France and Germany protested vigorously over the escalating price of petrol. In the UK, for example, oil refineries were blockaded by the protestors, resulting in a severe disruption of supplies to filling stations and to essential users of petrol. Unusually, there was strong support for the protestors from private motorists. These groups wanted the Government to reduce the tax paid on each litre of petrol.

To economists, it is changing world market conditions that have led to this crisis. In other words, the forces of demand and supply have been responsible for the price rises, not the actions of government as is widely believed by the protestors. The underlying reasons are twofold. First, the world demand for petrol has increased in recent years, largely as a result of the ever-increasing number of car owners. Manufacturing firms and other businesses have also increased their demand for petrol. Secondly, the supply of crude oil is effectively controlled by the producers' monoploy, the Organisation of Petroleum Exporting Countries (OPEC), which include all the world's major producers. By cutting supply, at a time of rising demand, OPEC producers have forced the price of crude oil up to over $36 per barrel, its highest price for 25 years. No major

British motorists queue for petol at Texaco petrol station in East London, 16 September 2000.   *Source:* Popperfoto/Reuters

producer, as yet, has broken ranks from OPEC, although it is widely rumoured that Iraq would like to do so in order to boost its economy, weakened by United Nations economic sanctions imposed following the Gulf War in the early 1990s.

For motorists, patiently queuing for fuel, the reality of the situation is that they need petrol to carry out their daily routine of work journeys, running children to school and making shopping trips. When prices rise, motorists have little choice but to 'pay up' or experience considerable inconvenience in their daily lives. Recent research based on a sample of 3,000 motorists has confirmed that this is true. Table 1 summarises how the estimated weekly demand for petrol changed with its price. The researchers also collected information to enable them to estimate appropriate income and cross elasticities of demand. These estimates are shown in Table 2.

Source: USA Today, 27 September 2000 (adapted).

Summary of results from sample survey

Price of petrol per litre (pence)	Quantity demanded ('000 litres per week)
90	89
85	91
80	95
75	100
70	106
65	112
60	119
55	125

Table 1

Elasticity estimates

Income elasticity of demand for petrol	+1.8
Cross elasticity of demand for bus journeys with respect to petrol prices	+0.2

Table 2

(a) ◆ With the aid of a diagram, briefly explain how the world market price of crude oil is determined. (4)

◆ With the aid of a diagram, analyse how the changing world market conditions have resulted in the increase in crude oil prices. (6)

(b) Following the Gulf War, sanctions by the United Nations have meant that Iraq can only sell a limited amount of its crude oil production.

◆ Explain how a substantial increase in Iraq's crude oil production might affect the world market price. (2)

◆ Using a production possibility curve, explain the likely consequences of using more resources to increase oil production in Iraq. (6)

(c) ◆ Define price elasticity of demand. (2)

◆ Use the data in table 1 to calculate the price elasticity of demand for petrol as the price rises from 75p to 80p per litre. Show your working. (2)

◆ 'When prices rise, motorists have little choice but to "pay up" or experience considerable inconvenience in their daily lives'. Does your answer to the question above support this assertion? Justify your response. (4)

(d) UK oil refineries are owned by oligopolistic firms such as Esso, BP, Texaco and Shell which are able to benefit from economies of scale.

◆ State **two** characteristics of an oligopoly. (2)

◆ Explain what is meant by the term economies of scale. (2)

◆ State and explain **two** possible ways in which oil refineries might benefit from economies of scale.

(e) Using the information in tables 1 and 2, discuss the extent to which a rise in the price of petrol is the main determinant of a change in its demand. (9)

Source: OCR, Paper 2881, January 2002.

Summary

In this section we have recognised that:

● A firm's costs of production can be broken down into fixed and variable costs.

● The marginal cost is the addition to total cost when producing one extra unit of output.

● Diminishing returns take place in the short run when the returns to variable units begin to fall.

● The benefits associated with a reduction in unit costs due to an expansion of output are known as economies of scale. Various sources of internal and external economies of scale can be recognised.

● A firm's revenue is the value of the output which is sold.

● Profit maximisation is the usual assumption made in economic theory as to how firms behave. It occurs at the output where the revenue from an extra unit of sales equals the cost of making this last unit, i.e. MR = MC.

● Firms do not always seek to maximise their profits and may pursue alternative objectives.

● Economists recognise various types of market structure in order to explain the behaviour of firms.

● The degree of competition in these markets is largely determined by the extent of barriers to entry.

● Perfect competition acts as a very important benchmark against which all markets can be measured.

● A monopoly is in theory a single firm controlling the entire output of an industry. Extensive barriers to entry are the source of monopoly power.

● Monopolistic competition and oligopoly are particularly relevant real-world market structures.

Key words

Definitions of Key words can be found in the Glossary on page 240.

abnormal or supernormal profit
average fixed costs
average revenue
average total costs
average variable costs
barriers to entry
collusion
concentration ratio
contestable market
diminishing returns
diseconomies of scale
economies of scale
firm
fixed costs
increasing returns
long run
managerial objectives
marginal cost
marginal revenue
market structure
monopolistic competition
monopoly
non-price competition
normal profit
oligopoly
optimum output
perfect competition
price taker
private costs
profit
profit maximisation
sales maximisation
sales revenue maximisation
satisficing
semi-fixed costs
short run
total revenue
variable costs

71

Unit 2

Market failure and government intervention

4 Economic efficiency within competitive markets

On completion of this section you should be able to:

➤ describe what is meant by efficiency in Economics

➤ explain what is meant by productive efficiency

➤ explain what is meant by allocative efficiency

➤ explain what is meant by Pareto efficiency

➤ illustrate how the concepts of efficiency can be applied to the production possibility curve

➤ understand how competition can lead to an efficient allocation of resources

Efficiency in economics

How might we judge whether any type of economic system (be it a market system or any other type of system) is 'doing a good job'? This is clearly a very important question. The answer to it might affect the whole way that we would want to try to organise the running of an economy. The answer that economists give to this question is to say that an economic system is doing well to the extent that it is delivering economic efficiency.

Efficiency is a word often used in our society. It is usually seen as 'a good thing'. However, it is important to think what it actually means. It probably has a range of different meanings when it is used by different people in different contexts.

The best way of understanding the term 'efficiency' is to return to the key issues of Economics, as discussed in section 1, unit 1. If Economics is a study of the use of scarce resources in order to meet our infinite wants, then efficiency is to do with using those scarce resources in the most effective way possible to meet the highest possible level of wants.

If resources are being used in this 'best' possible way, then economists are clear that this must imply that two different types of efficiency are being achieved, namely **productive efficiency** and **allocative efficiency**.

Productive efficiency

This type of efficiency is all to do with using the least possible amount of scarce resources to produce any particular product. To put it another way, it involves producing things at the lowest possible cost.

Productive efficiency can be understood through figure 4.1, which shows a firm's or an industry's average total cost curves.

In this diagram, the point marked 'x' indicates the point of productive efficiency. It is worth noting that productive efficiency can thus be seen as implying two things about the point of production by a firm or an industry. First, it implies that production takes place on the lowest possible cost curve. This means that the

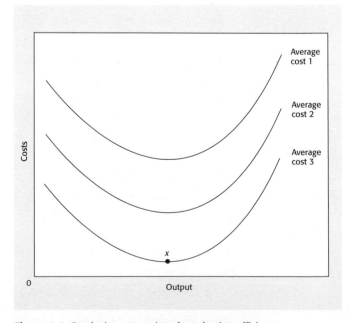

Figure 4.1 Producing at a point of productive efficiency

lowest possible cost techniques of production are being used. Secondly, it implies that production occurs at the lowest point on the lowest cost curve. Production at this point on an average cost curve is referred to as a point of 'technical efficiency' by economists.

Allocative efficiency

To achieve full economic efficiency, it is not enough simply to produce goods and services at the lowest possible cost. Even had the former command economies of Eastern Europe produced everything with full productive efficiency (which seems unlikely), it would be hard to argue that this represented efficiency in its full sense. Economies must not only produce things using the least possible resources, they must also make the products that consumers most want. There would be little of merit in an economy that produced many products at very low cost that nobody particularly wanted and yielded little satisfaction (see also section 5).

Allocative efficiency is all to do with producing those products that are most wanted by consumers, given their cost of production. This can be seen from the following:

1 Two products, x and y, cost exactly the same amount to produce. However, product x gives consumers twice as much satisfaction as product y. If allocative efficiency is to exist, product x should be produced in preference to product y.
2 Two products, a and b, yield the same amount of consumer satisfaction. However, product a costs half as much to produce as product b. It would be allocatively efficient to produce product a in preference to product b in this situation.

Allocative efficiency can be thought of more precisely than this. It will exist when the selling price of a product is the same as the marginal cost of producing that product. In this situation, the price paid by the consumer will represent the true economic cost of producing the last unit of the product. This should ensure that precisely the right amount of the product is produced.

The idea that when price is equal to marginal cost there will be allocative efficiency (the right amount of the product made) is best understood through a simple example:

Quantity	1 2 3 4 5 6 7

Price (£)	5 5 5 5 5 5 5
Marginal cost (£)	2 3 4 5 6 7 8

For this product, an output of one unit would not be allocatively efficient. Here, the cost of producing the product is less than the value put on it by the consumer (as represented by the price that the consumer is prepared to pay for that product). The product should clearly be produced, but there is scope for further worthwhile production from this point. This is also true when two or three units of the product are made. On the other hand, an output of seven units of the product should not be produced. Here, the seventh unit costs £8 to produce, but is only valued at £5 by the consumer. The same problem exists with output levels of 5 and 6. Thus, there is only one ideal output level (that is, one output level that will yield allocative efficiency) and that is an output of four units where price is equal to marginal cost.

Pareto efficiency

A related way of defining economic efficiency is in terms of what economists call 'Pareto efficiency' (named after an Italian economist, Wilfredo Pareto, who suggested the idea at the beginning of the twentieth century). This is said to exist when it is not possible to make any one person in society better off without making someone else worse off. If this situation exists, then there will be productive efficiency as nothing more could be produced with the resources available (and thus there is no possibility of any overall extra production). It also implies that allocative efficiency exists because, if it does not, then it may be possible to swap production in such a way that consumers can be made better off (without necessarily having to make any others worse off).

Efficiency and the production possibility frontier

One way to illustrate the concept of economic efficiency is to think in terms of the production possibility frontier. This is illustrated in figure 4.2.

Point a on the diagram can be considered to be productively efficient. At this point, nothing more can be produced in total than is currently being produced.

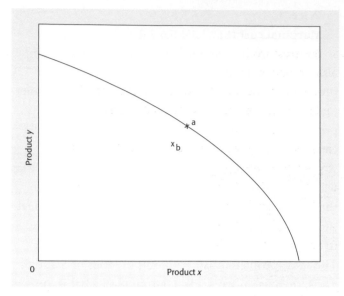

Figure 4.2 Efficient points on the production possibility frontier

This is as opposed to point b where it is possible to increase production with the scarce resources that are available in the economy. Equally, point a can be considered to be a possible point of Pareto efficiency as it is only possible to increase the production of one product by reducing the production of another (and hence potentially making someone worse off). This is not true about point b from where it is possible to increase the production of either product without sacrificing any other production. It is only possible to establish whether point a (or any other point on the frontier itself) is allocatively efficient by knowing consumer preferences. This information about consumer demand is not given by the production possibility frontier alone, and thus we cannot say for sure whether this point represents the point at which the combination of products *x* and *y* that are being produced is that which satisfies the maximum amount of wants (or gives the highest possible level of consumer satisfaction).

Competition and efficiency

It is often suggested by economists that efficiency, as defined above, will exist in a fully competitive market (specifically, a perfectly competitive market). This is seen as the crucial argument in favour of competition. It is why competition is seen as 'a good thing'.

Productive efficiency

A competitive market could lead to productive efficiency as it provides firms with the incentive to produce things at the lowest possible cost as represented by the lowest point of their average cost curve (see section 3). It does this by providing both a 'carrot' and a 'stick'. The 'carrot' of a competitive market is that, if a firm can produce at a lower cost than its competitors, then its profits will be higher. The 'stick' of a competitive market is failure to keep costs low will lead to the firm going out of business either because it cannot maintain competitive prices or, if it does, it is selling at a loss.

Allocative efficiency

Competitive markets could also force allocative efficiency upon an economy. The 'carrot and stick' of competition once more come into play. If firms wish to make maximum profit (the carrot), then they will only succeed in doing so by producing those products that are most demanded by consumers. Equally, the threat of bankruptcy (the stick) will force firms to produce only products that are clearly in demand, as a failure to do so will result in losses being made.

In perfect competition, it can be noted that the specific requirement of allocative efficiency, that the selling price is equal to the marginal cost of production, is always true. In other words, the price paid in the market is exactly equal to the cost of producing that unit of output.

Pareto efficiency

A free and competitive market can also be seen as leading to Pareto efficiency. The key to understanding this is to recognise that people will only trade with each other if they believe that trading is mutually beneficial. No one will trade with someone else unless they believe that they will benefit from that trade. If this is true, then it can be concluded that, in a totally free market, all trades that are advantageous to both traders involved will occur, but no trades in excess of this will take place. In other words, Pareto efficiency will exist. It will not be possible to improve on the situation described by making someone better off without making someone else worse off. The free market automatically leads to Pareto efficiency.

Self-assessment tasks

1 Discuss what type of efficiency each of the following might lead towards:

   (a) A firm uses a new machine that costs less than its old one but produces more.

   (b) A company swaps production to a different product that sells at the same price but is in greater demand.

   (c) A car plant makes 1,000 workers redundant because their jobs can now be done by robots that cost less over a period of time than paying workers' wages.

   (d) Following privatisation, firms in Eastern Europe have to change what they produce in order to make a profit.

Automatic robots weld parts of a Mercedes-Benz A class car in the new Mercedes-Benz plant at Juiz de Fora, 110 miles north of Rio de Janeiro. The new Mercedes-Benz plant is expected to produce 30,000 A class compact cars a year.
Source: Popperfoto.

2 Read the following newspaper article and then answer the questions that follow.

Consumers in a power struggle

Sparks will fly as the electricity revolution unfolds. Regional energy companies are now allowed to go looking for business on rival turf: but who will really benefit – the householder or the corporation?

The dream is that competition will drive prices down. The Office of Electricity Regulation (Offer) says: 'For typical domestic consumers, their electricity supplier will be charging among the highest prices in the area. They can save by switching supplier.'

But Offer's figures suggest the biggest saving possible for an average user is just £21.00 a year or 40p a week. Benet Middleton, who heads policy research at the Consumers Association, says: 'Until there is more competition in electricity generation, as opposed to sales, it is unlikely we will see anything like the savings in other utilities.'

John Over, Yorkshire Electricity's marketing director, believes domestic electricity prices are about as low as they are likely to get for some time and thinks that competition will centre on service instead. He says: 'Clearly, we've got competitive electricity prices. I think competition will impact not only on price, but also on the range of services you expect to get.'

Source: Paul Slade, *The Independent*, 19 September 1998 (adapted).

   (a) Explain why it might be expected that the price of a product, such as electricity, will fall when competition is introduced into a market.

   (b) Why might it be reasonable to anticipate that service to electricity consumers will improve now that consumers can choose their electricity supplier?

   (c) In what ways does the article suggest that consumers of electricity may not enjoy the benefits of the introduction of competition into electricity supply?

Summary

In this section we have recognised that:

- Efficiency is an important concept in Economics relating to how well scarce resources are used.

- Three types of efficiency are recognised: productive efficiency is achieved when firms produce at the lowest possible average cost; allocative efficiency is when the price paid is equal to the marginal cost; and Pareto efficiency occurs when it is not possible to make one person better off without making someone else worse off.

- The concept of efficiency can be applied to the production possibility frontier; a fully competitive market is the only one where all three types of efficiency are achieved.

Key words

Definitions of Key words can be found in the Glossary on page 240.

allocative efficiency   Pareto efficiency
economic efficiency   productive efficiency

5 Why markets may not work efficiently

On completion of this section you should be able to:

➤ describe what is meant by market failure

➤ understand why market failures arise

➤ describe what is meant by positive and negative externalities and explain these in terms of a divergence between private and social benefits and costs

➤ analyse why market dominance can lead to inefficiency, including x-inefficiency

➤ differentiate between public, quasi-public and private goods with an understanding of the terms 'non-excludability' and 'non-rivalry'

➤ explain why public goods may not be provided by the market

➤ explain the problems created by information failures, including the concepts of merit and de-merit goods and why these create market failures

➤ explain the possible inefficiencies caused by factor immobility, such as structural and regional unemployment

➤ understand that markets can lead to an 'unacceptable' distribution of resources such as 'unfair' access to health care and education

➤ apply these concepts of market failure to a range of possible economic issues

➤ comment upon their likely impact

Defining market failure

It is stating the obvious to say that market failures exist when markets fail. However, the question needs to be asked: 'Fail at what?' The answer is: 'Fail at delivering economic efficiency.' Market failure exists any and every time that a free market, left to its own devices and totally free from any form of government intervention, fails to lead to the best, or optimum, use of scarce resources. In terms of the previous section, it is when the interaction of supply and demand in a market does not lead to productive and/or allocative efficiency.

Here it was established that there are reasons to expect that freely functioning markets could lead to economic efficiency. There are also reasons why this may not be the case. The purpose of this section is to explain the different reasons for this failure of markets to work as well as might be hoped. Specifically, it will look at the following different reasons why markets fail:

1 The existence of externalities.
2 Merit and de-merit goods.
3 Public and quasi-public goods.
4 Occupational and geographical immobility of labour.
5 The concentration of power in markets.
6 Concerns about distribution and equity.

Externalities
Defining externality

If the market system is to work well and lead to economic efficiency, it is important that the people who make economic decisions are those who are affected by those decisions. A transaction between a supplier and a consumer for a product needs only to affect the supplier and consumer involved. As long as this is the case, then both sides will act only so long as both feel that they will benefit from any action – all is well in the market. However, a problem could clearly arise if someone else, not party to the economic decision, is affected by that decision. This is the economic concept known as externality.

An externality is said to arise if a third party (someone not directly involved) is affected by the decisions and actions of others. If you decide to shout loudly to your friend in public, then others (third parties) not involved in making that decision are affected by the assault on their ear drums.

Private and social costs

Another way of understanding the same concept is to define an externality as any divergence between private

79

and social costs or benefits. The social costs of any action are all of the related costs associated with that action. The private costs are those costs involved in an action that accrue to the individual or decision maker.

Negative externalities

It is quite possible that these private and social costs are the same: all of the costs of an action accrue to the decision maker and there are no further costs. If this is the case, then there are no externalities. However, it is possible that there will be a difference: private and social costs may not be equal to each other. For example, if you make a decision to take a journey in your car, you consider the costs of the petrol and the time taken. However, you do not consider the further costs that you may be imposing on others in terms of your contribution to road congestion, to environmental damage and to possible car accidents. In this situation, a negative externality, or an external cost, is said to exist. The situation is illustrated in figure 5.1. Here, private costs are part of the social costs involved in a decision. However, they do not represent all of the social costs. The difference between the two is the negative externality.

Private and social benefits

A similar situation can also exist with benefits rather than costs. The social benefits of a decision are all of

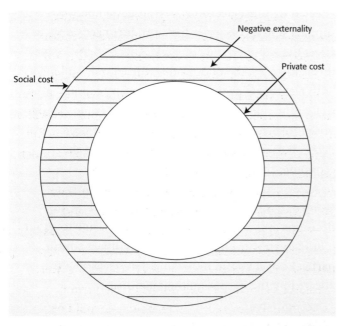

Figure 5.1 A difference between private and social costs: negative externalities

the benefits that accrue from that decision. The private benefits are those that accrue solely to the individual or decision maker. Again, these may or may not be the same.

Positive externalities

It is possible that the social benefits of a decision may exceed the private benefits. If this is the case, then a positive externality, or external benefit, is said to exist. For example, if you make a decision to go to the doctor to be inoculated against a particular disease, then clearly you receive the private benefit of not catching that particular disease against which you have been inoculated. However, you may not be the only one to benefit. The fact that you do not get the disease has some possible benefit to all others with whom you come into contact, who will now not catch the disease from you.

The problem created by externalities

The essence of the problem created by externalities is that they will lead to an inappropriate amount of the product involved being produced: the free market will lead either to too much or too little production.

Consider a firm that produces a chemical. There are costs that the firm will have to meet in producing a certain quantity of this chemical. These would include such things as:

◆ raw material costs;
◆ labour costs;
◆ energy costs.

All such costs would be termed 'private': they have to be paid for by the decision maker (the firm) (see section 3). These costs form part of social costs. However, there are further social costs likely to be involved as well. These might include any dumping of chemical waste, perhaps in a local river, which creates clean-up costs, any atmospheric pollution that creates clean-up costs and ill health, and possible road congestion that results from the transportation of the chemicals. These are negative externalities. The problem is that only the private costs of producing the chemical will be taken into account by the firm when making the pricing decision about its chemical. The further external costs, which are real costs to society, will not be taken into account. This will mean that the price will be lower than if all social costs were taken into account. In turn,

A coal-fired power station belching CO_2 emissions into the atmosphere: a typical case of negative externality
Source: Electricity Association.

demand and production will be higher than if the full social costs had been considered. Thus, a negative externality will lead to too much of a product being produced. The situation can be seen in figure 5.2.

The price that will occur in the market will be P_1 where the supply schedule that takes account of the private costs, S_1, is equal to demand. This price is

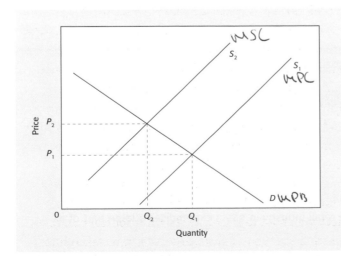

Figure 5.2 Over-production caused by a negative externality

associated with production of Q_1. However, if the supply schedule took into account all of the social costs, S_2, which are greater than just the private costs, then this would result in a price of P_2. This price is associated with a lower production of Q_2. Thus, the negative externality has led to $Q_1 - Q_2$ too much production. Too many scarce resources are being devoted to the production of this product. The market has failed.

The opposite problem is true of a positive externality. Here, the problem is that too little of the product will be produced. If only the private benefits, and not the full social benefits, are considered, then there will be under-production. This is illustrated in figure 5.3.

This time, the problem is with demand. If only the private benefits are registered, then demand is represented by the demand schedule D_1. This leads to a price of P_1 and an associated production of Q_1. However, if the further extra benefits to society were registered (which they will not be by the private decision maker involved), then demand would be greater at D_2. This would lead to a price of P_2 and a production of Q_2. Thus there is an under-production

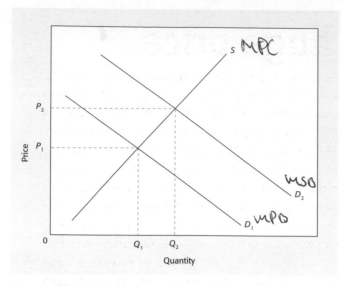

Figure 5.3 Under-production caused by a positive externality

of $Q_2 - Q_1$ associated with the positive externality. Insufficient scarce resources are being devoted to the production of this good or service. The market has failed.

We must, therefore, suggest that externalities are likely to be a source of market failure as they will mean that resources are not allocated in the ideal way: too few or too many resources are likely to be directed to the production of certain products.

Merit goods, de-merit goods and information failures

Defining merit and de-merit goods

Another way in which markets may fail is due to the existence of what are termed merit and de-merit goods.

Sometimes, merit and de-merit goods are simply seen as an extension of the idea of externalities in Economics, as discussed above. A merit good may be described as a good that has positive externalities associated with it. Thus, an inoculation might be seen as a merit good as others who may not catch the disease from the innoculated person also benefit. A de-merit good is seen as any product that has negative externalities associated with it. Thus, cigarettes can be seen as a de-merit good insofar as secondary smoking can be viewed as a possible cause of ill health (a clear negative externality). If this is all there is to merit and de-merit goods, then they cannot be seen as a separate category of market failure from externalities.

However, merit and de-merit goods can (and indeed should) be defined in a different way, which does make them clearly different from externalities. The essence of merit and de-merit goods in this definition is to do with a failure of information to the consumer. Consumers do not perceive, it is suggested, quite how good or bad a particular product is for them: either they do not have the right information or they simply lack some relevant information.

Merit goods

With this idea of a failure of information, a merit good is defined as a good that is better for a person than the person who may consume the good realises. Under this definition, education is often defined as a merit good. The individuals who make decisions about how much education to receive (or how much to allow their children to receive) do not fully appreciate quite how

Self-assessment tasks

1 Identify and explain whether each of the following involves a positive or a negative externality:
    ◆ a next-door neighbour playing his/her music loudly;
    ◆ a person being educated beyond the compulsory school leaving age;
    ◆ the dropping of litter;
    ◆ smoking in a public place;
    ◆ a new, well-designed and pleasant public building;
    ◆ the use of pesticides.
2 Read the adaptation of a newspaper article on the page opposite and then answer the questions below:
    (a) Explain what is meant by Professor Gershuny's phrase, 'The retail industry in effect externalises a large part of its costs.'
    (b) Identify and explain the different negative externalities arising from the development of out-of town supermarkets that are mentioned in this article.

Cheap food – at a huge price

Why do the British shop in supermarkets? Easy. Price, convenience, quality and choice: the mantra of the market economy. But is perception matched by reality?

Supermarkets are very cheap for some goods, but what you save on the loss-leading swings, you lose on the marked-up roundabouts. Take fruit and vegetables. Last summer we compared prices between supermarkets and street markets of the old-fashioned endangered variety. Like for like, the markets won on almost every count.

If they're not such paragons on price, at least supermarkets are safe, convenient and accessible by car. Or are they? If, like a third of the population, you don't have the use of a car, they are not. But even getting to the store by car may be far from convenient. Over the past 20 years, the number of shopping trips has increased by a third, and driver shopping mileage has more than doubled. Given Britain's congestion, more journeys of increasing length doesn't sound very convenient. Nor is it: in the Sixties, according to Professor Jonathan Gershuny of Essex University, consumers spent on average 41 minutes per day shopping and in related travel. In the Eighties this has risen to 70 minutes, with studies showing that food shopping accounts for more than three-quarters of total shopping time. According to Professor Gershuny, 'the increase in shopping time reflects the growth of "self servicing" and the growth in the size of supermarkets ... the larger the supermarket the more walking for the shopper and the greater the average distance from the shopper's home ... The retail industry in effect externalises a large part of its costs.'

On quality and choice, supermarket products may be varied and consistent – but is what you see what you really get, and are you paying the real costs? Supermarkets' huge buying power and demand for absolute consistency means that fruit and vegetable production are now industrialised processes. Multiples have 60 per cent of the market and suppliers who cannot supply 52 weeks a year need not supply. Your Brussels sprouts may be perfectly formed, but at what costs to the countryside? Biodiversity on the shelf is increasingly at the cost of biodiversity in the field.

While it has long been recognised that the perceived benefits of the supermarkets are not evenly spread between social groups (the chief executive of the supermarkets' own research organisation acknowledges that old and poor people will have serious problems over where to buy food because of the growth of superstores and the lack of town centre stores), our research leads us to believe that, even for the better-off and mobile, the advantages of supermarkets are beginning to be outweighed by the drawbacks.

The decline of the town centre is well documented and attributable, at least in part, to the development of out-of-town shopping centres. The big retailers' claims to efficiency in transport are bogus. Much freight transport is unnecessary – produce could be sold locally. More than a third of the increase in freight transport since the late Seventies has been food, drink and tobacco – which together account for less than one tenth of the economy. Next time you use a motorway, count the supermarket trucks. No wonder the big retailers are such lavish supporters of the British Road Federation.

It's the same story with packaging. According to the government, 'the stocking policies of supermarkets ... largely contributed to non-returnable [packaging] attaining [its] present share of the market', while MEPs reported that an EU directive to reduce packaging was 'the most lobbied issue in the (EU) Parliament's history'. The supermarkets are used to getting their way; the directive was duly changed.

Britain's retailing policies need a radical shake-up. We need more smaller shops, buying locally, and revitalised street and covered markets. We still need tougher rules on out-of-town development, and freight companies could pay the real cost of their operations.

Source: Hugh Raven and Tim Lang, *The Independent*, 10 January 1995 (adapted).

much benefit will be received through being educated. We do not appreciate how good education is for us. We do not perceive its full benefits at the time of making the decision about how much education to receive.

De-merit goods

De-merit goods, on the other hand, are those products that are worse for the individual consumer than the individual realises. Cigarettes are taken to be a good example here. It is suggested that, when a person makes a decision to smoke a cigarette, he or she is not fully in possession of the information concerning the harmful effects of smoking. If he or she were in possession of such information, then there would be a greater reluctance to smoke.

It is interesting to note that the example of a de-merit good given here, namely smoking, is the same as the example of a product that can be seen as having negative externalities associated with it. However, the reason for identifying the product is different. Here, it is not due to the damage done to others that the issue arises, but rather due to the unperceived damage done to the person through consuming the product.

Merit goods, de-merit goods and value judgements

It may have been noticed in the above definitions that a significant question poses itself with regard to merit and de-merit goods. Who is to say what is 'good' or 'bad' for a person? If an individual consumer makes a presumably rational decision to consume a product, what right has the rest of society to say that he or she is making a 'wrong' decision. It seems clear that if this is what is going on, we have entered the area of value judgements and thus normative economics. If society is able to say to consumers that they do not fully realise what is good or bad for them, then we are accepting that 'society knows best' and has some right to make such a judgement. In effect we are allowing paternalism to be a legitimate part of Economics. It is acceptable for us to say that society can judge what is, or is not, good for a person, regardless of what that person believes. In this area, then, we may have gone beyond our allegedly 'value-free' positive economics (see section 1).

The problems caused by merit and de-merit goods

Why, then, might merit and de-merit goods be identified as a failure of the market? The problem is that their existence will cause an inappropriate amount of the products concerned to be produced.

Merit goods will be under-produced in a free market situation. Insufficient scarce resources will be devoted to their production. The problem is that the lack of information about how good the product is for individuals will result in insufficient demand being registered for the product in the market. This is illustrated in figure 5.4. Here, the 'correct' level of demand, if consumers appreciated the true value of the product to themselves, would be D_1. This would lead to a market price of P_1, where D_1 is equal to the supply of product, S. This price would be associated with a level of production and consumption of Q_1, the ideal quantity of the good. However, because consumers undervalue the product, demand is only registered as D_2. This leads to a market price of P_2 (where D_2 is equal to supply S), which is associated with production and consumption of Q_2. This is below the optimum level: the market has failed.

Figure 5.5 illustrates the problem of a de-merit good. Here, the 'correct' demand should be at D_1, which will lead to a price of P_1 and a production and consumption of Q_1. As consumers over-value the product, demand is registered at the higher level of D_2. This leads to a market price of P_2 and a production and consumption of Q_2. Too many scarce resources are devoted to the production of this de-merit good: the market has failed.

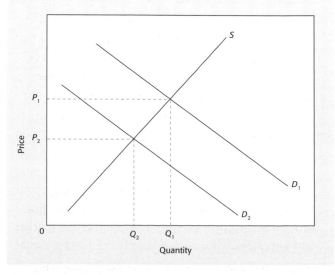

Figure 5.4 The under-provision of a merit good by the market

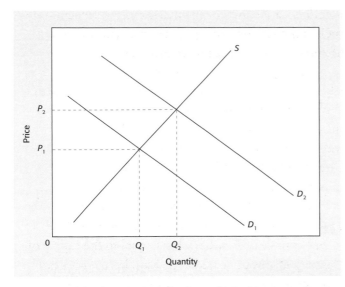

Figure 5.5 The over-provision of a de-merit good by the market

Further market problems caused by information failures

It is worth noting that there are other significant examples of market failure, as we have defined it, that can arise due to failures of information. Two specific examples are noted below:

The health care market Why does anyone go to the doctor? The most usual answer to that question is presumably because we are not sure what ailment we may have and/or are unsure what can be done about our ailment. To put it another way, we lack appropriate information. Thus we go the doctor to try to gain the necessary information. On the basis of the advice that we are given, we then make a decision about what to do. This system may be satisfactory as long as the doctor does not inadvertently or deliberately give us the wrong information. Our problem is that we have no way of knowing the veracity of the information that we are given. If it happens to be wrong, we may well make an undesirable choice about possible treatment. In economic terms, there will be a misallocation of resources. There is a market failure.

The insurance market It is suggested that markets for insurance may not work well because of information problems. The health care market could be an example again. This time it is the insurer who does not possess all the necessary information about the person who is to be insured. The insurer wishes to know how great a

risk the person seeking insurance may be in order to set an appropriate premium. They must rely on the person accurately disclosing information. If insurers are not made aware of relevant information about a person's state of health, then too low a premium is offered. In order to pay for the forthcoming health treatment, the premium that has to be paid by those who are healthy may rise. In the worst case, healthy people will no longer seek insurance as they consider the price to be too great and the insurance company is left with just the 'bad risks'. This could mean that the whole business becomes unprofitable and the market for health insurance in an entirely free market could collapse.

Public goods
Defining public goods

A different type of good from a merit or de-merit that may cause the market to fail is referred to as a **public good**. Here, it is not a matter of too much or little provision of the good in question, but rather whether the product will be provided at all.

There are two specific characteristics that a good must possess if it is to be classified as a public good:

1 It must be **non-excludable**. This means that once the good has been provided for one consumer, it is impossible to stop other consumers from benefiting from the good.

2 It must be **non-rival**. As more and more people consume the product, the benefit to those already consuming the product is not diminished.

Once one begins to think about these characteristics, there are a number of goods that can be seen as public goods. Take the example of a lighthouse. Once a lighthouse is built to warn one ship at sea away from a dangerous area of rocks, then, by its very nature, this service will automatically be provided to all ships that sail within a certain distance of the lighthouse. It is non-excludable. Equally, the fact that other ships see the light given by the lighthouse and are warned away from the dangerous rocks does not reduce the benefit that any one particular ship receives from that warning. It is non-rival.

Quasi-public goods

While there may be some goods that can clearly be defined as 'public' in nature, there are others that

Self-assessment tasks

1 Discuss whether each of the following may be considered to be either a merit or a de-merit good:
- ◆ wearing a seatbelt;
- ◆ visiting a museum;
- ◆ children eating sweets;
- ◆ listening to very loud music;
- ◆ the provision of health care.

2 Read the short newspaper extract below and then answer the questions which follow.

Museum charges will always be too high a price to pay

'If you wish to continue to look at this painting, please insert another compulsory donation token.' Can the day be far off when our museums and art galleries are cordoned off from the rest of public space and charges introduced across the board? That will be a shame. Either this country continues to glory in a series of great national art and cultural collections into which citizens can walk on a whim, in their lunch breaks or in between shopping. Or it slips and slides into a state of affairs in which 'culture' is seen as a segmented economic

Natural History Museum, London

activity, marked off, labelled as elite, and paid for.

Yes, of course this is an elitist issue. Many cultural institutions already charge. The Science and Natural History Museums in London are not cheap. You have to pay to go to a theatre or listen to a concert. Why are the fine arts and provincial museums different? Well, they are different because as communities we recognise that we all gained from them, even if we personally never understood why a photograph would not be a better likeness, or why we could not read about the Rosetta stone in a book.

Source: Leader article, *The Independent*, 1 December 1997 (adapted).

(a) In what way does this article suggest that fine art and certain museums might be viewed as merit goods?

(b) Many museums now no longer charge for entry. Discuss whether it can be justified to provide admissions to these museums free while consumers have to pay for virtually all other services.

have some of the nature of such goods without possessing fully the two required attributes mentioned above. Such goods are referred to as **quasi-public goods**. They are like public goods without truly being public goods.

In practice, it is not possible to classify all products as being either 'public' or 'private' (private goods being goods that are excludable and rival: others can be

excluded from their consumption and once more people start to consume the good, those already consuming it have their satisfaction reduced). Many products lie somewhere in between these two extremes. A good that is closer to a public good than to a private good, but is not fully a public good, is a quasi-public good.

A good example might be a sandy sea-side beach. Such a beach is available to all those who wish to use it.

It appears non-excludable. However, it is possible to conceive of ways of excluding consumers. Privately owned beaches have techniques of doing this. Equally, the beach is non-rival up to a point. If you are the first person on this pleasant beach on a warm sunny day, it does very little to diminish your enjoyment of that beach if a few more people arrive to enjoy the benefits. However, there may well come a point at which this is no longer the case. As the beach becomes crowded, space limited, and other people's conversations and music become ever more audible, enjoyment may be perceptibly reduced. Thus the beach has something of the characteristic of non-rivalry, but not the full characteristic. It is a quasi-public good.

The problem caused by public goods

The problem that may be caused in a free market by the existence of public goods is a serious one: the market may fail to produce them at all. There may be a consumer demand for such products (consumers are willing and able, in principle, to pay for the product's services), but the free market may not have a mechanism for guaranteeing their production.

The essence of the problem is summed up in the phrase free riding. Consumers attempt to gain a 'free ride' on the back of other consumers' purchases of the public good. It is entirely reasonable that they may attempt to do this. One of the key characteristics of public goods as stated above is that they are non-excludable. This implies that once one consumer has purchased the product, all other consumers cannot be prevented from benefiting from that product. Take the example of the lighthouse. Once one particular fisherman has provided a lighthouse close to some dangerous rocks for his benefit, then all other fishermen in the area will benefit equally from the lighthouse. Their advantage, however, is that they do not have to pay for this lighthouse: they have received a free ride on the back of someone else's purchase. The logical thing to do, then, would seem to be for all fishermen to sit back and to wait for one fisherman to be foolish enough to provide a lighthouse so that those not purchasing can benefit without paying. Unfortunately, the implication of this is that the lighthouse is never provided: everyone waits for everyone else to provide it, and nothing happens.

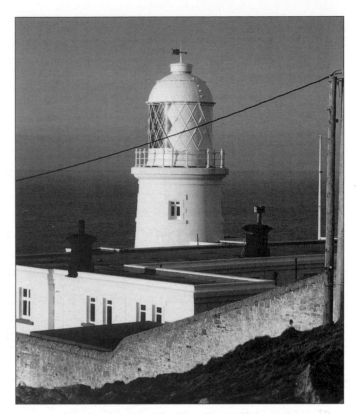

Pendeen Lighthouse, Cornwall – a classic example of a public good
Source: Turid Nyhamar and Roy Valentine photographers.

It could be argued that a more likely scenario to the one described above is that all fishermen in an area might agree to club together in order to make the purchase and thus the lighthouse would be provided. However, there is still a problem here as it is in the interest of any one fisherman to conceal his desire for the lighthouse, refuse to pay but still to gain the final benefit once it is provided. Again, if all fishermen behave thus, the lighthouse is not provided.

The existence of public goods may thus mean that scarce resources are not used in a way that would be desirable. People may wish for the provision of such goods (they yield utility), but the demand may never be registered in the market.

A further difficulty arises due to the existence of quasi-public goods. This is a specific issue with regard to concern over the environment. In many ways, the problems that appear to exist with the environment are due to the fact that it is a quasi-public good rather than a pure public good. If one thinks of the earth's atmosphere, it is non-excludable in terms of its use (for example, in terms of the production of greenhouse gases that are released into the atmosphere). Up to a point, it might be argued that the atmosphere is also non-reduceable; there are no costs to anyone due to its use by others. However, there clearly comes a point where this is no longer true and all may suffer due to the ever-increasing use of the atmosphere (for releasing greenhouse gases). A problem is created because the environment possesses some, but not all, of the attributes of a public good.

Failures in the labour market
The mobility of labour

If markets are to work with full efficiency, then labour markets must function well. There are a number of

---

Self-assessment tasks

1 Explain whether each of the following may be described as a private, a public or a quasi-public good:

- ◆ a nuclear defence system;
- ◆ a chocolate bar;
- ◆ a public park;
- ◆ a firework display;
- ◆ a motorway;
- ◆ street lighting.

2 Read the following short case study and answer the questions that follow.

Promises, promises: has Blair really been a friend of the environment?

When Tony Blair made his final speech to voters before the 1997 general election, the Labour leader promised to put the environment at the 'heart of government'. After Labour's victory, each government department was given its own 'green minister' and a Commons Select Committee was set up to provide proper scrutiny of environmental issues. How has the government matched up to its early promises?

Fuel prices The Environment Minister, Michael Meacher, had said the automatic fuel escalator (which significantly raised taxes on petrol each year) was valuable both in persuading people to use public transport and in helping to reduce pollution. Unfortunately, the huge rise in the price of crude oil in 2000 left the government vulnerable to fuel protests by lorry drivers and farmers. Ministers panicked and opted for cuts in duty on diesel for hauliers wihout any additional environmental safeguards.

Climate change Deputy Prime Minister, John Prescott, took a leading role in the agreement at the Kyoto climate summit in 1997 to reduce greenhouse gas emissions that cause global warming. However, by abandoning the fuel duty escalator and pandering to the haulage industry, greenhouse gas emissions are likely to increase.

Wildlife and the countryside The Countryside and Rights of Way Act introduced the so-called 'right to roam'. This allows visitors to the countryside to walk freely on all footpaths. There has also been action to defend peatlands from the destructive actions of fertilizer companies, and tough talk (but no legislation) about excessive leaks from water company pipes.

Nuclear power Tony Blair has given the nuclear industry strong support since taking office. He believes that the industry offers crucial jobs and skills in the depressed west Cumbrian region.

(a) ◆ Define the term 'externality'.
- ◆ From the article, identify **two** examples of a negative externality.
- ◆ From the article, identify **two** examples of a positive externality.

(b) The newspaper article talks about a large increase in fuel prices.
- ◆ Give **one** group who might suffer financial hardship due to a large rise in fuel prices. Explain the reasons for your answer.
- ◆ Give **one** type of transport business that might benefit through a large increase in fuel prices. Explain the reasons for your answer.

(c) ◆ State **two** characteristics of 'public goods'.
- ◆ How far does the 'right to roam' make the countryside more like a public good?

Source: OCR Paper 2882, June 2002 (adapted).

particular factors that will have to exist for this to be true. One important one is that labour must be fully mobile. Only if labour is fully mobile will labour markets function efficiently.

There are two types of labour mobility:

1 **Occupational mobility** of labour. This means that workers are able to move quickly and easily from one occupation to another. A redundant coal miner could rapidly move into a new form of employment.

2 **Geographical mobility** of labour. This means that workers are quickly and easily able to move from one part of a country to another in order to find employment. The loss of a job in one region means that the worker concerned rapidly moves to a different region in order to gain new employment.

The problem is that these two types of labour mobility often do not fully exist, or sometimes do not exist at all. This results in further examples of market failures.

Occupational immobility of labour

In practice, workers may not easily be able to move from one form of employment to another. It might make economic sense for a coal miner to leave the coal mining industry as it contracts and move into a job as a computer technician as that industry expands, but it may not be that simple. The redundant coal miner may possess few, if any, of the relevant employment skills to become a computer technician. Considerable re-training would be needed.

This can create a serious problem for a country. As some industries decline (such as coal mining) and others grow (such as computer management) due to changes in consumer demand and technological developments, workers need to move occupations. The problem is that they may not be able to do so. The redundant workers do not have the necessary skills to move. They can thus get 'stuck' and cannot get a new job: they are unemployed. This type of unemployment in Economics is referred to as 'structural unemployment'. If this occurs, it represents a very clear failure of the market. The scarce resource of labour is simply not being used. It is not a case of a scarce resource not being used as well as might be possible. The resource is not being used at all in order to meet infinite wants. It is the clearest possible case of a market failure (see section 7).

Geographical immobility of labour

Workers may also not easily and quickly be able to move from employment in one region of a country to employment in a different region. There are various possible reasons for this. Family and social ties may be very strong for people in a particular region and this may prevent geographical movement. House prices can differ greatly between different regions. This can make it very difficult for a worker to move from a low-cost to a high-cost housing region.

The effect of geographical immobility of labour may be that when employment contracts in one part of the country and expands in another, as may happen with changes in tastes and costs in a market economy, workers are unable to move from the region where employment is contracting to the region where it is expanding. Thus unemployment may once more be created. This type of unemployment is referred to as 'regional unemployment' in Economics. As with structural unemployment, it represents a clear market failure.

The concentration of power in markets
Competition and markets

For markets to work well, it is generally accepted in Economics that there must be a high level of competition. To work as well as is possible, the competition needs to be as great as is possible. Economists refer to this very high level of competition as 'perfect competition' (see section 3).

There are good reasons for believing that a high level of competition will mean that markets work well. Some of the following are important:

1 If there is a high level of competition between firms, then it is likely that these firms will produce exactly what consumers most want. There will be consumer sovereignty. Any firm that does not produce what consumers want will find itself out of business very quickly as there will always be plenty of other firms managing to produce what is most wanted.

2 A high level of competition will mean that firms will produce products at the lowest possible cost. The least possible scarce resources will be used to produce the products that consumers most want. Any firm that fails to do this will be in great difficulty as other

Self-assessment tasks

1 Explain whether each of the following is likely to experience occupational immobility or geographical immobility (or both):

 ◆ a redundant steelworker;
 ◆ a schoolteacher who loses his/her job;
 ◆ an unemployed doctor;
 ◆ a footballer forced to end his career early due to injury.

2 Read the following newspaper article and answer the questions which follow.

More artists than artisans in Britain by year 2006

Well-meaning parents should advise their children to head for the stage – or the screen, the music business, design, journalism or professional sport. The creative professions will be the fastest-growing source of new jobs between now and 2006, says a report published today.

The report's moral is that young people should be aiming high. Modern Britain offers better prospects in acting or football than in hairdressing or secretarial work.

The increase in demand for people with literary, artistic and sporting skills will even outpace the need for more computer technicians and lawyers, two other high-growth categories of employment. By the year 2006, there are likely to be nearly as many luvvies as construction workers in Britain and they will also outnumber engineers or security guards.

Within a decade there will be twice as many 'creative professionals' as car workers or doctors. The number is predicted to rise by 5 per cent a year, outstripping growth in all other job categories.

Traditional craft and manual jobs will shrink in number. Within three years there will be only just over three million in the traditional manufacturing craft-related occupations, and even demand for secretaries and hairdressers is falling.

Source: Diane Coyle, *The Independent*, 16 April 1998 (adapted).

(a) Why might a successfully functioning market economy expect to see the sort of changes in employment mentioned in the passage?

(b) Discuss the implications for geographical and occupational immobility of labour, given the projections for jobs stated in the passage.

competitors will have lower costs and be able to charge lower prices for the same product.

3 A competitive market will mean that firms have to charge a price to the consumer that is not much, if at all, above the cost of production. Any firm charging too high a price will soon lose out to others charging a price closer to the true production cost. Thus, when consumers buy a product, they pay a price that represents how much that product truly costs to produce in terms of scarce resources.

The problem is that in very many markets, nothing close to a high level of competition exists. This causes markets to fail.

Lack of competition and markets

There are two very valid reasons to expect many markets in developed economies to not be highly competitive:

1 The existence of economies of scale. Economies of scale imply that the larger a firm becomes, the lower the cost of producing any particular product is likely to become. In many industries, there are considerable economies of scale available and thus firms have to become very large to benefit fully from them. In some cases, this could mean that there is room for very few or even just one firm (a monopoly) to exist in any particular industry (see section 3).

2 The profit motive. As also stated in section 3 the dominant motivation of firms is seen as being to make maximum profits. Perhaps the most effective way that profit can be made by a firm is either to get rid of all competitors or to enter into agreements with those competitors. In either case, competition ceases to exist.

The implication of these two important forces in markets is that there is often a concentration of power in many markets, which means that the benefits of competition mentioned earlier are reversed:

1 Firms may not produce what consumers most want. Given the control that firms have in a market, firms may not have to produce those things that are most desired by consumers. Consumers cannot easily turn to an alternative. Thus, infinite wants may not be as fully satisfied as in a competitive situation. The market has failed.

2 Firms do not have to produce goods and services at the lowest possible cost. There is no constraint from competitors forcing firms to minimise their costs of production. Thus, firms may 'take it easy' and use more scarce resources for production than is necessary (economists refer to this as 'x'-inefficiency). The market fails.

3 Firms are able to charge a price that is higher than the cost of production. With no competitors, a firm does not have to worry that consumers will turn elsewhere if price rises above costs. In this case, the price paid by the consumer is higher than the cost of production in terms of scarce resources and the demand for the product will be lower than it should be. There will be an under-production of the product. The market has failed.

Self-assessment tasks

1 Explain why each of the following situations may well arise in a market that is dominated by one or just a few firms:
   ◆ a poor quality product;
   ◆ unnecessarily large expenditure on management perks;
   ◆ a selling price well in excess of the cost of producing a product.
2 Read the following article and answer the question that follows.

Important competition issues

One of our competitors, *The Times*, is next month planning to cut the cover price of its Saturday edition to 10p a copy. There is also some talk of it doing the same to its Thursday edition. *The Times* already charges just 10p for its Monday edition and sells at a significant discount in comparison to its main rivals throughout the rest of the week.

On a number of occasions Rupert Murdoch, proprietor of *The Times*, has expressed the view that there are too many national newspapers in Britain. An aim must therefore be to bring about the closure of a competitor. Why does this matter? It is because diversity of choice is the best and only reliable way of safe-guarding consumer and other public interests. It is in diversity and the innovation that flows from it that we find the greatest chance of economic success for all.

This is particularly important in newspapers and broadcasting, because diversity of opinion, information and reporting is such a fundamental part of the democratic process. But the same arguments also apply to other industries from supermarkets to banks, and from software providers to metal bashers where big companies use their greater clout and spending power to undermine and crush smaller competitors.

Source: Business Leader Article, *The Independent*, 30 December 1997 (adapted).

Discuss the ways in which consumers of daily newspapers in Britain might suffer if Rupert Murdoch were to succeed in reducing the number of competitors to *The Times* (as this article suggests he is attempting to do).

Distributive and equity issues
An economic democracy

One argument in favour of markets is that they can be seen as allowing the economic equivalent of a political democracy.

In the place of voters in our economic democracy, we have consumers. In the place of votes, we have money (claims on scarce resources). Our consumers (or voters) 'elect' those products that are to be produced by use of their money (or votes). The products that have most money votes are the 'winners'. These are the products that will be produced most and be most successful as these are the products that are most desired by consumers and thus those products that consumers will be most willing to purchase. Firms that wish to make a profit will produce exactly what consumers elect.

There is one important flaw in this analogy. One of the key tenets of a political democracy is 'One person, one vote'. This cannot be said to be true of the so-called 'economic democracy' that has just been described. Here, there are very greatly varying numbers of votes between different voters. In terms of £s or $s, some voters are able to cast millions of votes in order to elect those products that should be produced. Other voters have very few, if any, votes to cast. This is often seen as a major problem (or failure) of markets: a lack of fairness or equity. Both income and wealth may be very unevenly distributed.

'Fairness' and Economics

The concept of fairness or equity is one with which Economics as a subject has considerable difficulty. So-called 'positive' economics claims not to deal at all with value judgements (as mentioned in the discussion about merit goods). However, ideas of equity go straight to the heart of serious and important value judgements in society. We must therefore state here that the notion of 'market failure' with regard to concerns over the equity of the market system is a different idea of market failure from the others discussed in this section. While the others are to do with observations about how scarce resources are not being used as effectively as possible to meet the infinite wants of consumers, this 'failure' is to do with value judgements that the scarce resources are not being fairly distributed in a free market economy.

Income and wealth

There are two separate aspects of resources that could be unevenly distributed in a market system: income and wealth. They are not the same. Income is a flow of earnings over a period of time (perhaps a year) usually in return for services rendered. Wealth is a stock of owned assets or properties. The most important wealth owned by most people in the UK is their house. There may be considerable inequalities in both income and wealth arising from the operation of markets.

In a free market, income, in the form of wages for labour, will be determined by the forces of supply and demand. If a person is blessed with a particular talent that is in very high demand (perhaps the ability to score goals for a top soccer club), then the income commanded by that person will be very high. Others may not be so fortunate and may thus receive far lower incomes. This may be judged as 'unfair' (or inequitable).

The principal means of gaining significant wealth is through inheritance. This is sometimes seen as even more inequitable than significant inequalities in income. A person born into one family has a far greater ownership of scarce resources than one born into another family. The strength afforded by such wealth could allow inequalities to persist or even widen as better education and other opportunities may be available through the greater level of wealth. This might all be judged as an unacceptable aspect of the operation of markets.

Self-help in redressing the problem of equity

Self-assessment task

Read the following short case study and then answer the questions that follow.

Challenges facing the NHS

Whoever is in charge of the NHS has to choose how scarce resources are allocated among ever-increasing demands. Using the price mechanism to limit demand is out of the question. Medical care is free, although the price of prescription drugs, for those who have to pay, is currently £6. Although the Department of Health dislikes the word, 'rationing' (i.e. limiting the amount of health care available) is now the principal task of the NHS's managers. Of course, rationing has been part and parcel of the NHS since its birth in 1948. The range of national health care on offer has been limited by every government-run spending decision, every clinical guideline, and the price paid for every medical drug.

In addition to rationing across the country as a whole, there is a lot of 'postcode prescribing', i.e. local variation in what the NHS provides. Much of the strong criticism of the previous Conservative government stemmed from their attempt to introduce competition between hospitals and other providers of health care. What that did was to show clearly that some local health authorities restrict, or do not provide, certain services that are available in other areas. These include cosmetic surgery and some forms of cancer treatment.

The government, while notably silent about the ways and means of rationing, must nevertheless address its effects. It has promised to shorten hospital waiting times and to increase the number of intensive-care beds. It also wants to minimise regional differences in provision.

Source: *The Economist*, 26 February 2000 (adapted).

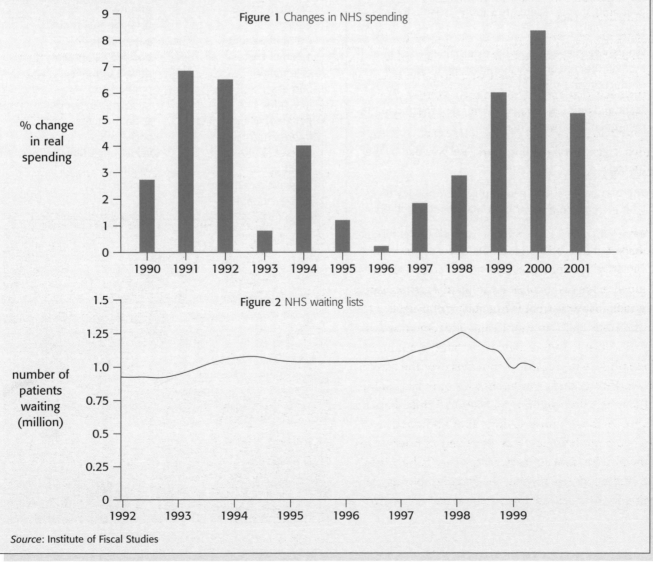

Figure 1 Changes in NHS spending

Figure 2 NHS waiting lists

Source: Institute of Fiscal Studies

(a) ◆ Define the term 'merit good'.

    ◆ Explain why health care is classified as a merit good.

(b) ◆ State **one** reason why it may be seen as 'unfair' if all health care were to be provided by the market system.

    ◆ Identify **one** reason from the article why the current provision of health care could be seen as 'unfair'.

(c) ◆ Using figure 1, describe what happened to health care spending between 1990 and 2000.

    ◆ The article states that 'medical care is free'. Consider the economic reasons why the government provides health care 'free'.

(d) ◆ Using figure 2, describe what happened to NHS waiting lists between 1992 and 1999.

    ◆ Explain why the free provision of health care by the NHS, together with ever-increasing demand for health care, must lead to 'rationing'.

Source: *OCR Paper 2882*, January 2001 (adapted).

Summary

In this section we have recognised that:

● Markets do not always operate as suggested by economic theory. There are various reasons why markets fail.

● Where negative and positive externalities exist in a market, the outcome is an inappropriate level of production and prices.

● Merit and de-merit goods will not be provided in the right quantities by the market.

● Public goods will not necessarily be provided by the market.

● The occupational and geographical immobility of labour creates particular unemployment problems.

● Where there is a concentration of power in particular markets, there is an undesirable effect upon consumers.

● Equity concerns over the distribution of income and wealth may arise from the operation of markets.

Key words

Definitions of Key words can be found in the Glossary on page 240.

de-merit goods
equity
external benefit
external cost
externality
fairness
free rider
geographical mobility
information failure
market failure
merit goods
negative externality
non-excludable

non-rival
occupational mobility
paternalism
positive externality
private benefits
public good
quasi-public goods
social benefits
social costs
value judgement
wealth
x-inefficiency

6 Making choices and the impact of government intervention on market outcomes and efficiency

On completion of this section you should be able to:

➤ understand what is meant by a cost–benefit approach

➤ understand and interpret information collected in a cost–benefit study

➤ understand the limitations of a cost–benefit approach

➤ describe the various methods by which governments intervene in markets

➤ analyse how the imposition of taxes and subsidies affects equilibrium in markets

➤ analyse the effects of price control and minimum wage control in product and factor markets respectively

➤ explain how state provision, regulation and standards can be applied in markets

➤ discuss the possible role of information provision in a range of possible market failures

➤ examine the role and analyse the impact of competition policy in tackling problems of market power

➤ discuss how governments may create inefficiencies when they intervene in markets due to such factors as political objectives distorting incentives and lack of information

The cost–benefit approach

The previous section of this unit identified various causes and consequences of market failure, in particular situations:

◆ where there is a divergence between private and social benefits and costs;

◆ where market dominance can lead to an inefficient allocation of resources;

◆ where public goods may not be provided by the market;

◆ where merit goods may be under-provided by the market;

◆ where there is factor immobility.

It is in such circumstances that a cost–benefit approach has been used by economists as a means of decision making, not least to ensure that the right choice of action is being made. Here we will be concerned with situations where major projects produce important and often controversial side effects, in particular where there are substantial costs and benefits which fall upon people and communities who have no direct connection with the particular project, either as consumers or suppliers.

A particularly relevant and widespread case of this occurring is where a new retail development is planned

(see Self-assessment task). The so-called **spillover effects** upon third parties (those not involved in the particular project) can be far-reaching and substantial. Cost–benefit analysis genuinely attempts to quantify the opportunity cost to society of the various possible outcomes or sources of action. It is therefore a procedure for making long-run decisions where present actions have implications far into the future.

The cost–benefit approach differs from private sector methods of appraisal in two main respects. These are:

◆ It seeks to include all of the costs and benefits, not just private ones.

A new housing development on former agricultural land

◆ It often has to impute **shadow prices** on costs and benefits where no market price is available. Very relevant examples here would be how to value the degradation of scenic beauty or the loss of agricultural land in the case (say) of building new houses on an attractive area of green belt. Other examples might be how to value the benefit of cleaner air or being able to live in a less noisy environment.

The framework of cost–benefit analysis

Whatever the problem under investigation, there are four main stages in the development of a cost–benefit analysis. These are shown in figure 6.1.

The first stage is to identify all of the relevant costs and benefits arising out of any particular project. Systematically, this involves establishing what are the private costs, the private benefits, the external costs and the external benefits (see unit 1, section 3 and unit 2, section 5 for details and definitions). On the surface this may seem a relatively simple task. In reality, and with a

little more thought, it is not so. There are particular problems when it comes to establishing external costs and benefits. These are often controversial, not easy to define in a discrete way and have the added difficulty that it is not always possible to draw the line in terms of a physical or geographical cut-off. The spillover effects of a new retail development, for example, are wide-reaching and often affect people and communities way beyond the immediate vicinity of the proposed development (see self-assessment task, question 1).

The second stage involves putting a monetary value on the various costs and benefits. This is relatively straightforward where market prices are available. For example, in the case of a new retail development, a monetary value can be put on the jobs created or the increased profits arising from the development. For other variables, though, a monetary value must be inputed for costs and benefits where no market prices are available. This particular measurement difficulty has occupied economists for thousands of hours over the years. It has also been a very controversial matter in situations where cost–benefit analysis has come under close public scrutiny. A particularly good example of this is the issue of valuation of time, especially travel time and savings in travel time. Another relevant example is how to put a monetary value on the cost of accidents, particularly where serious injuries or a loss of life is involved. (OCR's Transport Economics module looks at these in more detail in the context of the appraisal of new road schemes.)

The third stage of the cost–benefit analysis applies in situations where projects have longer-term implications which stretch well into the future. Here, economists have to employ statistical forecasting techniques, sometimes of a very crude nature, to estimate costs and benefits over many years. This particularly applies to proposed projects where massive capital expenditure is involved (see self-assessment task, question 3 for example). In other cases, this stage may actually not be needed, particularly if two alternatives are being considered (see self-assessment task, question 2).

The final stage is where the results of the earlier stages are drawn together so that the outcome can be presented in a clear manner in order to aid decision making. The important principle to recognise is that if the value of benefits exceeds the value of the costs, then the particular project is worthwhile since it provides an

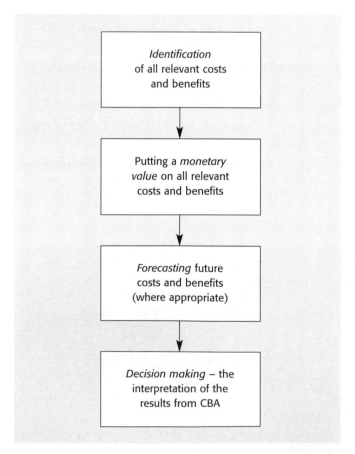

Figure 6.1 Stages in a cost–benefit analysis

overall net benefit to the community (see self-assessment task, question 2 for a simple example of such a situation).

The four stages in a cost–benefit analysis provide a coherent framework by which decisions can be made in situations of market failure. Students should therefore see any cost–benefit study or application in these terms. Of the respective stages, though the identification stage is in many respects not only the most interesting, it is also the one most relevant for OCR's examination of this unit, as the self-assessment tasks indicate. Students should also consider how the information which is required for a CBA might be collected (see the Introduction for information on how to plan an investigation).

Finally, to conclude, it is relevant to recognise that in practice cost–benefit analysis is fraught with many difficulties. Some have already been stated such as:

◆ which costs and benefits should be included;

◆ how to put monetary values on them.

Additionally, there are others, particularly when it comes to the acceptance of the outcome by the community as a whole. For example:

◆ CBA does not always satisfactorily reflect the distributional consequences of certain decisions, particularly where public sector investment is involved. In the case of a new retail development, external costs are likely to be highly localised whilst external benefits, in terms of employment creation for instance, are likely to be more widely spread.

◆ Many public sector projects (for example that analysed in self-assessment task, question 3) are very controversial and subject to much local aggravation from pressure groups. It may be the case that the outcome of the CBA is rejected for local political reasons, with the consequence that the most expedient decision may not be the one recommended by economists. Where this happens, it is easy to dismiss the technique of CBA as irrelevant. This is not a fair conclusion, not least as CBA has at least brought out the issues involved so that a decision can be taken on the basis of all of the information available. CBA is an aid and not a replacement for decision making.

Self-assessment tasks

1 Read the short case study below on Shopping in Bamfield, which is an adaptation of an A-Level question set by UCLES in March 1997, and then answer the questions which follow.

Shopping in Bamfield

Bamfield, a market town in the Cotswolds, is a thriving shopping centre, which attracts customers from many surrounding villages. It has various food and non-food shops, including a small privately owned supermarket trading as 'Cheap Away'. Virtually all of the shoppers travelling into Bamfield come by car as there are very few local bus services. Cheap Away does not have a car park of its own and consequently it is often difficult for shoppers to park on Bamfield's narrow streets.

Recently, Bamfield Town Council has received a planning application from a national supermarket chain, Fineways, to construct a new large store on agricultural land on the outskirts of the town. This proposed store would have a large car park and provide an extensive range of products. Many of the shoppers who currently use local shops and Cheap Away welcome the proposal. Others are against it, claiming that it will lead to the closure of existing shops, an argument which is endorsed by the local shopkeepers and the owner of Cheap Away.

Suppose you have been asked by Bamfield Town Council to produce a cost–benefit analysis of the Fineways supermarket proposal.

(a) What costs and benefits would you include in your analysis?

(b) How would you set about putting monetary values on this information?

(c) On what basis would you make a recommendation to the Town Council? Why might this recommendation not be entirely acceptable to all parties who have an interest in the proposed development?

2 This case study is an adaptation of an A-Level question set by UCLES in June 1997. Read it and then answer the questions that follow.

Cavalier Pet Products

Cavalier Pet Products is a large privately owned manufacturer of canned pet foods based in Bolton, Lancashire. The company, which employs 300 people, is long-established and has been on its present site since it was founded by its owners, the Fazackerley family, in 1906. It is a market leader, producing own-branded products, which are widely advertised and well known.

Through the nature of its manufacturing processes, the company is a polluter of the local environment. The nauseating smells from the factory, particularly in hot weather, are the main source of complaint; the firm also creates noise disturbance and quite recently was successfully prosecuted for discharging effluent into a local stream running alongside the factory. There is increasing local pressure from residents for something to be done about the whole question of the firm and its operations.

The obvious answer is for the firm to move to another location. The Managing Director of Cavalier Pet Products, Basil Fazackerley, favours such a move but is quite adamant that, 'We shall not pay the full cost. If the local council want us to move, then they will have to help us to do so.'

The decision to relocate the factory has long-term implications both for its owners and for the community. In particular, new jobs will be created as the firm increases output and the local environment within the vicinity of the present site will experience environmental gain.

The local authority have agreed to contribute to the relocation, as they can see a benefit to the community. Cavalier Pet Products remain concerned that they must also pay a contribution to the cost of relocation.

In order to sort out these difficulties, a local university was asked to carry out a cost–benefit analysis of the proposed relocation. A summary of their findings is given in the table below.

Costs		Benefits	
Private costs of the relocation	1,300	Private benefits	1,500
Contribution from local authority	300	External benefits	1,200
External costs	400		
Total costs	**2,000**	**Total benefits**	**2,700**

Estimated discounted[1] costs and benefits of the relocation of Cavalier Pet Products (£000)

Note: [1] Discounting is a procedure whereby a present value is given to costs and benefits that will occur some time in the future.

(a) What is the specific purpose of the cost–benefit analysis in this case?

(b) With reference to the proposed relocation, give an example of:
   ◆ a private benefit,
   ◆ an external benefit,
   arising from the proposed relocation. Explain your choice.

(c) Use the information in the table to state what conclusions you could draw from the cost–benefit analysis.

3 Read the two local newspaper articles on the opposite page on the problems of waste disposal in Huddersfield and then answer the questions that follow:

(a) Why has the decision been made to close the Vine Street incinerator?

(b) Use the evidence in the articles to identify:
   ◆ the private costs,
   ◆ the external costs,
   ◆ the private benefits,
   ◆ the external benefits,
   of the incinerator's operations. What additional information do you need in order to complete this task?

(c) You are required to produce a cost–benefit analysis on two alternative ways of disposing of Huddersfield's waste, namely:
   ◆ continuing to transport waste to landfill sites in the vicinity of Huddersfield;
   ◆ building a new 'state of the art' incinerator on the Vine Street site.
   What information would you require in order to carry out this study and on what basis would you reach a decision?

Vine Street waste site to close

Huddersfield's 330ft-high incinerator chimney is doomed to be a thing of the past, it was revealed today.

Waste officials confirmed the Vine Street rubbish plant would close in the next year.

And it could be replaced by extending a tip at Blackley on the Kirklees-Calderdale border.

Proposals went on show from today for public comment.

The move to shut the incinerator follows the failure to get backing for an ambitious plan to generate electricity from waste.

Cash was needed to update ageing furnace equipment because it did not reach Euro pollution standards.

Environmental group Greenpeace claimed last year that dioxin levels were 187 times higher than the safety limit.

Now West Yorkshire Waste Management says the site will be scrapped within a year.

An exact date has yet to be given for the shutdown.

Campaigners have long called for the incinerator to be closed because it is too close to the town centre – and only 500 yards from homes.

It opened in 1975 at a cost of £2m.

Two waste tips – at Cromwell Bottom, Elland, and Lower Spen Valley, Ravensthorpe – will also close around the same time.

Initial plans have been drawn up to replace them with a bigger tip at Hollins Hey, Blackley.

This would allow an extra 300,000 cubic metres of rubbish to be dumped over three years.

The exhibition of the proposals opened at Elland library today and runs until August 6.

But a West Yorkshire Waste Management spokesman said: "No decision has yet been taken on whether or not to submit a planning application."

The 330ft-high incinerator chimney which dominated the Vine Street plant has now closed. It opened in 1975 at a cost of £2m and stood just 500 yards from nearby homes. Anti-pollution campaigners succeeded in having it closed down in July 1996.
Picture by Julian Hughes

Source: Andrew Baldwin; this article and photograph appear with the kind permission of the *Huddersfield Examiner*, 19 July 1996.

Lorry plan as incinerator shuts down

A vast fleet of lorries is to be brought in to transport Huddersfield's waste when the Vine Street incinerator shuts this week.

The plant closes on Saturday and thousands of tons of rubbish will have to be transported by road to landfill sites across the county.

But speculation is growing that new talks could lead to a new incinerator being built on the site.

After 18 months of failed negotiations and scrapped plans, the incinerator at Vine Street is to shut.

In a move which has been branded "environmental nonsense", rubbish will be transported by road to two different landfill sites.

Euro laws are forcing the closure of the incinerator, which does not reach pollution standards.

And negotiations to get financial backing from a private company for an ambitious plan to generate electricity from waste at the site failed.

Environmental group Greenpeace claimed last year that levels of allegedly cancer-causing dioxins were 187 times higher than the recognised safety limit.

Campaigners have been calling for the incinerator – which deals with 55,000 tons of waste a week – to shut for many years. They claim it is too close to both the town centre and houses.

Strategy to take the area into 21st century

Kirklees Council's environmental waste services manager Steve Noble said from next week, waste will still be taken to the site but

there it will be compacted before being transported by road to landfill sites at Honley and just over the Kirklees/Calderdale border.

Mr Noble is drawing up a waste strategy to take Kirklees into the 21st century.

"We want our waste management to have the minimum environmental impact," he said. "And that could involve a new incinerator."

West Yorkshire Waste Management's engineering manager Dr David Baines explained two different groups were linked to the site.

While the collection of refuse is dealt with by Kirklees Council, whose binmen bring the waste to Vine Street, the incinerator itself and what happens next to the rubbish is the responsibility of West Yorkshire Waste Management.

"It all stems from the abolition of West Yorkshire County Council," he explained. "But ultimately I think Kirklees will have this land handed back.

"And the council will redevelop the site and build a new incinerator using private cash.

"Using landfill is environmental nonsense – especially if it is being sent to someone else's patch – and Kirklees knows that."

The incinerator plant was built by the former Huddersfield borough council and was brought into use in 1975. Since then it has handled the bulk of the town's household refuse.

Source: Claire Horton, *Huddersfield Examiner*, 26 November 1996.

Government intervention

You have only to glance at a newspaper, listen to the news or a political debate for a few minutes to realise that one of the more controversial areas of Economics is concerned with the extent and reasons for government intervention in markets. All governments in the world intervene to a greater or lesser extent and the reasons for intervention vary enormously between them. However, the justification for intervention is usually given under two broad headings:

> *market failure* and the desire to achieve a *fair or equitable distribution of resources* in the economy.

These have been analysed in section 5. The first intervention occurs when markets do not allocate resources efficiently and the second is concerned with ensuring that all members of society have fair access to goods and services. The role of the government is to intervene in markets that are not seen to be allocating resources in the most efficient or the most equitable manner. In attempting to achieve this aim it must also be recognised that there is also the possibility that governments will fail and create rather than remove distortions.

Methods of government intervention

Government policy and methods of intervention can be summarised under four broad headings: regulation, financial intervention, state production and transfer payments. The method chosen will depend to a large extent on whether the reason for intervention is concerned with market failure or with the desire to achieve equity.

Regulation

The government uses a large number of methods of **regulation** as a means of controlling a market. Legal and other methods are used to control the quality and quantity of goods and services that are produced and consumed. For example, the government may regulate the sale of certain drugs by making them only available on prescription from a qualified doctor. Hygiene laws set standards for the production of foods. There may be **controls** on shop opening hours or the setting of a minimum age at which a person can buy certain products, such as alcohol, cigarettes and lottery tickets.

Other forms of regulation may include the requirement for an individual to purchase an insurance policy before being legally permitted to drive a car, the age at which people are required to attend school and the payment of social insurance contributions.

Regulation may not only apply to the quantity and quality of goods and services sold but may also refer to prices. Examples of price controls include minimum wage legislation and rent controls.

Finally, the government has powers to control abuse of monopoly power through regulatory organisations such as the Competition Commission (CC) or bodies set up to investigate and regulate production and pricing policies by public utilities such as Oftel (telecommunications), Ofwat (water), Offer (electricity) and Ofgas (gas).

Financial intervention

Financial tools, such as taxes or subsidies, are also frequently used by governments to influence production, prices of commodities, incomes or the distribution of wealth in an economy. Price subsidies may vary. They might be in the form of a partial subsidy, as in the case of public transport, or total, as in the case of free eye tests for children in full-time education.

Tax instruments may also vary. For example consider two different forms of taxation that are currently applied to the use of vehicles in the UK. Vehicle Excise Duty is paid once every six months or year, unless the vehicle is more than 25 years old. The same amount is paid whether the car is used daily or only once a month. In addition vehicle users pay a tax on petrol. In this case the amount of tax paid rises with the number of miles driven. The first type of tax may deter ownership of a vehicle whilst the second deters use of the vehicle.

Governments also provide the finance that is needed to produce a good or service. It is very important to note at this early stage that, just because the government provides the finance for a product, it does not necessarily mean it has to produce the product too. For example, the government could finance education but all schools, colleges and universities could be privately owned and run. Health care may be provided free (financial intervention) but the drugs used in prevention and cure of illness could be privately produced.

State production

In addition to providing the finance it is also possible

for a government to take over the production of a good or service, either in whole or in part. State-owned industries are often referred to as **nationalised industries**. Industries such as the electricity, coal mining and railways are entirely owned and managed by the state in many countries. This is no longer the case in the UK following the major shift towards privatisation that took place in the 1980s and 1990s. It is also very common to find some goods and services being produced by both the state and the private sectors. Education and health care are particularly good examples of these types of service industries. NHS hospitals function alongside private hospitals and independent schools operate alongside state schools.

Income and other transfers

Income transfers are used by governments as a means of redistributing income or transferring income from one group in society to another group, for example from people in work to those who are retired or from relatively rich people to those who are in poverty. The justification for these transfers is to achieve fairness or equity in an economy. These transfers of income may be in the form of a cash benefit paid by the government to someone with a low income. Income transfers may also be used to cover the unexpected loss of income when a person is not working due to illness or unemployment. These cash transfers include social security benefits, such as income support, a job seeker's allowance or a state pension. The recipients of these benefits are free to spend this money as they see fit.

Other cash benefits are tied to specific areas of spending. An example of this would be housing benefits, which are given to low-income families to help with their housing costs. In this case the cash must be spent on housing.

It would be wrong to think that all transfers are in the form of a cash payment. **In-kind transfers** occur when a particular person is given a service or good free whilst other groups have to pay. An example of this type of transfer would be free dental check-ups, which are available to recipients of income support and to all children. In the first case free dental care is directed to those on low incomes whilst in the second it is directed to a specific age group.

Self-assessment task

Identify and explain the method of government intervention referred to in each of the following:

- the part of an MOT test that limits the amount of carbon particles that can be emitted from vehicle's exhaust pipe;
- the setting of a minimum wage rate;
- higher tax rate charged on lead substitute rather than unleaded petrol;
- free eye tests for pensioners;
- driving tests;
- age limits on individuals being able to purchase lottery tickets;
- reductions in the amount of job seekers' allowance paid to individuals with large amounts of savings;
- the building and staffing of schools.

The impact of government intervention on markets

The impact of these different methods of government intervention will vary according to both the reasons for market failure and the conditions facing the markets.

Public goods

Public goods, such as defence, need to be financed by the government but they do not necessarily need to be produced by the government. The government will decide upon the optimal amount of defence expenditure and raise revenue through taxation to fund it. The problem facing the government is deciding on the best or fairest method of raising the tax revenue required. One approach is to tax individuals according to their ability to pay tax. Thus those who have the highest incomes (or wealth) will pay most in taxation. Many governments use the 'ability to pay' principle as a basis for the tax system and it has a wide acceptance amongst the electorate as being the fairest means of raising tax revenue. In most countries the government takes a larger percentage of income in tax from the rich than the poor. This is called a **progressive tax** system.

An alternative approach is to tax individuals according to the benefits they receive from public goods. The main problem is valuing the benefits that an individual receives from a public good, defence being a particularly good example. Mrs Thatcher's government in the 1980s argued that all households received the same amount of benefit from local authority spending in the form of sewerage disposal, refuse collection, local road building, leisure centre and library facilities, parks and other such goods and services. All households were therefore required to pay the same amount of money to the local authority. This was called the Community Charge and it was in fact a 'poll' tax. Its introduction caused a lot of resentment and it was abandoned in favour of the Council Tax in 1991.

Externalities

Setting standards and regulation Governments frequently use regulation to overcome market failures caused by externalities. Let us consider the case of a chemical company that pollutes the surrounding countryside. The government might intervene by setting standards which restrict the amount of pollution that can be legally dumped. The government would then need to regulate and inspect the company to make sure that these restrictions are enforced. It can do this in several ways, for example by imposing large fines on any company that contravenes the law.

Exhaust fumes from cars pollute the atmosphere and to reduce this problem the government can set legal limits on the amount of carbon particles that is emitted from a car's exhaust pipe. This can be tested in the annual MOT test, although it also possible to conduct random on-the-spot tests. Regulations of this type are particularly effective when there are a large number of potential sources of the external cost. There are 17 million vehicles using Britain's roads and it is not possible to test individually every vehicle every day.

Financial intervention – taxes Financial intervention will take the form of taxes or subsidies and they can also be used in the case of externalities. A tax would normally be imposed on the individual or firm that causes the externality. If this happens then economists say that external costs are internalised.

In figure 6.2, in the case where there is no government intervention, the equilibrium occurs at point E, where supply, S_1, which is given by MPC or marginal private cost, equals demand, D, which is given by MPB or marginal private benefit. However, if external costs are included in this diagram, then the supply curve becomes

Figure 6.2 External cost and use of taxation

S_2 or MSC, marginal social cost. The vertical distance between these two supply curves is marginal external cost, MEC. The socially optimal level of output is therefore equal to Q_2, where S_2 cuts the demand curve. At this socially optimal level of output, the marginal external cost is equal to the vertical distance AB.

The government intervenes in this market and imposes a tax which is equal to the marginal external cost. This tax is added to the cost of producing the product and thus the supply curve S_2 is also equal to the MPC plus tax. Looking at the diagram, you can see that the price at which the product is sold has increased from P_1 to P_2. This is less than the tax applied by the government. At first sight this may appear a little strange, but the producer has accepted a cut in the price received from P_1 to P_3. The producer has borne the burden of part of the tax. The total tax paid is equal to the area P_2ABP_3, of which the consumer's share of the burden is P_2ACP_1 and the producer's share is P_1CBP_3.

Financial intervention – subsidies Financial intervention to overcome market failure caused by external benefits or positive externalities will take the form of a subsidy. This is shown in figure 6.3. The equilibrium without government intervention is at point F where MPC = MPB or $D_1 = S_1$. In this case marginal external benefit is added to the MPB curve to give the MSB or marginal social benefit curve. The MSB represents society's demand curve for the product.

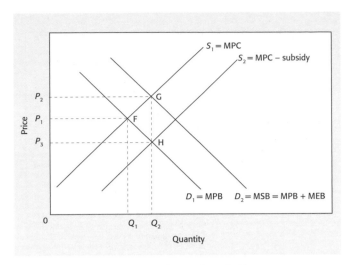

Figure 6.3 External benefits and use of a subsidy

If the government subsidises production of this product then the supply curve moves to the right from S_1, which equals MPC, to S_2, which equals MPC minus the subsidy. The marginal cost of supplying the good is reduced by the amount of subsidy and the vertical distance GH is equal to the value of the subsidy. Thus the equilibrium after the subsidy is given by point H, which is where D_1 crosses S_2 and the optimal amount of goods Q_2 is sold by the market.

As you might expect, there is considerable debate over which is the best method of government intervention when externalities are present in a market. If we accept the argument that education provides external benefits, then one solution would be to provide a subsidy to education. This can be seen in the UK where the government subsidises university education. Students still have to pay towards their education in the form of a fee, which can be represented by P_3 in figure 6.3. The government provides the difference between P_2 and P_3 in subsidy.

Information failures

Methods of intervention for market failure caused by information failures are varied. Consumers do not have perfect information about every good and service that is available on the market. The obvious question is why doesn't the government insist that correct and relevant information is made available to consumers and then they can correctly formulate their demand curve for the product. The short answer is that for many goods and services it does.

Providing information and government intervention

It is a legal requirement for shops and other suppliers to provide the consumer with information about the price of the product being offered for sale. Information about the product is also provided to the consumer. For example, food products are clearly labelled with details of weight, ingredients and the nutritional content of the product. Consumers are also protected against the possibility of buying products that have been sold using misleading information and against buying a faulty product. For example, it is not possible to tell by looking at the outside of a washing machine whether it has been manufactured to acceptable standards. The government therefore requires that products have a guarantee period, which protects the consumer against faulty manufacture. If a product needs repair during the guarantee period then consumers can claim their money back or have the good replaced.

Consumers may also be able to claim compensation if they are given misleading information, which led them to purchase the good or service. For example, a rail company may provide a timetable that gives the times a train is expected to deliver you at your destination. If you purchase a rail ticket for a train that is subsequently late, you are entitled to claim compensation if the delay is more than one hour.

In many cases, however, the information is either not available or it is so complicated that it cannot be interpreted by the consumer. In this case you could pay someone to provide and interpret this information for you. The consumer might buy a publication such as a car price guide or a computer magazine to obtain information about a product. These magazines usually give 'star' ratings for products, stating which is the best value for money in the eyes of the magazine. Alternatively you might pay an independent garage or the Automobile Association to send an expert to examine a second-hand car and provide you with a report before you purchase it.

When it comes to health care or the purchase of insurance, it is likely that the information is so complex that you need to obtain advice and information from an expert such as a doctor or an insurance broker. The government has to intervene in this market to make sure that the advice you receive is both good and appropriate to your needs. The consequences of poor or incorrect advice from a doctor could result in permanent injury or even death. Thus the medical profession is very strictly controlled and doctors are required to undertake regulated training before they can prescribe medicine and offer treatment to patients.

Over-consumption of a product and regulation It can be argued that a drug, such as heroine or tobacco, is over-consumed because individuals do not realise the true extent of the harm that the product causes. The government has several policy options that it can employ to try and limit the amount of the drug that is consumed.

For example, it can impose legal regulations on the market, such as an outright ban (as in the case of heroine), or limit the market, as in the case of alcoholic drinks and cigarettes, by restricting purchase to certain age groups. Such types of policy can cause anger amongst some consumers, who argue that these are infringements of civil liberties. The government could respond to this criticism by engaging in an advertising campaign to inform the consumer of the dangers of taking drugs and then allow individuals to decide how much they should consume. Warnings of the possible effects of smoking are printed on the side of cigarette packets. The success of this policy will be determined by the extent to which cigarette smokers take notice of these warnings. Thus the government attempts to control the behaviour of consumers by providing information.

Over-consumption and financial intervention Another option is to impose a tax on the good, which shifts the supply curve to the left. The government imposes a high tax (called a customs and excise duty) on both cigarettes and alcoholic drinks in order to reduce the consumption of these products. Figure 6.4 illustrates the case where a consumer over-values the product. The demand is incorrectly placed at D_1. The correct demand curve (with perfect information) would have been at D_2. Therefore an amount, Q_1-Q_2, is consumed that is above the correct equilibrium quantity, Q_2. The tax shifts the supply curve of the product from S_1 to S_2 and so as the prices rise the consumer moves along the incorrect demand curve to point A. The consumer now consumes Q_2, which is the optimal amount of the product.

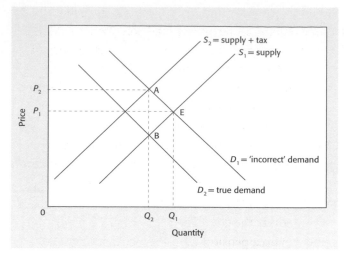

Figure 6.4 Over-consumption and the use of a tax

Under-consumption and regulation If a consumer underestimates the demand for a good then the policies are reversed. The government can make purchases of a good compulsory. Many of the compulsory purchase requirements are in insurance markets. All workers might be required by law to contribute to a state pension scheme or to a National Health Service via their national insurance contributions because the government estimates that they would under-consume these goods if purchase was not compulsory.

It is a legal requirement in the UK for all children to receive education between the ages of five and 16. In addition, state schools are required to follow a 'national curriculum' to ensure that all children receive a minimum standard of education. Thus the government considers that, without the legal requirement, some children would not attend school and thus education would be under-consumed.

Under-consumption and financial intervention
Financial intervention, in this case, will take the form of a subsidy or alternatively a financial incentive in the form of a tax reduction to encourage consumers to buy the product. Let us assume that the government believes that without government intervention individuals will not purchase sufficient pensions. The government could offer a subsidy to the pension providers. This subsidy may be offered to the customer in the form of a tax reduction.

A government may state that a consumer does not have to pay any income tax on the interest payments paid into a pension fund. (Income tax is normally payable on interest payments made on savings held in a financial institution such as a bank or building society.) This means that interest payments added to pension funds would be larger than those added to other forms of saving. For example if the interest paid on savings was 5 per cent per annum and the income tax rate was 25 per cent, the pension fund saver would receive the full 5 per cent whereas those saving money in a building society account would receive 3.75 per cent (5 per cent interest payment less tax at 25 per cent).

Alternatively the government could say that any payments into a pension fund that are made from a worker's income will not count towards that person's taxable income. An example illustrates how this works. An individual earns £20,000 and is in the basic income tax band. For simplicity assume that the income tax rate for this consumer equals 25 per cent. Now this individual decides to pay £1,000 into a pension fund. The Pension Company refunds the income tax that would have been paid on this sum and thus the individual has a refund of tax which equals £250. In this simplified example, the net cost (or price) of the pension therefore becomes £750. The individual pays the Pension Company £750 and the Pension Company claims back £250 from the tax authorities. The government has given a subsidy to the Pension Company which is equal to the tax rebate. The effect of this is illustrated in figure 6.5.

Without government intervention the equilibrium quantity of goods bought and sold will be Q_1; this is given by point M where S_1 crosses D_1 (the 'incorrect'

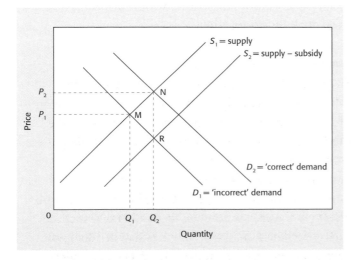

Figure 6.5 Under-consumption and subsidy

demand). However if information had been both made available and understood, the consumer would have purchased amount Q_2, given by the point where the 'correct' demand curve, D_2, cuts the supply curve.

The government intervenes by giving a subsidy to the pension company and this reduces the supply price by an amount equal to the amount of the subsidy. The supply curve shifts from S_1 to S_2 and equilibrium moves from point M to point R (note point R lies vertically below point N) and thus the equilibrium quantity bought and sold rises from Q_1 to Q_2. The supply shift means that the consumer has moved down the 'incorrect' demand curve from point M to point R.

Mixed goods and intervention

It is highly likely that many, if not all, of the product markets in which governments intervene have both externalities and imperfect information problems. These products can be referred to as **mixed goods**. The method of government intervention, therefore, has to allow for both potential causes of market failure. As an example, consider the case of drink driving.

Drivers may underestimate the effects of drinking alcohol on their ability to drive. If they do drink and drive they are more likely to be involved in an accident. It is often the case that drivers will underestimate the probability or likelihood of having an accident and thus over-consume alcohol. If as a result of excessive drinking they are actually involved in an accident they will incur both private and social costs. Private costs include both loss of earnings incurred by the driver whilst in hospital and also repairs to the driver's car. External costs will include injuries to others who were hurt in the accident or damage to another individual's property or vehicle. The government imposes legal limits on the amount of alcohol that can be consumed before driving a car.

Smoking not only affects the smoker, who may not fully appreciate the harm that cigarette smoking causes, but it also affects other individuals who inhale the smoke. Thus smoking has both elements of imperfect information and externality.

Concentration of power in markets

Governments intervene in situations in which market power is concentrated in a small number of firms. In these situations markets are not operating efficiently because firms abuse their market power. There are several methods that a government can use to prevent abuse of this market power. The government can use standards and regulation or financial intervention in the form of price controls. In some cases governments may also decide that market efficiency is best achieved if the product is produced by state-owned firms. Barriers to entry will protect the power of a monopolist. Some of these barriers may be artificial and the government can remove these barriers and thus make the market more 'contestable' (see unit 1, section 3).

Regulation and control of monopoly power

Governments have three key methods of controlling monopoly power. They can prevent the formation of monopolies by blocking the merger of companies that would potentially lead to one large company that is likely to dominate the market. Alternatively they can regulate firms that dominate the industry. Finally, the government can remove any artificial barriers that have allowed the monopolist to dominate the market.

All mergers that are likely to lead to a company gaining dominance in a market can be referred to the Competition Commission (CC). This government body is charged with ensuring that the merger is not against the public interest, in other words, that the result of the merger will not lead to a situation in which the consumer will be exploited through high prices and reduced output.

If a company already has a dominant position within the market, then this company can also be referred to the CC if it is considered to be acting against the public interest. A dominant position is usually seen to occur when a company controls more than 25% of a market. There are a wide range of methods by which these dominant firms can act against the public interest and against which the CC will act.

The dominant firm may charge prices that are considerably higher than the marginal cost of production, safe in the knowledge that there are no competitors to which the consumer can turn for a lower-priced product. As we have shown in Section 4, this leads to an allocatively inefficient use of resources. Price is also unlikely to equal minimum average cost, which leads to productive inefficiency. The government

may place price controls on a firm to ensure that prices are not set above a certain limit. Thus the maximum price that a firm in this situation can charge is set by the government. This type of price control is typical in the case of public utilities, such as privately owned gas, electricity and water companies.

The dominant firm may also exploit the consumer by offering a poor quality product or service. An example of this might by a train-operating company that frequently gives poor service in terms of the late running or cancellation of trains. Other companies may produce products with shoddy workmanship and lack the willingness to honour guarantees. The government can intervene and fine these companies or, in the case of rail companies, withdraw their franchises so that they are no longer able to operate train services.

As a final example, the firm may exploit consumers by using a practice that has become known as 'bundling'. In this case the company insists that if you buy their product then you *must* also buy other products that are associated with it. Thus a consumer has to buy a 'bundle' of products from the company. Until recently a tour operator could insist that if you bought their holiday product you also had to purchase their holiday insurance. Thus the holiday and insurance were bundled together. This practice has now been made illegal. Similarly a building society (or other mortgage provider) would insist that you could only have their mortgage if you also bought their life insurance policy and their house and contents insurance policy. A final example is given by the Microsoft company which insists that if you buy their 'Office' product you must also buy their Internet browser as the two are bundled together.

State ownership and monopoly power In many

countries, natural monopolies are placed into the hands of state ownership to avoid the problems of exploitation by dominant firms. The state-run, or nationalised, industry then charges prices that are equal to the marginal cost of production. Large economies of scale are present in special markets referred to as natural monopolies. These include public utilities and railways. In the UK many of these industries have been privatised because it was believed that privately run companies would be more efficient as a result of the discipline placed upon them by the profit motive. However, without control these privatised companies may abuse their dominant position and charge high prices or provide a shoddy product or service.

The government has a clear choice: state ownership or private ownership plus rigid regulation and control. Products such as water, gas and electricity are seen by some governments as being so important to the welfare of their population that their production cannot be entrusted to large privately owned companies. This appears to be a political rather than an economic decision.

Removal of barriers to entry and contestable markets

One possible barrier to entry that leads to monopoly power is the legal barrier that only allows a single company to supply the product. This was the case for the provision of most local bus services before deregulation in 1986. Local authority and state-owned companies were operating in a protected market which became contestable following deregulation. The Royal Mail's monopoly over 'last mile' mail deliveries is a more recent yet equally controversial example. As the market becomes more contestable, then private companies will tend to 'cherry pick' those parts of the former monopolist's business that will be likely to generate profits. It is highly unlikely that one of these companies will be tempted into taking over those postal activities that are loss-making.

Royal Mail van stops to collect post from a village post box

Self-assessment task

Explain how different methods of government intervention can be used to correct market failures caused in the following:

- the purchase of a technically complex good such as a computer;
- a national airline, which is given sole rights to fly certain routes;
- a chemical plant that discharges its waste products into the local river;
- street lighting;
- the potential health risk caused by BSE-infected cattle;
- noisy neighbours;
- inoculation against a disease;
- university education.

Equity, redistribution and government intervention

The methods of intervention used by governments to ensure a fair or equitable distribution of resources are different from those described earlier. First, if markets fail then the government needs to raise taxes in order to provide the finance to correct the market failures. For example, finance is needed to pay for public goods, such as defence, and it is also necessary to pay for goods and services, such as roads, education and health. These taxes should be raised in a fair and equitable manner.

Second, the government may want to redistribute income, wealth or other resources for social or political reasons. These involve value judgements but nonetheless require government intervention in markets. Society, through its elected members of government, decides that it is socially unjust to have a very unequal distribution of income or wealth. Thus these types of argument to justify redistribution are referred to as social justice reasons.

There are several possible strands to such equity objectives. The government may intervene to achieve any one or any combination of the following:

- the elimination of poverty (all individuals are entitled to a minimum standard of living regardless of personal circumstances);
- a reduction in unacceptable inequalities in the distribution of income and wealth;

◆ equal access, regardless of a person's income, to certain goods and services such as education, health and housing – for example, all children should have equal access to high-quality education regardless of their family background;

◆ the protection against a sudden and unexpected loss of income – for example, protection against loss of income due to an unexpected illness that prevents a person from being able to work.

If the government decides to intervene for social justice reasons it then has to decide how to redistribute these resources. It may do this in the form of cash payments or social security benefits. These benefit payments may be 'means-tested' (that is, only paid to people on low incomes) or 'universal' (that is, paid to everyone with a particular need regardless of their income).

Alternatively these benefits may be paid 'in-kind'. This means that government provides a good or service free of charge rather than give cash to individuals to arrange their own consumption. An example of this would be entitlement to free prescriptions or dental

treatment that is given to people on low incomes or to people in certain age groups, such as children or pensioners.

Redistributive taxes and paying for welfare The government needs to raise a considerable sum of money each year to pay for its expenditure. A tax that raises this money by taking a larger percentage of income from the rich than the poor was referred to earlier and is known as a progressive tax. Alternatively, if a larger percentage of income is taken from the poor than the rich, it is called a **regressive tax**.

Table 6.1 gives a simple example of both types of system. First note that the total amount raised in tax from both systems is £5,000 and, equally importantly, that the poor person has paid less in tax than the rich person in both cases. In the regressive tax system, Person A (the person on the lower income) has paid 20 per cent of their income in tax whilst Person B has paid only 5 per cent. By redistributing the tax burden it is possible to shift to a progressive tax system. Person B now pays a higher percentage in tax than Person A.

The last gathering of all peers in the House of Lords prior to its reconstitution. Although the distribution of wealth has become more equal, those, such as the hereditary peers, who inherit wealth still account for many of the country's rich. New wealth, however, has been created through privatisation sales, through increased housing values and through share prices. Nevertheless, statistics on the distribution of wealth still indicate much inequality, with the top 50 per cent of the population having 82 per cent of the wealth, the top 10 per cent have 33 per cent and the top 1 per cent have 10 per cent.
Source: Eddie Mulholland.

Type of tax system		Regressive tax system		Progressive tax system	
	Income	Tax Paid	Percentage of Income paid in tax	Tax Paid	Percentage of Income paid in tax
Person A	£10,000	£2,000	20%	£500	5%
Person B	£50,000	£3,000	6%	£4,500	9%
Tax Paid		**£5,000**		**£5,000**	

Table 6.1 Regressive and progressive tax systems

Redistributive taxes and social justice Redistribution for social justice reasons is achieved through a combination of taxation, benefit payments and in-kind transfers. Let us assume that the government wants to redistribute wealth because it believes that the current distribution is too uneven. It might do this by taxing inheritances. An example will illustrate how this might work.

Assume that the first £100,000 of an inheritance is free of tax but any additional receipt of an inheritance is taxed at 40 per cent. If someone dies and leaves £200,000 to say, Person A, then £40,000 is paid in tax and the person receiving the inheritance actually receives £160,000. However, if the person leaves the money to two people who receive £100,000 each then no tax is paid. This system of tax may encourage people to leave their money in smaller amounts to a larger number of people and thereby redistribute or spread the wealth over a wider number of people.

Although the British system of taxation of wealth is called an Inheritance Tax, it is confusingly named because it does NOT in fact tax the amount of money that a person inherits. In the British system the amount of tax paid is determined by the total amount of money in a person's estate (that is, left by a person after death). It does not matter whether the deceased leaves this money to one person or to several people as the amount paid in tax is exactly the same. This is more properly called an Estate Duty. Thus in table 6.2, the deceased's estate would be required to pay £40,000 in tax in both cases and £160,000 would either be paid to one individual or, in the second case, shared between the two individuals. There is no tax incentive to redistribute the wealth.

The income tax system in the UK is a progressive tax system and thus redistributes resources from the higher-income earners to those on low or no income. In our tax system expenditure taxes are either regressive or progressive. VAT is generally regarded as being mildly progressive in its current form, which is mainly because the UK government does not impose VAT on food. The rich spend a higher proportion of their income on goods and services that have VAT imposed on them than the poor and so pay a higher proportion of their income in VAT. If VAT was imposed on food then, because the poor spend a much higher proportion of their income on food than the rich, they would pay a higher proportion of their incomes in VAT and the tax would become regressive. The tax on beer and cigarettes (that is, excise duties + VAT) is regressive because the poor spend a higher proportion of their income on these items than the rich.

	Inheritance tax system				Estate duty system			
	All to Person A		Equal shares		All to Person A		Equal shares	
	Amount of inheritance	Tax paid	Amount of inheritance	Tax paid	Amount of inheritance	Tax paid	Amount of inheritance	Tax paid
Person A	£200,000	£40,000	£100,000	0	£200,000	£40,000	£100,000	£20,000
Person B	0	0	£100,000	0	0	0	£100,000	£20,000
Totals	**£200,000**	**£40,000**	**£200,000**	**0**	**£200,000**	**£40,000**	**£200,000**	**£40,000**

Table 6.2 Different wealth tax systems

Redistributive social security benefit payments The government uses a range of social security benefits or payments to redistribute resources, usually in the form of income, from one group in society to another. Different criteria are used to judge who is entitled to claim these benefits. Some benefits are targeted towards those on low incomes, some towards those with children and others towards those who are over a certain age.

Social security benefits that are used to transfer income from high-income earners to low-income earners are referred to as 'income-targeted' or 'means-tested' benefits. This is because the type of benefit, such as income support, is targeted towards low-income earners. There are two major problems with this type of redistributive benefit system. A considerable amount of information is required about an individual's financial position and thus long and detailed claims forms need to be completed by the claimant.

There are two problems associated with this type of benefit. First, it is administratively expensive to collect information about a person's income and, secondly, claimants are put off making a claim for several reasons. For example, the form is complex, they feel uneasy about releasing sensitive personal information and a certain amount of 'stigma' is attached to admitting publicly that you are poor. For this reason, many 'means-tested' benefits have very low 'take-up rates', that is, the number of people who claim the benefits as a proportion of those who are entitled to claim them is low. In the case

of a benefit such as income support only around 50 per cent of those entitled to make a claim will do so.

To overcome the problem of stigmatisation and low take-up rates the government frequently uses other methods of targeting benefits to those who are poor. For example, it is known that a very large percentage of people who are living in poverty in the UK are either over 65 (that is, pensioners) or have children. Benefits are therefore targeted to these groups. Old age and having children can be used as an 'indicator' of poverty. These benefits are known as 'indicator-targeted' benefits.

These benefits are not 'means-tested' but are given to everyone regardless of their income. The general name for a benefit that is given to everyone regardless of income is 'universal benefit'.

Child benefit, an example of a universal and indicator-targeted benefit, is paid to all families who have children regardless of income. Child benefit is very easy to claim – you make one claim soon after the baby is born and the benefit is paid until the child reaches a certain age or leaves full-time education. This is obviously very cheap to administer and has no stigma attached to it as everyone receives the payment. In consequence the take-up rate for child benefit is close to 100 per cent. However, many people argue that child benefit is poorly targeted because it is paid to many people who are not in poverty.

The government is willing to accept payment to all because the rich in effect pay more into the tax system than they claim in benefits, whilst the poor pay little or

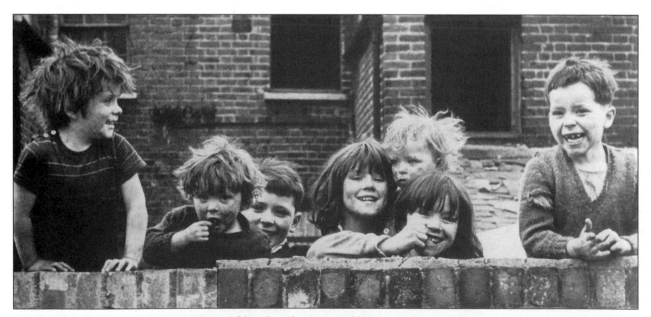

Two decades of rising poverty mean today's children face the same problems as earlier generations
Source: Family Service Units.

		Progressive tax system		Universal benefit		Table 6.3 Redistribution under a universal benefit system
	Income	Tax paid	Percentage of income paid in tax	Annual payment	Income after tax and benefit	
Person A	£10,000	£500	5%	£2,500	£12,000	
Person B	£50,000	£4,500	9%	£2,500	£48,000	
Tax raised		**£5,000**		**£5,000**		

nothing in tax and still receive the benefit. Thus a combination of a progressive tax system and a 'universal' benefit payment system means that income is redistributed from high-income earners to the poor. Table 6.3 gives a simplified example to illustrate how this works.

A total of £5,000 is paid in tax using the progressive tax system discussed earlier in table 6.1. This is used to pay a universal benefit of £2,500 to each of the taxpayers (half the tax raised). We can see clearly that Person A pays £500 in tax and receives £2,500 in benefits. Person A's disposable income after subtracting tax and adding benefits is equal to £12,000 – a rise of £2,000. However, Person B has a disposable income of £48,000, which is a fall of £2,000. Therefore, £2,000 has been transferred from Person B to Person A under this system. In the real world the tax and benefit system is much more complicated, but this simple example shows how universal indicator-targeted benefits can transfer income from one group to another.

Redistributive benefits paid 'in-kind' Not all redistributive benefits are paid in the form of cash. 'In-kind' benefits are usually provided in the form of entitlement to a good or service without the need for payment. Thus goods and services such as medical prescriptions, eye tests and dental care are given free of charge to children and pensioners. In this case the benefit is targeted towards certain age groups.

Benefits paid 'in-kind' are also targeted at those with low incomes and/or in receipt of certain means-tested benefits, such as a job seeker's allowance or income support. Receipt of one benefit therefore automatically acts as the ticket or passport to other benefits. A person on low income is therefore spared the indignity of filling in a multitude of forms.

Some 'in-kind' benefits are paid to every person in the country. All residents are entitled to free access to the National Health Service and to free education in a state school for their children. These universal 'in-kind' benefits are provided to allow everyone to have equal access to services that the government believes to be important. However, in this case they should not be seen as redistributing resources from the rich to the poor. In fact the opposite is probably the case as the rich tend to make greater use of both the health service and the education system. The economic justification for providing health care and education free of charge to all is based on market failure rather than equity arguments.

Self-assessment tasks

1 Explain which of the following are regressive and which are progressive taxes:
   - a Poll Tax which takes the same amount of tax from everyone regardless of income;
   - VAT on children's clothing;
   - income tax.
2 Explain which of the following redistribute resources and how this redistribution occurs:
   - free long-term care in residential homes for pensioners;
   - reduced bus fares for individuals receiving job seeker's allowance;
   - a state pension paid to everyone;
   - a tax on the purchase of houses costing more than £100,000;
   - tax on beer.

Government failures

It is not only markets that fail. It is important to recognise that government intervention can also fail. To illustrate this point we begin by considering an economy in which *all* of the decisions are taken by the state, the extreme opposite to an economy in which *all* decisions are taken by the market with no government intervention. Both extremes are unlikely to occur in reality as most economies can be considered mixed economies and thus we consider the case of **government failure** in a mixed economy too.

Government failure in a non-market economy In the state-controlled economy, all prices, all production levels and the allocation of all resources are decided by some central authority. This requires central planning, which is an extremely complex business. If planners make errors in determining production levels and demand exceeds supply at the government-set prices, then a shortage and queues will form. There will be unsold surpluses for goods where supply exceeds demand.

Although used extensively by many Socialist and Communist countries during the twentieth century, most of these countries, such as the Soviet Union, Poland, Bulgaria and China, have now abandoned central planning of this type. Four government failures were significant in this decision. First, a centrally planned process finds difficulty in coping with rapid change, such as technological advance or sudden harvest failure. Secondly, it proved difficult to control the quality of products produced. Thirdly, there was no incentive for workers to undertake training or move jobs as they were guaranteed employment at a fixed wage. Similarly, companies had little incentive to innovate and introduce new products or technology into their production processes. Finally, environmental degradation occurred on a massive scale as production plants were concerned only with meeting production targets and were not concerned at all with pollution (section 13 covers these issues in more depth and detail).

Government failure in a market economy
Governments intervene in mixed and market economies to correct market failures. Through intervention a government introduces a distortion or rigidity into a market. If the government makes a mistake with the type, size or extent of intervention, then rather than correct a market failure the government will itself create a more inefficient distribution of resources.

It takes time to change government policies and, if there is a sudden and unexpected change in the market,

then governments may be slow to react as policy changes have to pass through correct parliamentary procedures. For example, tax rates are usually only adjusted in an annual budget.

The government may use the best information available at the time the policy decision was made but the introduction of the policy will itself undoubtedly cause behaviour to alter. In a highly uncertain world, the government may not always be able to fully judge the effect of its policy change. The government may impose a tax on petrol to correct for the external cost that arises from the pollution that is emitted by car exhaust fumes, but, if car producers invent a new form of car engine that radically reduces the amount of pollution, then a lower tax rate will be required to correct for the market failure.

Many members of the public will always attempt to find legal (and sometimes illegal) ways of avoiding paying tax. Thus, if the government increases the tax rate on high incomes, the tax payers will attempt to find loopholes in the tax laws which allow them to reduce their tax liability or attempt to find alternative ways of receiving this income payment which avoids the tax payment. The government then has to play catch-up and close these loopholes or extend the tax to cover all other sources of income. For example, a company director may not take all of his earnings in the form of income but may accept perks, such as a company car. The government (as it does in the UK) will tax the company car as though it was an addition to the company director's income. The company director may then take payment in the form of free private health care. The government will need to close this loophole too. It could be argued that if the government has to keep altering the tax laws to close these loopholes then it has failed, *but* it has to be remembered that the government cannot work out how the public will respond to many of these policies and many of the loopholes will only be discovered once the policy is put into practice.

The government has political objectives as well as economic objectives. Governments have to face elections and the implication of some policies, such as those which involve increasing taxes or regulating the behaviour of individuals when an election is close, may have an influence on when and if to introduce the policy. It can be argued that a government is more likely to introduce unpopular changes at the start of its term of office rather than at the end.

Self-assessment tasks

1 (a) Explain why governments might fail to allocate resources efficiently in a command economy.

   (b) Explain how a government can fail in its attempt to achieve a more equitable distribution of income.

   (c) Explain how a government might fail in setting a tax to reduce the external costs caused by pollution.

2 Local residents claim that a planned pop festival will cause several problems for their community. They claim that roads will become congested, excessive noise will be created throughout the day and night, litter and waste products will be thrown into the local countryside and drugs introduced to the local community. The organisers argue that if the residents had good information they would realise that these claims were exaggerated and in any case the pop festival will bring benefits to the community in the form of increased expenditure in local shops and campsites.

   (a) Explain the potential causes of market failure in this case.

   (b) Comment upon the different policies that could be used to overcome the problems caused by market failure.

3 The government gives both child benefit and income-targeted benefits to families with children who are considered to be poor.

   (a) Explain why a government might want to redistribute resources from one sector of the population to another.

   (b) Comment upon the use of child benefits and income-targeted benefits as a means of achieving the aim of redistributing resources to families who are considered poor.

4 The market for education might fail if the provision of education was left entirely to the private sector.

   (a) Explain why the market for education might fail.

   (b) Comment upon the alternative policies that a government might use to correct for these market failures.

The following tasks bring together various concepts – they are typical of those that will be set by OCR in the examination for this unit.

5 Government intervention

The annual budget speech is a chance for the Chancellor of the Exchequer to explain why and how the government intervenes in the economy. It also enables the government to alter taxes and government expenditure in order to overcome problems generated from a freely operating market economy. This case study takes selected parts from the 1999 budget speech. As you read these highlights from the speech, it will become obvious that it is a political speech but it is also obvious that there are many reasons for government intervention in an economy.

Chancellor's Budget Speech, 10 March 1999

With this the last Budget of the 20th century – we leave behind the century-long sterile conflicts between governments of the left that have too often undervalued enterprise and wealth creation, and governments of the right, too often indifferent to public services and fairness.

The sharpest spur to enterprise, the ingredient too often missing in our country today, is competition… And it is time for more competition and lower prices in basic essentials like the utilities, financial services, indeed the whole range of consumer goods, where too often British people are paying more than they should for what they need to buy. It is wholly unacceptable that consumer goods can still cost up to twice as much in Britain as in America.

Tomorrow so that competition will be encouraged for the long-term needs of the economy and consumers, the Secretary of State for Trade and Industry plans to set out a new competition policy for Britain. The Office of Fair Trading will now be charged with a pro-active remit to root out cartels and restrictive behaviour. Wherever there is monopoly power we will open the way to competition… Britain will have the most open competition policy the country has seen.

As Britain works to lead in the new economy we must resolve to lead in respecting the environment. Our target is to reduce greenhouse emissions by 12.5 per cent by 2010. And today I will announce a programme of measures that will cut carbon pollution by 3 million tonnes.

My first proposal alone will reduce carbon pollution by 1.5 million tonnes… We will now… introduce a levy on business use of energy from April 2001.

We also intend to set significantly lower rates of tax for energy intensive sectors that improve their energy efficiency … We will also allocate an extra £50m to encourage business to invest in the new environmental technologies and in renewable fuels.

In line with the fuel escalator first introduced by the previous government at 5 per cent above inflation and now 6 per cent, petrol duty will rise from 6pm today.

Vehicle excise duty for smaller cars will, from 1 June this year, be cut by £55 – the first cut in the licence fee in 50 years. Other cars' rates are only increased in line with inflation.

Children are 20 per cent of the British people but 100 per cent of Britain's future. To build that future, this Budget provides a better deal for families and children …

In the Budget last year I set down the two principles that govern my approach: that we must substantially increase support to families with children and we must do so in the fairest way.

Every year a quarter of a million children, even at the moment they are born, are born into poverty. This too is wrong. … When we came into power, one child in every three in our country was in poverty. With our measures today 700,000 children are being lifted out of poverty. Families with children are better off…

On top of the £40bn extra we are already investing in education and health, we will today allocate increased resources for our key public services…

We are allocating an additional £170m for crime prevention in areas where crime is highest. The Home Secretary will make a detailed statement to the House. For public transport, in addition to the rural transport fund, we will make a further allocation to be announced by the Deputy Prime Minister.

The £190bn extra we are already providing for education will finance smaller class sizes, more nursery education, better pay for better teachers, our drive to improve literacy and numeracy – and we will help 700,000 more young people to go on to further and higher education.

I turn to the NHS: £21bn extra money is making possible the largest hospital building programme since the war: a £1bn investment in modern technology in the health service, the recruitment of 7,000 new doctors; 150,000 more nurses; and a fair pay award for nurses.

To enhance in every part of the United Kingdom the health care that people most urgently require we today make an additional and immediate cash allocation, to be spent in the next 12 months, for the upgrading of every single accident and emergency unit which needs it.

Today's Budget is a better deal for work, a better deal for the family, a better deal for business – for a Britain now united around values of fairness and enterprise, and I commend this Budget not just to the House but to the country.

(a) ◆ Why does the government want to intervene in markets whenever there is market power?

◆ How can the government open the way to competition?

◆ How can the government root out cartels and restrictive behaviour?

(b) ◆ Explain why the government is keen to reduce pollution tax.

◆ Using a diagram, show how you can determine the rate of tax that would need to be charged to reach the optimal level of production.

◆ How will the proposed changes in vehicle excise duties help?

◆ What other policies could the Chancellor choose to cut carbon pollution by 3 million tonnes?

(c) ◆ Explain two different methods by which the government could help families with children.

◆ Is increasing 'Child Benefits' the best way of helping children who are 'born into poverty'?

◆ What 'in-kind' transfers does the government use to help children? How would increasing expenditure on these help children 'born into poverty'?

◆ Discuss the advantages and disadvantages of the Chancellor using means-tested benefits to help children 'born into poverty'.

(d) ◆ Why does the government spend money on crime prevention, education and health care?

◆ Could the private market provide all or part of crime prevention, education or health care?

6 On completion of this unit, you should be able to answer all questions in the examination paper below.

Market failure, public services and government failure

When markets do not achieve economic efficiency (that is productive plus allocative efficiency), economists say that markets fail. There are several different examples of such failure, but they all arise owing to scarce resources not being used in the best possible way. Government may respond to such failures by intervening in these markets. One possible form of intervention is for the government to provide services to the general public. These are known as 'public services'. The article below looks critically at government provision of such services in the UK and considers the ways the government might end up running them. Table 1 focuses on the government provision of one particular service – health care.

Public services: time to stop prattling and start spending

The European Court of Justice has recently made a significant ruling in the field of health care. It decreed that UK patients facing 'undue delays' have a right to seek treatment elsewhere in Europe and to send their bills to Britain's health service.

The European Court's decision was reasonable and fair. It is just a shame that European judges cannot play a larger role in British government policy. When one reads of British children without qualified maths teachers, one wishes the judges could rule that such children have a right to seek education in Germany – and to send the bill to the Department of Education. And when one reads of the poverty of British pensioners, one wishes the judges could rule that British pensioners should enjoy the same pension rights as the Swedish – and send the bill to Gordon Brown, the British Chancellor.

Funding seems to be the main problem. The figures could not be more decisive. Take health care, for example. To reach the European average, Britain would have to increase spending from about 6 per cent of the country's total income to 9 per cent or more. And other public services – such as schools, universities and transport – are also chronically under-funded, but perhaps not quite to the same degree as health care.

Source: Michael Prowse, *Financial Times*, 1 September 2001.

The table below shows the ranking for each country in each category listed where 1 is best (highest) and 7 is worst (lowest).

Country	Health care spending	Female life expectancy	Male life expectancy
United States	1	7	7
Germany	2	5	6
France	3	2	5
Canada	4	3	2
Italy	5	4	3
Japan	6	1	1
United Kingdom	7	6	4

Table 1 The relation between health spending and life expectancy
Source: *Institute of Fiscal Studies.*

(a) ◆ Define the term productive efficiency. (2)
   ◆ Identify and explain **one** reason why a monopoly, such as a local hospital, might not achieve productive efficiency. (3)
(b) ◆ What evidence is there in table 1 that the UK spends less on health care than other similar developed economies? (2)

◆ Using the data in table 1, comment on the suggestion in the article that higher spending on health care will lead to a better service. (6)

(c) ◆ Define the term inequality of income. (2)

◆ Explain how the government provision of a pension to everyone over a certain age reduces the inequality of income in a country. (4)

(d) ◆ Define the term government failure. (2)

◆ Identify and explain **one** example of government failure mentioned in the article. (4)

(e) ◆ Explain why health care is classified as a merit good. (4)

◆ Health care is provided free in the UK. Identify and comment upon **one other** means by which the government could encourage the consumption of health care. (6)

(f) ◆ The article suggests that more money needs to be spent by the government on education. Discuss the costs and benefits, both to students and to society, of the government doing this. (10)

Source: OCR, Paper 2882, January 2003.

Summary

In this section we have recognised that:

● The cost–benefit approach through cost–benefit analysis is an important aid to decision making in situations where markets fail.

● The limitations and weaknesses of the cost–benefit approach should also be recognised.

● Government intervention can take various forms including regulation, financial intervention and the provision of public goods.

● Different methods of intervention can be used to achieve specific market outcomes.

● Financial intervention in the form of taxes and subsidies has been widely advocated for use in markets where there are negative and positive externalities.

● Where there is a concentration of power in a market, the government can use standards and regulation or financial intervention in the form of price controls to prevent the abuse of this power.

● Governments too may fail in market and non-market economies.

Key words

Definitions of Key words can be found in the Glossary on page 240.

controls
cost–benefit analysis
financial intervention
government failure
income transfer
in-kind transfer
mixed goods
nationalised industry
privatisation

progressive tax
regressive tax
regulation
shadow prices
social justice
social security benefit
spillover effect
subsidy

Unit 3

The national and international economy

7 Government macroeconomic policy objectives and indicators of national economic performance

On completion of this section you should be able to:

- define, in broad terms, employment and unemployment, inflation, the balance of payments account and economic growth
- understand the objectives of government economic policy in terms of the above and why it is necessary for governments to establish such objectives
- define GDP
- outline its measurement through the output, income and expenditure approaches
- explain the difference between real and nominal values of GDP
- define unemployment and explain how it is measured in the UK economy
- explain the difficulties of measuring unemployment
- define inflation, explain the main methods by which it is measured and its possible causes in the UK economy
- outline the broad structure of the balance of payments account of the UK economy
- define economic growth and explain how it is measured in the UK economy
- show an awareness of trends in these key policy indicators
- discuss the consequences of unemployment, inflation and balance of payments problems
- discuss the benefits and costs of economic growth
- explain the reasons for, and consequences of, possible conflicts in macroeconomic policies

Introduction

'Barclaycard cuts 1,100 jobs over three years.'
The Times, 3 September 1998

'The G7 must make some painful choices now if it is to halt the crisis in the world economy.'
The Financial Times, 16 September 1998

'No interest rate rise but respite may be short-lived.' *The Independent*, 10 July 1998

'Thousands face dole as the Chancellor admits: "It's grim."' *The Sun*, 7 October 1998

These are all recent newspaper headlines. Every day stories appear in the newspapers and on the television news about how the UK economy and other economies are performing. As the fourth headline shows even the tabloid press cover certain economic issues!

These stories appear in the media because people are interested in events which affect their lives. For example, when a company such as Barclaycard makes staff redundant it not only has an impact on the lives of the

redundant workers but also reduces demand in the area where they were previously employed. People working in other financial institutions may become concerned about their own job security. The redundancies may also be taken as an indicator that the economy is running into difficulties. Unemployment as an indicator of economic performance is starkly referred to in the fourth headline.

The global crisis mentioned in the second headline led to falling incomes throughout the Far East, Russia and Latin America. To minimise the impact of this crisis on the UK, the Bank of England initially held interest rates constant and then cut them. A fall in interest rates may benefit borrowers but reduces the return which savers receive.

So how the economy is performing can have a major impact on people's lives. It influences the types of jobs we have, indeed whether we have jobs at all, and the quantity and quality of goods and services we are able to buy.

Government policy objectives

The main government macroeconomic policy objectives are:

◆ low unemployment;
◆ low and stable **inflation**;
◆ a satisfactory **balance of payments** position;
◆ avoidance of excessive **exchange rate** fluctuations;
◆ steady **economic growth**.

Key indicators

To assess how successful a government is being in achieving its objectives and to judge the performance of an economy, economists examine a number of key indicators. These include:

◆ the level of **output**;
◆ economic growth;
◆ the inflation rate;
◆ the level and rate of unemployment;
◆ the balance of payments position.

In broad terms an economy can be judged to be performing well if it has a high and growing output, a low and stable inflation rate, low unemployment and a healthy international trade position.

There are a number of stages involved in analysing any of the key indicators. First, economists define what they mean by, for example, unemployment; then they measure it and then they interpret their findings (see Introduction). As discussed below these tasks are neither as easy nor as straightforward as they may first appear.

The level of output and economic growth

One of the main indicators of a nation's economic performance is its level of output. Tables are produced by a number of organisations, which rank countries according to their level of output or more commonly, level of output per head.

Output can be measured in terms of **Gross Domestic Product** (GDP) and **Gross National Product** (GNP). Gross means total, domestic refers to the home economy and product means output. So UK GDP is a measure of the total output produced by factors of production based in the UK.

There are three ways of calculating GDP. These are the output, income and expenditure methods. They should give the same total as they all measure the flow of income produced in an economy. Figure 7.1

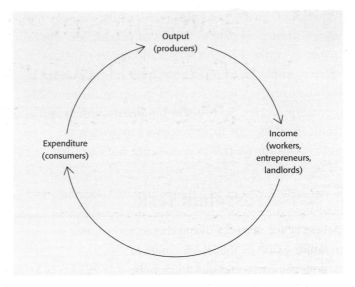

Figure 7.1 The circular flow of income in an economy

illustrates this **circular flow of income** in a simplified model of the economy.

The value of output is equal to the incomes which it generates, that is wages, rent, profit and interest. If it is assumed that all income is spent, expenditure will equal income and in turn, by definition, equal output.

The output method

This measures the value of output produced by industries including, for example, the output of the manufacturing, construction, retail, hotel and catering and agricultural industries.

In using this measure it is important to avoid counting the same output twice. For example, if the value of cars sold by car manufacturers is added to the value of the output of tyre firms, double counting will occur. So economists count only the value added by each firm. **Value added** is the difference between the sales revenue received and the cost of raw materials used. It is equal to the payments made to the factors of production in return for producing the good or service. So that if a TV manufacturing firm buys components costing £60,000 and uses them to make TVs which it sells for £130,000, it has added £70,000 to output. It is this £70,000 which will be included in the measure of output.

The income method

The value of output produced is based on the costs involved in producing that output. These costs include

119

wages, rent, interest and profits. All of these payments represent income paid to factors of production. For instance, workers receive wages and entrepreneurs receive profits. In using this measure it is important to include only payments received in return for providing a good or service. So **transfer payments**, which are transfers of income from taxpayers to groups of individuals for welfare purposes, are not included.

Self-assessment task

Decide which of the following should be included in measuring GDP by the income method:

- ◆ government subsidies to farmers;
- ◆ the pay of civil servants;
- ◆ the pay of nurses;
- ◆ supernormal profits;
- ◆ state pensions.

The expenditure method

As discussed above, the total amount spent in a year should also equal total output and total income:

Output = Income = Expenditure

What is produced in a year will either be sold or added to stocks. So, if additions to stocks are added to expenditure on goods and services, a measure is obtained which will equal output and income. In using this method it is necessary to add expenditure on exports and deduct expenditure on imports. This is because the sale of exports represents UK output and creates incomes in the UK, whereas expenditure on imports is spending on goods and services made abroad and creates incomes for people overseas. It is also necessary to deduct indirect taxes and add subsidies in order to get a value which corresponds to the incomes generated in the production of the output.

Nominal and real GDP

Nominal (or money) **GDP** is GDP measured in terms of the prices operating in the year in which the output is produced. It is sometimes referred to as GDP at current prices and is a measure which has not been adjusted for inflation.

Nominal GDP may give a misleading impression of how a country is performing. This is because the value

of nominal GDP may rise not because more goods and services are being produced but merely because prices have risen. For example if 100 million goods are produced at an average price of £5, GDP will be £500 million. If in the next year the same output of 100 million goods is produced but the average price rises to £6, nominal GDP will rise to £600 million. So to get a truer picture of what is happening to output, economists convert nominal into **real GDP**. They do this by measuring GDP at constant prices, that is, at the prices operating in a selected base year. By doing this they remove the distorting effects of inflation. For example, in 2000 a country's nominal GDP is £800 billion and the price index is 100. Then in 2001 nominal GDP rises to £864 billion and the price index is 105.

$$\text{Real GDP} = \text{Nominal GDP} \times \frac{\text{price index in base year}}{\text{price index in current year}}$$

So, for 2001:

$$\text{Real GDP} = \text{£864bn} \times \frac{100}{105} = \underline{\text{£822.86bn}}$$

To conclude, figure 7.2 shows the way in which the UK's real GDP has changed since 1980. As this shows, the overall trend has been upwards despite the **recession** between 1990 and 1992.

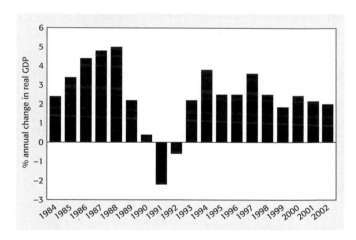

Figure 7.2 UK real GDP growth 1984–2002
Source: OECD.

Self-assessment task

In 2002 a country's nominal GDP is £1,000bn. In 2003 nominal GDP rises to £1,092bn and the price index increases by 4%. Calculate:

- ◆ real GDP;
- ◆ the percentage increase in real GDP.

Economic growth

If a country's output is increasing, this suggests that its citizens will be able to enjoy more goods and services and so a higher **living standard**. Most countries now measure changes in output by examining changes in GDP. Indeed the most common definition of economic growth is that it is an increase in real GDP. So that a growth rate of 3 per cent means that real GDP this year is 3 per cent greater than it was the year before.

Actual and potential growth

Increases in output can be referred to as actual growth whereas increases in the productive capacity of a country can be called **potential growth**. Figure 7.3 illustrates this distinction. A shift outwards in the production possibility curve from AB to CD means that the country is capable of producing more goods and services – potential growth (see section 1).

A movement outwards of the production point, for example from point D to point E or from point D to point F, means that the economy is actually producing more output. So actual growth, increases in GDP, can occur in the short run by utilising previously unemployed resources. Once all resources are being fully utilised output can only be increased as a result of more resources (factors of production) or better quality resources. So in the longer run, for output to continue to grow, there has to be an increase in potential output.

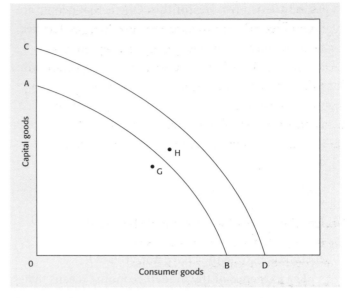

Figure 7.4 The output gap in an economy

Output gap

If potential output grows at a faster rate than actual output there will be an increase in spare capacity. Figure 7.4 shows that, as potential output increases from AB to CD but actual output only increases from G to H, the shortfall between actual and potential output widens.

Production and productivity

A country's output can increase either because more resources are employed or because **productivity** rises. Whereas production is output, productivity is output per factor of production. For example, labour productivity is output per worker. If productivity rises but fewer resources are employed production may actually fall. An increase in production means that actual growth occurs. An increase in productivity means that potential growth occurs but whether this is matched by an increase in actual output will depend on what happens to the level of employment of resources.

Measurement problems

The output, expenditure and income methods are all used in an attempt to gain an accurate measure of national output and changes in national output. However, in practice, a number of difficulties arise in achieving a completely accurate figure. The key difficulties are:

1 The existence of a **hidden economy**. The output of some goods and services are deliberately not declared.

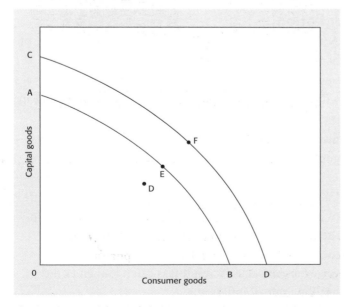

Figure 7.3 Potential growth in an economy

There are two reasons for this. One is that people are seeking to avoid paying tax. For example, a plumber may receive payment for undertaking jobs in his spare time and not declare the income he receives to the Inland Revenue. So some of the services he produces will not be included in GDP. Another reason for not declaring economic activity is that the activity is in itself illegal, for example prostitution and the trading in hard drugs.

Some idea of the size of the hidden or informal economy can be gained by measuring any gap between GDP as measured by the expenditure and income methods. This is because people will be spending income they have not declared!

The existence of the hidden economy means that the official GDP figures will understate the quantity of goods and services actually produced. However, if its size is relatively constant, the rate of economic growth can be calculated reasonably accurately.

The size of the hidden economy does vary between countries. It is influenced by the marginal rates of taxation, the penalties imposed for illegal activity and tax evasion, the risk of being caught and social attitudes towards, for example, drug taking, prostitution and tax evasion. Of course this can and does vary over time. A recent estimate has put the size of the hidden economy in the UK at 15–20 per cent of GDP and increasing.

2 **Non-marketed goods and services**. The GDP figures only include marketed goods and services, that is goods and services which are bought and sold and so have a price attached to them. Services which are produced and which are either not traded or which are exchanged without money changing hands go unrecorded. For example DIY activities, domestic services provided by homeowners and voluntary work are not included in the official figures. The proportion of goods and services which people produce for themselves and the proportion of voluntary work varies from country to country.

3 **Government spending**. In the expenditure method government spending on final goods and services is included. However, some government spending goes on producing public goods, for example defence and the fire service, which are not sold. In the past in the UK the output was valued at cost, normally in terms of the value of inputs. This gave a somewhat

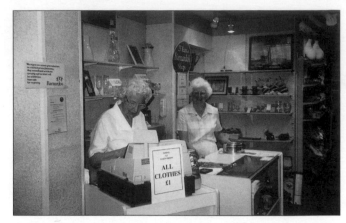

Charity shops – staff are usually unpaid volunteers and second-hand goods do not always command a true market price

distorted view of what was happening to output. For instance, if productivity increased in the fire service, fewer firemen and women might have been needed. This reduced the cost of providing the fire service. Output as officially recorded fell, although the level of service provided might have been unchanged or may even have increased. To overcome this problem, in 1998 the Office for National Statistics developed a system for measuring government outputs of services other than through the value inputs. This method covers education, health and social security, around 50 per cent of the public sector, and uses a variety of key performance indicators (such as student numbers for education and claimant numbers for social security) in order to estimate output.

Inflation

A low and steady rate of inflation provides a number of benefits for a country, in particular that of enabling businesses to forward plan with confidence. A country with a rapidly rising inflation rate in excess of that of its main trading partners will be likely to experience a number of problems, including difficulty in selling its goods and services at home and abroad.

One of the main measures of inflation used in the UK is the Retail Prices Index (RPI), which is a measure of changes in the prices of consumer goods bought in the UK. Much attention is paid to this index by the media, economists, business people, politicians and wage bargainers. As a result it is often known as the headline rate of inflation.

The RPI is a weighted price index and is calculated in

three main stages. These are:

1 A 'Family Expenditure Survey' of around 7,000 households in which families are asked to keep a record of what items they buy and how much they spend on them over a two-week period. This survey provides the weights for the calculation of the RPI.

2 A record of the prices of 600 selected items. These prices are collected from selected retail outlets and other sources. An average price is then calculated for each of the selected items.

3 The price changes and weights are then combined to give the RPI.

Two further measures of inflation should be mentioned. These are:

◆ RPIX, the underlying or target rate of inflation. This is the RPI minus mortgage interest payments. It is an important indicator from a macroeconomic policy perspective as the UK Government has set a target of 2.5 per cent plus or minus 1 per cent.

◆ RPIY, which is the RPI minus mortgage interest payments, indirect taxes and local authority taxes. This also shows the underlying rate of inflation but is not distorted by changes in interest rates or taxes on net income.

Measurement problems

Although measures of inflation in the UK economy are now much more sophisticated than say 20 years ago, there are various problems which should be noted when considering their accuracy. These problems include:

◆ Changes in quality. The price changes that are measured do not take quality into account. In the case of some consumer products, such as electronic goods, prices have fallen and yet quality has improved considerably.

◆ Special offers, prices of second-hand goods, retail sales at charity shops and car boot sales.

◆ Changes in the pattern of expenditure. New products are always coming on to the market and the weights used in the RPI may often lag behind what consumers are actually purchasing.

Causes of inflation

Figure 7.5 shows the trend in UK inflation (measured by the RPI) from 1979 to 1999. Since then, the underlying rate of inflation has been more volatile than RPIX,

which has generally been below the 2.5 per cent target. What we have seen since 1999, is the most sustained period of low inflation in the UK economy in modern times.

Over the years, economists have sought to explain the causes of inflation in two main ways. These are:

◆ Demand–pull inflation. This type of inflation tends to be associated with a situation of 'boom' in an economy, with a positive output gap (see figure 7.4). Demand for goods and services is rising faster than can be supplied from within; as a consequence, firms raise prices as they know they can sell almost anything they produce, so increasing their profits.

◆ Cost–push inflation. This type of inflation tends to occur when the costs of production are increasing. A good example of this is where the cost of oil and raw material imports increase, leading to firms raising their prices due to increased costs. This in turn can trigger off wage demands as real incomes have fallen. Consequently, a wage–price spiral can come about, fuelling further increases in the RPI unless these wage increases are matched by gains in productivity.

Monetary economists would disagree with the above explanation. They argue that inflation is simply a monetary phenomena, caused by a change in the money supply in an economy, particularly where governments act irresponsibly in the way in which they print money for their own purposes (see section 9).

Explaining the causes of inflation is therefore by no means as simple as it might seem, particularly with economists disagreeing amongst themselves. One conclusion though that can be made with confidence is that at any one time, a whole series of processes are at work resulting in changes in the RPIX.

The generally low rate of inflation in the UK economy in recent years can be attributed to many factors including:

◆ the effective management of the economy,

◆ greater competition in markets which has limited the ability of firms to raise prices,

◆ greater labour market flexibility,

◆ falling real prices of goods such as computers and certain consumer durable items.

Employment and unemployment

Countries measure both the numbers in employment and the numbers of those unemployed. If there is unemployment, output will be below its potential level, tax revenue will be lower and more state benefits will have to paid out. The unemployed, in addition to having lower incomes, may experience higher rates of divorce and mental and physical illnesses and will miss out on training and work experience. There is also increasing evidence of a link between levels of unemployment and crime.

The level of unemployment should be distinguished from the rate of unemployment. The level refers to the number of people who are unemployed whereas the rate of unemployment is the number of people unemployed as a percentage of the number of people in the labour force (that is, the employed and the unemployed).

Measures of employment

The Office for National Statistics collects data on employment. It carries out a 'Labour Force Survey', which asks people about their employment status and the nature of their main job. In addition it draws on information from employers and from administrative sources, for example those on government training schemes.

Measures of unemployment

One of the measures of unemployment in the UK is based on those in receipt of unemployment-related benefits, principally the job seeker's allowance. It is called the claimant count.

As a measure it has the advantage that it is relatively cheap and quick to construct since it is based on information which the government collects as it pays out benefits. However it has come in for criticism on the grounds of accuracy. Some of those who are receiving the job seeker's allowance may not be very actively seeking employment (although this is carefully checked) or they may be working and so claiming the benefit illegally.

On the other hand, a number of groups who would like to work but who are unable to find employment do not appear in the official figures. These groups include those who are over 60, those under 18, those on government training schemes, married women looking to return to work and those who choose not to claim benefits. As unemployment is a measure which is based on those receiving benefits, it changes every time there is a change in the criteria for qualifying for benefit.

An alternative measure is based on the 'Labour Force Survey'. This uses the International Labour Organisation definition of unemployment, which includes all people of working age who, in a specified period, are without work, but who are available for work in the next two weeks and who are seeking paid employment. Since April 1998 this measure has been given greater prominence whilst the claimant count has been downgraded.

As its name suggests the measure is based on a survey which is carried out four times a year. Sixty thousand people are asked whether they have a job and if not whether they are seeking employment and what steps they have taken to find employment. It picks up some

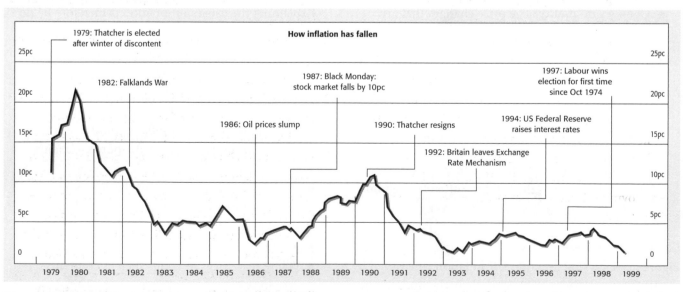

Figure 7.5 Inflation in the UK Economy, 1979–1999

of the groups not included in the claimant count and so measures unemployment rather than those eligible for unemployment-related benefits. It collects more information, for example on ethnic origin, qualifications and those seeking part-time as opposed to full-time employment. It also has the advantage that as it is based on internationally agreed concepts and definitions it makes international comparisons easier. However it is a more expensive and time-consuming method than the claimant count. Also as it is based on a sample survey it is subject to sampling error.

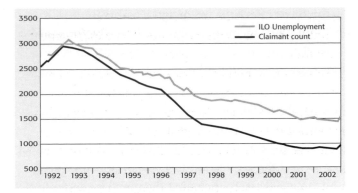

Figure 7.6 Unemployment in the UK, 1992–2002 ('000)
Source: Economic Trends, Annual Supplement, ONS.

Self-assessment task

Using any appropriate source, compare the UK unemployment rate with that of other EU countries at the present time and over the last five years.

Measurement problems

Among the problems involved in gaining an accurate measure of unemployment are:

◆ If the claimant count method is used, any government changes in the eligibility criteria for job seekers' allowance will affect the figure. For example, if it becomes more difficult to qualify, the official unemployment figure will fall even though there may have been no change in actual unemployment. Changes in the criteria will also make it more difficult to compare figures over time.

◆ If the 'Labour Force Survey' measure is used there is a risk that the sample may not be truly representative.

◆ Whichever measure is used it can be difficult to assess whether people claiming to be unemployed are genuinely seeking employment.

◆ It may also be hard to decide whether some people should be included in the unemployment figures or counted as sick or disabled. Some without a job may actually be physically or mentally incapable of keeping a job, whilst others receiving disability benefit may actually be capable of working.

Figure 7.6 shows the trend in the level of UK unemployment since 1992 as measured by the two indicators described above.

The balance of payments

The balance of payments is a record of the UK's economic activities with other countries. Economists,

politicians, the media and the business world study this account to gain information on the UK's current and future international competitiveness and net movements of income and assets. The first part of the balance of payments is in three main sections – the **current account**, the **capital account** and the **financial account**. These are a record of all money entering and leaving the country over the period of a year. There is also now a second part, the International Investment Position, which shows the level of external assets and liabilities at the end of the calendar year.

The current account

This in turn has four main headings:

1 Trade in goods. This covers the **exports** and **imports** of goods. For example, the export of toys to the USA brings money into the country and so is a credit item, whereas the import of video recorders from South Korea will result in money leaving the country and so is a debit item.

2 Trade in services. This covers exports and imports of services, for example financial services, insurance, transport, tourism and information services.

3 Income. The main item in this category is investment income. This covers profits, dividends and interest receipts from abroad minus profits, dividends and interest paid abroad. These receipts and payments arise from lending and borrowing money and from the sales and purchase of assets between countries.

4 Current transfers. These include central government and other sector transfers. The former includes the UK's net contribution to the EU and aid which is provided to developing economies. The latter covers items such as money sent back to relatives by UK citizens working abroad and taxes on income paid to

the Inland Revenue by foreign workers in the UK. Debit items include money sent home by foreign workers in the UK and taxes paid by UK citizens to foreign governments.

The capital account

A new capital account came into being in 1998. This shows capital transfers, including government investment grants, and the acquisition/disposal of non-produced, non-financial assets, including the purchase and sale of patents, trademarks and land for foreign embassies. This is now a very minor part of the balance of payments.

The financial account

Known previously as the capital account, this is concerned with investment leaving or entering the country. This can take many forms including the purchase and sale of companies, portfolio investment and reserve assets of foreign exchange. Outward investment will later generate income and will be shown as such in the current account, whilst inward investment is likely to result in certain income streams leaving the UK as debit items in the current account. This is an important part of the balance of payments and can involve huge flows of money.

Net errors and omissions

In theory the balance of payments should balance. In other words the net of the current account plus the capital account plus the financial account when added together should equal zero. This last part, formerly known as the balancing item, is included to reflect any discrepancies in what is a highly complex accounting system. Table 7.1 shows a highly simplified summary of the UK balance of payments in 1998.

The international investment position

Whereas the financial account shows the purchase and sale of external financial assets and liabilities in one year, this account shows the total of external assets held by the UK government, companies and individuals and the total UK assets held by overseas governments, companies and individuals.

Self-assessment task

Allocate each of the transactions (a)–(f)
   (a) interest paid by a UK company to a French bank,
   (b) the hiring of a UK tanker by an Arab oil company,
   (c) UK citizens travelling on an Australian aircraft,
   (d) the sale of UK cars to America,
   (e) the payment of dividends on Italian shares held by UK citizens,
   (f) the purchase by a UK company of raw materials from Germany
to one of the following parts of the UK balance of payments:
   1 trade in goods section;
   2 trade in services section;
   3 investment income section.

International competitiveness

In terms of the balance of payments most attention is focused on the trade in goods and services. A deficit on the trade in goods and services means that more has been spent on imports than has been earned from exports and may be a symptom of poor economic performance. The country's goods and services may be uncompetitive in terms of price and/or quality or the country may be concentrating on producing goods and services which are in low demand.

Other measures of international competitiveness

A number of international organisations now seek to measure comparative international performance. For example the OECD annually publishes a 'league table' based on countries' real GDP per head. In its 2002 report, which uses 2001 figures, the UK was placed twenty-first.

Whereas real GDP per head gives an indication of current economic performance, indexes of international

	£m	£m
Current account		
Trade in goods and services	−22,461	
Income	9,162	
Current transfers	−7,154	
Current balance		−20,453
Capital account		1,499
Financial account		19,291
Net errors and omissions		−337

Table 7.1 Summary of the UK balance of payments in 2001
Source: ONS, *Economic Trends Supplement*, 2002.

competitiveness seek to throw light on future economic performance. The World Economic Forum and the International Institute of Management Development (IMD) compile lists of world competitiveness. Whilst they use different methods to measure competitiveness, they both base their indexes on a range of indicators including progress on growth, trade, investment, employment, education and technology. In 2001, the World Economic Forum reported that the UK had fallen from eighth to twelfth position in its league table, the fall being largely attributed to poor relative levels of technological innovation.

Self-assessment tasks

1 Study the table below and then answer the questions which follow.

	Gross domestic product								Gross product per person employed						
	US	Canada	Japan	France	Germany	Italy	UK	OECD	US	Canada	Japan	France	Germany	Italy	UK
	Constant prices														
1994[a]	37.1	3.4	14.1	6.3	9.2	5.9	5.9	100.0							
1989	91.7	94.0	89.8	94.3	80.6	95.3	94.4	90.8	96.2	95.5	94.5	93.6	106.1	91.5	90.3
1990	92.8	94.3	94.4	96.7	85.3	97.4	95.0	93.2	96.2	95.2	97.5	95.1	109.4	91.8	90.2
1991	92.0	92.5	98.0	97.4	96.7	98.5	93.6	94.5	96.1	95.2	99.3	95.8	94.0	92.0	91.1
1992	94.5	93.3	99.0	98.6	98.5	99.0	93.6	96.2	98.1	96.6	99.3	97.5	97.0	93.5	93.7
1993	96.7	95.5	99.3	97.3	97.3	97.9	95.8	97.3	98.9	97.5	99.4	97.4	97.0	95.9	96.7
1994	100.0	100.0	100.0	100.0	100.0	100.0	100.0	100.0	100.0	100.0	100.0	100.0	100.0	100.0	100.0
1995	102.3	102.6	101.4	102.1	101.3	102.9	102.8	102.0	100.8	100.9	101.3	101.2	101.4	103.3	101.5
1996	105.8	103.9	106.6	103.7	102.6	103.6	105.4	105.0	102.8	100.9	106.1	102.6	103.2	103.4	102.6
1997	110.0	107.8	108.1	106.1	105.0	105.2	109.1	108.3	104.5	102.8	106.4	104.5	106.1	105.0	104.4

Gross product and productivity in industrial countries and OECD (*Seasonally adjusted, Index numbers, 1994 = 100*)
Note: [a] % of OECD total.
Source: Table 13, page 124, *National Institute Economic Review*, 167, January 1999, National Institute of Economic and Social Research.

(a) Explain what is meant by GDP at constant prices.

(b) Estimate which country experienced the most rapid economic growth in the period shown.

(c) Estimate which country experienced the most rapid increase in productivity in the period shown.

(d) Comment on the other economic data it would be useful to examine in assessing the UK's comparative international competitiveness.

2 Study the short case study below and then answer the questions that follow.

The death of inflation?

In December 2001, the UK saw its annual inflation rate fall to 0.7%, its lowest level since April 1960. In 2001, the UK economy was in a generally healthy state, particularly compared with other industrialised countries (see table below). Economic growth was relatively high, and unemployment, estimated by both the claimant count and the Labour Force Survey measures, was below that of many other industrialised countries.

Some economists argue that low inflation is here to stay. They point to lower inflationary expectations, increased international competitiveness and technological advances as proof of this. They also claim that measures of inflation tend to exaggerate its level.

If inflation does remain low, the government will have more opportunity to concentrate its policy measures on achieving its other macroeconomic objectives of economic growth and low unemployment. In pursuit of these objectives, Gordon Brown, the Chancellor of the Exchequer is particularly keen to increase productivity. Higher productivity would raise the UK's long-run economic performance and increase its ability to achieve a sustained rise in production without inflation. Other economists, however, argue that inflation remains a real risk. If consumer spending remains high, investment increases or the value of the pound falls, there may be upward pressure on prices.

A comparison of economic performance in 2001

	Germany	Ireland	Japan	UK
% change in real GDP (economic growth)	0.7	5.1	−0.4	2.2
% unemployment rate	7.9	3.8	5.0	5.1
% change in consumer prices (inflation rate)	2.4	4.0	−1.6	1.2

Source: National Institute Economic Review, April 2002

(a) Distinguish between:

♦ production and productivity,

♦ the claimant count and the Labour Force Survey measures of unemployment.

(b) ♦ Give **one** macroeconomic policy objective **not** mentioned in the passage.

♦ Selecting information from the table, and excluding the UK from your answer, discuss which of the remaining three economies performed best in 2001.

(c) ♦ Explain what is meant by a fall in the inflation rate.

♦ Describe how the retail price index (RPI) is calculated.

Source: OCR, Paper 2883, January 2003 (adapted).

3 Study the article below and then answer the questions which follow:

Quality of life gets a higher profile

A radical move to extend the yardstick of progress from economic output alone to quality-of-life measures, such as education, pollution, and even the number of birds in the countryside, was yesterday unveiled by the government.

A series of 13 new headline indicators [see below] intended to reflect everyday concerns will for the first time allow the government's performance to be judged not only by growth rates but by the effect of policies on the environment and social welfare.

Launching the indicators yesterday, the Deputy Prime Minister, John Prescott, said, 'Sustainable development links the standard of living and the quality of life, not just in Britain, but right across the world.'

Charles Secrett, executive director of Friends of the Earth, said, 'Often policy has been driven by the idea that more is always better...'

The 13 quality of life indicators:

Economic growth: Total output of the economy. Standard measure is gross domestic product (GDP). Since 1970 output has increased by 80 per cent in real terms.

Social investment: Measures investment in 'public assets' such as railways, buses, roads, hospitals, schools, water and sewerage. Accounts for 10 per cent of all capital spending and about 2 per cent of GDP.

Typical 1960s high-rise flats – now often unpopular with those who live in them

Employment: Income enables individuals to improve living standards. Since 1994, the employment rate has increased slowly to 73 per cent of the population of working age.

Health: Average life expectancy is now around 74 years for men and 79 for women, but the time people can expect to live in good health is some years less.

Education and training: Based on qualifications at age 19.

Housing quality: Measures numbers of homes unfit to live in. In 1996, the private rented sector had the highest proportion of unfit stock – 15.1 per cent.

Climate change: Based on greenhouse gas emissions. UK emissions of the 'basket' of greenhouse gas fell by 5 per cent between 1990 and 1996.

Air pollution: In urban areas, the average number of days when pollution was recorded as moderate or worse fell from 62 days in 1993 to 40 in 1997.

Transport: Motor vehicle traffic in 1997 was more than eight times the level in 1950, and car traffic was over 14 times higher.

Water quality: According to number of rivers of good or fair quality – currently 95 per cent of UK river network.

Wildlife: Based on population of wild birds – regarded as a good indicator of wildlife and the health of the wider environment. Populations of farmland and woodland birds have been in decline since the mid 1970s.

Land use: New homes built on previously developed land. In England, about 55 per cent of homes are built on brownfield sites, against a government target of 60 per cent by 2008.

Waste: An estimated 145 million tonnes of waste are produced in the UK each year, of which over 60 per cent are disposed of in landfill sites.

Source: Lucy Ward, *The Guardian,* 24 November 1998 (adapted).

(a) What do you think is meant by 'sustainable development'?

(b) Does more growth always mean that 'things get better'?

(c) What evidence is there in the comments on the 13 quality of life indices that social welfare may have improved in recent years?

(d) Discuss two additional quality of life indicators you would like to see added.

Macroeconomic problems

In managing the economy, governments are acutely aware of the problems that can arise when (say):

- the rate of inflation is higher than they would like;
- there is a recession and the rate of unemployment is excessive;
- there is a surge of imported goods into the country.

Such problems as these have consequences for the economy as a whole. In managing these problems, though, the dilemma governments face is that not all of their stated policy objectives can be achieved simultaneously. Choices and priorities must therefore be established.

For many years, economists and governments took it for granted that a high rate of economic growth was a very appropriate objective to follow. Growth does of course bring many benefits; it should also be recognised that when not managed effectively, a high rate of growth is not without its costs. Issues such as these will be discussed in the remainder of this section.

Consequences of inflation

The effects of inflation depend on:

- the rate at which it is rising;
- whether the rate is accelerating or stable;
- whether the rate is the one which had been expected;
- how the rate compares with that in other countries.

The inflation rate

An inflation rate of 20 per cent is likely to cause more problems than an inflation rate of, say, 2 per cent because money will be losing its purchasing power at a rapid rate. A very high rate of inflation is known as **hyperinflation**. When this occurs people will lose confidence in money and may even go back to barter.

In Germany between 1913 and 1923 the price level rose 755,700 million times and people switched from using cash to using cigarettes to buy goods. More recently in Georgia in 1994 when inflation reached 15,000 per cent, a wheelbarrow was needed to carry enough money to purchase a loaf of bread.

Hyperinflation can also cause political instability. People become dissatisfied with the government's failure to control the high rise in prices and may look to parties offering radical solutions to the problem. Even less dramatic inflation rates of, say, 10 per cent can cause problems. People who are on a fixed income or on an income which does not rise as fast as inflation will experience a fall in their purchasing power.

High rates of inflation also mean that people and companies may lose considerable purchasing power if they keep money lying idle and not earning interest. Economists refer to this as shoe leather costs. These are the costs involved in moving money from one financial asset to another in search of the highest rate of interest. The term can also be applied to firms and consumers spending more time searching out the lowest prices.

Inflation makes it more difficult to assess what is happening to the price of goods and services. A rise in the price of a good may now not mean that it has become more expensive relative to other goods – indeed it may have risen by less than inflation and so have become relatively cheaper. This tendency for inflation to confuse price signals is referred to as inflationary noise. It can result in consumers and producers making the wrong decisions. For example, producers seeing the price of their good rising may increase output when this higher price is the result of inflation rather than increased demand. This will result in the misallocation of resources.

Firms will also suffer from menu costs. These are the costs involved in changing prices. For example, catalogues, price tags, bar codes and advertisements have to be changed. This involves staff time and is unpopular with customers.

Whilst there are clear disadvantages of a high rate of inflation there can be advantages of a low, stable rate of inflation of, say, 2 per cent. If the rise in the general price level is caused by increasing demand firms can feel optimistic about the future. They will also benefit if prices rise by more than costs since this will mean that profits will increase.

Inflation may also stimulate consumption. This is because real interest rates may be low or even negative as the nominal rate of interest does not tend to rise in line with inflation. So debt burdens may fall and people may be able and encouraged to spend more. For example, those who have borrowed money to buy a house may experience a fall in their mortgage interest payments in real terms. At the same time the price of their house is likely to rise by more than inflation, which may make them feel better off, and so they may spend more.

The existence of inflation may also help firms which need to reduce costs to survive. For most firms the major cost is wages. With zero inflation firms may have to cut their labour force. However, inflation would enable them to reduce the real costs of labour by either keeping nominal (money) wages constant or not raising them in line with inflation. During inflation workers with strong bargaining power are more likely to be able to resist cuts in their real wages than workers who lack bargaining power.

Accelerating versus stable inflation

An accelerating inflation rate is likely to have more serious consequences than a stable rate. If, for example, inflation three years ago was 5 per cent, two years ago was 8 per cent and last year was 15 per cent, people and firms will be likely to expect a further rise in inflation. The way they react is likely to bring about what they fear. For example, workers may press for higher wages, firms may raise prices to cover expected higher costs and consumers may seek to purchase goods now before their prices rise further. Accelerating, or indeed fluctuating, inflation will also cause uncertainty and may discourage firms from undertaking investment. The need to devote more staff and effort to estimating future inflation will also increase administration costs. Whereas if inflation is stable it will be easier to predict future inflation and hence easier to plan and protect people from the harmful effects.

Self-assessment task

The rate of inflation in France was reported to have been 8 per cent in 1996. Explain what this figure means and how it might have been calculated.

UCLES, Modular A Level Economics, The National Economy, 4382, June 1997.

Anticipated versus unanticipated inflation

Anticipated inflation is when the rise in the general price level is the one, or close to the one, expected. If firms, workers, consumers and the government have correctly predicted the inflation rate then, as mentioned above, they can take measures to avoid the harmful effects. For example, firms can adjust their prices, nominal interest rates can be changed to maintain real interest rates if considered desirable, consumers may be able to distinguish between changes in the general price level and relative prices, and the government can adjust tax thresholds and index-linked pensions, benefits and civil servants' pay (that is adjust them upwards in line with inflation).

In contrast **unanticipated inflation** occurs when inflation was either not expected or is higher than had been expected.

Unanticipated inflation can bring with it a number of problems. As people and firms have been caught unawares they are likely to be uncertain about future inflation. This can result in a fall in consumption and investment.

Fiscal drag may also occur. With no adjustment of tax thresholds, higher nominal pay will drag incomes into higher tax bands and workers' disposable real income will fall.

There can also be an arbitrary redistribution of income. Borrowers tend to gain and lenders to lose. This is because nominal interest rates usually rise more slowly than the inflation rate. So real interest rates often fall with inflation. Indeed in some years they have been negative.

Income may also be transferred from the old to the young as the former tend to be net savers whilst the latter tend to be net borrowers. It is also because, whilst state pensions are raised in line with inflation, they fall behind wages, which usually rise at a faster rate than inflation.

International price competitiveness

Inflation may make a country's goods less price competitive. This may result in balance of payments problems. Consumers at home and abroad may switch away from buying the country's goods and services, which may cause a deficit to arise or get larger in the trade in goods and the trade in services sections. The uncertainty that arises from inflation may also discourage financial and capital investment in the country.

In a **floating exchange rate** system, a fall in demand for a country's goods and services and a reduction in the inflow of investment from abroad will reduce the exchange rate. This in turn will lower export prices and, at least initially, restore price competitiveness. However, there is danger that a vicious cycle will develop with inflation causing a lower exchange rate which in turn

results in higher import prices, cost–push inflation and then a fall in the exchange rate. Also, if the root cause of the inflation is not tackled, it will continue.

However, inflation will not necessarily have adverse effects on the country's international trade position. If the country's inflation rate is below that of its main competitors, its goods and services will become more price competitive. In addition, if a country's goods and services were originally cheaper than their rivals, even with a higher inflation rate they may still be at a lower price.

It also has to be remembered that, whilst price is an important influence on demand, it is not the only one. A country may be able to sustain its output and sales at home and abroad even with inflation if the quality of its goods and services is rising or if, for example, its marketing is improving.

Consequences of unemployment

The consequences of unemployment will depend on its rate and duration. A high rate of unemployment will tend to have more significant effects than a low one. However, the length of time which people are unemployed also has to be considered. An unemployment rate of say 12 per cent with an average duration of two months will have less serious consequences than a 6 per cent unemployment rate which lasts on average for a year. Unemployment will have consequences not only for the unemployed themselves but also for firms and the economy.

Consequences for the unemployed

There may be some benefits of being unemployed. It may encourage those who are unemployed to reassess their career objectives and provide them with the time to search for a job which may be better paid and/or which they may enjoy more. It may also provide them with more time to pursue their leisure activities. However, whilst they may have the time, they will lack the income. Indeed, for most, any advantages of being unemployed are likely to be outweighed by the disadvantages.

Most of the unemployed will experience a fall in income. The amount they receive from benefits is likely to be lower than the amount they were earning when in work. This fall in income will lower their living

One of the many 'drop-in' centres where the unemployed can get help in obtaining work

standards and can make people more prone to certain forms of physical illness. In addition the loss of status and the stress involved can lead to mental illnesses and the break-up of relationships.

The longer someone is unemployed, the more they will miss out on training, changes in technology and changes in work practices. The chances of regaining employment diminish as the duration of unemployment increases.

Consequences for firms

If unemployment is high the demand for a firm's goods and services will be relatively low. High unemployment may also reduce workers' morale, which in turn may reduce labour productivity.

However, some firms may gain some benefits from unemployment. They may find it easier to recruit staff and the people applying for jobs may possess higher skills. The existence of unemployment may make workers fearful of losing their jobs. As a result they may reduce their wage claims, be more willing to agree to adopt flexible working practices and be more reluctant to take industrial action.

Consequences for the economy

The most significant disadvantage of unemployment is the opportunity cost involved. Having people out of work means that output and hence living standards are lower than they could be. The output is lost for all time. Even if unemployment falls next year, the output can never be regained.

Higher unemployment increases government

Self-assessment task

Discuss why a government might allow significant levels of unemployment to exist.

Adapted from UCLES, Modular A Level Economics, The National Economy, 4382, June 1996.

expenditure on unemployment-related benefits, health and possibly the police force whilst it reduces revenue from direct and indirect taxes. Crime levels may increase with some of the unemployed feeling disaffected from society. A positive correlation has been found between unemployment rates in young men and crime levels.

The distribution of income will become more uneven and, if the rise in unemployment is not evenly spread, regional differences will increase.

There are few benefits of unemployment for the economy, which is why governments usually seek to keep unemployment at a low level. However unemployment provides some slack which can permit the economy to expand. Some economists also claim that the existence of unemployment can put downward pressure on inflation by reducing wage claims and limiting increases in aggregate demand (see section 8).

Consequences of instability of exchange rates

Countries, or groups of countries, may operate fixed, managed or floating exchange rate systems (see section 9 for details). A fixed exchange rate system is one determined by the government or international body. The rate is maintained by the purchase and sale of the currency and by changes in interest rates. A managed exchange rate system is usually one in which the exchange rate is permitted to move within bands. A floating exchange rate is one which is determined by market forces and which varies with changes in the demand and supply of the currency. In a floating exchange rate system there is a risk of frequent and large changes in the value of the currency. Speculation on changes in the value of currencies and interest rates can result in large changes in demand and supply of the currency and hence the exchange rate (see section 10 also).

Planning problems

Frequent changes in the exchange rate may create a number of problems. Firms will find it difficult to plan if there are frequent changes in the price of exports and imports, particularly if these fluctuations are unpredictable. They will be uncertain about how much they will earn from export sales and how much they will have to spend on imported raw materials and components. To overcome this uncertainty they may seek to agree in advance the price at which they will buy or sell the currency.

Effect on international trade

Frequent changes may even discourage firms from engaging in international trade. If they are worried about how much they will earn from exporting they may decide to concentrate on the home market. This will reduce their potential market and hence their opportunity to take advantage of economies of scale. Uncertainty about the amount that will have to be paid for imports may mean that the highest quality raw materials and components may not be purchased.

Effect on productive potential

The uncertainty created may also reduce investment. This will have consequences for current output and for future economic growth. The productive potential of the economy may also be reduced as a result of firms going out of business when the exchange rate is high.

The ratchet effect

Changes in the exchange rate can push up costs of production and cause inflation. When the exchange rate goes down import prices rise and this increases the cost of living. As a result workers may press for wage rises. If these are awarded the price level will rise further. In contrast, when the exchange rate goes up and import prices fall workers do not ask for a wage cut. This

tendency for exchange rate movements to move the price level in only one direction is known as the **ratchet effect**.

Consequences of a balance of payments deficit

The effects of a balance of payments deficit will depend on

- its size;
- its duration;
- its cause.

The size and duration

A deficit will mean that more money is leaving the country than entering it. This will reduce the country's money supply and may also reduce inflationary pressure as there will be less money to spend on more goods and services. The country's citizens will enjoy more goods and services than the country is producing. However it will mean that the country is adding more to the demand and hence output and employment of other countries than to its own demand, output and employment. It also means that the country will be getting into debt with other countries.

However these may not be serious problems if the deficit is small and/or is of short duration. If a deficit is relatively quickly followed by a surplus, some of this can be used to repay any debt and it may indicate that there are no fundamental problems in the economy.

Cause

A deficit which arises as a result of an increase in imports of raw materials may be self correcting. When the raw materials are converted into finished goods at least some are likely to be exported.

A deficit may also arise because of cyclical factors. When income levels are rising demand for goods and services will increase. More imports are likely to be purchased and goods and services, originally intended for the export market, may be diverted to the buoyant home market.

More significant is a deficit caused by structural problems. There may be fundamental weaknesses in the economy, which means that foreign goods and services are more attractive than domestic ones. For instance, the

---

Self-assessment task

Plot the movements in the value of the £ sterling against another major currency such as the $US or the euro over the last year and discuss the likely consequences of fluctuations in its value.

quality of the domestic goods and services may be low, they may not be price competitive, after sales service and marketing may be poor and the country may be making goods and services which are not in high domestic nor world demand.

With a floating exchange rate, a deficit would result in a fall in the value of the currency. However, without measures being taken to make the domestic goods and services more attractive, the deficit will reappear again and the country's output and employment are likely to be below their potential levels.

Benefits and costs of economic growth
Benefits
The main benefit of economic growth is the increase in goods and services which become available for the country's citizens to enjoy. This raises their material living standards. If you have difficulty in believing this, ask your parents what life was like when they were your age!

Economic growth also makes it easier to help the poor. Without any increase in output and income, the only way in which the living standards of the poor can be raised is by taking income and hence goods and services from higher income groups. Whereas if economic growth occurs at least some of the extra income can be given to the poor in the form of higher benefits, thereby enabling them to enjoy more goods and services.

A stable level of economic growth increases firms' and consumers' confidence. This makes planning easier and encourages investment. Economic growth may also increase a country's international prestige and power. For example, China's rapid growth in the early 1990s increased its status in world politics.

Costs
Economic growth may bring with it a number of costs. If the economy is operating at the full employment level there will be an opportunity cost involved in achieving economic growth. To produce more capital goods, in order to increase the country's productive capacity, some resources will have to be moved from producing consumer goods to producing capital goods. So current consumption of goods and services will have to be reduced. However, this will only

be a short-run cost since in the long run the increased investment will increase the output of consumer goods and services (see also figure 1.5).

Economic growth may also bring increased stress and anxiety. A growing economy is a dynamic economy with changes in the structure of the economy. Workers may have to learn new skills and may have to change their occupation and/or where they live. Some workers may find this difficult to cope with. Economic growth may also be accompanied by increased working hours and pressure to come up with new ideas and improvements. When Japan was growing rapidly in the 1980s some workers put in very long hours and students felt under considerable pressure to pass examinations.

Economic growth may also be accompanied by the depletion of natural resources and damage to the environment. Higher output may, for example, involve firms using more oil, building on greenfield sites and creating more pollution. However, this does not have to be the case. Output can be increased in ways which do not damage the environment.

Sustainable economic growth
Very rapid growth may be achieved but this may be at the expense of the living standards of future generations if it results from the reckless use of resources. Countries are now becoming more concerned to achieve sustainable economic growth. This occurs when output increases in a way which means that increases in output can continue into the future. Materials such as aluminium, paper and glass can be recycled. More use could be made of renewable energy resources in preference to non-renewable resources and improvements in technology may increase both output and reduce pollution.

Conflicts in macroeconomic policy objectives
Government policy objectives may not be compatible. A government wishing to raise employment may seek to increase aggregate (total) demand. Higher demand is likely to encourage firms to expand output. As well as reducing unemployment this will also accelerate the rate of economic growth. However the higher demand may lead to demand–pull inflation. The increase in spending may also result in more imports being purchased, and

goods and services being diverted from the export market to the home market. To reduce inflationary pressure and correct a deficit on the current account a government may seek to restrain or reduce aggregate demand. This tendency for governments to seek to expand economic activity and then, when their other objectives are threatened, to limit it is sometimes referred to as a **stop–go policy** – although a more appropriate term might be a 'go–stop policy'.

As policy aims can conflict, a government may have to decide, at any particular time, what is its priority.

To achieve its key aim or aims it may be prepared to sacrifice other objectives. For example if unemployment is very high a government may be prepared to raise aggregate demand even if it means a rise in the inflation rate. It is prepared to trade off higher inflation for lower unemployment.

Due to the difficulty of achieving a number of objectives a government may follow Tinbergen's rule, which states that a different policy instrument should be employed to achieve each objective.

Self-assessment tasks

1 Discuss which government macro-economic objective is currently receiving the highest priority.
2 Read the short case study below and then answer the questions that follow.

Balance of payments concerns

In the second half of the year 2000, it was generally thought that the UK economy was performing well with low and stable inflation, falling unemployment and high economic growth. However, concerns were raised about the UK's international trade performance. In July 2000, the trade in goods deficit with the rest of the world increased from £2.4bn to £3bn as imports rose and exports fell.

Some UK producers blamed the high value of the pound, especially against European currencies, for this situation, claiming that it was making their goods and services uncompetitive at home and abroad. Support for

this view came in August 2000, when the value of the pound against the dollar fell below $1.45 for the first time since 1993. Exports to the United States of America (USA) rose to their highest level for three years. This was attributed to both the fall in the exchange rate and a rise in US incomes.

However, despite the higher exports to the USA, UK exporters still faced a number of actual problems and potential problems at the end of 2000. The value of the pound remained high against the euro, the single currency of twelve of the European Union (EU) members.

Trading areas	Destination of UK exports of goods (£bn)	Source of UK imports of goods (£bn)
European Union (EU)	97	103
Other Western Europe	7	11
United States of America (USA)	28	28
All other countries	34	50

Geographical pattern of UK trade in 1999

Source: Office for National Statistics, 2002

(a) Define what is meant by:
   ◆ an exchange rate,
   ◆ low and stable inflation.

(b) Explain the likely effect of a **high** exchange rate on:
   ◆ UK exports,
   ◆ UK imports.

(c) Explain **two** benefits of 'low and stable inflation'.

(d) Using the table, compare the UK's trade position with the European Union and its trade position with the USA.

Source: OCR, Paper 2883, June 2001 (adapted).

3 Read the short case study below and then answer the questions that follow.

Interest rates set to stay on hold

A surprise fall in unemployment and the latest signals from the Bank of England left the City predicting yesterday that interest rates are set to stay on hold well into 2003. The headline jobless total of those out of work and claiming benefit dropped unexpectedly by 3,100 last month to just 949,600 – only 4,000 short of February's 25-year low, official figures showed.

Official data also showed the sharpest rise for more than two years in the numbers of those in work, taking employment levels to a record high.

Bank of England minutes of this month's meeting of its Monetary Policy Committee (MPC) revealed that its members were in no hurry to move rates up or down. The MPC voted 9–0 to hold rates this month. Base rates have been unchanged since last November.

The MPC minutes showed that the nine members did consider easing rates to prop up the economy. But they decided that they were not ready to do so, with arguments against 'seen as more compelling'.

Mervyn King, the Bank's hawkish Deputy Governor, who voted for a rise in rates in June and July and is the favourite to take over as Governor next year, fell into line with the rest of the MPC to back unchanged rates.

'The minutes suggest that a move in rates looks a long way off, unless there is a marked deterioration in the economic outlook or a further retrenchment in equities,' George Buckley, of Deutsche Bank, said.

Source: Gary Duncan, *The Times*, 15 August 2002 (adapted).

In the UK the Monetary Policy Committee of the Bank of England has the responsibility of keeping inflation in line with the target set by the Government
Source: Popperfoto.

(a) Use the information provided to analyse the change in UK employment by sector from July 2001 to July 2002.

(b) Describe how:

◆ unemployment,

◆ employment

can be measured.

(c) Explain how the rise in employment in the UK could have been greater than the fall in unemployment.

(d) Comment upon the variation in the employment rates for the UK, France, Germany, USA and Japan.

(e) Discuss how 'easing rates (of interest) to prop up the economy' were not seen as an appropriate action at that time.

Summary

In this section we have recognised that:

● The four main government policy objectives are low unemployment, low and stable inflation, a satisfactory balance of payments position and steady economic growth.

● Among the indicators of a country's economic performance are its growth rate, its inflation rate, its unemployment rate and its balance of payments position.

● Production is output whereas productivity is output per factor of production.

● Economic growth is measured in terms of percentage annual increases in GDP.

● GDP is measured by the output, income and expenditure methods.

● Real GDP is nominal (money) GDP adjusted for inflation.

● Countries with high inflation may experience problems in competing on price with other countries.

● Various measures of inflation are used by economists.

● The main causes of inflation are an increase in total demand or a rise in costs in an economy.

● The main cost of unemployment is foregone output.

● The three main sections of the balance of payments are the current account, the capital account and the financial account. The section which receives the most attention is the current account.

● A deficit on the current account may indicate a lack of price or quality competitiveness.

● A whole range of indicators can be used to assess the international competitiveness of an economy relative to those of others.

● The effects of inflation on an economy depend on the rate, whether it is fluctuating or stable, whether the rate has been anticipated or not and its rate relative to that of other countries.

● High, unstable, accelerating and unanticipated inflation will involve more costs than low, stable, declining and anticipated inflation.

● Low and stable inflation may bring advantages including encouraging producers to increase output and permitting real wages to be adjusted downwards.

● The effects of unemployment will depend on its rate and duration.

● The costs of unemployment for the economy include lost output, lost government revenue and increased expenditure on benefits.

● Instability of exchange rates creates uncertainty, makes planning more difficult, may discourage international trade, may cause inflation and may lead to upward or downward spirals.

● The effects of a balance of payments deficit depend on its size, its duration and its cause. A deficit is particularly serious where this is caused by structural weakness in the economy.

● Economic growth increases material living standards and makes it easier to help the poor but may involve some costs.

● Policy conflicts may occur with unemployment and economic growth benefiting from increases in aggregate demand whilst higher aggregate demand may cause inflation and a balance of payments deficit.

Key words

Definitions of Key words can be found in the Glossary on page 240.

aggregate demand	fiscal drag	living standard	recession
anticipated inflation	fixed exchange rate	managed exchange rate	shoe leather costs of
balance of payments	floating exchange rate	net errors and omissions	inflation
capital account	government spending	nominal GDP	stop–go policy
circular flow of income	Gross Domestic Product	non-marketed goods and	sustainable economic
cost-push inflation	Gross National Product	services	growth
current account	hidden economy	output	transfer payments
demand-pull inflation	hyperinflation	output gap	unanticipated inflation
economic growth	imports	output method	unemployment
exchange rate	income method	potential growth	value added
expenditure method	inflation	productivity	
exports	international	ratchet effect	
financial account	competitiveness	real GDP	

8 Aggregate demand and aggregate supply

On completion of this section you should be able to:

➤ define aggregate demand (AD)

➤ explain why the AD curve slopes down from left to right

➤ describe the main components of AD and explain what determines each of them

➤ account for why the AD curve in an economy shifts outwards or inwards

➤ define aggregate supply (AS)

➤ distinguish between the short-run and long-run aggregate supply curve

➤ explain why AS curves may shift

➤ explain what is meant by equilibrium in the macroeconomy and how the equilibrium output and price level is determined

➤ analyse how the equilibrium is affected by changes in aggregate demand and aggregate supply

➤ explain how changes in AD and AS may affect output, unemployment and inflation

➤ show a broad awareness of the multiplier effect and the concept of leakages and injections

➤ use AD and AS analysis to illustrate the macroeconomic problems in an economy

Introduction

Economists often disagree, particularly when it involves macroeconomic policy issues. This section provides an introduction to the basic workings of the economy and, in so doing, provides a perspective on one of the most controversial areas of economic policy, namely whether the economy is best managed through the application of demand-side or supply-side policies. Central to this debate is the role of government in managing the economy.

The traditional view, advocated by J. M. Keynes almost 70 years ago and applied for many years in the UK, is that governments must intervene in the affairs of the economy if the objectives stated in section 7 are to be met. The management of aggregate demand through both **fiscal** and **monetary policies** (see section 9) is crucial to achieving full employment, low inflation, balance of payments stability and economic growth. Other economists, especially since the election of Mrs Thatcher's Conservative government in 1979, have taken a different view. Their belief is that macroeconomic objectives can be best met when the economy is allowed

John Maynard Keynes, the creator of modern macroeconomics

to function naturally, with little interference from government. In other words, the forces of aggregate demand and **aggregate supply** combined will allow the market economy to operate in the most effective way to allow governments to meet their objectives for the macroeconomy. **Supply-side policies**, which focus explicitly on managing the total amount of output in the economy, are combined with policies which manage aggregate demand, in order to provide the most appropriate ways of allowing governments to meet their macroeconomic objectives. This particular approach is the one which will be applied in this section and in section 9. In order to understand its operation and relevance, it is first necessary to establish and define its basic parameters.

Aggregate demand

Aggregate demand is the term used by economists to denote the total spending on goods and services produced in an economy. It consists of four elements:

- consumer spending (C),
- investment expenditure (I),
- government spending (G),
- net expenditure on exports and imports ($X–M$),

and is usually represented by means of the following expression:

$$AD = C + I + G + (X - M)$$

Figure 8.1 shows a typical aggregate demand curve. In certain respects this is very similar to the demand curves introduced in section 2. It is for example downward sloping. The axes of this graph are of course different – real GDP is shown on the horizontal axis and the average price level is on the vertical axis. Any point on the AD curve therefore shows total real GDP required in an economy at a specific overall price level. Because the curve relates to *real* GDP, it takes into account the effects of inflation. Unlike the demand curves seen in section 2, though, the downward-sloping nature of the curve cannot be explained by inflationary changes.

There are three main reasons why the AD curve is downward sloping. These are:

1 Exports of goods and services are likely to be greater if the domestic price level is lower, as long as there is no compensating adjustment in the exchange rate to offset the lower price level. In addition, imports are likely to appear more expensive in these circumstances. Consequently, domestic demand may switch from imported commodities to home-produced ones, so increasing aggregate demand. The international economy is highly competitive and those economies with a low and stable rate of inflation may find it easier to sell their products in their own domestic markets. For example, in such circumstances, a Rover car made in the UK is likely to appear cheaper than a Volkswagen made in Germany, so demand for UK-produced cars may remain strong. Exchange rate fluctuations though may often have a more important bearing on this particular factor, often wiping out the benefits of low domestic inflation.

2 It is fair to assume that a reasonable proportion of domestic consumers possess a stock of wealth, in the form of savings in banks and building societies and holdings of stocks and shares. If the overall price level were to fall it would mean that this wealth would be capable of being used to buy an increased quantity of goods and services. People would feel better off. When this occurs there will be a tendency for them to go out and buy more, so the aggregate demand increases. Essentially this argument supposes that peoples' savings are for a 'rainy' day in the future – such as wanting to buy a new car or a house, or keeping a stock of money in case they need to go into a nursing home when they become elderly. When the price level is lower their savings or wealth has a greater real value. It seems less essential either to keep so

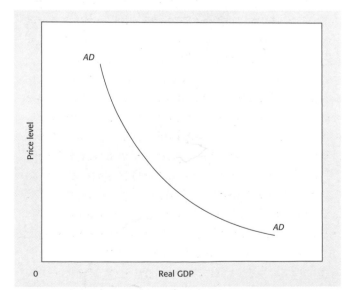

Figure 8.1 An aggregate demand curve

much money in the bank, or to save quite as much of their income as they have been doing. So consumers' expenditure and aggregate demand will be greater.

3 The third reason for a downward-sloping demand curve arises from the relationship between the price level and the rate of interest. When the price level falls, the rate of interest usually falls. A lower rate of interest is likely to stimulate consumption and investment and so raise aggregate demand.

These three ideas, based on exports, wealth and the rate of interest, provide a sufficient reason to expect the aggregate demand curve to slope downwards from left to right.

Using aggregate demand curves

The use of AD curves follows a similar approach to the discussion of microeconomic curves in section 2. There are some circumstances that lead to movements along the AD curve, and some that cause shifts in the AD curve. Movements along the AD curve were discussed earlier above when considering the rationale for its downward slope. Three basic reasons were given for the curve sloping down from left to right. If the basic circumstances underlying those causal factors alter then there will be shifts of the AD curve. For example, if the world economy moves into a boom there will be a boost to UK exports at any given price level, and the AD curve may be said to shift to the right. On the other hand, if a tax on wealth holdings is imposed so that stocks of monetary assets fall dramatically, then the AD curve may be said to shift to the left. If, at any given price level, interest rates fall then the AD curve will shift (figure 8.2).

On the other hand, more dramatic changes in aggregate demand may arise from changes in the underlying constituents of aggregate demand – that is, consumer spending, investment, government spending, exports and imports. To see the factors that may cause changes in these categories it is necessary briefly to consider their underlying determinants. Let us look at each in turn.

Determinants of consumer spending

Consumer spending (or consumers' expenditure as it is more technically known) is the most important

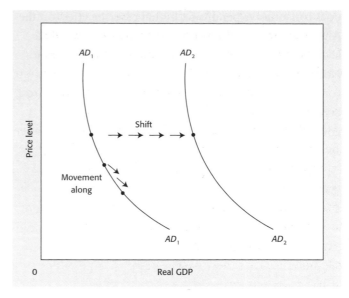

Figure 8.2 Shifts of and movements along the aggregate demand curve

component of aggregate demand. It is the amount of money spent by individuals on goods such as food, clothing, drink, cars, personal computers, housing, travel, entertainment and so on. A key determinant of consumer spending is the level of income or, more correctly, the level of **disposable income** (income after the payment of compulsory direct taxes and social security contributions). It is very obvious that as one's income level increases so too does spending on the above items. For the economy as a whole, therefore, an increase in the level of income will lead to an increase in consumer spending.

This is though a great simplification. What is often important is the **marginal propensity to consume** (mpc) – that is, the proportion of any increase in income that is spent on consumption. The general belief is that at low levels of living any increase in incomes is taken up entirely on increased consumption – the mpc is 100 per cent. That is, if you are very poor additional funds are likely to be spent on food, clothing, shelter and other essential items. Even at living standards beyond this it is still likely that the mpc may be high – 90 per cent or so – although it will decline a little because some provision is now made for saving. However, when income levels are so high that there is general affluence people become less concerned about spending any additional income, and the mpc falls to 60–70 per cent or so. The rest of the increase in incomes is saved and adds to wealth.

But the key thing is that when incomes increase, so

does consumer expenditure. In that case, the effect on the AD curve is that it shifts to the right. At any given price level, consumers have more income and demand more. Note that a key way in which consumers may receive more (or less) disposable income is through the effects of direct taxation and social security contributions. If the government raises income tax, incomes decline, consumer spending declines, and the AD curve shifts to the left.

Two further important factors affecting consumer spending are:

1 Government policies which affect the distribution of income. For example, if the government increases old age pensions and increases tax thresholds for low-income earners whilst increasing income taxes for the high-income earners, total disposable income may remain the same. Consumer spending, though, will increase, as will aggregate demand. The effect will be a shift outwards of the AD curve.

2 Interest rate changes. Some forms of consumer spending are sensitive to variations in interest rates, particularly expenditure on consumer durables and housing. Higher interest rates will deter consumer spending and require mortgage borrowers to make higher monthly repayments. Consumer spending overall falls, as does aggregate demand. Consequently, the AD curve shifts inwards.

Self-assessment task

Read the article below and then answer the questions which follow.

High points of Japan's recession

It feels like a Golden Recession. The official Japanese statistics may be dismal: the economy contracted by 1.4 per cent in the six months to September last year, new vehicle sales last month fell 24 per cent while supermarket sales figures for 1997 fell 2.8 per cent. But the streets are not filled with the homeless, high street shops are not boarded up and there is evidence of pockets of spending.

Yumino Tanaka, a 24-year office worker, recently spent Y3.5m (£16,600) on a four-wheel-drive Mitsubishi and has also taken a holiday to Hong Kong on a shopping tour. 'I didn't like the car I bought a year ago so I decided to change it for a new one', she says blithely.

Ms Tanaka is not the only one with the propensity to spend. In Shibuya, one of Tokyo's main shopping areas popular with the young, the streets are packed and there is a five-minute queue to pay for a compact disc at Tower Records.

'The young are among the few groups supporting consumption in Japan at the moment', says Ken Egusa, retail analyst at UBS in Tokyo. Those in their twenties with jobs but no dependants and teenagers who work part-time are buying personal items, including clothing, footwear and accessories, and taking trips abroad.

European luxury goods manufacturers are still experiencing steady demand. Bulgari, the up-market jewellers, for example, expects turnover for the past year to increase 26 per cent and plans to open more stores.

Although not spending as lavishly as during the economic 'bubble' of the late 1980s consumers in the top income brackets have not turned the tap off completely either, say analysts. Toshiko Binder, retail analyst at HSBC in Tokyo, says that over the past couple of years, low income households have cut their spending, while those with higher incomes seem to have been less affected by the downturn.

But spending by the rich and young has not offset the fall in consumption by the country's core spenders – people in their thirties and forties. Comprising a third of the population, they have been the main buyers of household goods, electronic equipment and cars. Faced with declining incomes and increasing uncertainty over jobs, many households have deferred spending on high priced items.

Office workers, who bought property and have mortgages – often lasting more than 30 years – have become especially cautious.

Economists warn that things could get worse, especially unemployment, now at a record high of 3.5 per cent and expected to rise. Although the government has announced cuts in income tax of Y26,000 per worker over the next month, scepticism is rising over its effectiveness in fuelling consumer demand.

Source: Emiko Terazono, *Financial Times*, 5 February 1998.

(a) List all the factors mentioned in the passage that have an effect on the level of consumer spending.
(b) Obtain data on the age distribution of the population in the United Kingdom and the spending patterns of different types of UK households. (Population figures are given in the Annual Abstract of Statistics and spending patterns in the Family Expenditure Survey, both published by the Office of National Statistics (ONS). Also check the ONS website.) What value are these data to an economist?
(c) Do you think that consumer spending in the United Kingdom would be as difficult to boost as it seems to be in Japan?

Determinants of investment expenditure

This is a very complex area of Economics. Let us therefore look very briefly at some of the issues involved. **Investment expenditure** can be split into three main categories – private investment, public investment and household investment in houses, flats and other types of accommodation.

Investment by the private sector, in say a new factory or distribution centre, varies inversely with the rate of interest, the cost of borrowing money. If interest rates rise, businessmen will find that fewer projects will earn a sufficient rate of return for the investment to be profitable. In this instance, the AD curve will shift inwards. On the other hand, if interest rates fall, projects become more profitable, investment expenditure increases and the AD curve shifts outwards to the right.

Another relevant factor to consider is the role of **expectations** of the future. Firms often base investment plans on all sorts of external factors which might affect business well-being, such as the outcome of an impending election or England succeeding in its bid to host the Olympic Games in 2012. These expectations are very volatile and investment expenditure may fluctuate quite markedly, leading to shifts outwards and inwards of the AD curve.

Public investment is rather less volatile, given that on-going investment is necessary to ensure the future viability of the armed forces, the road network, hospitals, schools and other important areas of capital investment. Such investment is very much dependent on the state of the economy. For household investment in dwellings, the rate of interest has a substantial effect on mortgage payments and, in turn, on disposable income and aggregate demand.

Determinants of government spending

This element of aggregate demand mainly includes current expenditure on goods and services and spending on employment in central and local government services. It is particularly sensitive to a change in economic policy on the part of government in order to achieve their macroeconomic objectives (as stated in section 7). On a wider basis, the pattern of taxation and expenditure may be manipulated in line with political beliefs and aspirations. Changes in government spending act directly to cause a shift in the AD curve. However, as we have seen, in recent years, when government spending has been restricted in real terms, there has been little change in the AD curve as a consequence of changes in this particular component. A sudden boost in government spending would alternatively lead to an outward shift in the AD curve.

Determinants of net expenditure on exports and imports

It is quite difficult to summarise these determinants in a simple way but one key aspect is the nature of a country's resources and the structure of its industries. If a country possesses oil or cheap labour supplies, or has strength in industries, such as car manufacture or pharmaceuticals, then it will have a greater chance of being a successful exporter than if it does not. However, possession of desirable characteristics is not sufficient in itself. The industries must also be efficient and competitive in many different dimensions: good quality products, swift delivery, a steady stream of product innovations based on research and development, well-thought-out marketing campaigns, salesmen with an ability to converse in several languages and so on. All these characteristics are needed to make a success out of exports. In addition, exporting will be easier at times of a world boom than when there is a global recession.

The other key element in export success is the level of the exchange rate. If US importers are purchasing Scottish knitwear they will be offering US dollars for the goods, whereas the Scottish producers will seek to be paid in pounds sterling. There therefore needs to be some way of exchanging dollars for pounds. This is achieved through banks and other financial intermediaries, who use the foreign exchange market. Through this market system there will arise an exchange rate of dollars for pounds. The level of the exchange rate is crucial for the exporter. The Scottish producer may be selling sweaters at £30. If the exchange rate is $1.50 for £1 the US importer will pay $45 for each sweater. If the exchange rate is $2 for £1 they will have to pay $60. Clearly, export sales will be much more difficult to achieve in the latter case. (See section 9 for details of exchange rate determination.)

Many of the factors which determine exchange rates in the modern world are beyond the power of a government to influence. International capital flows or **hot money** have a significant effect, as witnessed in the SE Asian currency crisis of 1997/98, when certain currencies experienced substantial depreciation in value over a very short period of time. Such unplanned and unexpected variation in the exchange rate had a major impact on trade and on most of the world's economies.

Imports of goods and services do not contribute to aggregate demand directly, but they do indirectly by diminishing its size. If imports make substantial inroads into the home market then there is less scope for domestic industry to respond to home demand. The extent to which this is possible will clearly depend upon the relative success of exports, and the factors that contribute to that success. Of these the key one will be the level of the exchange rate.

Beyond this the key element that determines imports is the overall level of demand in the economy. When GDP rises there is an automatic increase in imports. This is particularly the case for those imports that are needed for the production process. If the manufacture of cars needs steel, copper and rubber, all of which are imported, then an increase in the production of cars will require additional imports. In addition, growth in standards of living tends to increase demand for imported products, often more than proportionally so, as consumers seek greater variety and quality of commodities from other countries. It is difficult for a government to resist this trend other than by manipulating the exchange rate.

Self-assessment task

Study the table below, which brings together each of the main components of aggregate demand, and then answer the questions which follow:

	£ billion			Growth rates per cent per annum	
	1980	**1990**	**1997**	**1980–1990**	**1990–1997**
Household final consumption expenditure[2]	303.7	427.4	490.6	3.5	2.0
Government expenditure on goods and services	121.9	133.0	142.9	0.9	1.0
Investment	73.9	117.8	132.4	4.7	1.7
Exports of goods and services	111.1	156.6	236.0	3.5	6.0
Imports of goods and services[4]	−104.9	−176.4	−245.2	5.3	4.8
GDP at 1995 market prices[1]	504.8	658.5	756.1	2.7	2.0

	Per cent of GDP		
	1980	**1990**	**1997**
Household final consumption expenditure[2]	60.2	64.9	64.9
Government expenditure on goods and services[3]	24.1	20.2	18.9
Investment	14.6	17.8	17.5
Exports of goods an services	22.0	23.8	31.2
Imports of goods and services[4]	−20.8	−26.8	−32.4
GDP at 1995 market prices[1]	100.0	100.0	100.0

UK gross domestic product at constant (1995) prices[1]

Notes: 1 The term 'at constant 1995 prices' means that the statisticians have tried to eliminate, as far as possible, the effects of inflation. Other ways of expressing this are to say that the data are in *real* or *volume* terms.   2 Including the expenditure of non-profit institutions serving households.
   3 Individual and collective government final consumption expenditure.   4 Including the statistical discrepancy.
Source: United Kingdom National Accounts, 1998, Office for National Statistics.

(a) Briefly describe how the composition of the UK's Gross Domestic Product changed between 1980 and 1997.

(b) Discuss the likely reasons for the changes in composition which you have identified.

(c) Suppose in 1997 the government wished to reduce aggregate demand in the UK economy. What possibilities were available to it and what problems would it have experienced in carrying out such a policy.

Aggregate supply

So far in this section we have been concerned with aggregate demand or the demand side of the economy. Let us now turn our attention to aggregate supply or the supply side of the economy.

Aggregate supply is the total output of the economy. In our modern economy this would be anything that is produced by the factors of production (as described in section 1). Aggregate supply is simply the total output of the economy at a given price level and at a given point in time.

The key factors needed to produce aggregate supply are those needed to produce any good or service. Usually there is a need for land, some input of labour and capital equipment. We must also consider the level of technology as this is a very specific input into the production of goods and services. The role of enterprise and entrepreneurship must also be included. It is, though, beyond the scope of this book to look at these key factors other than in this very cursory way. To help you grasp the idea of aggregate supply, and what factors underpin it, look at the self-assessment task below.

Self-assessment task

Consider any particular production or service activity known to you. This could be where one of your relatives or friends works, where you work or possibly somewhere you have visited from school or college. Try listing the production inputs in terms of land, labour, capital and specific forms of technological input. Also, think about some of the problems you experience in classifying inputs in this way.

The aggregate supply curve

The aggregate supply curve shows the relationship between the total quantity supplied in an economy and the price level. Given this we would expect it to resemble the supply curve introduced in the microeconomic context of section 2 and slope upwards from left to right.

We can also rationalise this picture of the supply curve quite easily, in the same way as we do for the microeconomic curve. At low price levels businessmen collectively do not feel that it is worth producing commodities, because they do not expect to be able to sell them and make a profit, or break even. As the overall price level increases, more and more businessmen feel that it is worthwhile to start producing, or produce more, and so supply expands. However, again as in the case of the individual businessman, we must expect that, in the short run at least, as supply expands it starts to meet bottlenecks and this carries on until, eventually, the economy is running at full capacity. Given the stock of land, labour, capital and entrepreneurship, it is not possible to produce any more. At this point the AS curve will become vertical. Whatever the price, only a fixed amount can be produced. On this basis, the aggregate supply curve is shown in figure 8.3. Note that the axes are the same as for an aggregate demand curve (figure 8.1) and, like all supply curves, it is upward sloping.

It is now necessary to distinguish between the short-run and long-run aggregate supply curves. Thinking

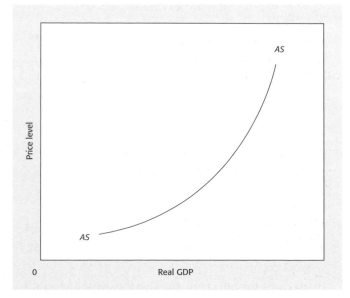

Figure 8.3 An aggregate supply (AS) curve

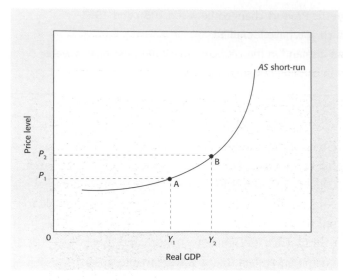

Figure 8.4 The short-run aggregate supply curve

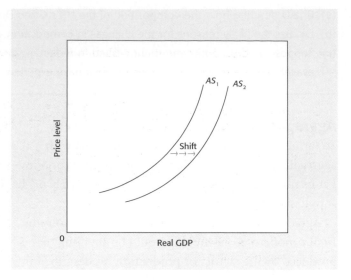

Figure 8.5 An outward shift of the aggregate supply curve

back to the factors which might affect aggregate supply, it becomes clear that almost all of them are relatively long term in nature. Any change in these factors will lead to shifts of the aggregate supply curve. In the short term, though, we are looking at a movement along the curve – this would be as a consequence of a change in the overall price level in the economy. If there is spare capacity in the economy, any increase in demand will have a much bigger effect on output than it will have on prices. Looking at figure 8.4, this is shown by the movement along the AS curve from A to B. Beyond B, though, as firms are reaching their full capacity and costs are rising, the AS curve becomes steeper. Further increases in demand will have a bigger effect on prices than output.

From a long-run standpoint there are many factors which may shift the whole of the aggregate supply curve. Some examples are:

- an increase in the capital stock due to a reduction in interest rates;
- an improvement in the expectations of businessmen;
- continuing technological change;
- increased investment in education and training;
- a reduction in direct taxation or unemployment benefits which may increase the incentive to work;
- schemes to increase the geographical mobility of workers.

In all cases the effects of such actions will be to shift the aggregate supply curve outwards, as shown in figure 8.5. The last twenty years or so have seen a strong commitment on the part of the government to create economic conditions which favour such a shift (see also section 9).

The problem is that all these actions are relatively uncertain in impact and will take a long time to have any marked effect. In addition, their use is likely to impinge on other government policies because they may involve greater government expenditure, interfere with other social objectives, involve foregoing tax revenue or reduce interest rates when other government objectives require that interest rates be raised. Consequently, government supply-side policies are intrinsically difficult to introduce, uncertain in their impact and may take a long time to have an effect. The only policies that may have a short- to medium-term impact will be changes in income tax levels and unemployment benefits and eligibility for them. However, some of these may have a 'once-and-for-all' impact. Once instituted, they will be hard to repeat.

Equilibrium in the macroeconomy and the determination of output and prices
The AD/AS diagram

We are now in a position where the aggregate demand curve of figure 8.1 can be combined with the aggregate supply curve of figure 8.3. The outcome is shown in figure 8.6.

Self-assessment task

Read the article below and then answer the questions that follow.

Rates cut to 3.75%

The Bank of England yesterday surprised the markets by cutting its primary interest rate by a quarter of a percentage point to 3.75 per cent, the lowest rate since 1955 and the first change for 15 months. The Bank said 'prospects for demand, both globally and domestically, are somewhat weaker than anticipated'. The cut was not matched at the European Central Bank, which held its basic rate at 2.75 per cent.

Although the cut was welcomed by maufacturers, there were fears it might strengthen imbalances in the economy between a weak manufacturing sector and strong consumption. House prices have risen 25 per cent over the past 12 months and household debt has risen sharply.

'No one should mistake this for good news', said Peter Wyman, president of the Institute of Chartered Accountants in England and Wales. The reduction 'runs the risk of turning the heat up further, heightening the risk of a subsequent crash'.

Wim Duisenberg, ECB president, said the ECB had held back, fearing a cut now would have been 'drowned' in the 'sea of uncertainty' caused by tension over Iraq. Most economists said they expected an ECB reduction in the spring following its half percentage point reduction to 2.75 per cent in November.

European interest rates are determined by the European Central Bank in Frankfurt
Source: European Central Bank.

Source: Adapted from an article in the *Financial Times*, by Scheherazade Daneshkhu, 7 February 2003.

(a) How does a cut in interest rates affect
- ◆ aggregate demand,
- ◆ short-run aggregate supply?

(b) Explain why 'the cut was welcomed by manufacturers'.

(c) Why did the Bank of England 'surprise' the markets by cutting interest rates to their lowest level since 1955?

Inevitably, the AS and AD curves cross at a point, marked as P_1 and Y_1. These indicate the *equilibrium* price level and real output, in exactly the same way that microeconomic supply and demand curves cross to give an equilibrium price and output. The price level P_1 is the only price level which will lead suppliers to produce exactly the right output to satisfy the aggregate demand from consumers, government, overseas customers and investors in fixed capital, at that price level. At any other price level there will be an imbalance between aggregate supply and aggregate demand. If some other price level is somehow set up, then there will either be excess demand or excess supply. If price is below equilibrium there will be excess demand, but those demanding goods and services will become more willing to pay higher prices, and the price level will be bid back up

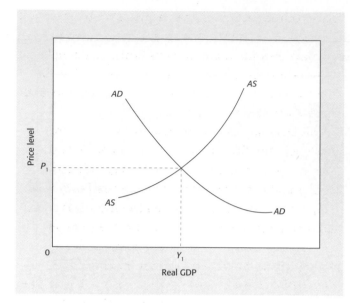

Figure 8.6 Equilibrium between AD and AS

towards the equilibrium. If price is above equilibrium there will be excess supply, stocks will start to build up, and suppliers will be forced to cut prices in order to sell stocks. So the price level will be forced down towards equilibrium.

Changes in aggregate demand and supply

The accepted relationship between output and employment is that, as output increases, employment also increases and unemployment falls. Particularly in the short run, this is valid although in practice by no means as simple as might be assumed. In the long run, if aggregate supply increases, the situation is complicated by the factors that cause this shift. Take for example an improvement in technology or a better-educated workforce; these may enable output to increase without there being an increase in employment. Indeed, a firm that installs some new high-tech machinery may be likely to make some workers redundant and add to unemployment. Overall, a 10 per cent increase in output capacity caused by increased capital investment might imply only a 3 per cent increase in labour requirements and a lesser impact on unemployment. This is the reality of how the economy works although, for the time being, the earlier accepted relationship is the one that will be assumed.

Figure 8.7 shows that a shift in aggregate demand from AD_1 to AD_2 will raise output (real GDP) but at the

same time increase the price level from P_1 to P_2. This shift can be due to an increase in any one of the components of aggregate demand. For example:

- Consumer spending would increase if the government reduced the rate of income tax.
- A reduction in interest rates is likely to stimulate investment expenditure by business.
- The government could increase its own spending by giving more money for new teachers and textbooks.
- Exports could increase if our labour costs were more competitive relative to some of our EU trading partners.

There are many other possibilities. The effect though is a shift of the AD curve to the right in an AD/AS diagram. If the economy is running below capacity, there is likely to be an increase in output, a fall in unemployment and probably an increase in prices.

Some economists would argue that the AS curve should be vertical, indicating that any increase in aggregate demand can only increase prices (see figure 8.8). The reasoning behind this is the time it takes to move additional resources into supply following an increase in demand. They would further argue that the only way to increase output in the long run is by increasing aggregate supply, not by boosting aggregate demand.

Figure 8.9 shows that an increase in aggregate supply, shown by the AS curve shifting to the right, is likely to have the general effect of leading to an increase in

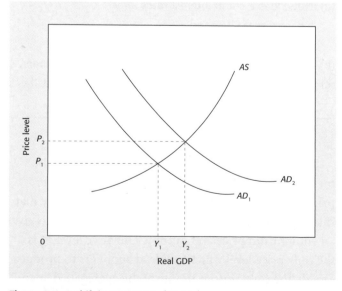

Figure 8.7 A shift in aggregate demand

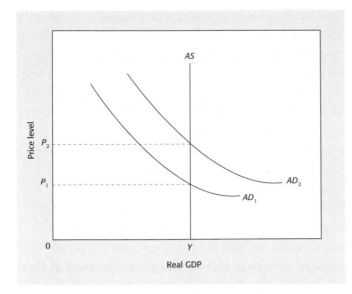

Figure 8.8 Equilibrium with a vertical AS curve

output and a lower price level. As mentioned earlier, the short-run impact will be very small. The longer-run effects may be more substantial but take a considerable time before they are anything other than modest in size. Factors which might be responsible for the shift in the AS curve have already been stated.

Injections and leakages and the multiplier effect

We have so far looked at aggregate demand and aggregate supply or aspects of total spending and total output in the economy. In producing this output,

factors of production receive payments for their services (see section 1). In turn these payments are used to purchase the output produced by firms. This simple relationship was referred to earlier in section 7 as the circular flow of income. Figure 8.10 is a development of figure 7.1 for a simple economy.

This economy consists of households which are consumers and firms which are producers. The two flows between them are physical flows (goods and services and factor services) and monetary flows. It is assumed that all output is sold and all income is spent and that in this simple representation, there are no **injections** or **leakages**. This is unrealistic as in the modern economy there are various injections and leakages, which have to be recognised since they add or remove income from the circular flow. All have been considered at some point in this section.

The three injections into the circular flow of income are:

- investment expenditure (I);
- government spending (G);
- exports (X).

Each represents an autonomous addition to the circular flow. Leakages, on the other hand, represent a withdrawal of income and expenditure from the circular flow and are:

- **savings** (S);
- **taxation** (T);
- **imports** (M).

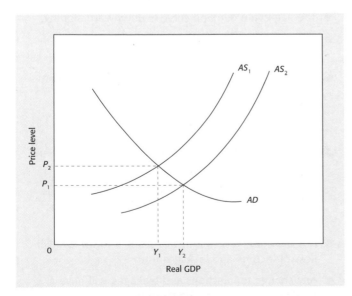

Figure 8.9 A shift in aggregate supply

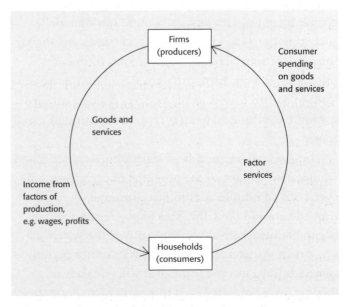

Figure 8.10 The circular flow of income and expenditure

At any one time, all of these are likely to be operating in the economy, making for a much more complex situation than might at first be obtained from the earlier analysis in this section.

It should also be recognised that changes in AD and AS may have a larger total effect on GDP than the particular tax reduction or increase in government expenditure that set it off. This is known as the **multiplier effect** and can be used to explain why, say, a reduction in income tax of £500m may produce an expenditure boost of £800m to the economy.

The rationalisation for this result is as follows. Suppose that government increases expenditure on health and education. This means not only that the salaries of teachers and nurses increase but also that there is new expenditure on school buildings and hospital wards, new computer facilities, new brain scanners and so on. Consequently there is a big boost to consumer spending and to investment expenditure, equal to the value of the additional government expenditure. This is known as the **first-round effect**.

However, the pattern of increased expenditure does not end there. Teachers and nurses, with increased salaries, go off to cinemas and nightclubs, drink beer and whisky, and buy new curtains for the home. As a result, the cinemas, nightclubs, breweries and distilleries, curtain manufacturers and others are soon faced with increased demand. This is also true of the building industry, manufacturers of computers and brain scanners. All these manufacturers have to increase output, which may mean employing more labour (who receive incomes) and buying in more raw materials, such as hops, cotton fabrics, computer cases and digital imagery software. This sets up a second round of purchases. In their turn, the second round of purchases leads to a third round, as the workers making curtains get more overtime, have an increased income and spend more.

These successive rounds of expenditure carry on, and would seem to have all the potential of carrying on for ever, with an infinite addition to consumers' expenditure and the GDP. This happy result does not occur, because there are leakages out of the system at every turn. As referred to earlier, every time a person gets additional income some of it will be taken as income tax before they even receive it; in any case they will not spend all of the income they receive because

they will save some of it; when they spend it, some of the expenditure may return to the government as VAT or excise duty; and they may purchase imports, which do not add to the domestic GDP. Consequently the first-round impact of expenditure is less than the full value of the increased income, the second round expenditure is only a fraction of the first, and so on. Eventually successive rounds are so small as to add nothing to the multiplier effect, and it peters out.

In principle multiplier effects result from any additional expenditure, whether it be through changes in government taxes or expenditures, the result of a spontaneous increase in investment expenditure, or the result of a boom in exports. They may also operate on a small scale in an area, for example when a large new factory employing a lot of previously unemployed workers is set up, and they can also operate in reverse, so that a rise in income taxes may lead to a *reduction* in consumer expenditure greater than the original amount. Regardless of how they might have occurred, multiplier effects have to be taken into account by policymakers when investigating the impact on the economy of a change in aggregate demand.

Summary

In this section we have recognised that:

- Aggregate demand refers to the total spending on goods and services produced in an economy. It consists of consumer spending, investment expenditure, government spending and net expenditure on exports and imports.
- The aggregate demand curve is downward-sloping.
- Each of the components of aggregate demand is in turn determined by various economic variables.
- Aggregate supply is the total output in the economy. It is determined by factors of production and the level of technology.
- The aggregate supply curve is upward-sloping.
- Equilibrium output and prices are determined where the AD and AS curves intersect.
- Any change in AD or AS will lead to a shift in these functions and will have an effect upon the level of output, unemployment and inflation.
- Any economy has various injections into the circular flow of income and leakages from it.
- Any change to injections and leakages will have a multiplier effect on expenditure in the economy.

Key words

Definitions of Key words can be found in the Glossary on page 240.

aggregate supply
consumer spending
disposable income
expectations
first-round effect
fiscal policies
hot money
injections
investment expenditure

leakages
marginal propensity to consume
monetary policies
multiplier effect
net expenditure on imports and exports
savings
supply-side policies

9 The application of macroeconomic policy instruments

On completion of this section you should be able to:

➤ describe what is meant by fiscal policy

➤ define monetary policy and understand the basic relationship between money supply and interest rates

➤ outline how exchange rates are determined by the supply and demand for currencies

➤ explain how interest rates are determined by supply and demand for money

➤ discuss how the AD/AS model may be used to analyse the way fiscal, monetary and supply-side policies and exchange rate changes can affect the levels of employment, rate of inflation, economic growth and the balance of payments position

Fiscal policy

Previous sections have, rather casually, referred to instruments of fiscal policy, such as variations in income taxes and social security benefits, without discussing them in any depth. This section remedies this deficiency by considering fiscal policy in more detail. In doing so it will stress the ways in which variations in fiscal policy instruments may affect aggregate demand and supply.

Fiscal policy refers to the use of taxation and government spending in pursuit of particular policy objectives. It is used by governments to influence the level of aggregate demand in the economy and it can also affect aggregate supply through changing incentives facing firms and individuals. In simple terms it is best seen as referring to changes in the income or expenditure sides of the government accounts.

Table 9.1 shows the UK government's sources of income for the period 1993–2002, and table 9.2 shows the pattern of its expenditures over the same period. In each case the data are at current prices, so it must be assumed that some of the variations in the relative importance of some of the tax and expenditure items in the tables will reflect differences in the rate of inflation. For example, it is possible that the pay of the armed forces could increase more rapidly than that of nurses, so defence expenditure might rise more rapidly than expenditure on health. Or it could be that prices for electronic goods, on which VAT is levied, rise more rapidly than incomes, on which income tax is paid, so VAT receipts rise more rapidly than income tax.

However, many of the trends shown in the tables stem from changes in government policy, together with changes in the economy and society. For example, as was discussed in section 5, government has a responsibility to the public for arranging for the provision of public goods and merit goods, or for limiting the effects of negative externalities. As a

	£ billion		
	1993	**1997**	**2002**
Primary incomes			
Operating surplus, (deficit)	2.9	4.1	(11.2)
Value added tax (VAT)	38.3	52.3	63.9
Other taxes on products	28.4	40.7	42.6
Other taxes on production	15.0	16.7	33.2
Property income	9.7	9.6	8.2
Balance of primary incomes (gross)	*94.3*	*123.4*	*136.7*
Secondary incomes			
Taxes on income and wealth	80.7	110.5	134.1
Social contributions	42.9	54.4	65.0
Other	7.0	6.3	7.6
Total resources (gross)	*224.8*	*294.4*	*343.4*

	Percentage of total resources		
	1993	**1997**	**2002**
Value added tax (VAT)	17.0	17.8	18.7
Other taxes on products	12.6	13.8	12.4
Other taxes on production	6.7	5.7	9.6
Taxes on income and wealth	35.9	37.5	39.0
Social contributions	19.1	18.5	18.9

Table 9.1 UK Central government: sources of income
Note: The data is for financial years.
Source: Economic Trends, 2002. Office for National Statistics

	£ billion		
	1993	1997	2002
General public services	12.0	15.1	19.4
Defence	24.4	23.4	24.6
Public order and safety	14.5	16.3	23.0
Economic affairs	20.7	21.7	16.0
Environmental protection	2.6	2.6	3.2
Housing and community services	9.5	6.3	5.8
Health	37.0	44.0	55.8
Recreation, culture and religion	4.6	4.1	4.2
Education	30.7	36.2	54.0
Social protection	115.3	113.2	109.0
Other	20.0	30.1	49.0
Total outlays	291.3	331.0	364.0

	Percentage of total outlays		
	1993	1997	2002
General public services	4.1	4.6	5.3
Defence	8.4	7.1	6.8
Public order and safety	5.0	4.9	6.3
Economic affairs	7.1	6.6	4.4
Environmental protection	0.9	0.8	0.9
Housing and community services	3.3	1.9	1.6
Health	12.7	13.3	15.3
Recreation, culture and religion	1.6	1.2	1.2
Education	10.5	10.9	14.8
Social protection	39.6	39.6	29.9
Other	6.9	9.1	13.7
Total outlays	100.0	100.0	100.0

Table 9.2 UK Central government: total outlays
Source: Economic Trends, 2002, Office for National Statistics.

'Steady Eddie' – one of many transport operators using central government funded motorways

consequence it may alter its expenditures on health and education, or change excise duties on whisky, tobacco and petrol, for general political reasons that have nothing to do with using them as part of macroeconomic policy. Again, a change in government from a political party of one set of beliefs to another party with a different view of the responsibilities of government may produce a slow, but steady, turn-round of the government's expenditure pattern. The final column of Table 9.2 for example clearly shows New Labour's stated commitment to education and health. In addition, a boom in the economy will raise employment and hours worked and reduce unemployment. Without lifting a finger, because of the increased incomes and expenditures, the government automatically receives more revenue from income tax, excise duties and VAT.

Because of the reduced unemployment the government automatically pays out less in social security benefits, such as unemployment benefits.

The instruments and their effects

In practice the government is aware of the different instruments of fiscal policy and their effects. On the income side, the key areas that may be manipulated are income tax rates and allowances; Value Added Tax (VAT); excise duties, such as those on tobacco, alcohol and petrol; social security payments, such as National Insurance contributions. On the expenditure side, there is no key area as such. An increase in almost all types of government expenditure will have an impact on aggregate demand, but increases in some areas may have a greater impact on aggregate supply than others. Expenditure on fighter aircraft will not add much to productive capacity; new motorways will.

To boost aggregate demand the government essentially has two options. It can either *cut* taxes, or it can *increase* expenditure. In either case the net effect is the same. The general public have greater real incomes than before, consumer expenditure rises and aggregate demand is boosted (shown by the AD curve shifting to the right). In more detail, a reduction in income tax will mean that large sections of the population will receive more money in their pay packets or as salary payments. Not unnaturally, a high proportion of this increased income will be spent, the exact proportion depending upon the marginal propensity to consume. Consequently, consumer expenditure will rise. Alternatively, a fall in excise duty on petrol means that people have to spend less on petrol. As petrol is a good inelastic in demand, expenditure on petrol will fall, implying that people have more money to spend on other things, whilst buying at least as much petrol as before. Consequently consumer expenditure rises. Finally, if the government increases its expenditure on health and education, it is possible that the salaries of nurses and teachers will increase and in turn, therefore, consumer expenditure will increase.

The discussion above has concentrated on the impact of fiscal policy instruments on aggregate demand. In addition, there may also be an impact on aggregate supply, and this should not be neglected. Such impacts may occur in two ways.

First, changes in income taxes and social security benefits may have *incentive* or *disincentive* effects on workers. This may cause aggregate supply to increase, or to decrease, in the short to medium term. Secondly, depending upon the nature of the change in government expenditure, there may be long-term effects on aggregate supply. This is most obviously the case for direct expenditures on roads, but it can also occur in a multitude of other ways. Changes in subsidies to capital, or for research and development, may lead to increases in the size and productivity of the capital stock. Improved education and training will improve the efficiency and productivity of the workforce.

The result of this is that some areas of fiscal policy have fairly direct, short-term impacts on aggregate demand whilst also affecting aggregate supply in the long run. Both effects need to be considered when analysing fiscal policy.

Self-assessment task

What will be the effects of the following on both aggregate demand and aggregate supply in the short and long run?
(a) a reduction in income tax allowances;
(b) an increase in compulsory pensions contributions;
(c) an increase in VAT;
(d) an increase in expenditure in further education colleges;
(e) an increase in unemployment benefits;
(f) a reduction in expenditure on subsidising firm's expenditures on investment in capital goods.

Monetary policy

Monetary policy in principle involves government induced changes in either the supply of money or interest rates. Over the last twenty years or so it has become the dominant means of macroeconomic policy; since 1997 in the UK it has been independently managed by the Monetary Policy Committee of the Bank of England.

A simple definition of money was introduced in section 2. Although this is a great simplification compared with the real world, it will suffice. Defining the **money supply**, though, is far more complex (see the A2 module, the UK Economy).

Clearly it must include notes and coins, but nowadays many purchases are not paid for with such currency. Instead people pay with Visa cards, Switch cards or personal cheques. What is happening is that they are paying using money balances that stand in their name in banks and building societies. The effect of the cards or cheques is to transfer some of their bank balance from their account to the payee's account. Obviously these bank balances are serving as money, and they are therefore counted as part of the money supply. Taken together currency in the form of notes and coin, plus balances that are available for use in normal transactions, is often called **narrow money**. Beyond this amount of money there is an additional vast amount of balances at banks and building societies that stand in the names of individuals, but which is not so immediately accessible and cannot be used for direct transactions. This is usually called **broad money**.

As referred to in section 7, economists view the growth of the money supply as a prime cause of inflation, particularly where this involves the cavalier printing of notes by the monetary authorities. Changes in the money supply will affect aggregate demand indirectly. So, if the supply of money increases, people will have more spending power and they will demand more goods and services. What we are saying here is that aggregate demand has increased and the AD curve has shifted to the right. This will put pressure on suppliers, bottlenecks will appear and prices will rise. It also follows that a means of keeping underlying inflation at a low level is to restrict the supply of money. Consumer spending in turn is restricted, so there is less danger of the economy over-heating and prices will be relatively easy.

A change in the money supply, though, can also affect

aggregate demand in less direct ways:

1 Individuals may not necessarily spend their income on goods and services; instead they may decide to purchase a security in the form of a **government bond**, which is usually issued at a given face value and pays a fixed annual sum as a rate of interest. For example, it may be a £1,000 bond paying £80 per year – representing 8 per cent on the face value of the bond. However, such bonds may be traded in financial markets, in the City of London, New York, Frankfurt or Tokyo. If the markets move the price of the bond down, so that it now only has a value of £800, but it is still paying £80 per year, then the rate of interest is now effectively 10 per cent. If the market price of the bond rises to £1,600, but it is still paying £80 per year, the rate of interest is now effectively 5 per cent. Hence the market price of bonds and the rate of interest are inversely proportional. So, when the supply of money increases, the demand for such securities will rise and, in turn, their price will rise.

2 Individuals may spend some of their income on imported goods and services (see section 10). So when the money supply increases, so too will the demand for imports, necessitating an increase in (say) pounds on the foreign exchange market. With floating exchange rates, the price of pounds will fall, in turn making exports rather more competitive and imports rather more expensive. In turn, some consumers will switch their expenditure from imports to home-produced goods, so eventually increasing aggregate demand.

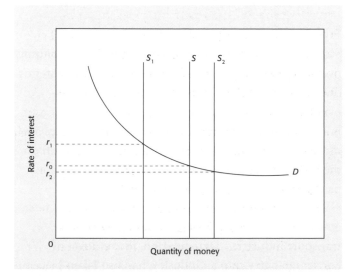

Figure 9.1 Relationship between money supply and interest rates

The basic theoretical relationship for the determination of interest rates was shown in figure 2.24 in section 2. Building on this a change in the money supply will in turn affect interest rates, as figure 9.1 shows. So, when the money supply is reduced from S to S_1, the rate of interest increases from r_0 to r_1. On the other hand, if the money supply were to increase from S_1 to S, the rate of interest would fall from r_1 to r_0. Any further increase, to say S_2, would lead to a very slight fall in the rate of interest to r_2.

This relationship between the money supply and the rate of interest has very substantial implications for macroeconomic policies, as we shall see at the end of this section.

Supply-side policies

As mentioned in section 8, there are various policies which can result in a shift of the aggregate supply curve. Collectively these measures are referred to as supply-side policies in so far as they seek to increase the aggregate supply available in the economy. When combined with policies to manage aggregate demand they provide an effective means for allowing governments to meet their stated macroeconomic objectives. A wide range of supply-side policies are potentially available. Unlike the relatively blunt instruments of fiscal and monetary policy, these policies are much more focused in their objectives, although they can be expensive to introduce and have limited and relatively uncertain long-run effects on the economy. In promoting these policies the role of government is to remove market imperfections and restrictive practices so that the economy can operate in a more efficient manner. A few examples are outlined below.

Providing incentives to work

The guiding principle here has been to encourage more people to join the labour force and so bring about an increase in output. Underlying this particular approach is the idea that direct taxation and the welfare payments system can actually act as a disincentive to work and through evading taxation, promote the growth of the 'hidden economy' (see also section 7). It should be emphasised though that this relationship is by no means clearly evidenced from an empirical standpoint, although, in theory, it is more obvious.

The last Conservative government in the UK firmly believed that high rates of direct taxation were very much a disincentive to work. When elected in 1979, the top rate of income tax was a massive 83 per cent – systematically and deliberately this has been reduced to a top rate of 40 per cent and the basic income tax rate has now fallen from 33 per cent to just 22 per cent. Tax thresholds for low-income earners have also been revised with the objective of encouraging more people to join the labour force. Lowering income tax in this way will shift the AS curve to the right (see figure 8.9).

The Conservatives also reformed the unemployment benefit and social security system, a process which has been continued by the Labour government elected in 1997. The Conservatives' objective was to encourage low-income earners and the unemployed to seek work rather than rely on state handouts. Because of the system some individuals actually received more in benefits than they would be paid if they were in a job. This so-called **unemployment trap** acts as a clear disincentive to work. The objective of supply-side policies here is one of widening the gap between the wages received through working and the welfare payments received whilst unemployed or economically inactive. Its effect on the AS curve is the same as indicated by figure 8.9.

Education and training

Many people who are unemployed lack the skills that are necessary to obtain a job. This particularly applies to many sixteen-year-old school leavers and some people who have been unemployed for a long time. By providing opportunities for such people to train, wider skill shortages in the economy can be addressed and the workforce can become more effective, more mobile and more flexible, so enhancing the country's international competitiveness compared with our trading rivals.

In recent years there have been many schemes designed to promote this particular objective. Many of these are managed by local Skills Councils, which provide vocational training and work placements for teenagers and unemployed adults. Job clubs, Restart schemes, Access courses and personal counselling, managed by the local offices of the Employment Services Agency, provide opportunities for the longer-term unemployed to rejoin the labour market. The theoretical impact of all such schemes is once again as shown in figure 8.9.

Interviewing and assessment are an important role of staffing agencies
Source: Select Appointments plc.

Trade union reform

This has been another area where the last Conservative government pursued a vigorous supply-side policy, in this case aimed at reducing the power of trade unions in the labour market. By restricting the supply of workers, trade unions seek to increase the wages of their members but at the cost of a decrease in the numbers employed. Such action, it is argued by supply-side economists, increases costs, impairs efficiency and reduces international competitiveness. During the 1980s, a mass of new legislation was introduced to reduce the power of the trade unions and consequently produce a more flexible, adaptable and responsive labour force. The number of working days lost through strike action, for example, has fallen remarkably and in many companies highly restrictive working practices have been removed. The outcome again has been to shift the AS curve to the right.

Privatisation and deregulation

Structurally the most important change in the economy over the past twenty years or so has been the transfer of ownership of former state-owned activities to the private sector. This is a supply-side policy in so far as it is argued that, under private ownership, companies are more efficient, more competitive and less of a drain on the public purse. As a consequence market conditions provide for a shift to the right of the AS curve.

Privatisation in the UK economy since 1979 has been extensive, particularly for the fuel and power and transport industries. **Deregulation**, the removal of barriers to entry into an industry, has also taken place on an extensive scale, as indeed has the contracting-out of activities normally undertaken by the public sector. Although we cannot ignore the political motive, the outcome has arguably been the creation of a much more competitive market in many areas of the economy where previously there had been a public sector monopoly.

It is beyond the scope of this text to look at the arguments for and against privatisation. The significance of privatisation and deregulation though cannot be ignored from a supply-side standpoint.

Self-assessment task

Study the short article below and then answer the questions that follow.

Benefit 'will not provide work incentives'

Only between 30,000 and 45,000 families are likely to be tempted back to work by the government's new flagship benefit for the low paid, the Working Families Tax Credit (WFTC), the independent Institute for Fiscal Studies said yesterday.

As the government launched the bill to replace family credit with WFTC, the Institute said most of the gain from the new, more generous credit would go to people already in work.

Relatively few individuals are likely to be tempted into the labour market, despite the estimated £1.5bn extra cost of the credit, because for those on housing benefit the combined means-tests will still not leave them markedly better off, the Institute said.

While people who do not receive housing benefit will make significant gains, those who do will lose 89p of each extra £1 they earn as they start to pay tax and national insurance and begin to lose WFTC itself and housing and council tax benefit as their earnings rise. Under the present system they lose 92p in the £1.

Alan Duncan, a senior researcher at IFS, said some further reform to housing benefit and its interaction with the new credit would be needed to provide bigger work incentives.

The estimates have been made for the Bank of England's Monetary Policy Committee, which wanted to know the likely labour market effects of the new credit.

Source: N. Timmins, *Financial Times*, 27 January 1999 (adapted).

(a) With the aid of a diagram, briefly explain the economic logic underpinning the Working Families Tax Credit (WFTC) scheme.

(b) Comment upon the views made by the Institute for Fiscal Studies about this new scheme.

Exchange rate determination

As stated in the early part of section 8, net receipts from exports and imports are one of the four contributors to aggregate demand in an economy. Section 10 will look at the international economy in detail but, in order to complete our perspective of macroeconomic policy instruments, it is now necessary to understand how exchange rates are determined. The concluding part of this section will then explain how exchange rate changes can affect the performance of the macroeconomy.

The exchange rate of a currency, as its name suggests, is the rate at which one currency is exchanged for another. For example, £1 can be exchanged for (say) $1.6 US or 1.54 euros at any one time on the foreign exchange market. It is therefore the price of one currency expressed in terms of any other tradable currency.

Foreign exchange is needed because of the nature of international trade. If a UK resident buys a good which has been produced abroad and imported into the UK, currency exchange must take place. This is because the producer of this in, say, France will require payment in their own currency, euros. At some stage of the trading process currency exchange must take place. The buying and selling of foreign exchange takes place on the foreign exchange market. Importers of goods into the UK will use £s to buy the currency of the country from which they are purchasing the goods, so providing a supply of £s to the foreign exchange market. Similarly, those who have bought products from the UK will be using their own currencies to purchase £s on the foreign exchange market. This action creates a demand for £s.

The exchange rate of a currency is determined by the relative strength of the supply and demand for a currency. Figure 9.2 shows the supply and demand for £s on the foreign exchange market. For simplicity, the relationship between just two currencies, £s and $USs, is shown. In this diagram the demand for £s ($D£$) slopes down from left to right because when the price of the £ in terms of $USs is high, UK goods are relatively expensive to US consumers. As a result the demand for British goods and services will be low, with few £s being demanded on the foreign exchange market. As the value of the £ falls against the $US, American consumers can gain more £s for their $USs and so more £s are demanded on the foreign exchange market. The supply

Figure 9.2 The simple determination of an exchange rate

curve for £s ($S_£$) in figure 9.2 is upward sloping from left to right, as when the value of the £ against the $US is low, American goods are relatively expensive in the UK. Fewer British consumers will buy such goods and, as a result, few £s will be supplied to the foreign exchange market. As the value of the £ rises against the $US, however, American goods become more affordable to British consumers and therefore more £s are supplied to the foreign exchange market.

Suppose the price of the £ on the foreign exchange market moves from the position shown in figure 9.2 to one where £1 = $2 US. The £ is now overvalued and British exporters find it difficult to sell their goods in the US market. The demand for £s is low but in contrast, because American goods are relatively cheap in the UK market, British consumers have increased their demand and more £s are being supplied. At this exchange rate therefore there is an excess of £s on the foreign exchange market. In such a situation the usual principles of market economics apply – the excess supply results in a fall in price until it reaches the equilibrium rate of £1 = S1.60 US, where once again supply equates to demand.

The above analysis is a great simplification of how the foreign exchange market really operates. It is necessary, though, to understand these basic principles to be able to analyse how exchange rate changes can affect the level of employment, rate of inflation and the balance of payments position in the economy.

Applications of the AD/AS model

Let us conclude this section with a brief overview as to how the policies described so far can be applied through the AD/AS model to allow governments to achieve the objectives given in section 7. First, though, a few words of warning!

1 The policies described so far in theory might seem relatively easy to comprehend. Unfortunately in practice their outcome is far from easy to predict and, on occasions, very uncertain.

2 The policies themselves do not operate independently. At any one time, a whole mass of fiscal, monetary and supply-side policies are being applied by governments in pursuit of their objectives. It is also the case that indirectly one policy may trigger off an unwanted reaction. For example, if the government tries to boost aggregate demand in the economy by lowering taxes, this increases the demand for money with the resulting effect that interest rates must rise. In turn, this reduces aggregate demand. So, fiscal policy designed to expand aggregate demand leads to interest rate rises that reduce investment expenditure and demand, cutting back the positive effects of fiscal policy. These interest rate changes may also lead to a higher exchange rate and lower exports. Overall, the effect of reduced investment and exports is referred to as **crowding out**, that is exports are crowded out by increased consumption.

3 The application of fiscal, monetary and supply-side policies involves a time lag. Some policies tend to be more immediate than others in their effects. Changes to indirect taxes on fuel, drink or VAT are relatively quick to apply and relatively immediate in their impact. Other fiscal changes, say to government

spending or direct taxes, take much longer both to be applied and to have an effect on the macroeconomy. Monetary policies are in general more longer term in their effects than fiscal policies.

4 Supply-side policies tend to be long term and uncertain in their measurable outcome since they require structural changes to be made to increase aggregate supply in the economy. They therefore have little relevance from the point of view of short-term economic management.

Table 9.3 provides a summary of the main applications of fiscal, monetary and supply-side policies that governments can use in pursuit of their macroeconomic objectives. In terms of the AD/AS model, you should refer back to figures 8.7 and 8.9, which show how the equilibrium position is affected by shifts in AD and AS respectively.

Policies to reduce unemployment

It might seem easy to reduce unemployment. All the government needs to do is to create more jobs and produce a greater output. In terms of the AD/AS model, it means shifting either the AD curve to the right or the AS curve to the right or both simultaneously.

In the short run, as table 9.3 indicates, fiscal and monetary policies can operate to increase aggregate demand and so reduce unemployment. The only adverse effect would seem to be the increase in prices that will follow such an expansion in the economy. If interest rates are lowered, this could lower the exchange rate, allowing export prices to fall but leading to higher import prices, in turn feeding domestic inflation. In the long run the main hope for reducing unemployment must lie with supply-side policies targeted at the labour force. Some examples of such policies are also shown in table 9.3. If effective these will shift the long-run AS curve to the right. As figure 8.9 showed, this has the added benefit of reducing the price level. As section 8 explained, by definition, fiscal and monetary policies are ineffective in dealing with the problem of long-term unemployment – only policies designed to enhance training and skills or improving home circumstances will make it easier for such people to obtain work.

Policies to control inflation

It follows from the above that appropriate short-term policies to bring down prices are the reverse of those to reduce unemployment. In the case of fiscal policy this

Problem	Short-run policies	Long-run policies	Difficulties
↓ Unemployment	Fiscal and monetary e.g. ↓ indirect taxes ↑ government spending ↓ rate of interest → shift AD to right	Supply-side e.g. retrain long-term unemployed, reduced welfare payments → shift AS to right	Higher prices in short run Not all unemployed can realistically re-join labour force
↓ Rate of inflation	Fiscal and monetary policies e.g. ↑ direct taxes ↓ government spending ↑ rate of interest → shift AD to left	Supply-side e.g. remove restrictive practices, deregulation → shift AS to right	Reduced output and increased unemployment in short run Appreciating exchange rate Politically unpopular Increasing indirect taxes is likely to be inflationary
↓ Balance of trade deficit	Fiscal and monetary policies e.g. ↑ direct taxes ↑ rate of interest Exchange rate policies e.g. depreciation → shift AD to left	Supply-side e.g. measures designed to promote increased international competitiveness → shift AS to right	Increased unemployment in short run Businesses could suffer in short run Depends on price elasticity of demand of imports and exports

Note: ↓ decrease, ↑ increase, → leading to

Table 9.3 A summary of macroeconomic problems and policy options would mean raising income taxes, reducing social benefits or cutting government spending. These are by no means popular measures politically, but have often to be used to control inflation. On the monetary policy front, raising interest rates is an obvious measure to keep down the rate of price increases. The AD/AS model is the reverse of that shown in figures 8.7 and 8.9 (see self-assessment task below). Unfortunately all of these policies have the unpopular side effect of reducing output and increasing unemployment.

In recent years the UK government has had as its principal economic objective, that of stabilising the rate of inflation. This has been necessary for it to meet its macroeconomic objectives (as outlined in section 7) and the convergence criteria set for Economic and Monetary Union (EMU) (see section 12). Conservative and Labour governments have turned away from fiscal measures to control inflation; the consequence is that monetary policy in the form of regular changes in interest rates has been the means of controlling inflation. This task is in the hands of the specially created Monetary Policy Committee which since 1997 has been given a target rate of 2.5 per cent per annum. Their response was initially to raise interest rates in small cautious steps. Inevitably, as table 9.3 shows, this led to an upward movement of exchange rates against the US dollar and major European currencies. Good news for UK holiday-makers but not good news for exporters! It was only when the inflation rate was seen to be reaching its target that interest rates were reduced to a low of 4 per cent by the end of 2001 (see also section 7).

The only effective long-run policy of reducing the price level, avoiding the above problems, is to use supply-side policies to expand aggregate supply. Such policies, as mentioned on numerous occasions, are designed to improve international competitiveness and economic efficiency. Like all supply-side policies, they are very slow to have any measurable impact.

Policies to promote economic growth

Economic growth is an objective in all modern economies as, through growth, living standards can improve as more goods and services become available to the population. To achieve this is difficult and the effects of policies to promote growth are by no means certain. One thing that economists do agree, though, is that an increase in the quality and quantity of factors of production is essential if a positive rate of growth is to be achieved through an outward shift of the PPC (see figure 1.4).

It follows from the analysis of actual growth and potential growth in section 7 that the two main factors contributing to the latter are:

◆ an increase in the quantity of resources available;
◆ an increase in the efficiency with which these resources are being used, for example through increased labour productivity and advances in technology.

One of the most important ways to foster economic growth is to increase labour productivity. In other words, the amount of goods and services produced per worker must increase. This can be achieved by making the capital stock more efficient, either by replacing old outdated machinery and buildings by improved new ones or expanding the stock with new efficient capital. Alternatively, it can be achieved by making the labour force more efficient through education and training as we discussed earlier.

In modern economies, it is essential that improved technology through better equipment, improved organisation and management is used to achieve this important objective. It can, though, be a difficult process not least because the introduction of new technology invariably seems to lead to job losses and unemployment. One can see this process quite clearly in activities such as banking and retailing as well as in manufacturing where robots and mechanised production have taken over from process workers.

How best governments can achieve growth is a complex matter and subject to certain disagreement amongst economists. On the one hand, policies can focus on the demand side, in particular to create conditions where demand is strong, firms wish to invest and potential output is achieved. On the other hand, supply-side policies can be used to increase potential output through measures such as those referred to earlier. The disagreement really centres on how best to implement such policies. Some economists argue very strongly that this has to be done through the free market; others are not convinced, arguing that planning and control can best lead to the high levels of investment needed to sustain long-term growth.

Policies to affect the balance of payments

In recent years the balance of payments in the UK, including the balance of trade, has been rather low key and down-played as a policy objective. The reasons for this are quite complex and complicated by the UK's membership of the European Union (EU). The flow of capital in response to interest rate changes has had an important bearing on the exchange rate. As a result, if the exchange rate is 'too high', and the balance of trade in goods and services is out of balance, a massive deficit is caused by increasing volumes of imports from the rest of the EU and the rest of the world (see section 10). In such circumstances, firms in the UK will find it difficult to export goods, output will be affected and workers made unemployed. Under such circumstances, the government finds it necessary to consider policies that affect the exchange rate in order to move a deficit on the current balance of trade away towards a more balanced position.

In theory, the most effective way to redress this situation is to apply fiscal and monetary measures to depress the economy by cutting aggregate demand. So, if consumer spending and capital investment are cut back, imports will fall. In other words, UK consumers will buy less French wine and fewer German cars, less sports clothing from China and Taiwan and firms will cut back on purchases of machinery from the USA. Imports of raw materials should also fall as there will be less domestic output being produced. The shift of the AD curve to the left will be indicative of a rise in unemployment. Such policies are unpopular and do nothing to enhance the 'feel good' factor which politicians openly like to promote.

Otherwise the possible policies to address balance of payments problems are long-run supply-side ones, which seek to improve the efficiency and competitiveness of the UK economy. These imply making factories and services more efficient, cutting costs, improving the quality and design of products, putting more effort into marketing and after-sales service and so on. This is a long and slow process, carried out against the background of a global economy where all other countries are following the same set of procedures.

Self-assessment tasks

1 Look back at figure 8.7. Re-draw this to show how a shift to the left of AD affects the equilibrium position. Briefly say what this means, how it might apply and what are the consequences for the economy.

2 The level of capital investment in the UK is currently below that of many other EU countries. Briefly explain what fiscal, monetary and supply-side policies could be used to improve this position and how these might be represented on the AD/AS model.

Summary

In this section we have recognised that:

- Fiscal policy, which involves the use of taxation and government spending, has an important bearing on the level of aggregate demand in the economy. It can also affect aggregate supply.

- Monetary policy involves the manipulation of the supply of money or interest rates in the economy.

- Supply-side policies are longer term in their effects and their outcome is less certain than fiscal and monetary measures. They are designed to affect the total output in the economy.

- All three types of policy tend to be in operation at any one particular time.

- The exchange rate in simple terms is the price of one currency in terms of another currency.

- The AD/AS model can be used to show how fiscal, monetary and supply-side policies can affect the level of employment, the rate of inflation, economic growth and the balance of payments in the economy.

Key words

Definitions of Key words can be found in the Glossary on page 240.

broad money	government bond
crowding out	money supply
deregulation	narrow money
exchange rate	unemployment trap

10 Structure and essential determinants of international transactions

On completion of this section you should be able to:

➤ recognise the similarities and differences between internal and external trade

➤ understand the main types of goods and services traded internationally, the main destinations of UK exports and the main sources of UK imports

➤ describe the broad impact of EU membership on the pattern of UK international trade

➤ explain the gains from international trade in general terms

➤ understand the meaning and advantages of free trade

➤ explain tariff and non-tariff methods of protection using relevant diagrams

➤ discuss the arguments for and against protection

The UK and the international economy

Many of the goods and services produced in the UK will not be consumed by domestic households. They will be exported to satisfy the wants of consumers in foreign economies. Similarly, many British consumers' wants will be satisfied by goods and services which are produced abroad and imported into the UK. In addition, many UK firms will import capital goods from abroad, just as some British firms will produce capital goods for export. Buying and selling goods and services across national frontiers is called international trade. It is based upon international specialisation and has led to a tremendous growth in world living standards over the years. Because goods and services are traded across national frontiers, different currencies are involved and it is necessary at some stage to exchange one currency for another. This takes place in the foreign exchange market. The flows of currencies to pay for imports and exports of goods and services are recorded in a country's balance of payments account. In addition to recording receipts and payments for exports and imports of goods and services, the balance of payments account also records international flows of currency for other reasons. These include, for example, flows of funds for investment in other economies and the receipt of income from these investments (see section 7).

Overseas trade and investment is particularly important to the UK economy. In 2001, the population was 59.8 million which represents only about 1 per cent of the world's population and yet the United Kingdom was the fifth largest trading nation, accounting for around 5 per cent of world trade in goods and services. This is a considerable decline since the mid nineteenth century when Great Britain was responsible for over 25 per cent of the world's exports of goods and services, but this declining share has only occurred as a result of the tremendous expansion in world trade over the years as other countries have begun to import and export goods and services. The volume of goods and services exported by the UK economy continues on a steady upward trend.

Just as the UK remains an important nation in international trade, so trade has had a very great impact upon the UK economy. The significance of international trade can be assessed by the degree of 'openness' of an economy. Openness is measured by the proportion of total final expenditure in an economy which is taken up by sales abroad of goods and services.

In 2001, this proportion was about 33 per cent of GDP for the UK compared with 10 per cent for the

United States and 9 per cent for Japan. This means that although the United States and Japan are responsible for more exports than the UK, they are relatively more 'closed' economies. Consequently, international trade is less significant for the average US or Japanese citizen than it is for a citizen of the UK. This is emphasised by the fact that the UK exports more per head of the population than both the United States and Japan.

The UK is also the world's second biggest foreign investor with a higher percentage of overseas investment relative to Gross Domestic Product than any other leading economy. It should also be noted that the United Kingdom, as a major economy within the European Union, is part of the world's largest established trading group with access to a market of over 390 million citizens (see unit 4). Through its membership of the European Union, the United Kingdom has significant influence on world international trade policy.

The pattern of UK trade

The United Kingdom was the first industrial nation and the first economy to take off into self-sustained economic growth. The traditional pattern of UK trade was related to this early industrialisation and the fact that much trade was with former or existing colonies. Although the UK was deficient in certain raw materials, it was able to import these from the Empire, which also provided a market for British manufactured goods. Although the trade in goods section might be in deficit, the trade in services was often sufficient to provide a surplus on the Current Account. There was an inevitability about this pattern of trade given Britain's political dominance of her Empire and the fact that new entrants to world markets in the second half of the nineteenth century, such as the United States and Germany, imposed tariffs on British imports to protect their infant industries.

So the traditional pattern of UK trade was the import of raw materials and foodstuffs from the Colonies and the export of manufactured products. Trading links with Europe developed gradually during the twentieth century, but in 1955 the rest of Europe was the destination for only about 25 per cent of UK exports, and approximately 25 per cent of imports. By contrast the less-developed economies, including the Colonies, accounted for just

	Value (£ millions)			%	
	Exports	Imports	Balance	Exports	Imports
European Union	97,293	103,719	−6,436	58.7	53.9
Other Western Europe	6,514	10,629	−4,115	3.9	5.5
North America	27,872	28,116	−244	16.8	14.6
Other OECD countries	9,159	15,934	−6775	5.5	8.3
Oil exporting countries	5,552	3,269	2283	3.4	1.7
Rest of the World	19,286	30,765	−11,479	11.7	16.0

Table 10.1 Distribution of trade in goods, 1999
Source: Office for National Statistics, 2002.

under 40 per cent of both imports and exports.

In more recent years (see table 10.1) there have been very significant changes in the United Kingdom's pattern of trade:

◆ The greatest proportion of trade is now with other developed economies. Other countries in the OECD took over 80 per cent of UK exports and supplied 83 per cent of imports into the UK in 1997.

◆ Imported manufactures have taken an increasing share of the domestic market in recent years. Import penetration ratios in some products have risen to over 90 per cent. (The United Kingdom has not had a surplus in manufacturing since 1982.)

At the same time:

◆ The surplus on trade in services continues to be important. In 2001 the surplus was £11,700m, reflecting large surpluses in insurance, financial services and other business services.

◆ Manufactured goods continue to provide the biggest proportion of exports. The balance of trade in manufactured goods has deteriorated since 1997, reaching over £20,000m in 2001. The UK does though have reasonable surpluses for trade in chemicals, beverages and oil.

Causes of the changing pattern of UK trade

The changing pattern of UK trade in recent years has been caused by two very closely related issues:

1 The entry of the UK into the European Economic Community (EEC) in 1973 and the development of this community into an Economic Union (EU).

2 The decline in the competitiveness of the UK manufacturing sector, leading to extensive deindustrialisation.

In assessing the significance of these changes, we need to consider how each has affected the pattern of UK trade. We then need to consider how this has affected resource allocation and to consider whether resources are put to their best use. This is known as optimal resource allocation. Another way of expressing this is that we need to consider whether the UK's pattern of trade reflects comparative advantage which is predicted to lead to maximum economic welfare. We then need to consider the costs and benefits of a movement to optimal resource allocation to assess whether, on balance, the changes have been beneficial to the United Kingdom economy and its people.

The gains from international trade

It is generally acknowledged today that international trade based upon specialisation and exchange will lead to an increase in world economic welfare. The guiding principle in trading relationships between nations is that trade should be based upon co-operation and any barriers to trade which exist should be removed. Several organisations such as the World Trade Organisation (WTO) exist to promote free trade between nations. Government support for free trade between nations has not always existed. In the seventeenth and eighteenth centuries, the dominant view was that nations should aim for self-sufficiency and an excess of exports over imports. This body of thought was known as mercantilism and was based upon the idea that a nation's wealth and power were directly related to the gold and silver circulating in the economy and in the state's reserves. The greater the gold and silver in circulation, the greater the prosperity of the citizens of the country.

Modelling the gains from international trade is discussed in depth in OCR's A2 modules. For the time being, in general terms, international trade, free of restrictions, provides various important benefits for participants. These include:

◆ *Benefits of specialisation*. Trade allows countries to specialise in those commodities that they can produce most efficiently. This produces important gains in terms of cost and resource use compared with when each country is trying to provide everything that they need.

◆ *Wider choice of commodities* for consumers. International trade gives consumers a much wider choice of food (one has only to visit a good supermarket to see this) and other items. It also provides consumers and businesses with the latest range of products that are being made in the global economy

◆ *Closer links between economies*. International trade makes countries more economically dependent upon each other, and, in turn, this can promote better political understanding

◆ *Best use of scarce resources*. This is the outcome of specialisation. Waste is minimised and the world's scarce productive resources are used in their most efficient way. This arguably is the most important gain from the economist's perspective.

Free trade and protection

Since free trade leads to a rise in world economic welfare, why should any country adopt policies which prevent free trade? Sometimes policies are adopted which distort market forces in order to give a competitive advantage to the domestic industry of an economy. Such policies are called **protectionist** policies because they provide some degree of protection from foreign competition. There are various methods of protecting domestic industry.

Tariffs

A **tariff** is a tax on imports. It can be either specific, that is so much per unit or *ad valorem*, which is a percentage of the price. Like all indirect taxes, tariffs have the impact of reducing the supply and raising the equilibrium price of the import. This gives a competitive advantage to home-produced goods and services, which become more attractive to consumers, resulting in a fall in imports.

Consider the economy in figure 10.1. If it did not engage in world trade, consumers would pay price P

A modern UK-registered container vessel
Source: Bibby Line Group.

and consume quantity Q. This would be determined by the domestic supply and demand for the commodity. If the economy engaged in international trade, then consumers would benefit from international specialisation. World supply is shown as supply (world). Under these circumstances prices would fall to P_1. Consumption of the good would rise from Q to Q_4. At this price, however, only Q_1 would be supplied by the domestic producers. This means that domestic production has fallen from Q to Q_1. Lower-cost overseas producers have free access to the market, which has benefited consumers, but domestic producers have

suffered, leading to a fall in employment in the industry. The imposition of a tariff, like all indirect taxes, would shift the supply curve upwards. This would increase the price to domestic consumers from P_1 to P_2. Production by domestic producers would increase from Q_1 to Q_2. Some jobs in the domestic economy would be saved.

Clearly, tariffs distort market forces and prevent consumers from benefiting from all the advantages of international specialisation and trade.

Quotas

Quotas are restrictions on the maximum quantity of imports. Their effect will be to reduce the supply of imports on the domestic market. This will lead to a higher equilibrium price than would occur in a free market. Just as with tariffs the impact is to prevent the domestic consumer from benefiting from all the advantages of international trade. One difference is that, whereas the government gains revenue as a result of tariffs, with quotas the increased price paid by consumers results in the foreign firm which supplied the imports earning higher profits. One answer might be for the government to sell licences to foreign firms to allow them to sell some allocation of the quota on the domestic market. The prospect of raised profits would ensure a market for the import licences.

Although tariffs and quotas are the most widely used methods of protection, two others can be noted. These are:

- ◆ **Exchange control**. Through this governments seek to prevent excessive spending on imports by legally restricting the amount of foreign currency that is available to pay for imported goods.
- ◆ Export subsidies are a type of hidden protection in so far as they give an unfair competitive advantage to domestic producers, allowing them to reduce their prices below the free market equilibrium.

The above four methods of protection are sometimes called **expenditure switching policies** since they aim to switch expenditure, domestic and foreign, to the output of goods and services of the economy that imposes them.

Let us conclude by discussing the arguments for and against protection. It is often argued by developed and developing economies that protection is justified when:

1 *There is a need to safeguard employment in the*

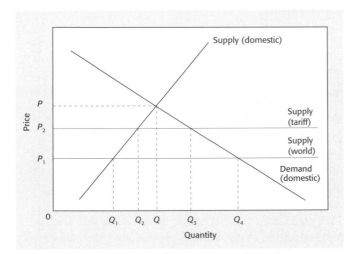

Figure 10.1 The effects of a tariff

domestic economy. This argument has certainly been advanced over the years for the UK economy, especially to stem **de-industrialisation**. The absolute and relative loss of manufacturing jobs has been taking place since the mid-1960s when over 11m people were employed in manufacturing. By 2002, this figure was well below 4m, less than 20 per cent of the working population.

2 *There is disequilibrium in the balance of payments.* As referred to in section 9, fiscal and monetary policies can be used to try to prevent consumers purchasing imports. **Expenditure dampening** policies such as raising income taxes and interest rates may have a short-term impact but in the long term, the root cause of the disequilibrium remains. In such cases, to prevent the drain of foreign currency, it is often argued that protection is justified.

3 *There is a need to prevent unfair competition.* This often occurs through **dumping**, whereby producers sell goods in an overseas market at below the cost of production, whilst consumers in the home market have to pay a higher price. The purpose behind this might be to destroy a competitor or gain market share with a view to increasing prices once the competition has been removed.

4 *There is a need to set up a new industry.* Setting up a new or **infant industry**, particularly in developing economies, can be quite difficult due to competition from long-established, powerful competitors that are experienced in global markets.

There are seemingly sound arguments for countries seeking to protect their domestic markets from the full force of the competition. These arguments though must be seen in the light of the earlier arguments that have been put forward for multilateral free trade. The economist's role in this debate is to assess the respective costs and benefits; in particular, these should be evaluated in terms of world resource allocation and consumer welfare.

World trade in the twenty-first century

The reality of international trade is that it is far from being free of restrictions (see self-assessment task for example). The latest round of talks between WTO members, scheduled to finish in 2005, has brought considerable hope that protectionist tariffs will be reduced in the future, so producing increased liberalisation in the global economy. In particular, restrictions on trade between developed and developing economies are being addressed in the light of what are positive mutual benefits for all 142 WTO members.

Self-assessment task

Read the newspaper editorial below and then answer the questions that follow.

Free trade is fair

'Fair trade, not free trade' is the banner carried by protestors outside the World Trade Organisation conference. It is code for quotas, tariffs and prohibitions. So when Britain's man in Seattle blathers approvingly about 'fair trade', it matters. By adopting the language of the protectionists, Stephen Byers, the DTI Secretary, advertised before the hard bargaining had even started that this Government will not exert leadership to defeat obscurantism. Nor will President Clinton, who is backing away from America's commitment to free trade in order to appease the rioters and their friends in the media. If the two powers that built the world's open trading system – and are still seen as its custodians, even if Britain has surrendered trade policy to the EU – do not have the gumption to face down Dyke Action and the Raging Grannies, God help us.

Free trade does not happen of its own accord. The natural condition of the world is protectionist: the gains of increased commerce are spread widely, and to some degree invisibly, while the losses are concentrated heavily in sectors that mobilise quickly for political action – as French farmers and Detroit's motor industry have shown in their time. Trade barriers are rarely reduced without a Herculean effort by far-sighted leaders, acting in concert, at grand summits like this one in Seattle. So far, it looks as if the current generation of leaders is incapable of making such an effort.

The European Union is seeking to do little more than protect its ruinous system of farm subsidies, while suggesting otherwise with disingenuous demands for a comprehensive agenda. President Clinton – already electioneering for Al Gore – has abruptly changed US trade policy in a sop to the trade unions, calling for the WTO to extend its power into the area of labour rights.

Mr Clinton is making emotive noises about 'child labour', but the real issue is cheap labour, which is the one competitive advantage left to poor countries. The gambit is rightly regarded as an invidious form of rich world protectionism by most of the WTO's 134 members. If pressed, it will wreck the meeting.

It is lamentable that the governments of the world's richest countries cannot find the political will – in the easiest of conditions, at the height of a long economic boom – to uphold the system that made them so rich. The best that can now be expected from this miserable summit is a fudge that does no damage.

Source: Daily Telegraph, 3 December 1999.

(a) What is meant by 'fair trade'?

(b) Discuss why the EU is reluctant to reduce its quotas, tariffs and prohibitions on trade with developing economies.

(c) On completion of this unit, you should be able to answer all questions in the examination paper below.

Past experience though has shown that what may be good in principle does not always turn out to be the case. Two important events appear to have acted as a catalyst this time around for more liberalisation. These are:

◆ The slowdown in the world economy following the 9/11 terrorist attacks on New York. This served to show yet again how the well-being of the global economy is dependent on the health of the US economy and that how, increasingly, the prosperity of all economies is very closely interrelated.

◆ The admission of China to the WTO. Given a sluggish global economy, it makes a lot of economic and political sense to include this powerful trading country, with an emerging domestic market, in the WTO group.

◆ The World Bank have concluded that if all trade barriers are removed, global income will rise by almost £2,000 billion and over 300 million people will see their own incomes rise above the poverty level. This surely has to be a target that must be realised.

Self-assessment task

On completion of this unit you should be able to answer all the questions in the examination paper below.

Boom, Boom...Bust?
A Tale of Two Economies

In 2001, for the first time in eight years, the annual change in real GDP of the United States (US) economy was negative. As the domestic US economy experienced a downturn, the number of people out of work increased. The Federal Reserve, the US central bank, reacted to the decline in economic activity by cutting its interest rate to just 2 per cent in October 2001, the lowest level for forty years.

In the United Kingdom (UK), the Monetary Policy Committee of the Bank of England responded by reducing its interest rate to 4 per cent. High levels of consumer spending, in particular, were helping to keep UK aggregate demand rising. It was feared that falling business confidence would have a negative effect on consumption and investment, and that aggregate supply, as well as aggregate demand, would be affected by the expected downturn. Compared to the US, the economic performance of the UK was relatively strong at this time but the Bank was concerned that the UK economy would be adversely affected by the US recession.

The table below shows the annual growth rate in real GDP and the average unemployment rate for the US and the UK economies from 1996 to 2001. Here, the US unemployment measure is based on the Labour Force Survey approach, whereas the UK unemployment figure is based on the claimant count.

	UNITED STATES		UNITED KINGDOM	
	% change in real GDP	% unemployment rate	% change in real GDP	% unemployment rate
1996	3.6	5.4	2.6	6.2
1997	4.4	5.0	3.5	5.5
1998	4.3	4.5	2.6	4.7
1999	4.2	4.2	2.3	4.3
2000	5.0	4.0	3.0	3.7
2001	−0.1[1]	4.6[1]	0.6[1]	3.5[1]

Note: [1] forecasts

Table 1: Selected statistics on the US and UK economies, 1996 – 2001

(a) What is meant by the following economic terms as they appear in the text:
   ◆ investment; (2)
   ◆ aggregate supply; (2)
   ◆ recession? (2)

(b) ◆ What is meant by 'real GDP' (see table)? (2)
   ◆ Use the data in the table to compare what happened to real GDP in the US and the UK economies between 2000 and 2001. (4)

(c) ◆ Describe what is meant by the 'claimant count' measure of unemployment. (2)
   ◆ To what extent is it possible to compare the unemployment rates between the US and UK economies as shown in the table? (2)

(d) ◆ Explain how changes in an economy's real GDP would usually be expected to affect its rate of unemployment.
   ◆ To what extent does the data relating to the UK economy (see table) support this relationship? (4)

(e) In 2001, the US Federal Reserve cut interest rates on various occasions, reaching a 40-year low in October.
   ◆ What evidence is there in the table to suggest why these interest rate cuts were made? (2)
   ◆ **Apart from a cut in interest rates**, explain **two** other measures that the US government could have used to stimulate aggregate demand. (6)
   ◆ Using an aggregate demand and aggregate supply diagram, analyse the effect of a **fall** in aggregate demand on an economy. (6)

(f) **Either**
   ◆ discuss the effectiveness of monetary policy in achieving an increase in aggregate demand in an economy, (20)
   Or
   ◆ discuss the alternative policies a government may use to improve a deficit in the balance of payments. (20)

Source: OCR, Paper 2883, June 2002.

Summary

In this section we have recognised that:

- International trade is extremely important for the UK economy.

- The pattern of the UK's trade has changed much over the past 150 years; at the present time it is strongly focused on the EU and on other developed economies.

- Tariffs, quotas, exchange control and export subsidies distort the picture of free trade in the world economy.

- Under certain circumstances, the application of protectionist policies may be appropriate in the short term.

- From a global perspective, multilateral free trade produces the best allocation of the world's scarce resources and the best deal for consumers.

Key words

Definitions of Key words can be found in the Glossary on page 240.

de-industrialisation	import penetration ratio
dumping	infant industry
exchange control	international trade
expenditure dampening policies	mercantilism
	protection
expenditure switching policies	quota
	self-sufficiency
free trade	tariff

Preparing for examinations

On completion of this section you should be able to:

➤ Know how to plan your work and how to use your study time effectively before an examination

➤ Know what sort of examination questions to expect and how to apply a simple method to understand what they mean

➤ Know what OCR Economics examiners are looking for when marking your examination script

➤ Know the most common errors students make in Economics examinations

Introduction

In many respects this is the most important section in the book. To make a sporting comparison, the examination is your FA Cup Final, your Wimbledon tie break or your Superbowl decider. If you approach it in an appropriate way, it should be the means by which you realise the grade you were expecting, consistent with helping you achieve a result based on the effort you have put into your work. For some students, though, this is not the case. It can be like missing a penalty in the last minute or serving a double fault at match point. When this happens it is very unfortunate and examiners do not derive pleasure in witnessing it. For many students who are in this situation it is *not* that:

- they have failed to complete the work for the module;
- they have not understood the main concepts involved.

The principal cause of under performance or even failure can be bad examination technique. Experience has shown over and over again that some students make basic errors in their Economics examinations. The consequence of these errors is that they can make at least a grade difference in the final assessment or, in some cases, the difference between a pass grade and an unclassified result.

These common faults are explained at the end of this section. But before you get to this, it is important that you know what you need to do to succeed in OCR AS Economics. The seeds for success are sown well before you enter the examination room. The key to success is preparation! A well-used and highly relevant phrase for you to remember is:

'A FAILURE TO PREPARE IS A PREPARATION TO FAIL'

For many years, this was on the office wall of Howard Wilkinson, the former Leeds United Manager, and one of the longest serving football club managers in the UK. Why not put it on your wall? But, if you do, remember to practise what it says.

How to plan your work and study effectively

Get into the study habit and plan ahead

As a student, study is something you do from the first day of your AS course. The process of study involves the gradual accumulation of knowledge and should also include its regular review. Revision is not something you should do just before an examination. *Make study a habit. Make revision a habit.*

Each of us has our own preferences for when and where to study in an effective manner. Some people are most receptive to study in mornings; others prefer to work late and 'burn the midnight oil'. Think about what is best for yourself and do it.

At school or college, *use your time effectively*, particularly if you are in a situation where you have only to attend for time-tabled classes. Think about how much additional time there is at your disposal; by all means have a social life, but reserve regular periods for your own private study *and do it*. In other words, build breaks into your study time – not the other way around. So, get into a routine of regular study. Have a set time and place to work, and stick to it.

Adaptation from an original drawing by Emily Bamford

A second important aspect of time management is that of *planning*. As a student, this is something you should try to do. It is particularly important where you are taking AS subjects on a staged basis, as there is only about four and half months time between the start of teaching and you taking the first examination. So, here are a few simple things you should do:

- Read through your class notes on a *daily* basis; follow this by reading about the subject matter in this text. You will also find it useful to use some of the other texts on the recommended reading list, particularly to obtain other examples and applications of economic concepts.

- Make a *weekly* plan of what you have to do and what you have actually done. Tick off items as you complete them. Table 1 shows an example of a simple planner you might like to use.
- Above all, *think and plan ahead*. Find out when mock examinations are to be held; know precisely when your actual examinations will be taking place.

And remember what was said earlier: 'A failure to prepare is a preparation to fail.'

Week commencing 16 October	Lesson topic	Homework due	Study tasks
Monday			Homework for 19 October completed
Tuesday	Price elasticity of demand – definition, calculations, meaning		N R
Wednesday			
Thursday	Business relevance of price elasticity of demand. Other elasticities – income and cross elasticities	Essay on how prices are determined	N
Friday			
Saturday			
Sunday			OCR assessment task from Section 2 completed
Outstanding work for next week	Read up about topics from Thursday's lesson. Look at past papers for other questions on elasticities of demand.		

Table 1 A daily and weekly study planner pro-forma
Notes: N – notes checked through
R – topic read up in text books

A few hints on how to study effectively

Each of us has a preferred study environment where we can work in an effective and efficient way. For most of us it is likely to be a bedroom or a school library where the distractions going on around us can at least be shut off for an hour or two. The best time for study may also vary – much will depend upon your family circumstances and how you can arrange to study in relation to these and other commitments on your time. Whatever the best time, the following advice should help you.

◆ Put yourself in a position where you can *concentrate on your work*. This is most unlikely to happen if your CD player is turned on or there is your favourite television programme being broadcast in the same room.

◆ The *attention span* of most people is 40–60 minutes. After such a period, have a drink and a rest, maybe watch a short television programme before studying for a further period.

◆ When reading, *make notes* on what you have read and incorporate these into your class notes on a particular topic. You will also find it useful to do the self-assessment exercises in this book and work through sample examination questions on a topic. Writing and working in this way greatly enhances your understanding of a topic. *Do not just read material on its own* – the problem with this approach to study is that you will very quickly forget what you have read. The big advantage also of making notes is that they will be there for future revision when you need them.

◆ Once you have completed the study of a particular topic, condense your notes down onto a *revision card*, which you will find invaluable for use shortly before examinations. An example of such notes is shown in figure 1.

So, it is not so much how long you study but how effective you are in your studying. Make sure you use your time effectively so that you *feel in control of your own learning experience.*

And remember: 'A failure to prepare is a preparation to fail.'

Figure 1 Example of revision card

The OCR examinations

All AS Economics question papers consist of themes or a case study from which a series of questions are drawn. These represent a concise, self-contained economic situation indicative of the subject content of the module. The Self-assessment tasks include many examples of the kinds of questions and topics you can expect in OCR's examination papers. In addition the appendix to this section shows some typical examples of complete current specimen examination papers.

There are two types of theme or case study. These are:

1 Those which are 'synthetic' in so far as they have been produced specifically for examination purposes. This type will only be used on the Market System paper and when used will have been derived from an actual situation, involving real economic problems and issues.

2 Those which contain 'actual' or 'real world' information, which is reproduced in the same way as it appears in the original source or some adaptation of this. The other specimen papers are of this form. All examination papers have an actual theme or

themes, drawn from the subject content of the module. When you read through the paper, you should think carefully and deliberately about the following:

(a) Look for the economic theory or concepts around which the material has been compiled and from which questions have been derived. If the paper contains data, think about how these concepts are embedded in the data.

(b) Look at the title of the material – this may well give you some clues.

(c) Where the case study contains real data, look for any dates, labels or footnotes and if there is a stated source. Again, these may help you to understand its context. If the data are in the form of a table, look for any trends and important features. Questions are likely to be drawn from these. (Refer back to the Introduction for more advice.)

(d) If the case study contains a chart or diagrams, look to see if you can identify any patterns or outstanding features. If there are, then there is likely to be a question on these. (Again, refer back to the Introduction.)

Once you have done these simple yet fundamental tasks, you will feel more confident to answer the questions that follow.

Self-assessment task

Spend ten minutes reading through each of the appended question papers. When you have done this, ask yourself the following questions:

(a) What is the key economic concept or concepts in the paper?

(b) Is this confirmed by the title? Or is the title of little relevance?

(c) Can you identify any important features in the data provided?

(d) Do you recognise how these features can support your knowledge of the key concept or concepts? Make a few notes on each.

Examination questions

Types of question

The appendix contains specimen question papers for each of the three OCR AS Economics units. These papers contain the following general types of question:

- short answer questions;
- questions where continuous prose is required;
- questions which require you to interpret the data provided in the case study.

In all instances the mark allocation is clearly shown in brackets. This indicates how many marks are allocated to each part out of the total marks available for the examination.

Short answer questions require short answers. It is important for you to remember this. In some cases, the answer required may be no more than a single word, a phrase or a number. In other cases, it may be a diagram with a sentence or two of explanation. What is required for a particular question should be clear from:

- the precise wording of the question;
- the marks allocated to it, relative to others on the question paper.

Questions where continuous prose is required will always be those at the end of the set of questions in a particular examination paper. For example, part (e) on the Market System specimen paper is this type of question. In the case of questions which have 12 marks available, two or three paragraphs of writing is normally needed to answer the question effectively. This should broadly equate to around 15 minutes of writing time.

Questions which require you to interpret the data provided. The use of data and their interpretation is a very important part of the economist's 'tool kit'. Some of the basic data handling skills you need were outlined in the Introduction. Each of OCR's AS papers may contain some data, either in the text or in a separate table, graph or diagram.

In all AS units, these data will be actual information, usually from a published source, or data which have been compiled specifically for the examination.

Whatever the type of question, all of the AS units are seeking to examine your knowledge and understanding of the material. It is therefore very important for you to use this material as directed in your answers and draw upon it consistently throughout your examination script. This skill is a very important one for you to acquire.

The wording of questions

A lot of care, thought and attention goes into the final production of all OCR examination papers. So, when you sit an examination, it is important to appreciate that the questions which are on the examination paper have been set by an examiner who is requiring you *to answer these questions.* Put another way, examination papers never contain questions such as:

Write all you know about ... or:

Write as much as you can remember about ...

Unfortunately, this point is not always appreciated by some students.

All examination questions contain two very important instructions. These are called:

- *Directive words* – these words indicate what form the answer should take. For example, it could be in the form of a description, a discussion, an explanation or merely a statement. These words are there for a purpose, namely that they have been used by the examiners to say what they are looking for (in skill terms when you answer a particular question).
- *Content words* – these are much more diverse in nature since they cover the whole of the subject area of the AS syllabus. Their aim is to make clear to you, the candidate, what is the focus of the question being set, and indeed, what examiners expect you to write about.

Table 2 shows a list of key directive words which will be used in OCR AS Economics examination questions. *You should study these carefully and understand what each means.* You will then appreciate that a question which asks:

Define price elasticity of demand

is not the same as

Explain what is meant by price elasticity of demand

is not the same as

Discuss the relevance of price elasticity of demand in business

Directive word	What it means	Where you can expect it to be used
Calculate	Work out using the information provided	All AS units, usually in the early parts of the questions
Define	Give the exact meaning	
Describe	Give a description of	
Give (an account of)	As 'describe'	
Give (an example of)	Give a particular example	
How	In what way or ways	
Illustrate	Give examples/diagram	
Outline	Describe without detail	
State	Make clear	
Summarise	Give main points, without detail	
Which	Give a clear example/state what	
Analyse	Set out the main points	All AS units
Apply	Use in a specific way	
Compare	Give similarities and differences	
Explain	Give clear reasons or make clear	
Account for	Give reasons for	
Consider	Give your thoughts about	
Assess	Show how important something is	All AS units but usually in the *later* parts of questions
Comment upon	Give your reasoned opinions on	
Criticise	Give an opinion, but support it with evidence	
Discuss	Give the important arguments, for and against	
Evaluate	Discuss the importance of, making some attempt to weight your opinions	

Table 2 Key directive words

A simple method for understanding and interpreting examination questions
Short answer questions

The appendix to this section gives typical OCR AS question papers for each of the three units. You will now find some valuable advice on how you can understand what the questions mean and therefore, how you can be expected to answer them.

Look at the Market System specimen paper. The early questions are asking you for some basic knowledge of the unit. For example:

(a) (i) Define the term opportunity cost [2]

If you look at table 2, then 'define' means 'give the exact meaning'. In other words, the question requires you to 'give the exact meaning of the term opportunity cost'. The allocation of two marks to this question indicates that this task requires a short answer of one or possibly two sentences.

So, if you refer back to section 1, you can find the information you need.

Moving on, the next question is:

(ii) Explain how opportunity cost could be applied to a family deciding on whether to visit a particular theme park such as Chessington's World of Adventures. [2]

Looking at table 2, you will see that 'explain' is in the second block of words. This indicates that the task is that bit more challenging than part (i), and requires you to 'give clear reasons or make clear' in this case how opportunity cost could be applied to a family deciding on whether to visit a particular theme park such as Chessington's World of Adventures. The wording of the question, and being in the same part as the previous question, is a clear indication that both questions are linked.

So, refer back to your definition of opportunity cost and apply it to explain this situation. A competent answer is one that refers to the monetary cost or benefit foregone in visiting another attraction rather than Chessington. The two marks indicate that as before only one or two sentences will be needed.

In this simple way you should be able to know and interpret what you need to do to make an effective response to short answer questions.

Questions where continuous prose is required

Again look at the specimen paper for the Market System unit. Part (e) is typical of this type of question. Twelve marks, almost one quarter of those available, have been allocated to this question. You should try to write for about 15 minutes. If you want to do well, then a good, clear answer to this question is essential. So, let us take a close look at it.

> (e) Chessington's World of Adventures aims to maximise its profits each year; economists have stated that this is not the case with most smaller family-owned theme parks.
>
> Discuss whether profit maximisation is the **only** objective for all firms in the theme park industry.

Going back to table 2, you will see that 'discuss' means 'give important arguments for and against'. This requirement is further supported in the question by the bold type used to emphasise 'only'. This type of question is to be found as the last one in all units – it is important that you structure your answer in such a way that alternative arguments are being clearly put forward and discussed.

Figure 2 shows a simple but effective method that you can use to understand this type of question. Refer back to section 3 for content details.

If you do this then you have the basis for a good, meaningful answer to the question: you will also have a logical structure to follow when writing your answer.

Questions where a data response is required

AS question papers contain only small amounts of data. These data may be in the form of a separate table or diagram (see the National and International Economy specimen paper) or 'embedded' into the theme material or subsequent questions (see the Market System specimen paper).

Done well, data response questions can be an easy way of achieving marks. You must therefore tackle such questions in a positive way using your knowledge of the five basic data-handling skills stated on page 5. Above all, do not be frightened by such questions – they are invariably straightforward.

Table 1 in the National and International Economy specimen paper contains a simple set of time series data for the UK economy. These data are for two economic variables, the percentage change in real GDP and the percentage unemployment rate. Looking at the table for the first time:

◆ Make sure you have a reasonable idea of what the column headings mean.

◆ Look for the trend in each of the two columns.

◆ Broadly see if you can tell how they are related.

If you spend a couple of minutes doing this you will be able to answer question (b) (ii), assuming of course that you have understood the theoretical relationship between the two variables (in the previous answer).

Glancing at table 1, you can see:

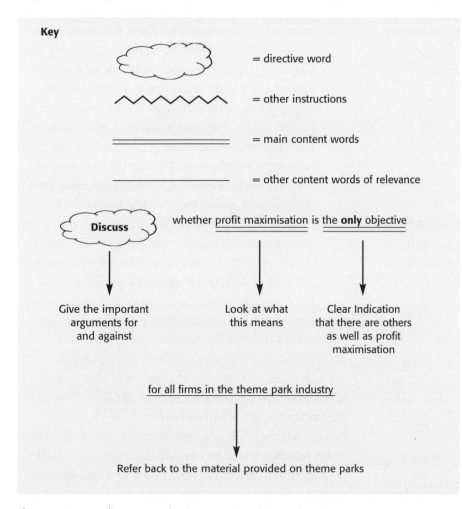

Key

= directive word

= other instructions

= main content words

= other content words of relevance

Discuss whether profit maximisation is the **only** objective

Give the important arguments for and against

Look at what this means

Clear Indication that there are others as well as profit maximisation

for all firms in the theme park industry

Refer back to the material provided on theme parks

Figure 2 How to dissect a continuous prose question

- real GDP (output) is increasing throughout the period;
- unemployment is falling throughout the period;
- there is therefore evidence to indicate that the normal expected theoretical relationship applies.

You might like to quote some broad evidence from the data to enhance your answers. Beyond this, the 'to what extent' directive in the question is telling you that some simple evaluation is needed. For example:

- the relationship between the rate of growth and the unemployment rate is not always proportionate;
- a time lag appears to apply.

Either of these points will be sufficient to meet the question requirement – by including such a statement in your answer you are indicating to the examiner that there are grounds for believing that the normal theoretical relationship does not necessarily apply in full.

How to impress AS economics examiners

Let us start with a few typical comments that OCR examiners will write on some of the examination answers they read:

'Does not answer the question'
'Too vague'
'Misses point of question'
'No application'
'Commentary not made'
'Ignores second aspect of question'

These comments clearly indicate that the candidates have not done what was expected from them in the question. So, the first way to impress any examiner reading your examination scripts is:

To answer the question

In other words, produce an answer as directed by the question. The information above, in particular the simple method for dissecting examination questions, should help you to write your answer in a clear, well-structured manner as directed by the questions. This point cannot be emphasised too much!

There are various other ways in which you might impress an AS examiner. For example:

- *Diagrams* These are very important and a relevant means of economic explanation. Many of the topics you come across in AS Economics can be illustrated by a diagram or by means of an explanation supported by a diagram. You have only to glance at the sections in this book to see this. So, a relevant correctly drawn diagram, used effectively in your answer, will impress an examiner reading your examination script. An example of good technique is shown in figure 3, which is a variation of figure 6.3 in unit 2.

  The diagram shows how the price of theatre tickets will be affected by the introduction of a subsidy. As this indicates, the subsidy will lead to an increase in supply, shifting the supply curve downwards and to the right. The price which theatre goers will have to pay falls from P_1 to P_2 – it does not fall to P_3 as part of the subsidy (that shown between P_3 and P_2) will be retained by the theatre owners to offset the higher costs incurred due to the increase in the number of theatre visits demanded.

- *Current issues and problems* One of the reasons for studying AS Economics is to help you understand some of the things that are taking place around you. So, when you get the opportunity, do so! For example, if you are answering a question on the negative externalities associated with environmental pollution, you might refer to a local case which is known to you or something you have seen in a newspaper or magazine. Most of the topics in the syllabus can be supported by additional up-to-date material, not always found in text books.

- *Refer to things you have read* It follows that there are instances where it would support your answer if you referred to this source material by name, for example an article, an example from a text book or the views of a particular economist. This is clearly only possible in answers where you have to write two or three paragraphs.

Common mistakes made in OCR Economics examinations

In addition to a failure to answer the question, the other main mistakes made by candidates are:

1 A failure to allocate writing time in an appropriate way.
2 Confusion over similar terms.

Taking the specimen examination paper for the National and International Economy (see pages 189–91), 60 minutes is available for this question paper.

You need to spend a few minutes looking at the case study and getting a feel for what the questions mean. Thereafter, allocate your writing time directly in relation to the marks available.

5 minutes (Initial reading)		Scan through the case study. Read the material, highlighting main points; make sure you understand any data and try to pick out basic trends.		

	Approx. minutes			
55 mins (Writing)	10	(a)	(i) (ii) (iii) (iv)	8 marks
	10	(b)	(i)	4 marks
			(ii)	6 marks
	20	(c)	(i)	2 marks
			(ii)	6 marks
			(iii)	7 marks
	15	(d)		12 marks
				45 marks

Try to leave a couple of minutes for	**Final check**; have a go at any parts where it was necessary to move on where a question could not be answered.

Table 3 A simple method for allocating time in an examination

3 Meaningless, wrongly drawn diagrams or diagrams which add nothing to an answer.

Let us conclude this chapter by looking at each in turn.

1 The time available for each AS examination is relatively short – one hour only. You must therefore make sure you allocate your writing time in the examination in a meaningful way.

Table 3 shows how you can do this. The following important principles should be applied:

◆ Roughly speaking, allocate your writing time in direct proportion to the marks available.
◆ Do not exceed the time you have allocated for each part.
◆ If you cannot do a particular question, leave it and

move on to the next part. (You can always return to it later on in the examination if time permits.)

◆ You will only get marks for the questions you answer – your script, though, will always be marked out of the total marks which are available.

2 A second problem in Economics examinations is that,

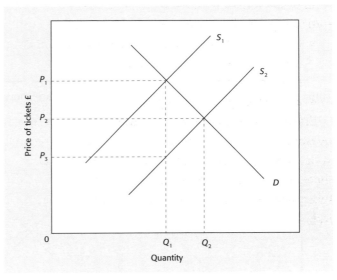

Figure 3 How to use a diagram effectively in your answers
Notes: D – Demand curve for theatre tickets
S$_1$ – Supply curve of theatre tickets
S$_2$ – Supply curve after introduction of subsidy

Topic	Often confused with
elastic demand	inelastic demand
allocative efficiency	productive efficiency
prices	costs
merit goods	public goods
direct taxation	indirect taxation
external costs/benefits	social costs/benefits
real income	nominal income
rate of interest	exchange rates
fiscal policy measures	monetary policy measures
aggregate demand	aggregate supply
balance of trade	balance of payments
income	wealth

Watch out also that you express formulae correctly – in particular elasticity formulae

Table 4 Common errors over terms and topics in the OCR AS Economics specification on occasions, candidates sometimes confuse terms which are similar (in terms of content) or which have similar names (but mean something different). Table 4 contains a few common examples from the AS Economics specification.

3 Finally, a common mistake which candidates often make is in the ways in which they use diagrams in their answers. Common errors are:

◆ to label axes incorrectly or not to label them at all;
◆ to make diagrams too small;
◆ to draw lines and curves incorrectly, usually through being wrongly sloping;
◆ to fail to use a diagram in an answer when asked to do so;
◆ to include a diagram when one is not needed and where it does not enhance an answer at all.

Self-assessment task

Three examples of badly drawn/incorrect diagrams are shown in figure 4. How many improvements can you make to them?

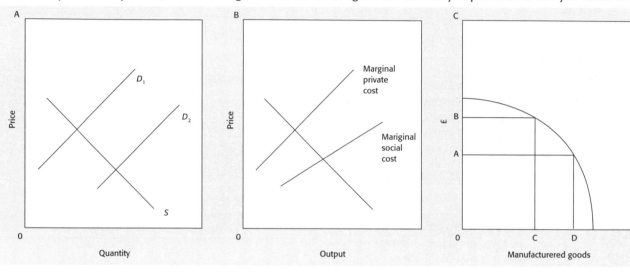

Figure 4 Examples of badly drawn diagrams

Self-assessment task

When you have completed studying each of the three AS units, see if you can do the specimen examination papers which follow on from this section. Do this under examination conditions and in the time allocated.

Remember to think about the matters raised in this section when you are completing this task.

Summary

In this concluding AS section we have established that:

● It is very important for you to be well-organised and to be able to plan ahead if you are to succeed in OCR Economics.

● Revision should be an ongoing process, not just a last-minute activity you carry out just before a written examination.

● OCR's examinations at AS contain a variety of forms of external assessment, with three main types of question.

● Candidates who underperform in examinations have usually not been adequately briefed on the type and style of question.

● A lack of time and an inability to understand the relevance of directive words are the most common causes of underperformance.

Sample examination papers

Pages 182–190 contain copies of typical examination papers that will be set by OCR from June 2003 onwards.

For each examination, you will also be provided with a separate answer booklet. This booklet will contain each question and the marks that have been allocated to it. An amount of space is provided in the answer booklet for you to write your answers. This is broadly in line with the marks available. You should see this as helping you to know how much (or how little) you should write.

All examination papers are of one hour duration. This is not long. It is therefore absolutely essential that you allocate your writing time effectively as suggested in table 3. Do make sure that you attempt the last question and devote an adequate writing time to it. This is very important if you want to get a good mark.

On completion of each unit, you should attempt each of the specimen papers in full. Try to do this under 'examination conditions'. In this way you should have a reasonable idea about how much you know …or indeed whether you will need to do more work on the unit.

OXFORD CAMBRIDGE AND RSA EXAMINATIONS

Advanced Subsidiary GCE

ECONOMICS   **2881**

THE MARKET SYSTEM

Revised Specimen Paper

Additional materials:
    Designated Answer Booklet [2881/AB]

TIME   1 hour

INSTRUCTIONS TO CANDIDATES

Write your name, Centre number and candidate number in the spaces provided on the answer booklet.

Answer **all** questions.

Write all your answers in the separate answer booklet provided.

INFORMATION FOR CANDIDATES

The number of marks is given in brackets [ ] at the end of each question or part question.

The quality of your written communication will be taken into account in marking your answer to the question labelled with an asterisk(*).

The total mark for this paper is 45.

7812/3812/SP/EN/02

_____

This question paper consists of 4 printed pages.

Economics
Revised Specimen Paper 2881

An Industry Riding for a Fall

High investment, stiff competition and the unpredictable British weather mean that theme parks are a rollercoaster sector of the economy. Many companies are struggling to survive in a market which economists claim has now reached saturation point. One of the exceptions is Chessington's World of Adventures, part of the Tussauds Group, owners of the famous waxworks museum along with theme *5* parks at Thorpe Park and Alton Towers. This company now dominates the theme park market.

Chessington's star attractions are the Samurai ride and the more sedate Beanoland, which together cost a massive £4.5m to build. These are the major attractions for the visitors who pay an average of £15 for entrance to a park which *10* can accommodate 15 000 visitors per day.

Economists estimate that most of the smaller family-owned theme parks do not operate at a profit. 'It costs a great deal to build theme parks. This is in addition to labour costs and other operating costs. Despite having loads of visitors, they make little or no return for their owners,' said Simon Lake of ABN Amro. Another *15* economist, Pat Aston of Mintel, said, 'There is little doubt that as a theme park opens new attractions, the demand for visits increases. However, it should be recognised that the London Eye has lured some visitors away from theme parks. Disneyland Paris, despite the cost and journey involved, also plays a part in reducing demand for visits to UK theme parks.' *20*

Source: Daily Telegraph, 19th August 2000 (adapted).

© OCR 2003
Oxford, Cambridge and RSA Examinations

Economics
Revised Specimen Paper 2881

1.(a)(i) Define the term opportunity cost. **[2]**

(ii) Explain how opportunity cost could be applied to a family deciding on whether to visit a particular theme park such as Chessington's World of Adventures. **[2]**

(b) Use a diagram **in each case** to explain how the demand for visits to Chessington's World of Adventures might be affected by

(i) a general increase in household income **[4]**

(ii) the opening of a new leisure attraction such as the London Eye. **[4]**

(c) Chessington's World of Adventures attracts an average of 15 000 visitors per day. Each visitor pays an average ticket price of £15. Research by the company indicates that the estimated price elasticity of demand for visits is (–) 0.4.

(i) What is price elasticity of demand and what does an estimate of (–) 0.4 mean? **[4]**

(ii) Explain **two** factors that might affect the price elasticity of demand for visits to Chessington's World of Adventures. **[4]**

(iii) The company is considering increasing the average ticket price from £15 to £18 but is concerned about the effect that this increase might have on its revenue. What advice can you provide? **[5]**

(d) All theme parks have high fixed costs which might deter new firms from entering the industry. Chessington's Samurai ride, for example, cost £3m to build.

(i) Explain the difference between the fixed and variable costs of the theme park industry. **[4]**

(ii) Excluding the high costs of entry, state and explain **two** other likely barriers to entry into the theme park industry. **[4]**

(e)* Chessington's World of Adventures aims to maximise its profits each year; economists have stated that this is not the case with most smaller, family-owned theme parks.

Discuss whether profit maximisation is the **only** objective for all firms in the theme park industry. **[12]**

OXFORD CAMBRIDGE AND RSA EXAMINATIONS
Advanced Subsidiary GCE

ECONOMICS   **2882**

MARKET FAILURE AND GOVERNMENT INTERVENTION

Revised Specimen Paper

Additional materials:
    Designated Answer Booklet [2882/AB]

TIME   1 hour

INSTRUCTIONS TO CANDIDATES

Write your name, Centre number and candidate number in the spaces provided on the answer booklet.

Answer **all** questions.

Write all your answers in the separate answer booklet provided.

INFORMATION FOR CANDIDATES

The number of marks is given in brackets [ ] at the end of each question or part question.

The quality of your written communication will be taken into account in marking your answer to the question labelled with an asterisk(*).

The total mark for this paper is 45.

7812/3812/SP/EN/02

This question paper consists of 4 printed pages.

Economics
Revised Specimen Paper 2882

Answer **all** parts of this question in the designated answer booklet.

Government and the environment

There are several serious concerns about our environment. These include pollution of various sorts, the effects of global warming and fears over the future of the countryside.

All environmental problems can be seen as examples of market failure. They are problems created by some individuals and groups that impact upon others who are not involved in the decision-making. As such, these problems may require government action if they are to be tackled. The following article considers the Government's recent record in tackling some of these issues.

Promises, promises: has Blair really been a friend of the environment?

When Tony Blair made his final speech to voters before the 1997 general election, the Labour leader promised to put the environment at the 'heart of government'. How has the Government matched up to its early promises?

Fuel prices

The Environment Minister, Michael Meacher, had said the automatic fuel escalator (which significantly raised taxes on petrol each year) was valuable both in persuading   5
people to use public transport and in helping to reduce pollution. Unfortunately, the huge rise in the price of crude oil in 2000 left the Government vulnerable to fuel protests by lorry drivers and farmers. Ministers panicked and opted for cuts in duty on diesel for hauliers without any additional environmental safeguards.

Climate change

Deputy Prime Minister, John Prescott, took a leading role in the agreement at the   10
Kyoto climate summit in 1997 to reduce greenhouse gas emissions that cause global warming. However, by abandoning the fuel duty escalator and pandering to the haulage industry, greenhouse gas emissions are likely to increase.

Wildlife and the countryside

The Countryside and Rights of Way Act introduced the so-called 'right to roam'. This allows visitors to the countryside to walk freely on all footpaths.   15

Nuclear power

Tony Blair has given the nuclear industry strong support since taking office. He believes that the industry offers crucial jobs and skills in the depressed west Cumbrian region.

Renewable energy

It is believed that renewable energy creates less pollution as well as providing a sustainable energy source. A subsidy of £100 million for solar, wind, wave and   20
biomass forms of power generation has recently been announced but many experts claim wind power should be boosted with bigger capital grants.

Source: The Independent, 7th March 2001 [adapted]

Economics
Revised Specimen Paper 2882

1.(a)(i) Define the term 'externality'. **[2]**

   (ii) From the article, identify **two** examples of a negative externality. **[2]**

   (iii) From the article, identify **two** examples of a positive externality. **[2]**

(b) The newspaper article talks about a large increase in fuel prices (lines 4–9).

   (i) Give **one** group who might suffer financial hardship due to a large rise in fuel prices. Explain the reasons for your answer. **[4]**

   (ii) Give **one** type of transport business that might benefit through a large increase in fuel prices. Explain the reasons for your answer. **[4]**

(c) **(i)** State **two** characteristics of 'public goods'. **[2]**

   (ii) How far does the 'right to roam' (line 14) make the countryside more like a public good? **[5]**

(d) **(i)** Define the term 'subsidy'. **[2]**

   (ii) Using a diagram, explain how a government subsidy paid to the renewable energy industry might increase the consumption of renewable energy. **[10]**

(e)* Discuss the advantages and disadvantages to the government in using taxes to improve the quality of the environment. **[12]**

OXFORD CAMBRIDGE AND RSA EXAMINATIONS

Advanced Subsidiary GCE

ECONOMICS   2883

THE NATIONAL AND INTERNATIONAL ECONOMY

Revised Specimen Paper

Additional materials:
  Designated Answer Booklet [2883/AB]

TIME   1 hour

INSTRUCTIONS TO CANDIDATES

Write your name, Centre number and candidate number in the spaces provided on the answer booklet.

Answer **all** questions.

Write all your answers in the separate answer booklet provided.

INFORMATION FOR CANDIDATES

The number of marks is given in brackets [ ] at the end of each question or part question.

The quality of your written communication will be taken into account in marking your answer to the question labelled with an asterisk(*).

The total mark for this paper is 45.

7812/3812/SP/EN/02

This question paper consists of 4 printed pages.

Economics
Revised Specimen Paper 2883

Boom, Boom ... Bust? A Tale of Two Economies

In 2001, for the first time in eight years, the annual change in real GDP of the United States (US) economy was negative. As the domestic US economy experienced a downturn, the number of people out of work increased. The Federal Reserve, the US central bank, reacted to the decline in economic activity by cutting its interest rate to just 2% in October 2001, the lowest level for forty years. *5*

In the United Kingdom (UK), the Monetary Policy Committee of the Bank of England responded by reducing its interest rate to 4%. High levels of consumer spending, in particular, were helping to keep UK aggregate demand rising. It was feared that falling business confidence would have a negative effect on consumption and investment, and that aggregate supply, as well as aggregate demand, would be *10* affected by the expected downturn.

Table 1 below shows the annual growth rate in real GDP and the average unemployment rate for the UK economy from 1996 to 2001. Here, the UK unemployment figure is based on the claimant count.

Source: Daily Telegraph, 19th August 2000 (adapted).

Selected statistics on the UK economy, 1996–2001

	UNITED KINGDOM	
	% change in real GDP	% unemployment rate
1996	2.6	6.2
1997	3.5	5.5
1998	2.6	4.7
1999	2.3	4.3
2000	3.0	3.7
2001	0.6^1	3.5^1

Note: [1] forecasts

Source: The World in 2002, economist.com

Table 1

1. (a) What is meant by the following economic terms as they appear in the text:

   (i) investment (line 10); [2]

   (ii) aggregate supply (line 10); [2]

   (iii) real GDP (line 12); [2]

   (iv) the claimant count (line 14)? [2]

(b) (i) Explain how changes in an economy's real GDP would usually be expected to affect its rate of unemployment. [4]

   (ii) To what extent does the data relating to the UK economy (see Table 1) support this relationship? [6]

(c) In 2001, the US Federal Reserve cut interest rates on various occasions, reaching a forty year low in October (see lines 3–5).

   (i) What evidence is there in the passage to suggest why these interest rate cuts were made? [2]

   (ii) Apart from a cut in interest rates, explain **two** other measures that the US government could have used to stimulate aggregate demand. [6]

   (iii) Using an aggregate demand and aggregate supply diagram, analyse the effect of a **fall** in aggregate demand on an economy. [7]

(d)* Discuss the alternative policies a government may use to improve a deficit in the balance of payments. [12]

A2 Unit

Economics in a European context

11 The 'New Europe'

On completion of this section you should be able to:

➤ understand how the 'New Europe' has evolved over the last decade or so

➤ understand how the EU is being geographically extended

➤ describe the nature of free trade areas, customs unions and economic unions and the differences between them

➤ explain why these forms of integration do not always work in reality as economic theory may suggest

➤ analyse how Europe compares with other major economic forces in the global economy

The origins of the European Union

The origins of European economic integration are largely political and are rooted in the immediate aftermath of the Second World War. With so much of Europe ravaged by the effects of war there was a pressing need for economic reconstruction. The UK participated wholeheartedly in these plans through the US-sponsored Marshall Aid programme and was an important architect of the Organisation for European Economic Co-operation (OEEC), the forerunner of the OECD.

Around the same time other schemes for European co-operation were also being implemented. The most important of these were the formation of a Customs Union between Belgium, Luxembourg and The Netherlands in 1948 and the Schuman Plan for the pooling of the coal and steel industries in Western Europe, which led to the European Coal and Steel Community (ECSC) in 1951. The important point about this alternative route to European unity was that it was to be pursued by economic means. The founders of the ECSC went on to sign the Treaty of Rome in 1957 creating the European Economic Community (EEC). The Treaty of Rome committed the 'Six' to create a Customs Union, involving agreement on a 'common market', a common external tariff against non-members, and with national policies to be replaced by Community policies in certain areas of economic activity (notably agriculture). Britain stood apart from this movement and instead formed the looser European Free Trade Area (EFTA) with Austria, Switzerland, Sweden, Norway, Denmark and Portugal (the 'Seven'). It was to be the former version of integration which was to win the day

with enlargements in 1973, 1981 and 1986 moving the EEC from Six to Nine to Twelve.

The development of economic integration since 1990

The 1990s have witnessed an unprecedented momentum in the European integration movement. Following the acceptance of the Delors Report in 1989, moves towards Economic and Monetary Union (EMU) began on 1 January 1990. Alongside, the Single European Market (SEM) was 'completed' on 31 December 1992, leading to greater freedom of movement of goods, services, labour and capital, and in 1993 the Treaty on Economic Union (The Maastricht Treaty) came into effect, committing the member states of the European Union (EU) to the launch of a single currency by January 1999. The European Economic Area (EEA), from 1994, extended the single market to the remaining members of the European Free Trade Area (EFTA). Further enlargement of the EU occurred in 1995 with the accession of Austria, Finland and Sweden. On 1 January 1999, in a blaze of publicity and celebration, the Euro was launched with eleven of the fifteen members of the EU joining a single currency area.

European integration has not been without its problems and challenges since 1990 nor has it been solely a Western European phenomenon. The early years of the 1990s saw the Exchange Rate Mechanism (ERM) of the European Monetary System (EMS) run into difficulties in a period of currency instability in 1992/3. Major devaluations of sterling, the lira, the French franc, the Irish punt, the Spanish peseta and the Portuguese escudo contributed to the collapse of the EMS. The dramatic events in Central and Eastern Europe Countries (CEEC) in the late 1980s ushered in an era in which the EU could not ignore developments in its own backyard. With the collapse of the Council for Mutual Economic Assistance (Comecon), CEEC began to look for new markets in Western Europe. From an initial fear of cheap CEEC imports the EU has done much to help these countries in their transition to the market economy and to aid their integration with the EU. Poland, Hungary, the former Czechoslovakia and Slovenia formed the Central European Free Trade Area (CEFTA) in 1992 and a series of Europe Agreements have been signed with the EU to promote free trade in a number of 'non-sensitive' goods. By 1993, a set of criteria (the Copenhagen Criteria) had been agreed by which to judge the readiness of former command economies to join the EU. After much delay, disappointment and not without aggravation, ten new members (eight CEECs plus Cyprus and Malta) join the EU from May 2004. Figure 11.1 shows the changes which have led to the map of Europe being redrawn from that which might appear in a conventional atlas.

Figure 11.1 The New Europe

The EU in the global economy

Forty years on from the Treaty of Rome, the EU is the dominant trading bloc in a world economy where multilateral trade has proliferated on a 'regional' rather than global basis. A few general statistics illustrate this dominance:

- With 390m relatively high-income consumers, the EU 15 is the most important consumer market in the world; a further 75m consumers join in 2004.
- Through trade, the economies of the individual member states are increasingly dependent upon each other.
- The EU 15 had a 42 per cent share of world exports in 2001; its nearest rival, the North America Free Trade Area, consisting of the USA, Canada and Mexico, had 17 per cent.
- The value of the EU's exports was approximately ten times greater than those of Japan and the Asian Tigers, and 30 times greater than for China.

The aim of rest of this unit is to examine the nature and meaning of economic integration and change in both Western and Eastern Europe by applying the economist's 'tool kit' of concepts, theories and techniques which have been built up in the specification.

The meaning and nature of economic integration

What is meant by the term economic integration? Healey defines it as follows:

> Economic integration refers to the merging together of national economies and the blurring of the boundaries that separate economic activity in one nation state from another.
>
> N. Healey, *The Economics of the New Europe* (Routledge, 1995)

The importance of the boundaries which economic integration seeks to 'blur' is that boundaries reduce the free movement of goods, services and the factors of production between member states (see section 10). The result is a reduction in economic efficiency due to:

Tariffs Tariffs create a barrier to the free movement of goods and services by raising the price of imported goods and services relative to those produced domestically. This increase in the relative price of imports causes a reduction in demand and an increase in domestic supply (see figure 10.1).

Quotas Quotas are physical limits on the quantity of imports and can be thought of as having very much the same effect as a tariff. Their outcome is to restrict the quantity of imports and to force up domestic prices.

Government subsidies Government subsidies are a more subtle form of protectionism but, nevertheless, restrict the free movement of goods and services (see section 10). They enable domestic producers to compete with foreign producers where otherwise such competition would be difficult. This is shown in figure 11.2.

In this diagram UK producers could only produce Q_1 if they were to compete head-to-head with foreign producers at the world price (P_W). Given UK consumers demand quantity Q_3, the difference is made up by foreign imports. If the UK government were to subsidise producers in the UK by s per unit of output, the supply curve would shift to $S_{UK} + s$. UK producers are now able to supply Q_2 at the world price and the subsidy succeeds in reducing imports without raising prices to UK consumers. Once again the protection of the domestic market from international competition is separating economic activity in one nation state from another.

Taxation The tax systems of economies can differ in a number of ways:

(a) The tax base

The tax base refers to what is actually taxed in a country. The UK's tax base differs from that in other EU countries with children's clothing, newspapers and books, for example, being exempt from VAT (see section 6).

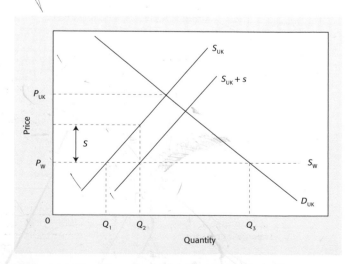

Figure 11.2 The effect of subsidising domestic producers

(b) The tax rate
Even if the tax base were the same in all countries, there may be different rates of taxation depending upon the role taxation plays in governments' fiscal policy (to discourage de-merit goods consumption and internalise negative externalities). UK indirect taxation of alcohol and tobacco is one of the highest in the EU. In the early 1990s excise duty on cigarettes in the UK was twice that in France, the duty on beer was eight times higher than in Germany and the duty on wine 50 times higher than in France. Differences in tax rates can therefore affect the relative prices of goods and services in an economy, which may hinder trade. For example, UK excise duties on wine are almost double the duties levied on beer. By increasing the price of wine relative to that of beer the UK taxation system discourages the consumption of wine. Since most wine is imported into the UK the tax system acts very much like a tariff, altering the terms of trade between countries or, as figure 11.3 shows, reducing the size of the UK market for French wine producers.

The extent to which variations in indirect tax regimes distort trade and consumption depends upon the way in which taxes are levied. If taxes are levied at the production stage (the so-called *origin* principle), the country with the lowest rates of taxation enjoys an artificial advantage over other countries. Where taxes are levied at the consumption stage, the distortions are removed, yet there needs to be a complex system of refunding taxes on goods exported and taxing imports.

If countries have removed boundaries, such as border controls as part of the integration process, different tax regimes add to the costs of trade.

Differences in taxation regimes can have other important effects on the allocation of resources in addition to the distortions on trade mentioned above. Differences in corporation tax, for example, could affect the location of economic activity as firms seek out low taxation economies and different taxes on incomes and savings distort the free movement of labour and business capital.

Exchange rates Exchange rates impose costs on those firms that trade internationally. Such costs are often termed *transaction costs*. The most obvious example of a transaction cost is the financial cost to firms of exchanging currencies. Transactions costs also include the time spent drawing up contracts or the time and effort spent 'hedging' against currency fluctuations. Such fluctuations in exchange rates also create uncertainty in international transactions, perhaps limiting the volume of trade between countries where individuals and firms are 'risk averse'. In addition some economists have suggested that the argument can be taken one stage further to consider how different macroeconomic policies can add to the boundaries separating economic activity.

Public procurement Public procurement refers to the power that central and local governments have as consumers of goods and services. The size of the public sector varies between economies, but, in the UK, public expenditure on goods and services alone currently accounts for approximately 21 per cent of GNP. In purchasing defence equipment, office equipment and cars or contracting out for waste collection and disposal services central and local governments may give preference to domestic suppliers. This clearly separates economic activity between nation states by closing off important markets to foreign producers.

National qualifications Differences in national qualifications clearly distort the free movement of labour between countries. For

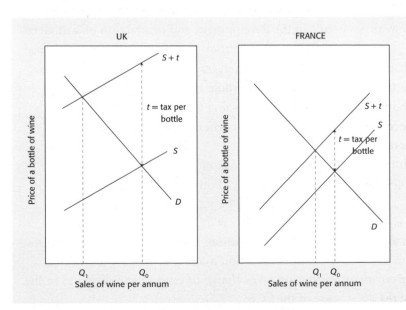

Figure 11.3 The effect on demand of different excise duties

example, if French accountancy qualifications are not recognised in the UK and vice versa, there will be a barrier to the movement of accountants and, to some extent, accountancy firms. Each country's accounting services market will be distinct and separate, resulting in a reduction in potential competition.

Self-assessment task

Non-Tariff Barriers (NTBs) are important obstacles to the free movement of goods, services and factors of production.
(a) Add to the types of NTBs given above using European examples where possible. Divide your list of NTBs into the following two categories:
   ◆ cost increasing barriers;
   ◆ barriers to entry.
(b) How might economic integration seek to eliminate such NTBs?

Levels of integration

Given the large number of boundaries between economies, economic integration is often thought of as a process. Economists analyse integration in terms of stages or levels, ranging from very weak forms of integration to very strong. The different levels of integration do not imply that countries need to move through each stage in sequence. For example, the Treaty of Rome called for the creation of a customs union (a stronger form of integration than a free trade area) from the start and the eventual development of a weak form of common market in its requirement for members to adopt common policies in areas such as agriculture and transport. Some would argue that the launch of the Euro (a Monetary Union) in 1999 has taken place before the EU has fully completed the Single Market or taken any significant steps towards creating an Economic Union. The five levels of integration most commonly used are presented in table 11.1.

Economists also use four terms to distinguish between different types of integration. They are:

1 Market integration Market integration refers to the idea that consumer and producer behaviour is governed by demand and supply conditions in the whole of the geographical area covered by economic integration. It implies that there will be significant flows of goods, services, labour and capital between nations. As such integration deepens price disparities although these will be reduced as a result of competition and trade. Rather than national markets being segmented and fragmented, nations will become part of a larger, single market.

2 Policy integration Policy integration refers to the idea that integration brings about greater co-operation and co-ordination of economic policies between member states. It does not have to mean that economic policies are centralised. For example, the introduction of the Euro has led to the centralisation of monetary policy, with the European Central Bank (ECB) determining Euro area interest rates, but fiscal policy has not been centralised. Instead, national governments conduct their own fiscal policy subject to the constraints of the Stability and Growth Pact which limits a country's budget deficit to 3 per cent of GDP. The EU has developed the notion of subsidiarity to determine whether economic policies require co-operation, co-ordination or centralisation. According to the notion of subsidiarity, economic policies centralised at the EU level are only justified when the policy involves significant externalities or economies of scale. External trade policy is determined centrally in the EU because if each member were to determine its own trade policy there would be important negative externalities on neighbouring economies. The Eurofighter for instance is a joint EU project because of the large economies of scale in the development and production of a modern jet fighter. Competition policy only applies in the case of monopolies, mergers or anti-competitive practices which affect the whole EU market, with national governments pursuing their own competition policy within their own borders.

3 Negative integration This refers to measures designed to remove boundaries and distortions in economic activity between nation states.

4 Positive integration This arises when there is some 'pooling' of decision making or when a centralised institution takes charge of economic policies, as in the case of the ECB.

Level of economic integration	Key characteristics	Comments
Free Trade Area (FTA)	1 Removal of tariffs and quotas on trade between member states. 2 Member states reserve the right to determine their own trade policy towards non-members.	*The weakest form of economic integration which only involves negative integration. There is little in the way of market integration as NTBs may distort trade and the FTA may be restricted to a limited range of goods and services. There is a danger that trade may be 'deflected' as imports from non-members enter the FTA via the country with the lowest tariffs and then are re-exported tariff free.*
Customs Union (CU)	3 Removal of tariffs and quotas on trade between member states. 4 Member states agree to a common external tariff on trade with non-members.	*Avoids the problems of trade deflection but goes beyond negative integration since countries must sacrifice some of their economic sovereignty with respect to external trade policy. Only introduces a limited amount of positive and policy integration. Market integration is not developed as NTBs may arise to replace tariffs and quotas.*
Common or Single Market (SM)	5 Removes restrictions on the free movement of labour and capital between member states. 6 Removes NTBs by harmonising product standards, employment laws, taxation policies, competition policies, public procurement policies, state aid to industry, etc. 7 Adoption of common policies in one or more areas.	*By creating the conditions for a genuine single, borderless market, the degree of actual and potential competition is increased. There should be an increase in flows of goods, services and factors of production between member states and a reduction in price disparities. A significant increase in the amount of positive and policy integration occurs.*
Economic Union (EU)	8 Greater degree of harmonisation and co-ordination of economic policies. 9 Some degree of centralisation of economic policies, in particular macroeconomic policies.	*This is a rather vague concept and is really just an extension of the degree of integration found in the SM. There is not much agreement amongst economists of the precise definition of an Economic Union, although most would tend to stress the introduction of a degree of centralisation of economic policy making.*
Monetary Union (MU)	10 Extends macroeconomic policy co-ordination to the monetary field. 11 The degree of monetary union can differ from a system of semi-fixed exchange rates (EMS) to the adoption of a single currency.	*In its strongest form (single currency) MU involves centralised monetary policy. Eliminates exchange rate uncertainty, the transaction costs of dealing in exchanging currencies and gives rise to price transparency increasing trade flows and competition amongst member states. Requires greater co-ordination, harmonisation or centralisation of fiscal policy with respect to the business cycle, taxation and borrowing requirements.*

Table 11.1 The five levels of economic integration

Long delays at one of Poland's border crossing points into Germany. From May 2004, the checkpoint will move over 600 miles eastwards to the frontier between Poland and Russia
Source: Popperfoto.

Self-assessment task

Read the boxes below and then answer the questions that follow.

Call for minimum wage in constitution blocked by Britain and Spain

Provisions for a minimum wage across the EU are not likely to be included in a future European constitution, following opposition led by the UK and Spain.

Georgos Katiforis, chairman of the 'social Europe' working group in the Convention on the future of the EU, said a call by French socialists for guaranteed minimum incomes had failed to win widespread support. A majority of members preferred the Anglo-Spanish stance, aimed at achieving market flexibility, he added. The clash between French-led support for minimum social standards and the more liberal approach driven by the UK has split the Convention group. In a joint paper, representatives of the UK, Spain and Estonia warned against a 'crude policy of harmonisation of social standards' which would 'constrain the adaptability' of Europe's economies. They claim the present diversity of national traditions concerning trade unions, social insurance schemes, pensions, health care and welfare is a source of strength for the EU.

Source: Dana Spinant, *European Voice*, 16 January 2003.

Ryanair to face EC investigation

Ryanair's business model is to come under embarrassing and minute scrutiny after the European Commission launched a formal investigation yesterday into claims that one of the low-cost airline's main continental hubs is being illegally subsidised to the tune of millions of pounds.

Acting on a complaint from an unknown competitor, the Commission disclosed it had 'certain doubts' about the legality of aid received by Ryanair to encourage it to use Charleroi airport in Belgium as a continental hub.

Source: Andrew Osborn and Helena Smith, *Guardian*, 12 December 2002.

Commission gets tough with EU law dodgers

Frits Bolkestein, the internal market commissioner, this week announced legal action against every member state except Sweden over the failure to implement EU laws. The European Commission is taking eight member states to task for yet another lackadaisical legislative transgression: failure to implement a directive protecting shoppers' rights. Belgium, France, Ireland, Luxembourg, the Netherlands, Portugal, Spain and the UK have all missed a 1 January 2002 deadline to translate the 'guarantees directive' into national law. This sets out certain minimum legal rights for EU consumers, including a right to return defective goods, or have them repaired or replaced, up to two years after delivery. 'If consumers cannot be confident that their rights will be protected they are not going to shop across borders', said David Byrne, the health and consumer protection commissioner.

Source: *European Voice*, 9 January 2003.

(a) With reference to the Ryanair case, comment upon whether economic integration in the EU should seek to abolish all state aid to industry.

(b) With reference to the guarantees directive,
◆ Explain why European economic integration is likely to increase cross border shopping.
◆ Comment upon the extent to which European economic integration is in the national interest of member states.

(c) With reference to the call for a minimum wage,
◆ Explain what is meant by the term market flexibility.
◆ To what extent does the success of economic integration in Europe depend upon whether it is accompanied by common minimum social standards, such as those preferred by France, or the market flexibility preferred by the UK?

12 The Single European Market and Economic and Monetary Union

Economic analysis of integration

In section 10 you learned that free trade, based on comparative advantage, resulted in various benefits to all parties. The European Union, however, represents only a step towards free trade as tariff and non-tariff barriers between the members of the union are abolished but a uniform tariff is imposed against non-members. So, the EU promotes free trade amongst its member states but discriminates in trade with the outside world. What are the economic effects of such discrimination?

The static effects of a customs union

A customs union is one of the levels of integration introduced in the last section. Whilst the EU has begun the process of moving beyond this stage of economic integration, important non-tariff barriers have still to be eliminated. The costs and benefits of European economic integration can still be analysed using the theory of customs unions.

A customs union replaces the individual tariffs of member states with a common tariff against countries outside the union. Economists distinguish between two effects of the formation of a customs union:

◆ trade creation;
◆ trade diversion.

Let us look at each in turn.

1 Trade creation Trade creation refers to the replacement of high-cost domestic production with imports from a more efficient source. The source of imports is from a partner within the customs union. The effect is that countries in the customs union engage in more trade with each other and this gives rise to an increase in economic welfare. Figure 12.1 helps to illustrate this effect. It assumes that the UK is currently outside the EU and that the UK imposes tariffs on imports that raise the prices of goods from EU suppliers from P_{EU} to $P_{EU} + t$ and the goods from suppliers in the rest of the world from P_{ROW} to $P_{ROW} + t$. Both EU

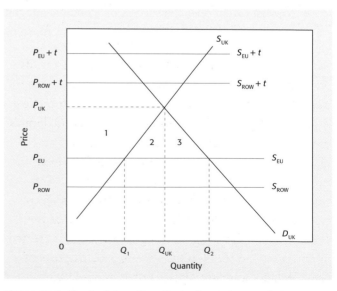

Figure 12.1 The trade creation effects of a customs union

suppliers and those from the rest of the world are priced out of the UK market, such that UK producers supply everything UK consumers demand (Q_{UK}) at a price of P_{UK}. When the UK joins the EU it must abolish tariffs on trade with its Union partners. The UK can now import from the EU at a price of P_{EU}. The UK must also adopt the Common External Tariff (CET) of the EU – here we assume that this is equal to the UK's existing tariff. The result is that UK consumers now increase consumption to Q_2. UK producers, however, are forced to reduce their supply to Q_1 at the lower price. The difference between Q_2 and Q_1 is made up by imports from countries in the EU, and in this way trade which previously did not exist is *created*.

What are the economic effects of this creation of trade? UK consumers are clearly much better off, since they consume more at a lower price. The increase in consumer surplus measures this benefit to UK consumers (areas 1 + 2 + 3). Domestic suppliers in the UK have lost out, however. The reduction in producer surplus of area 1 measures this loss. The net gain in economic welfare is represented by areas 2 + 3. You might notice that, although trade creation is a benefit to the UK, this benefit is not as large as if the UK had abolished all tariffs and bought at the world price. Trade creation is a step towards free trade and, therefore, the benefits are similar to those you learnt about in principle in section 10.

2 Trade diversion Trade diversion occurs when joining a customs union causes trade to switch, from a low-cost supplier outside the union to a higher-cost supplier within it. In reality the effect of a customs union will be both to create and *divert* trade, as figure 12.2 shows.

Take the case of the UK's trade in lamb with New Zealand. Before joining the EU, the UK placed a tariff on lamb's meat equal to t. This tariff raised the price of imports of lamb from the EU to $P_{EU} + t$ and from New Zealand to $P_{NZ} + t$. UK consumers consumed Q_2 lamb's meat in total, with Q_1 produced by UK farmers and Q_2Q_1 imported from the lowest-cost supplier (New Zealand). Once in the EU, tariffs on European lamb were abolished but tariffs on New Zealand lamb were replaced by an identical CET. The result was that the price of lamb fell to P_{EU}. Although extra trade is created by this price fall (Q_4Q_3 rather than Q_2Q_1), imports of New Zealand lamb are replaced by imports from Europe. The impact on economic welfare is now much

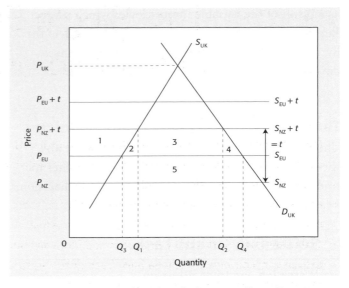

Figure 12.2 Trade creation and trade diversion effects of a customs union

less straightforward than the case of pure trade creation above. Consumers are once again better off, this time gaining an area of consumer surplus equal to 1 + 2 + 3 + 4. UK farmers are worse off, as producer surplus in the UK has fallen by area 1. The impact on the UK government must now be considered, since tariff revenue is lost. This revenue loss is equal to the area 3 + 5. The net result is a change in welfare of areas 2 + 4 minus area 5. The customs union no longer leads to an unambiguous increase in welfare. Whether European economic integration, in the form of a customs union, raises or lowers a country's economic welfare therefore depends upon:

- how inefficient EU producers are in comparison to world producers (the more inefficient they are, the bigger will be area 5 in figure 12.2);
- how price inelastic the demand and supply curves are for the commodities affected by the CET (the more inelastic they both are, the smaller will be areas 2 and 4 in figure 12.2).

Trade creation and trade diversion are obviously responsible for much of the changing pattern of trade of European economies. This has been especially true of agricultural trade. Exports of Australian butter and fruit to the EU have all but been wiped out. Less-developed countries have also suffered badly from the trade diversion caused by the Common Agricultural Policy. Uruguay, Argentina and the Philippines, for example, have lost valuable markets for beef, wheat and sugar as a result of the variable import levies which protect European agriculture. This can dramatically affect the livelihoods of those engaged in agriculture in these developing economies.

The dynamic effects of a customs union

The welfare effects of the European integration are, therefore, ambiguous. They depend upon whether the trade creation effects outweigh those of trade diversion. Economists, however, identify other important economic consequences of integration which occur over a period of time. Such dynamic effects include:

1 Reduced monopoly power
  In an enlarged market, with no tariff or non-tariff barriers, there will be an increase in effective competition. Domestic monopolies can no longer abuse their market power in the way described in sections 3 and 5.

2 Other effects of competition
  Competition is also likely to result in more innovation and greater levels of research and development. UK

Self-assessment task

Trade creation and trade diversion

On the basis of the information given in the tables below decide where production takes place before and after a customs union is formed between countries A and B. Decide which of the situations relates to the trade creation effects of a customs union and which to the trade diversion effects.

Situation 1

Country	Cost of production	Price in home country before customs union (100% tariff)	Where does the home country buy from?	Price in home country after customs union (CET of 100%)	Where does the home country buy from?
A (home country)	€60				
B (customs union partner)	€40				
C (rest of the world)	€34				

Situation 2

Country	Cost of production	Price in home country before customs union (50% tariff)	Where does the home country buy from?	Price in home country after customs union (CET of 50%)	Where does the home country buy from?
A (home country)	€60				
B (customs union partner)	€40				
C (rest of the world)	€34				

Self-assessment task

Study the data below and then answer the questions that follow. The table below shows the UK's trade in goods (visible trade) with selected EU and non-EU countries in 1991 and 2000.

	Exports				Imports			
	1991		2000		1991		2000	
	£m	%	£m	%	£m	%	£m	%
Rest of EU	63,118	60.7	107,600	57.3	65,463	57.3	111,188	51.0
– Germany	14,513	14.0	22,701	12.1	17,312	15.2	27,724	12.7
– France	11,739	11.3	18,512	9.8	10,771	9.4	18,227	8.3
– Netherlands	8,166	7.9	15,109	8.1	9,802	8.6	15,111	6.9
North America	13,645	13.1	33,845	18.1	15,457	13.5	33,591	15.4
Japan	2,246	2.2	3,682	2.0	6,269	5.5	10,191	4.7
Australia	1,341	1.3	2,708	1.4	808	0.7	1,539	0.7
Rest of World	23,589	22.2	39,821	21.2	26,165	23.0	61,527	28.2
Total	103,939		187,656		114,162		218,036	

(a) ◆ Compare the UK's total trade in goods with Germany with its trade in goods with France.
  ◆ How might you account for the difference?
(b) Explain what other data you would need in order to make a full evaluation of the UK's pattern of external trade over this period.
(c) Discuss the extent to which the data match the static effects of the UK's membership of the customs union.
(d) Comment upon how the data might be used in an argument against the UK joining EMU.

consumers, for example, will be faced with enhanced choice of products from which to choose and greater non-price competition. The result will be that demand will increase and firms will be forced to eliminate waste and inefficiencies (so-called *x*-inefficiencies).

3 Economies of scale
Being part of a larger market is also likely to bring the benefits associated with economies of scale. It has often been argued that European firms cannot effectively compete with large American firms, because of their smaller size. The removal of tariff and non-tariff barriers expands the size of the European market. Without economic integration, markets in Europe would be fragmented into small national sub-markets, with competition stunted by the existence of non-tariff barriers even after the formation of a customs union.

In section 3, economies of scale were divided into internal and external economies. The arguments above apply to internal economies. There are also reasons to suggest that European integration could also bring benefits in terms of external economies of scale. The American car industry is much more geographically concentrated than that in Europe. When industries concentrate geographically, cost advantages are likely to result. Witness the benefits in terms of research and development, access to specialist suppliers, skilled labour and the dispersion of knowledge in Silicon Valley in California. Europe has many financial centres (London and Frankfurt being the largest) and would benefit from greater geographical concentration as markets become less fragmented.

4 The costs of economic integration
The above discussion of the dynamic effects of European integration should have set some alarm bells ringing. Surely, all this economic integration is not without its costs?

In fact, many of the dynamic gains also pose

potential costs. Greater geographical concentration of industry implies that some regions of Europe will expand as others decline – a booming European 'core' and a 'periphery' which increasingly diverges in terms of output and employment. Adjusting to the changes implied by economic integration could cause severe declines in output and employment in particular regions of the EU. The result could be regional, structural and technological unemployment. Many have argued that Europe lacks the necessary mobility of labour to avoid these costs of integration (see section 5). The search for economies of scale has already seen a number of European-wide mergers in the pharmaceutical and motor industries. To avoid the problems that this would cause, there is a need for an enhanced role for European regional policy.

Rather than integration enhancing competition, it could well lead to greater oligopoly and monopoly power. European steel producers have repeatedly been found to have engaged in price-fixing cartels. In 1994, Tetra Pak (the major EU supplier of drinks cartons) was deemed to have abused its market dominance by restricting supply, segmenting the EU market, engaging in predatory pricing and forcing an Italian dairy magazine to agree not to carry advertisements for its main competitors. In 1996 six European companies were alleged to have carved up the market for contracts for the supply of district heating pipes across Germany, Denmark and Sweden. Clearly, economic integration implies that competition needs to be policed by a European competition authority if the costs of integration are not to exceed the benefits.

Factor market integration

In terms of the stages of economic integration, the European Union has progressed beyond the stage of a Customs Union. The Treaty of Rome (1957) called for the free movement of not only goods and services but also of the factors of production (labour, business capital and enterprise). The abolition of exchange controls, the Single European Act (SEA) and the movement towards Economic and Monetary Union (EMU) have all helped to create some of the conditions for the free movement of capital and enterprise. The different ways in which national governments treat taxes on savings means that genuine free movement does not really exist, yet much

more progress has been made on the free movement of financial capital than on the free movement of labour.

Up until the Single European Act, limited steps had been taken to ensure that labour was freely mobile between member states. A number of important barriers to the free movement of labour in Europe continue to exist. Indeed, it makes little sense to talk about a European labour market. There are big differences in unemployment rates between member states with modest convergence since 1994 (see figure 12.3). If labour were truly mobile, such differences would be reduced over time. Negative integration, then, has done little to remove the barriers to the free movement of labour and much more positive integration needs to take place. The problem is that the positive integration measures introduced (or proposed) have led to a great deal of tension in the EU, with past UK governments 'opting out' of measures like the Social Charter (see table 12.1). In the social aspects of integration, there is very much a 'pick and mix' Europe.

Why is integration of the European labour market important? The main reason is that integrating markets for goods and services makes little sense without labour market integration. The free movement of goods, services and enterprise will create problems in some member states as resources are re-allocated within Europe. Whilst there are benefits to economic integration, as identified above, not all countries or regions will benefit equally and some will lose out (rural areas and those regions in which declining industries are located). Without labour market integration there is a danger that governments will engage in dangerous competition with each other, watering down labour protection laws for example. If employment conditions and social standards are not harmonised, labour will migrate to the country with the lowest rates of income tax or the highest social security provisions – so-called social 'dumping'. More 'laissez faire' economists argue that such competition is desirable, since it will weaken the powers of governments to interfere with market forces and create labour market flexibility in Europe. Such flexibility and mobility, they argue, is vital if Europe is to make a success of the euro – an argument we will return to later.

The European Union has taken steps to try to encourage the mobility of labour by:

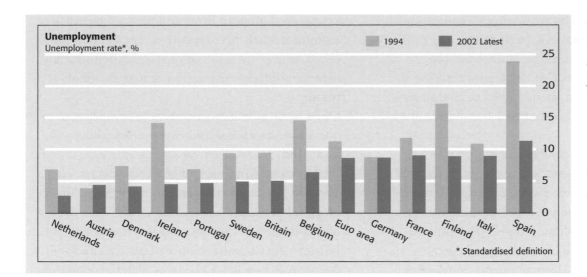

Figure 12.3
Unemployment rates in
13 EU member states
Source: Economist,
May 28 2002.

1 **Living and working conditions**
'The development of a single European labour market must result in an improvement in the living and working conditions of workers within the EC.'
This provision calls for, amongst other things, a maximum working week.

2 **The right to freedom of movement**
There must be no discrimination between workers on grounds of nationality.

3 **The right to social protection**
'Subject to the arrangements proper to each member state, any citizen of the EC is entitled to adequate social protection.'
A reference to social security or a minimum wage.

4 **The right to freedom of association and collective bargaining**
'Every employer and every worker has the right to belong freely to the professional and trade union organisation of their choice.'

5 **The right to vocational training**
This includes the provision of leave for training.

6 **The right of men and women to equal treatment**

7 **The right to information, consultation and worker participation**

8 **The right to health and safety protection at work**

9 **The protection of children and adolescents**
Establishes a minimum working age of 16 years and entitlement to training in work hours after two years of work.

10 **Disabled persons**
Calls for measures to fully integrate disabled people in working life, including improving accessibility to places of work.

Table 12.1 The main provisions of the Social Charter

1 abolishing work permits;

2 improving job information in the EU;

3 allowing entitlement to social security benefits like unemployment benefits to be transferable between member states;

4 allowing workers who cross national frontiers to choose to be taxed in their place of residence to avoid differences in income tax rates acting as a barrier to the free movement of labour;

5 drawing up directives which insisted that national professional and vocational qualifications were acceptable in all EU states;

6 harmonising working conditions, such as paid holidays, maximum working week, minimum paid maternity leave, extending employment rights to part-time workers; and

7 establishing minimum European health and safety standards.

Despite these measures the flow of labour between national labour markets remains low, causing potential problems in the era of a single European currency as we shall discover later in this section.

The Single European Market

The Single European Act (SEA) of 1986 was an attempt to eliminate many of the non-tariff barriers which restricted competition and trade in the European Union. The Act highlighted some 200–300 measures that would create a genuine Single Market in Europe by the end of 1992. There were three guiding principles:

1 Non-discrimination

National regulations, as we discovered earlier, can act as important boundaries separating economic activity in one nation state from that is, another. The principle adopted was that regulations should not discriminate between goods and services produced domestically and those produced elsewhere in the EU.

2 Mutual recognition
Countries in the EU should accept products produced in other countries, despite differences in product standards. Two important cases led to the adoption of this principle. One was the Cassis de Dijon case, involving the French liqueur of that name. Under German law, it did not meet the regulations to be classified as a liqueur, thereby preventing imports into Germany. A successful European Court of Justice (ECJ) ruling established that, if the French classified Cassis as a liqueur so too must the Germans and therefore restricting imports was illegal. A similar case involved the German beer purity laws. These laws effectively stopped imports of foreign-produced beers because they contained chemicals and preservatives. The ECJ rejected the claims of the German government that such beers endangered health. If other countries allowed their citizens to drink mass-produced beers, so must Germany.

3 Burden of proof
This principle meant that any national restriction based on grounds of health and safety must be proved by scientific evidence if it was to be allowed to continue. The long drawn out case of British beef and its acceptance by other EU members, notably France, is a very good example of this.

The SEA, therefore, implemented measures in four main areas to eliminate non-tariff barriers to trade in the European Union:

1 Removal of frontier controls
Customs checks increase the cost of trading by lengthy formalities and form-filling, raising the cost of imports relative to domestically produced goods. Customs controls were, therefore, abolished between the frontiers of the member states of the EU.

2 Removal of technical barriers
Technical barriers include differences in product regulations and standards and the checking of imports for conformity with national standards. Harmonisation of technical standards has led to cost-savings for European firms and the opening up of national markets to competition. The EU now has the power to over-rule any national legislation which it believes results in the creation of new technical barriers.

3 Opening up public procurement to competition
National and local governments are major buyers of goods and services. They can use this power to favour their domestic firms over other EU companies. The Cecchini Report into the benefits of the Single Market identified public procurement as a major non-tariff barrier in the EU. The SEA proposed that public procurement contracts be opened up to competition from suppliers in other EU states, with the result that public sector contracts are now much more contestable.

4 Removal of fiscal frontiers
As seen earlier, differences in taxation rates amongst the member states can create barriers to the free movement of goods and services and trade. The problem arises with excise duties and rates of VAT (indirect taxes on goods and services). If France has a rate of VAT of 15 per cent and the UK a rate of 17.5 per cent, how are exports to be treated? If French exports are taxed by the French when they are produced and then taxed by the UK authorities when they are sold in the UK, French exports will be more expensive relative to UK-produced goods. The SEA envisaged using the so-called 'destination principle' of taxation. That is, tax should be applied at the rate where the goods are sold. Before the SEA, exports

British lorry heading for central Paris
Source: EST Trucking.

were zero-rated for VAT and excise duties when they crossed borders. The SEA abolished border controls so that UK importers, for example, pay VAT at (say) French rates and then reclaim this VAT from the UK government. It does not get around the form-filling problems but means that UK consumers have an incentive to shop in France to avoid the higher VAT and excise duties in the UK. To reduce these fiscal barriers to trade, European VAT and excise duties need to be brought more closely into line – a process known as tax harmonisation.

Self-assessment task

Study the material below and then answer the questions that follow.

Examples of European Commission action against anti-competitive behaviour in 1997–99

Belgian brewer under investigation

Belgium's largest private brewer, Interbrew, is under investigation by the European Commission amid allegations that it has been staving off competition in its home country by rewarding loyal customers with discounts and selling products below market prices.

British Airways fined €6.8 million

British Airways was fined €6.8 million for offering travel agents commission which unfairly restricted sales by other airlines. The European Commission said the rebate scheme discouraged travel agents from selling other airlines' services and warned that others running similar schemes could face similar fines.

Action against price cartels

Six stainless steel producers, together accounting for 80 per cent of European production, were fined a total of €27.3 million for jointly raising prices. Four sugar producers, together controlling 90 per cent of the UK market, were fined €50 million for colluding to fix prices. Ten producers of district heating pipes were found to have engaged in price fixing, market sharing and bid rigging throughout the whole of the EU and were fined a total of €92 million. Seven ferry companies operating services between Greece and Italy were found to have met regularly to fix prices and were fined €9 million.

Volkswagen (VW) group fined €102 million

The European Commission fined the German car manufacturer €102 million for restricting trade within the European Union (EU) by preventing its Italian dealers from selling Volkswagen and Audi cars to EU customers resident outside Italy. The Commission had concluded that VW, Europe's largest car manufacturing group, had been segmenting the EU market for ten years.

(a) With reference to the cases presented, explain the ways in which competition in the European Union's Single Market may be restricted.

(b) Economic theory strongly advocates the concept of competitive or contestable markets as the best ways to achieve an efficient allocation of resources. Analyse why the activities in the boxes above might be of concern to national governments in the EU and to the European Commission.

Macroeconomic policy co-ordination

As we have seen in table 11.1, the weakest form of economic integration is the free trade area, since this does not involve things like common external tariffs, free movement of factors of production, economic policy harmonisation or any centralisation of economic policy making.

It is argued that for member states to take the fullest advantage of a common market, some degree of policy co-ordination and monetary union is necessary. For example, the benefits of a common market may be offset by exchange rate uncertainty and volatility. Policy co-ordination is necessary once economies begin to be integrated. As economies in the European Union become more closely dependent upon each other for trade, one country's macroeconomic policy can have positive and negative spillover effects on other countries in the EU. As shown in table 9.3, when a country expands its economy using fiscal policy it will have to raise interest rates to attract the money markets to fund its budget deficit. Higher interest rates will put upward pressure on its exchange rate. This is the same thing as saying other countries' exchange rates depreciate, stimulating their trade and increasing aggregate demand. Such countries effectively 'free ride' on the fiscal expansion elsewhere in the EU. Similarly a monetary expansion reduces a country's interest rates and its exchange rates, raising the exchange rates of its partners in the EU – their aggregate demand falls and they suffer from the policy decisions made elsewhere in the EU.

If macroeconomic policies are not co-ordinated, then, there is an incentive to wait for others to stimulate demand by fiscal policy and to engage in competitive devaluations against those countries that conduct monetary expansion. The European Economic Community first attempted macroeconomic policy co-ordination by choosing to 'fix' their exchange rates against each other. In 1979, it launched the European Monetary System which had at its heart a semi-fixed exchange rate regime, known as the Exchange Rate Mechanism (ERM). Countries in the ERM agreed to fix their exchange rates within a band of no more than 2.25 per cent (the 'ceiling') and no less than 2.25 per cent (the 'floor') around a central parity against the DM.

Many commentators have argued that the experience of the ERM should act as a warning siren to countries like the UK, contemplating signing up to a single European currency. So, how successful was the ERM?

Despite the currency upheavals of the early 1990s, the ERM was a success in achieving external and internal monetary stability. There was a considerable reduction in exchange rate volatility (between 1980 and 1986 sterling had varied by 30 per cent), and member states' inflation rates had converged towards the lowest rate in the EU.

As for sterling's ignominious withdrawal from the ERM in 1993, it is difficult to see with hindsight how the ERM could have been expected to support what most economists agreed was an overvalued currency: the UK had entered the ERM at a time when interest rates needed to be reduced for domestic reasons to improve our international competitiveness. The key feature of the ERM, namely relatively stable exchange rates, had been responsible for its success in achieving inflation convergence but in turn this became the system's enemy. As a consequence, there was a period of intense monetary turbulence in 1992–1993, resulting in sterling and the lira suspending their membership of the ERM, the devaluation of the peseta and the escudo and a forced movement to wider bands of ±15 per cent. At a time of recession in the European economy, the weaknesses of the ERM were clear for all to see.

Economic and Monetary Union (EMU)

The process towards full economic and monetary union was accelerated by the signing of the Maastricht Treaty in December 1991. It is argued that for the full benefits of the single market to be realised there must be both economic **and** monetary union. These terms were defined earlier in table 11.1 but it is worth recapping on how they have been achieved.

1 Economic Union

   This has meant the creation of a single market in Europe through the dismantling of artificial trade barriers, the development of competition and regional policies, and the co-ordination of macroeconomic policy making.

2 Monetary Union

   This has come to mean a monetary association which results in common inflation and interest rates within Europe. It implies the integration of the financial sectors of the Union, the free movement of capital between member states and the permanent fixing of exchange rates or the creation of a single currency. Table 12.2 gives the post-Maastricht timetable for the

Euro-timetable

June 1989	Delors report on economic and monetary union
July 1990	Stage one, abolition of capital controls
December 1991	Maastricht treaty negotiated
January 1994	Stage two, European Monetary Institute created
December 1995	Euro chosen as name of single currency
May 1998	Euro members chosen, bilateral conversion rates fixed, European Central Bank established
December 1998	Euro conversion rates fixed
January 1999	Stage three, Euro is launched
January 2002	Euro notes and coins introduced
July 2002	National notes and coins withdrawn

Convergence criteria

1 Price stability: a rate of inflation no more than 1.5 per cent above the average of the three best-performing states.

2 Interest rates not more than 2 per cent above the average of the three member states that had the lowest inflation rates over the previous year.

3 The government deficit (that is, the budget deficit) should not exceed 3 per cent of GDP.

4 The public sector debt (that is, the national debt) should not exceed 60 per cent of GDP.

5 Exchange rate movements within the ERM should not exceed their allowed margin of fluctuation for at least two years. Also, there should be no devaluation.

Table 12.2 The countdown to EMU

realisation of EMU. The Treaty also set out the criteria to determine which countries could join. Those meeting the so-called 'Convergence criteria' would join automatically – the UK, Sweden and Denmark, though, negotiated a special opt-out allowing them to buy time in order to determine their participation.

The benefits and costs of European monetary union

To many, the success of the Single Market was always dependent on the adoption of a single currency because of its impact on competition. The microeconomic advantages of Economic and Monetary Union are widely recognised by many but not all economists, politicians and businesses. At the macroeconomic level, however, the advantages of EMU are less than clear-cut.

At the microeconomic level the logic of a single currency is rooted in three distinct advantages:

- reduced transaction costs;
- the elimination of exchange rate risk;
- increased price transparency.

In the context of the Single Market it is argued that these advantages will stimulate intra-eurozone trade and competition. But greater competition in product markets also has a *macroeconomic* dimension in terms of improving the supply side of the economy.

At the macroeconomic level there are a number of questions which, following the launch of the euro, have yet to be answered:

- How is the eurozone economy managed by the ECB?
- Is it managed well?
- How can monetary, fiscal and supply-side policies be co-ordinated in a single currency zone?
- Are the problems of a 'one size fits all' monetary policy offset by advantages in terms of trade and supply-side improvements?

Both the micro- and macroeconomic issues need to be analysed using the economist's toolkit and evaluated in the light of the experience since January 1999.

The microeconomic pros and cons of the euro

Three main advantages of a single currency such as the euro were identified above.

Reduced transaction costs

Trade between countries using different currencies requires firms to change currencies, thereby incurring costs. It has been estimated by the European Commission that the savings on such costs brought about by the introduction of the euro represents 0.5 per cent of the EU's GDP per annum.

The elimination of exchange rate risk

The daily changes in exchange rates, witnessed on the foreign exchange markets, introduces an element of risk and uncertainty to trade between nations. Businesses 'hedge' against these risks by purchasing a range of financial instruments like futures, options and swaps. With a single currency these additional costs for business are no longer necessary and trade becomes less costly and more risk free.

Increased price transparency

Now that prices in the eurozone are all expressed in the same currency, consumers and firms can compare prices more easily across the single currency zone and source the lowest cost supplies. In the past, exchange rates could 'hide' quite substantial price differences in the EU. Firms could take advantage of this lack of transparency by 'segmenting' the supposedly single market, charging different prices in different EU countries.

These three advantages ought to mean that the full benefits of the single market can be realised.

Consumers should benefit from the lower prices brought about by greater competition and price transparency, raising consumer surplus. In some markets, where price differences are greatest, these benefits could be substantial. Cross-border shopping should increase as consumers seek the best bargains. Some economists have argued that, at present, these benefits have been limited because of the small amount of cross-border shopping which takes place in the eurozone but that the potential exists for more significant benefits to arise in the future in the form of, say, greater internet shopping. For most eurozone consumers the obvious and immediate way in which lower transaction costs have benefited them is when they become international tourists.

Producers benefit from the single currency through their ability to source inputs at cheaper prices (price transparency). For some this may mean higher profit margins, for others it will realise new market opportunities from reduced entry barriers. Competitive forces in the eurozone should be enhanced and intra-eurozone trade boosted. Theoretically this should lead to a greater level of foreign direct investment in the eurozone, not only from outside the zone. A benefit of price transparency for eurozone firms is the incentive to locate economic activity where unit labour costs are lowest. There has been a substantial increase in intra-eurozone foreign direct investment since the launch of the euro (see It's official – the euro is a success). In addition, the launch of the euro has enlarged the size of the market for many firms leading to cross-border mergers in telecommunications and pharmaceuticals as firms seek the benefits of economies of scale. Competition itself should expose inefficiencies and reduce monopoly power, leading to increases in both productive and allocative efficiency in the eurozone.

The extent to which the euro promotes competition and efficiency is dependent upon a number of factors. The euro unleashes forces which both intensify competition amongst eurozone firms and, by encouraging cross-border mergers and acquisitions, promotes greater market concentration. The microeconomic advantages of the euro depend, therefore, on the ability of the European Commission to effectively police competition. The role of the EC's Competition Policy becomes much more critical in ensuring that the gains in productive efficiency from mergers are not compromised by the allocative inefficiencies that might arise through greater market concentration. In the case of some industries, such as financial services, market concentration may be desirable in order for European business to compete in world markets. As you saw in section 3, the critical consideration is not just the degree of actual competition but the potential competition (the contestability of markets) and the behaviour of firms in terms of restrictive practices and collusion. The positive impact of the adoption of the euro may be reduced, too, by the distortion of competition by national governments' policy on state aid favouring domestic industry (see Collision course). In addition, the microeconomic effects of the euro will be limited in those markets which have not yet been fully opened up to competition under the single market programme, such as energy, postal services and telecommunications.

There are costs of adopting a single currency which consumers and firms will incur in the short term. These include the costs of changeover to the new currency, such as the costs of changing prices (menu costs), the need to change accounting systems, staff training costs and the initial lack of information on the part of consumers which may allow firms to take advantage of the changeover to raise prices. These costs are not to be underestimated (see Poorer, yes – but by how much?). Some have claimed that, for the UK, this could be as much as £3.5bn. Since these costs are largely fixed they represent a heavy burden for small- and medium-sized firms and the retail sector in particular. However, they are a one-off cost and to some extent are faced by EU countries that choose to remain outside the eurozone but trade with it.

It's official: the euro is a success

Britain would benefit immensely from joining as soon as possible

Until now, the euro debate has been between two visions of the future, neither of which could be proved right or wrong. Now, though, evidence is coming in of the real economic impact of the euro on the 12 countries that have adopted the single currency. Although we have only five months of euro notes and coins, we have three years of experience with risk-free fixed exchange rates, and the benefits of the euro are evident.

The two most important areas of debate have been over whether a single currency would remove an obstacle to business and hence to prosperity. If the euro-advocates are right, there should now be increases in both investment and trade across borders within the euro area. With no such increase, the central economic argument favouring the euro – that it completes the single market and enables competition and productivity gains – fails.

Take investment, the crucial ingredient is secure jobs, rising productivity and long-run growth in living standards. Businesses cannot insure against currency movements if they invest in a country with a different currency. The company's profits on its foreign investment go up and down with the exchange rate. Separate currencies increase investment risk and reduce cross-border investment.

So we should have seen a noticeable increase in cross-border investment in the euro area. The figures for foreign direct investment – whenever a business takes a substantial stake in another business across border – are now available for the whole of the EU for the first two years of the euro. There is a dramatic increase of 384 per cent to €601bn in the two years to 2000. Over the same period, the increase in foreign direct investment into Britain, Sweden and Denmark – non-euro area countries – was an eighth as much. By reducing risks, the euro has dramatically raised investment.

Businesses have a clear preference for investing in the euro area. Investment into the euro area increased most sharply from the non-euro countries. Alarmingly, the investment from countries outside the EU to Britain, Sweden and Denmark has actually fallen.

Businesses are voting with their feet. This was predicted by the euro-advocates, as it closely mirrors economic history. This happened in that older monetary union – the Gold Standard from 1880 to 1914 – when international capital flows were far higher than they are today.

The euro also succeeded in boosting trade within the euro area. This was not meant to happen, because businesses can theoretically insure against currency changes for the lifetime of an export contract, which is much shorter-term than investment.

But this forgets that many businesses operate on very small profit margins of perhaps only 2 per cent of sales, which is often not a big enough profit margin to pay the insurance costs. Either insurance costs wipe out profits, or the business feels that it is simply too risky to undertake an export contract where profits could be wiped out by a couple of days' movement in a volatile exchange rate. Moreover, many businesses cannot predict their foreign exchange receipts with certainty.

Exports and imports of goods to the rest of the EU in both France and Germany have grown far more sharply than Britain's EU trade. They have risen by more than 4 per cent of national output in each case. This is a dramatic increase in just three years in what is normally one of the most slothful of economic series. By contrast, British trade with the rest of the EU has stagnated as a share of GDP. There has been no increase in our integration with the rest of the EU over this period. On average, EU trade in the euro area countries has grown three times as rapidly as EU trade in the non-euro area countries.

The significance of a steady increase in economic integration between the euro area countries is that people benefit from lower prices. Markets become more efficient because prices will tend to align with prices in the most competitive parts of the area. This is good for consumers, and in the UK would put an end to 'rip-off Britain'.

That is also the evidence from a recent study which shows that the prices of a selection of goods now vary by no more than 3 per cent among the cities of the euro area, whereas the same goods cost 16 per cent more in the UK. Cars are the most notorious example – a Ford Focus now costs 32 per cent more in the UK than in the euro area.

Germany and France are already about 1 per cent better off each year as a result of their euro membership. These are substantial economic gains reminiscent of the huge benefits derived by the original six member states from their creation of a customs union (and hence abolition of internal tariffs) in the 1950s. The euro is living up to the highest expectations of the economists who advocated it, and Britain is missing out.

Source: Chris Huhne, *Guardian*, 6 June 2002.

Collision course

The 15 member states of the European Union are poised to inflict an unprecedented humiliation on the European Commission today by insisting that national governments – not unelected officials – should call the shots in an area in which the EU executive had regarded itself as sovereign.

The confrontation revolves around tax breaks to hauliers, granted by France, the Netherlands and Italy in the heated atmosphere after the September 2000 fuel tax protests. The Commission was preparing to declare the rebates on excise duty on fuel an illegal state aid. National governments have activated a long-dormant article of the EU treaty in an attempt to overrule it.

For at least a decade, the Commission has regarded as a key task reducing government subsidies to business throughout the EU, which it has helped bring down from €104bn six years ago to €80bn (£49bn) in 1999.

The competition authorities in Brussels have a particular scorn for government payments they believe waste taxpayers' money, create unfair competition and prop up national rivalries. Boosted by the growth of the competition department's powers and the effects of monetary union in tightening tax-and-spend rules, the Commission has claimed some notable scalps over the past ten years. In return for authorisation for subsidies, Credit Lyonnais, France's flagship bank, was whittled down to a fraction of its size. Last year Belgium's Sabena

Source: Daniel Dombey, *Financial Times*, 2 May 2002.

airline was forced to file for bankruptcy and Germany agreed to wind down controversial guarantees for national banks.

According to Mario Monti, competition commissioner: 'Every single reduction of aid clearly reduces the distortion of competition in the internal market and increases the benefits of economic and monetary union'.

What the Commission finds most disconcerting in the case of haulage is the way it has been bypassed by member states in the bargaining over subsidies. Germany says that, in return for supporting France, Italy and the Netherlands on their fuel concessions for trucks, it has received reassurances that other countries will not stop it propping up its coal industry with more subsidies. Austria's delay in announcing its position on the trucks issue is linked to its quest to win support for prolonged restrictions on the transit of heavy goods vehicles through its territory – a move that could hurt new EU entrants from central and eastern Europe.

The tax breaks on offer to Dutch, French and Italian truck owners are not really the issue. They amount to a fraction of the state aids still on offer in the EU. What is at issue is a principle – the Commission's power, insulated from national political pressures, to adjudicate on questions of unfair subsidies. In seeking to block the Commission on such a clear question of state aids, the member states have served clear notice of their intentions.

Hauliers protest over fuel tax on 11 September 2000 on the M62 motorway near Bradford
Source: Popperfoto/Reuters.

Poorer, yes. but by how much?

Italians don't know, but they blame the euro

HOW much did the price of oranges go up in 2002? By 7% or 41%? Bread: 2.5% or 19.5%? Veal: 2.6% or 10.6%? The official statisticians of Istat put last year's overall inflation at 2.8%, with the price of food up 3.2%. Tosh, says the woman on the Milan tram, and a rival institute, Eurispes, puts food inflation at 29%. Istat is threatening to sue.

For its part, a consumers' organisation, Altroconsumo, says the price of oranges rose by 18.5%, meat 6.5%. And that of jeans by 14%, laundry services and public transport about 10%, a cappuccino 5%. And so on: in short, a lot. Just how far or why, no one really knows. But one thing is sure: as shopkeepers in January converted to the euro – at, in theory, 1,936 lire to euro – prices in the new currency were not just quietly rounded up (that was illegal) but leapt. And Italians, says one poll, went from being the euro's most enthusiastic fans to its most disappointed.

Source: The Economist, 9 January 2003.

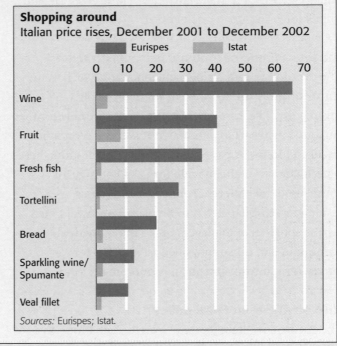

Shopping around
Italian price rises, December 2001 to December 2002

Sources: Eurispes; Istat.

The macroeconomic pros and cons of the euro

The microeconomic advantages analysed above have implications for the performance of the eurozone economy as a whole. There should be higher AD in the eurozone as a result of:

◆ an expansion of trade amongst eurozone economies – this represents an increase in eurozone consumption caused by increased price transparency, elimination of exchange rate uncertainty and reduced transactions costs;

◆ the enlarged market attracting higher levels of investment, both from within the eurozone and from outside;

◆ economies of scale raising the competitiveness of eurozone firms and thereby increasing eurozone net trade.

The euro should also lead to an improvement in the supply side of the eurozone economy through:

◆ lower costs of production,

◆ greater factor mobility,

◆ the impact of competition on productivity.

Figure 12.4 shows how the eurozone economy should

be affected by the introduction of the euro. The combination of the above effects is a rightward shift of both the AD and AS curves, an increase in real GDP and, in the long run, an increase in GDP growth rates, without the consequences of inflation.

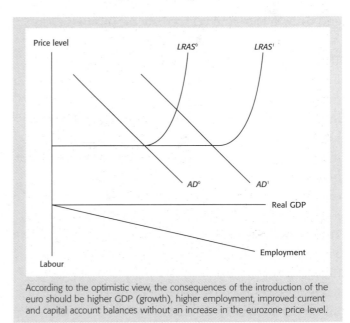

According to the optimistic view, the consequences of the introduction of the euro should be higher GDP (growth), higher employment, improved current and capital account balances without an increase in the eurozone price level.

Figure 12.4 Likely theoretical effects of the euro on eurozone economy

If the introduction of the euro is likely to bring such important economic benefits, why is it that the whole venture, at least from the UK perspective, has been so controversial? The controversy is centred around the potential costs of a single currency. These costs are said to include:

The loss of macroeconomic policy instruments

The decision to join a single currency zone such as the eurozone gives rise to a loss of monetary policy sovereignty. The euro interest rate is set centrally for the eurozone by the ECB and may not suit the economic circumstances of a particular country. In addition, there is no longer an exchange rate for each country to compensate for differences in competitiveness. As a result, greater reliance has to be placed on fiscal policy for the short-term management of the individual economies and on supply side instruments for longer-term improvements in economic performance.

The constraint on fiscal policy

The eurozone's 'Stability and Growth Pact' limits an economy's public sector borrowing to 3 per cent of GDP and its national debt to 60 per cent of GDP. For individual economies within the eurozone this is a further constraint on their macroeconomic policy. If their economic performance is such that a boost to aggregate demand is required or their budget deficit is 'cushioning' the impact of a recession then the Stability and Growth Pact could exacerbate the business cycle.

The lack of fiscal transfer between countries

In adopting the euro, countries effectively become 'regions' of the eurozone as a whole. Where an individual country's economic performance diverges from that of the eurozone there is no significant mechanism for fiscal transfers to boost the performance of low growth 'regions' as there is within a national economy. This can result in persistent unemployment.

The deflationary bias of eurozone monetary policy

The early days of the euro have been an experiment in the economic management of an area comprising 12 national economies. There has been much criticism of the conduct of eurozone monetary policy. Whilst independent of national governments and political control, the ECB has conducted much of its monetary policy making 'behind close doors'. Unlike the Bank of England's Monetary Policy Committee no minutes of ECB interest rate decisions are made public. There is said to be a lack of transparency in monetary policy leading to a loss of credibility – as a result the ECB needs to be seen to be 'tough' on inflation to restore confidence in financial markets. Some economists cited this as a reason for the euro's relentless depreciation against the US dollar in the first two years of the euro's existence. Other concerns centre on the reliability of eurozone data, on which monetary policy decisions are made, and the deflationary bias caused by an asymmetric inflation target. This latter point concerns the ECB's mandate to keep inflation below 2 per cent per annum. This compares unfavourably with the Bank of England's central target of 2.5 per cent within a band of 1.5 per cent – 3.5 per cent. Unlike the Bank of England, the ECB has no mandate to worry about **low** inflation, so that eurozone growth suffers from ECB interest rate decisions.

These disadvantages of membership of Europe's single currency zone need to analysed and evaluated in the light of economic theory and experience.

The loss of monetary policy sovereignty is significant when an individual country differs in either its economic performance or structure from the average of the other members of the eurozone. Such a lack of convergence might occur, for example, when one country is in the boom phase of its business cycle whilst another is in a recession phase. The former requires high interest rates to curb the growth of aggregate demand whilst the other requires low interest rates. A single interest rate set to manage the performance of the eurozone as a whole is unlikely to suit either. This was the case in 2000/01 for Ireland (the high-growth economy of the eurozone) and Germany (the low-growth economy). Here, in the event of a lack of business cycle convergence it is unlikely that, in the case of the eurozone interest rate, 'one size fits all'.

Economies with different economic structures to the eurozone 'average' are also likely to experience problems. For example, a change in the euro interest rate will have different effects in Germany than it would in the UK (if it were a member) because of differences in the structure of their borrowing. In the German economy, for example, most borrowing is undertaken at fixed rates whereas in the UK borrowing is conducted at variable rates. Changes in interest rates have more impact in the UK than they do in Germany.

The costs of eurozone membership are also increased when a country is subject to different (asymmetric) 'shocks' as a result of their different economic structures and characteristics. Without an independent monetary policy to cushion the blow and with constraints placed on fiscal policy, unemployment takes the strain of an economic downturn, especially in the absence of labour market flexibility.

What all of this boils down to is the idea that the costs of membership of a single currency regime such as the eurozone are greatest when there is:

- a lack of economic convergence between countries,
- countries suffer from asymmetric shocks,
- there is a lack of labour market flexibility and mobility.

Some economists have argued that the sheer fact that the euro now exists has altered the status quo regarding the costs of membership. They suggest that membership of the eurozone will actually *cause* economies to converge, increasing the benefits and reducing the costs of membership. A country, such as the UK, which has delayed entry into the eurozone in the belief that the costs exceed the benefits, might well have made the 'wrong' policy choice.

Many of the costs of membership have been over-emphasised by opponents of the euro project. Take for example the constraints on fiscal policy imposed by the Stability and Growth Pact and the loss of monetary policy sovereignty.

The logic behind the fiscal constraints of the Stability and Growth Pact is to prevent the centrally set monetary policy being undermined by the fiscal policies of individual member states. For example, expansionary fiscal policies in one country may lead to inflationary pressures which have a knock-on effect in other parts of the eurozone. In other words, the monetary consequences of high and sustained budget deficits may undermine the ECB's anti-inflationary policy. By increasing a country's rate of inflation, budget deficits also raise the eurozone average rate of inflation requiring an increase in the eurozone rate of interest. In this way other countries would pay the price of fiscal expansion in one part of the eurozone.

The loss of exchange rate policy may not, in itself, be significant. For example, depreciation or devaluation of

a currency does nothing to address the root cause of the lack of competitiveness, risks imported inflation and, within an economically integrated area such as the EU, may lead to 'competitive devaluations'. As with other elements of both monetary and fiscal policy, exchange rate policy is really only a shock absorber for the economy. In Section 8 you learnt that some economists view the economy's Long Run Aggregate Supply Curve as being vertical – in the long run neither fiscal nor monetary policy can influence the real performance of an economy. Improvements in long-term economic performance, then, are only likely if measures are introduced to tackle supply-side/productivity problems. The loss of, or constraint on, economic policy instruments such as the interest rate, exchange rate and budget deficit are of little long-term consequence.

The performance of the eurozone economy

The key to the success of the eurozone's economic performance is the convergence of its member countries' economies. The Maastricht Treaty set a number of Convergence Criteria (see table 12.2) which are, at best, a partial measure of convergence. Figures 12.5–12.7 present a range of data on the eurozone economies which measure not only the monetary convergence indicators targeted by Maastricht but broader measures of 'real' convergence.

The UK and the euro

UK policy is that 'in principle, the government is in favour of UK membership of EMU; in practice the economic conditions must be right' (HM Treasury, 1997). Membership is, therefore, subject to the UK passing the Treasury's Five Economic Tests:

- Are business cycles and economic structures compatible so that we and others could live comfortably with euro interest rates on a permanent basis?
- If problems emerge is there sufficient flexibility to deal with them?
- Would joining EMU create better conditions for firms making long-term decisions to invest in Britain?
- What impact would entry into EMU have on the competitive position of the UK's financial services

Self-assessment task

Study the data in figures 12.5–12.7 and then answer the following questions.

(a) For each of the variables, make a broad comparison of the performance of countries with the eurozone as a whole.

(b) Look specifically at the data for Ireland(IRL) and Germany(D):
- ◆ Compare their experiences between 1999 and 2001.
- ◆ How might you explain what has happened to their economies?

(c) What other data would you require in order to make a full evaluation of the economic performance of the eurozone and its members over this period? You may like to obtain these data and repeat the tasks that are given above.

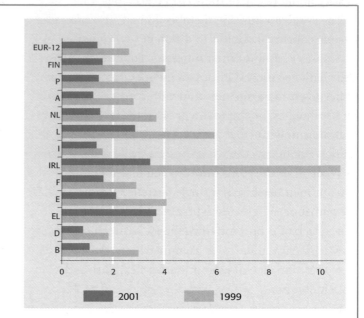

Figure 12.5 Eurozone real GDP growth rates

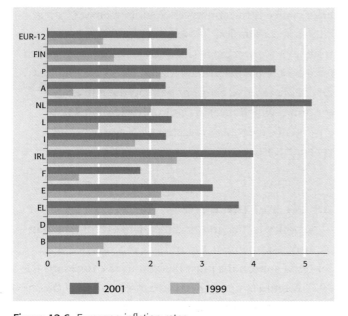

Figure 12.6 Eurozone inflation rates

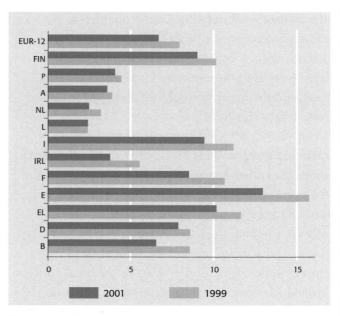

Figure 12.7 Eurozone unemployment rates

industry, particularly the City's wholesale markets?
- ◆ In summary, will joining EMU promote higher growth, stability and a lasting increase in jobs?

Membership of the euro is also subject to the UK meeting the Maastricht convergence criteria which, adapted for the existence of the eurozone, would now be that applicants should have:
- ◆ an inflation rate of no more than 1.5 per cent above the eurozone rate;

- ◆ long-term interest rates of no more than 2 per cent above the eurozone rate;
- ◆ a national budget deficit less than 3 per cent of GDP;
- ◆ a national debt less than 60 per cent of GDP;
- ◆ a stable exchange rate against the euro prior to entry which would be sustainable once the exchange rate is locked in by entry into the eurozone

With the possible exception of the question of the sustainability of the current £/euro exchange rate, the UK meets the other criteria for membership and could, therefore, join (see table 12.3 below).

On what basis, then, should the UK make its decision? The Maastricht convergence criteria focus on measures of monetary convergence and tend, therefore, to be biased towards the success of the euro project itself rather than the interests of each individual member. They do not guarantee that the benefits of membership will outweigh the costs and only provide a 'snapshot' at one point in time. In other words, monetary convergence can occur without real convergence and they do not employ the logic of optimal currency area theory.

Gordon Brown's Five Economic Tests are superficially better since they focus on whether UK membership would be in the UK's best interest. They imply an optimal currency area framework (that is, real convergence, flexibility to deal with asymmetric shocks, etc.). However, it is not clear that there are objective measures against which the tests can be judged (that is they are unquantified and subjective). The tests, therefore, fulfil a political function as much as an economic one.

The convergence framework which we identified above as useful for assessing the performance of the eurozone, can be employed to look at whether the UK could or should join the eurozone's existing 12 members. Figures 12.8 to 12.13 present a comparison of a range of monetary and real convergence indicators.

	Inflation rate (%)	Long-term interest rate (%)	Budget balance* (% of GDP)	National debt* (% of GDP)
Criteria for 2001	4.2	7.0	−3.0	60.0
Eurozone	2.7	5.0	−0.8	69.5
UK	1.3	5.0	+1.9	46.1

Note: * figure for 2000.
Source: European Central Bank (quoted in *One currency for Europe: the next steps*, Nigel M. Healy, *Developments in Economics*, Volume 18, Causeway Press 2002).

Table 12.3 The UK and EMU Convergence Criteria in 2001.

Summarising the data we might observe that:

1 Interest rate differentials have now converged to 0.5 per cent points:
 ◆ the UK 'could live comfortably with euro interest rates' but whether 'permanently' depends on other measures of real convergence;
 ◆ the value of sterling against the euro is likely to decline, making membership more viable.

2 There would appear to be a good degree of business cycle convergence over a sustained period:
 ◆ growth rates have been synchronised since 1998, although with a time lag;
 ◆ there is evidence of even greater convergence since 1999.

3 Inflation performance shows a very different picture:
 ◆ inflation rates diverged from mid-1999;
 ◆ the Bank of England has been more successful in keeping inflation low than the ECB.

4 Unemployment figures show a divergence, even though eurozone unemployment has fallen:
 ◆ in 1996 eurozone unemployment was 1.4 times higher than that in the UK;
 ◆ at the beginning of 2002 it was 1.7 times higher;
 ◆ the UK has an increasingly 'tight' labour market;
 ◆ some eurozone economies have significant long-term unemployment, which means that inflationary problems emerge at higher rates of unemployment;
 ◆ eurozone unemployment has a significant bearing on ECB monetary policy since inflationary pressures from the labour market can only be moderated by greater supply-side/labour market reform;
 ◆ evidence on the relative sizes of eurozone and UK 'output gaps' would help to assess whether business cycles have converged on a permanent basis.

5 The UK continues to have a competitiveness problem relative to the eurozone economies:
 ◆ its productivity is much lower than the average of the eurozone economies, that is GDP per hour worked in the UK is about 11 per cent lower than in the eurozone;
 ◆ the loss of the exchange rate as a policy instrument places greater emphasis on supply-side reform to tackle relative uncompetitiveness;
 ◆ at least by being in the eurozone, this competitiveness problem cannot be exacerbated by

Figure 12.8 UK and eurozone interest rates

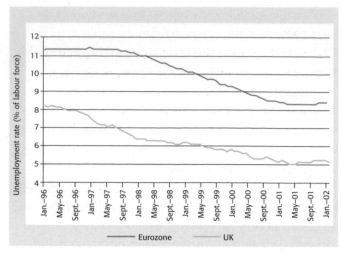

Figure 12.11 UK and eurozone unemployment

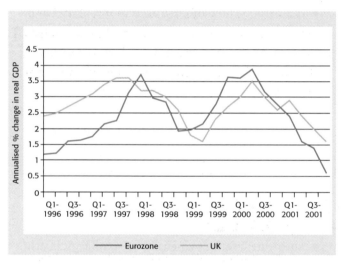

Figure 12.9 UK and eurozone real GDP growth

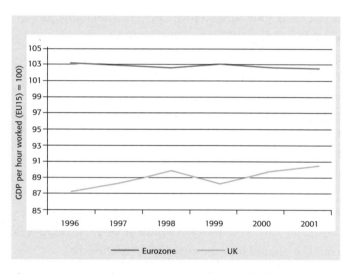

Figure 12.12 UK and eurozone GDP per hour worked

Figure 12.10 UK and eurozone inflation rates

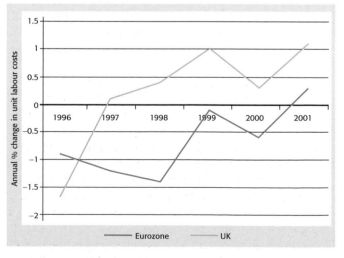

Figure 12.13 UK and eurozone unit labour cost growth

an appreciation of sterling as has happened since 1999;

- the UK is beginning to close the productivity gap, so the problems are not as severe as they would have been in 1999;
- the lack of competitiveness is also reflected in the growth in UK unit labour costs relative to the eurozone, although there would appear to be some convergence since 1999.

Whilst economic data allow us to make a case for UK membership it also suggests some potential problems. So, is the UK better off being 'in' or 'out'? This is a very difficult question to answer (see Ins and outs article below). There are certainly likely to be potentially large costs from a single currency for the UK. However, it is not clear that the UK will be substantially better off outside the Eurozone. Whilst it is probably true that the EU does not meet the conditions for an optimal currency union, the single currency has gone ahead. Outside the Eurozone area, the UK has to choose whether to continue to pursue its own independent interest rate policy or to stabilise its exchange rate against the euro countries, its main trading partners. If it opts to continue its battle against inflation, the exchange rate could fluctuate widely, damaging British business just as the high pound did in 1999.

There may be longer-term effects, however, as the eurozone will involve a combined GDP five times bigger than that in the UK. The eurozone will be very attractive to foreign and domestic European firms, which may wish to locate new investment or relocate to the eurozone from the UK. In such a scenario, the UK could become a peripheral part of Europe. This, of course, must be set against the very real risk that the single currency will continue to have problems due to a lack of real convergence in the Euro area. After the shock of 9/11, the eurozone economy has had to withstand its biggest test yet (see Self-assessment task at end of section). In turn, the UK's attitude towards EMU has softened and a full appraisal is expected to be published in summer 2003. Notwithstanding, there is a widely held view that it is now more a question of 'when' not 'if' we join.

Ins and outs

Perhaps the biggest omission in the Maastricht treaty was the failure to clarify the status of the 'outs' – the countries that decline to take part. (Britain, Denmark and Sweden have chosen to stay out; Greece would love to join but is nowhere near satisfying the Maastricht criteria for membership.) This was not an oversight but a deliberate gap, much in accord with the way Europe's architects have tended to proceed.

The EU's members are pledged to move towards 'ever closer union'. Implicitly, the idea is that they will approach this goal (as yet undefined) at about the same speed – so the four countries not taking part in EMU at the outset are expected to join as soon as they can. To have designed a durable relationship between the ins and outs might have encouraged further delay.

It often happens in European politics that if you do not want a contingency to arise, you ignore it, hoping it goes away. Sometimes it does – and this time-honoured approach may also work in the case of EMU's outs. If monetary union is a success, the qualifying outsiders will warm to the idea. But the collapse of the ERM in 1992–93 showed that the head-in-the-sand method is not infallible. If EMU works badly, outsiders such as Britain are likely to become even more reluctant.

There is also the question of EU enlargement. Prospective new members in Eastern Europe may not be ready, or may not choose, to join EMU at the beginning. Indeed, they would be wise to be cautious. Their economies are still struggling with the legacy of socialism. For many years yet they are likely to remain structurally different from their western neighbours, leaving them more exposed to the danger of asymmetric economic shocks. This only adds to the case for lasting arrangements allowing EU countries to opt out of EMU indefinitely.

The main economic problem posed by a permanent division of the EU into EMU and non-EMU countries is that the outs will be seen by the others as cheats. It is easy to imagine circumstances in which the euro will strengthen against other European currencies, putting euro countries at a competitive disadvantage in trade. If this happens (as well it might) at a time of slowing growth in the euro zone and briskly expanding output elsewhere in the EU, the euro-zone governments will be obliged to object.

In due course, therefore, some form of 'monetary co-operation' will probably be required of the outs, if only as a mark of good faith. One possibility would be a revived ERM, albeit a looser arrangement than the one that collapsed. (For instance, governments might promise to limit variations in their real, as opposed to nominal, exchange rates: this would preserve a measure of monetary discretion while ensuring that governments did not use it to pursue a policy of competitive devaluation.) Failing some such accord, the discussion may move to other ways of correcting the 'unfair' advantage of the non-euro countries' depreciated currencies – and that is a

discussion that could endanger the EU itself.

A permanent union of ins and outs would also raise a host of day-to-day political difficulties. The outs' great fear – and what eventually may force them into EMU – is that the centre of decision-making for the EU as a whole will move to the committee of euro-zone finance ministers. This seems certain to happen if EMU runs into trouble, and the euro-zone countries adopt remedies such as collective fiscal policy and/or increased harmonisation of taxes and economic regulations. Even if all goes well, though, a dimunution of the outs' political sway seems likely. The ins will surely want to punish the outs, with or without a show of regret. How better to encourage the laggards to change their minds?

Source: *The Economist*, 2 January 1999.

Self-assessment task

Testing times for the eurozone

On 1 January 2001, the eleven original participants in Economic and Monetary Union (the eurozone) were joined by Greece. This left Denmark, Sweden and the United Kingdom as the only European Union (EU) members not signed up to a single currency. 2001 also saw the eurozone banks preparing for a massive logistical exercise in the launching of euro notes and coins on 1 January 2002. After shaky beginnings, characterised by a sustained period of depreciation of the euro, the realisation of the single currency appeared to be back on course. No-one could have predicted that the eurozone's first real test would come from the external shock of a terrorist attack on the world's largest economy.

In 1998, economists Christopher Allsopp and David Vines commented that the eurozone's biggest test would be how economic policy would work and adapt in response to a major shock. The economic uncertainty which followed the tragic events in New York and Washington provided this shock – share prices tumbled, airlines folded and tourism slumped in the aftermath of the terrorist attack of 11 September 2001. European business called for financial compensation and subsidies from the European Commission and from national governments. Economic well-being in Europe had changed and commentators talked of a global economic downturn, if not outright recession, which might cause the eurozone's still high rate of unemployment to increase.

In managing the performance of an economy, economic policy-makers have traditionally had a number of policy instruments at their disposal. In the eurozone there is a 'separation' of these macroeconomic powers. Responsibility for monetary policy lies solely with the European Central Bank (ECB), yet fiscal measures are implemented by national governments. As such, there is no real co-ordination of the macroeconomic policies of the members of the eurozone. Instead members of the eurozone have to abide by rules which constrain their ability to run truly independent fiscal policies. The Stability and Growth Pact limits the size of members' budget deficits to 3 per cent of GDP in an attempt to minimise the problems that the 'separation of macroeconomic powers' between the ECB and national governments might create. With regard to the eurozone's high unemployment, the consensus amongst economists is that it is mainly caused by structural factors. Effective monetary policy therefore requires supply-side reforms to make the eurozone more responsive to changes in aggregate demand and supply. But without policies to promote growth no one individual country has much incentive to introduce appropriate supply-side measures. Yet the ECB's over-riding objective is to deliver for the eurozone price stability (annual inflation less than 2 per cent), not growth.

The most important test for the eurozone, then, is

whether the 'new Europe' and its new macroeconomic regime performs well or badly, particularly in the aftermath of an external shock such as the terrorist attacks on the USA. In deciding its interest rate stance, though, the ECB is hampered by a lack of reliable economic data on the performance of the eurozone as a whole – for example, there is a delay of over two months in the publication of GDP figures. Testing times they may be but, above all else, the months and years ahead are highly uncertain.

Now read the extracts below and then answer the questions that follow.

Extract 1.
Economic peformance in EU countries

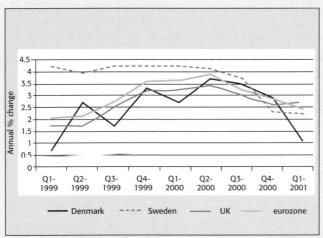

Figure 1 Real GDP growth (annual % change)

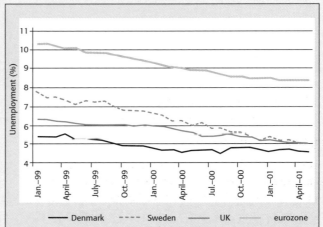

Figure 2 Unemployment (% of labour force)

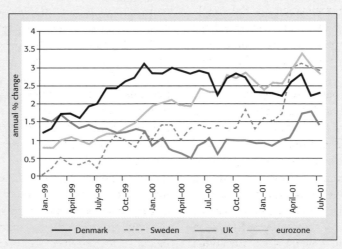

Figure 3 Inflation (annual % change in consumer prices)

Source: *ECB Monthly Bulletin*, September 2001.

Extract 2.
It's no carnival for Germany

The euro entered uncharted and potentially dangerous waters after the European Commission flexed its muscles yesterday and came out in favour of issuing an unprecedented and highly embarrassing warning to Germany, the EU's largest economy, over the alarming size of its budget deficit.

Less than a month after the ultra-smooth rollout of euro notes and coins, a grim-faced Pedro Solbes, the Commissioner in charge of the single currency, ended weeks of speculation by saying that the economic situation in Germany was now so serious that the Commission had no choice but to recommend an official warning. Portugal's budget deficit was also in a bad way (2.2 per cent last year), he said, and Lisbon too should be warned.

Hinting that he had agonised over the decision long and hard and describing the last two weeks as among 'the most difficult' in his life, Mr Solbes said that the very credibility of the rule book which underpins the euro – the so-called Stability and Growth Pact – was at stake. 'In the Commission's view', he said 'an early warning should be issued to Germany and Portugal. The situation is sufficiently serious for this to be triggered.

'This is the first time we have talked about it (the early warning mechanism) and it is the first time we have used it. We have arrived at an important juncture in the process of economic policy coordination. The credibility of the Stability and Growth Pact is at stake.

'If the Commission and Council (member states) fail to take action in these clear-cut cases it is difficult to imagine when an early warning could ever be used. The whole process of multilateral (budgetary) surveillance would be called into question. The success of the euro changeover has raised the stakes. We have no alternative – we have to press ahead.'

The early warning is the first stage in a process which could lead to Germany being fined 0.5 per cent of Gross Domestic Product.

The EU has a strict limit for budget deficits of 3 per cent of GDP but has forecast that Germany will run a 2.7 per cent deficit this year, a figure which it argues is perilously close to that threshold.

Ironically, it was the Germans, worried about throwing their lot in with the likes of Italy and Greece, who insisted on the 3 per cent rule in 1997 and who have now become the first to fall foul of it.

Predictably, the Commission's decision has not gone down well in Berlin. Signs emerged last night that the government, which is facing an election later this year, is hoping to muster enough support from EU partners to block the warning.

If the Commission's recommendation is thrown back in its face there is a serious risk that the Stability and Growth Pact will look meaningless and the value of the euro against the dollar, already languishing at a six-month low, is likely to fall still further.

Mr Solbes made a thinly veiled plea to Germany yesterday to go along with his recommendation or risk opening a Pandora's box whose contents are unknown.

'I particularly hope', he said 'that the member states involved take a long-term view and act in the best interests of the Union and the euro.'

One of Germany's most distinguished economists also warned Berlin against weakening the euro with a diplomatically contrived cover-up. In a reference to Germany's past insistence on fiscal discipline, Norbert Walter, the chief economist of Deutsche Bank, said: 'The head teacher must now show stature and accept a clip around the ear.'

The atmosphere at the Commission's headquarters in Brussels yesterday was in stark contrast to that of just a few weeks ago when officials were breezily exchanging jokes about the launch of euro notes and coins. So-called 'europhoria' has evaporated and as Mr Solbes delivered the bad news Europe's media, long-faced, listened in stony silence.

Source: Andrew Osborn and John Hooper, *Guardian*, 31 January 2002.

Extract 3.
Variations on a euro theme

Survey evidence released yesterday shows business confidence across the eurozone is at its lowest since 1996 as firms prepare for a difficult start to 2002. With little sign of the USA staging a quick recovery and stepping in as importer of last resort, Europe's economic difficulties look set to continue.

The current downturn is the first synchronised contraction in the world's three largest economies since the 1970s, and even the weakness of the euro over the last year could not have been expected to protect the single currency zone as a whole from the fallout. The European Central Bank has been loudly criticised for placing its inflation-busting credentials ahead of quick-footed interest rate-cutting in the style of the USA's Federal Reserve.

Deteriorating economic conditions are informative because the different way in which eurozone economies are being affected strikes at the heart of the project of establishing a single currency zone across a continent.

Take Germany, Europe's largest economy. Analysis by David Brown of Bear Stearns suggests that, if measured in terms of industrial output, Germany entered recession in the early months of 2001, even before America. Official figures show GDP growth slipped into reverse in the third quarter of 2001, and there were reports yesterday that the government is about to downgrade its estimate for expansion in 2002 from 1.25% to an anaemic 0.75%.

Fresh data published yesterday showed the unemployment rate climbing to 9.6%, with the jobless total just below the politically sensitive 4m mark, and expected to break through it soon. The pressure is already telling on Chancellor Schröder, who is facing re-election in September, and announced new job creation measures yesterday in a bid to head off criticism that his economic policies are failing.

Analysts give a number of specific reasons for the fact that global slowdown is hitting Germany especially hard. Although its economy is no more export-dependent than that of neighbouring France, where growth in the third quarter of 2001 held up at 0.5%, its exports are disproportionately made up of capital goods – machine tools, manufacturing equipment, and so on.

And a collapse in business investment has been a key feature of this downturn, as the hi-tech bubble has burst. So as firms across the world retrench, the German

Source: Heather Stewart, *Guardian*, 10 January 2002.

economy suffers. Secondly, the construction sector is still struggling with over-capacity, the legacy of the post-unification building frenzy, which subsequently folded.

There are more reasons than this – David Brown more controversially cites the conservative nature of the German consumer, rushing to put money under the mattress at the first sign of a cash crunch, for example. What this quick glance at the German economy illustrates, though, is that the eurozone is made up of a jigsaw of quite different economies.

Spain is likely to be disproportionately affected by the devaluation of the Argentine peso, because its banks are heavily exposed there; France (where there are also elections this year) may escape the worst of the slowdown in the rest of Europe if its consumers can keep their nerve; Ireland could insulate itself if it can continue to attract inward investment and maintain its healthy growth rates.

The eurozone governments have surrendered their ability to offset the differences between their economies by adjusting interest rates; and the markets can no longer offset those differences with movements in the exchange rate. The differences are significant, however, as a simple comparison of growth rates shows. And when the region as a whole is suffering from a slowdown, differences between growth rates hurt much more, because they can translate into higher jobless figures – or a longer recession.

So eurozone politicians may have a fight on their hands in 2002 to persuade their electorates that signing up to the euro was worth the price.

If, as expected, the apparently unstoppable spending spree of the British consumer helps the UK economy to escape the worst of the downturn across the channel – and across the Atlantic – in 2002, convincing the electorate here that they are losing out by missing the euro-party could be a difficult task.

Extract 4.
Low fares bid to boost Irish tourism

The Irish government is examining ways of encouraging low-fare carriers to start new routes to Europe amid concern the terrorist attacks on America will devastate the tourism industry next year.

Jim McDaid, the tourism minister, is likely to recommend that landing charges be cut with a view to

making Dublin airport a hub for no-frill airlines.

Government and tourist officials are reluctant to quantify the impact of recent events on the industry, but privately they forecast the number of American visitors to Ireland could be cut in half. That would put 12,000 jobs in jeopardy.

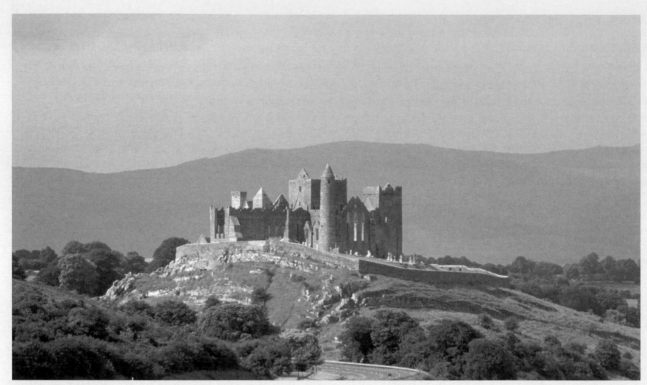

Source: Bord Failte Images.

The addition of new low-cost flights would attract tourists from Britain and Europe, helping to make up the American shortfall.

Among other measures, they are likely to place renewed emphasis on getting Irish people to holiday at home next year, and on devising packages to win visitors from Britain and Europe.

Irish tourism supports 145,000 jobs (one in 12 of the workforce) and the industry is heavily dependent on America. In 2000, about 6.3m people visited Ireland – about 1m from the United States – generating IR£3.8bn in revenue. For every pound spent by a tourist, the government got 57p.

Eoin Fahy, chief economist at KBC Asset Management Ltd, said: 'This is a test and it will be interesting to see if we pass. Hotels in Dublin have been full for the past few years without even trying. Now they're going to have to get out and look for business; to sell their product.'

Ashford Castle, a 772-year-old mansion in County Mayo, is one of the country's most exclusive hotels and, in normal circumstances, its prices reflect that. The cheapest room costs £254 per night, while the presidential suite, in which Pierce Brosnan and Keely Shaye Smith recently spent their wedding night, is priced at £642 a night.

These are not normal times though, and last week the luxury hotel was offering rooms for a third of that – £75 per person – on selected dates.

Like many upmarket resorts in the west of Ireland, Ashford depends on the dollar. Half of its guests come from North America, but non-essential travel is declining. That leaves hotels such as Ashford with plenty of beds to fill. Dromoland Castle, Ashford's sister hotel in County Clare, is also feeling the pinch. It says it lost £500,000 worth of business when all American flights were grounded for five days following the attacks on the twin towers and the Pentagon. The cancellations stretched into December.

Few can predict what will happen beyond that, into next year, but Irish businesses are bracing themselves for the worst. While tourism and aviation are the industries likely to be worst hit, the fall-out from the attacks could be widespread. The government has already moved into emergency mode. Charlie McCreevy, the finance minister, has ordered colleagues to cut day-to-day spending. Some large-scale infrastructure projects, such as the National Development Plan, are likely to go ahead, but other plans may be scaled down or shelved. Stadium Ireland may not be as grandiose as first envisaged, while the Abbey Theatre is unlikely to get £100m to relocate.

Although the problems are piling up, economists say there is no need to hit the panic button yet. The Irish economy remains among the world's strongest, and can therefore afford some slack.

'We are lucky because we are starting from a high base. Even if there were a considerable slowdown, we would maintain respectable growth', said Dermot O'Brien of NCB stockbrokers. The outcome is mostly dependent on

America and the duration and shape of its declared war on terrorism.

Commentators note that America's Federal Reserve, along with its counterpart, the European Central Bank, has cut interest rates and is likely to reduce them further over the coming months. That will provide a monetary boost to the economy, putting extra cash in people's pockets.

'This is a bad shock to the economy, but it is not an apocalyptic event', said Dan McLaughlin, chief economist at Bank of Ireland. 'Irish companies are flexible – they can cut costs quickly – and that will help them to get out of a recession fast.'

Most agree that the next six months will be 'horrible' but predict that, excluding the impact of a possible war, world economies should start to recover by the second half of 2002.

Either way, the future will be challenging. The Irish economy is coming down to earth faster than expected; keeping it on the right path is bound to be trying.

Source: Brian Dowling and John Burns, *Sunday Times*, 23 September 2001.

Extract 5.
ECB believes eurozone will bounce back quickly

The European Central Bank expressed confidence on Thursday that the eurozone would recover quickly from an economic slowdown made worse by last week's terrorist attacks in the USA.

In its monthly bulletin for September, the ECB held out the possibility of future interest rate cuts, but cautioned governments not to use the slowdown as an excuse for loose budgetary discipline.

The ECB report was the first tentative assessment by an authoritative international institution of the possible impact of the attacks on the world economy.

While offering no precise forecasts, the ECB said: 'The recent events have increased uncertainty about the USA and the world economy. They are also likely to weigh on confidence in the eurozone and on the short-term outlook for economic growth.'

It went on: 'Given the strong fundamentals of the eurozone, the Governing Council remains confident that the slowdown in economic growth will be short-lived.'

The report's wording was almost identical to that used by the 18-member council on Monday when it cut interest rates by 0.5 percentage points to 3.75 per cent.

However, in contrast to language used by the ECB after previous rate changes, the report pointedly avoided suggesting that the new level of interest rates was appropriate for the foreseeable future.

'We think this leaves the door wide open for further easing in coming months', said Neville Hill, economist at Credit Suisse First Boston.

The ECB report made clear that, even before the attacks on 11 September, several factors were causing the bank to lower its expectations for European economic growth.

First, the economic slowdown in the first half of this year had been worse than expected a few months ago.

Next, the negative impact of high oil and food prices on real disposable income had been stronger than expected. Last, the US economic downturn, Japan's weakness and the spillover effect on other parts of the world had been greater than foreseen.

Confirmation of the slowdown came on Thursday from Italy, where official figures showed a much weaker than expected 0.7 per cent month-on-month fall in industrial output in July.

The ECB said its quarterly survey of professional forecasters, conducted in August, estimated eurozone economic growth at 2 per cent this year and 2.4 per cent in 2002. In May, the survey produced estimates of 2.5 and 2.6 per cent respectively.

The report said annual inflation in the eurozone would probably fall below the ECB's target ceiling of 2 per cent 'in the not too distant future'.

The ECB urged governments to try to meet targets on budget deficit reduction set in line with the European Union's Stability and Growth Pact. This pact is the fiscal cornerstone of European Monetary Union, designed to ensure that no government destabilises the euro with excessively high deficits. 'A re-interpretation of the pact must not be considered', the ECB said.

Nevertheless, it showed some understanding for governments grappling with a sharper than expected economic slowdown. It said they should ensure that 'the deviation from (budgetary) targets . . . remains limited'.

Private sector forecasters agree with the ECB that the attacks on the USA will delay the eurozone's recovery.

ABM-Amro, the investment bank, says the area's economic growth could be 2 per cent next year, rather than 2.5 per cent as it had predicted before the attacks.

Source: Tony Barber, *Financial Times*, 20 September 2001.

(a) ◆ Using Extract 1, compare the economic performance of the eurozone with that in non-eurozone EU countries.
   ◆ Explain the additional data you might use in order to make a fuller comparison of the economic performance of the eurozone with that of non-eurozone EU countries.

(b) ◆ Comment upon the implications for a country's macroeconomic policy of its decision to participate in EMU.
   ◆ Comment upon the problems faced by economic policy makers in managing the performance of a single currency zone such as the eurozone.

(c) Discuss the possible economic consequences of an external shock, such as the terrorist attacks in the USA in September 2001, for
   ◆ European industries, and
   ◆ the EU economy as a whole.

Source: OCR, Economics in a European Context, 2888, January 2003 (adaptation).

13 The transition economies of Europe

On completion of this section you should be able to:

➤ describe the characteristics of centrally planned economies

➤ explain how and why central planning has failed

➤ analyse how economic reforms have been applied in transition economies

➤ discuss the costs and benefits of economic reforms for transition economies

➤ analyse the economic performance of the former centrally planned economies during transition and how they compare with EU economies

➤ discuss the reasons why some transition economies are joining the EU

Introduction

Since 1989 some 28 independent states of Central and Eastern Europe (CEE) and the Commonwealth of Independent States (CIS) have embarked on a journey along the road 'from Marx to the market'. Whilst these states differ markedly in many economic respects (population size, GDP per capita and the structure of the economy), they share one thing in common: a legacy of a planned economic system. For some countries like Russia this legacy is a long one that affected most aspects of economic life: the planning process determined what was produced, how production was organised and the distribution of production (for whom to produce) (see section 1).

The results of the transition to the market have been mixed. This is due, in no small measure, to the enormity and complexity of the task of turning a centrally planned economy (CPE) into a market economy. Whilst economists at the end of the 1990s were beginning to formulate theories of transition, at the beginning of that decade the transition economies, themselves, were stepping out on a path that none before them had trod. Much has been written on how to turn a market economy into a planned economy but, in the early 1990s, no-one had formulated a blueprint for planned economies wishing to move towards a market economy.

In order to understand the complexities and likely problems of transition it is first necessary to understand the legacy of planning which the CEE and CIS states were left with in the late 1980s and early 1990s. This section then goes on to examine the reforms required during transition before considering why the experience of transition has been so varied. Finally, the realities of integrating such economies into the EU are considered.

The problems and inefficiencies of planning

How well did central planning work as a means of allocating scarce resources? Steffens once said of communism, 'I have seen the future and it works'. In many respects communism and planning have some astonishing achievements to their credit: in their early days they provided some of the fastest rates of economic growth the world has witnessed; industrialisation in Eastern Europe was achieved without the consequent gross inequalities and mass poverty experienced in the West; it guaranteed full employment and a reasonable standard of living for its citizens. President Kennedy admitted in 1961 that the Soviet Union had achieved parity in space technology; and it was a phenomenal military power, particularly with respect to nuclear weapons.

Despite these achievements there were a number of problems with the planned approach to resource allocation. For example, the differences in collective ownership of the means of production and the lack of property rights created many economic inefficiencies. In the market system private ownership brings rewards and creates incentives. A firm which manages to reduce costs below those of its competitors is able to charge lower prices and is rewarded with higher market share and

227

profits. Incentives are, therefore, created to produce efficiently and to innovate products and production processes. In the socialist economy such incentives are absent causing productive inefficiencies.

The planning process itself caused economic inefficiencies. In order to draw up material balances, planners needed information about the resource requirements of each SOE and their 'capital–output' ratios: that is, the amount of output which could be produced with each unit of capital. Such information was passed on to the planners by the enterprise managers, leading to a 'principal–agent' problem. Enterprise managers are the agents of the planners (the 'principals') responsible for implementing the plan. The managers have more information than the planners and are therefore able to pursue their own interests given this asymmetry of information. The managers of SOEs would put in bids for more inputs than they required and bargain for production targets which were easier to achieve than those proposed by the planners. Incentives and penalties were weakly linked to performance and tended to encourage 'satisficing' behaviour on the part of managers (see section 3). One measure of the resulting inefficiency was that energy use per unit of output was up to four times higher in the CPEs than in the West. Most planned targets were expressed in volume (e.g. numbers of tractors) or weight and production took little account of the quality of what was produced. Soviet agriculture, for example, used more tractors per hectare than Western agriculture yet they frequently broke down. Since the plan for tractor production was expressed as a target for total production, SOEs produced lots of tractors but very few spare parts. This was common in much of industry, which was subject to frequent and long production stoppages.

Incentives for workers were also very crude. In order to raise levels of production in the quest for economic growth, workers were often given bonuses related to the total production of the factory rather than to individual effort. The consequence of this was that individual workers could 'free-ride' off the efforts of others by shirking, for example, or by gaining the benefit of the bonus with minimum effort. As you learned in section 5, free riding gives rise to under-consumption in the case of public goods. In this case, free riding caused low output per worker or productive inefficiency.

CPEs also suffered from a misguided belief in

economies of scale. In the former Soviet Union almost two thirds of industrial products were produced by a single SOE. The large-scale production favoured by CPEs resulted in cost inefficiencies. This inefficiency, and the monopoly position of firms, has had an important bearing on such businesses during the transition to a market economy, as we shall see later.

Finally, we can argue that the system of administered, as opposed to market determined, prices gave rise to allocative inefficiency (see section 4). In a planned economy prices bear little relationship to costs and consumers had no way of signalling their preferences since excess demand could not raise the price as in a market system. Instead scarce resources were allocated by queues. Consumers, then, had no way to influence the plan, and the bias towards heavy industry and military goods production in much of Central and Eastern Europe indicated allocative inefficiency.

In short, command economies suffered from numerous problems and inefficiencies: chronic shortages of consumer goods and inherent supply side weaknesses; repressed inflation due to the under-pricing of scarce goods and services; hidden unemployment due to the over-manning of industry and the guarantee of full employment; 'soft' budget constraints caused by the lack of financial control exercised over SOEs.

As these economies began to open up politically (*glasnost*), before the planning system was effectively reformed (*perestroika*), the low level of utility was channelled into political forces for change, culminating in the collapse of both the political and economic systems associated with communism.

The transition to a market economy: reforms and problems

The task of transforming a centrally planned economy into a market economy is enormous. Not only must the foundations of a fully functioning market economy be put in place but the government needs to react to the inevitable problems during transition. If these issues are not complex enough, governments must conduct this transformation lacking any prior experience on which they can draw. Although the major reforms can be identified, there is little guidance on the speed or the sequence in which the reforms should be implemented.

Some countries chose to follow the 'shock therapy' approach as recommended by some economists. This approach involves extensive privatisation, strict monetary and fiscal policies to reduce inflation and the forces of supply and demand to determine internal market prices and the external exchange rate. Others chose to adopt the 'gradual' approach to transition, arguing that consumers and producers needed time to adapt to the new economic system and that, to maintain public support for the reforms, the pain of transition needed to be softened. The transition to the market is arguably the largest economic experiment which has been conducted in the twentieth century.

The reforms which are needed on the road to the market economy include:

Price liberalisation

The key to microeconomic reform is to allow prices to be determined by supply and demand. By freeing prices from state control former command economies should enjoy benefits in the long term. In a command economy prices bore no relationship to demand and supply. Energy was, for example, massively under-priced in the CEE and CIS states, with the world price exceeding the plan price by as much as 150 per cent. By liberalising energy prices, gains in economic welfare of up to 10 per cent of GDP could be shown, more than the entire gains from the Single European Market in the EU.

Removal of subsidies

In order to fully realise the gains from price liberalisation the government must also remove the various subsidies to SOEs which kept prices low. As these subsidies are removed prices will 'jump' even further. Some governments, most notably the Russian government, delayed the introduction of such price reforms for fear of the effect of price rises on the real wages of workers. Sensitive prices, such as food, housing and energy, were not fully liberalised. Another fear was that, if prices were liberalised before competition was introduced, the former SOEs might take advantage of their monopoly power and raise prices even further. Some countries, therefore, delayed price liberalisation.

Privatisation

To create a fully functional market economy, SOEs need to be turned into profit-motivated, private sector firms.

The privatisation of small-scale SOEs created few problems – shops, restaurants and bars have largely been handed over to their former managers or, where they could be identified, their former owners. Where those who manage the firm are also its owners and free to make profit, changes can be rapid. Such small-scale privatisation has been the visible sign of transition for many consumers, with a rapid change in the appearance of the 'high street' in terms of window displays and the range of goods and services on offer. Outside the major cities, the typical Central and Eastern European 'restaurant', often part of a large-scale SOE, may still exist, but the growth in fast food outlets and trendy bars is apparent nevertheless. Small-scale privatisation has been an important source of employment generation, much needed as large-scale SOEs shed labour in the quest for greater efficiency.

Large-scale privatisation has been much more of a problem. Those governments that have privatised large-scale SOEs have had to think carefully about how to privatise. A number of different ways have been used:

- auctioning them to the highest bidder for cash;
- issuing privatisation vouchers to the general public and then auctioning the SOEs in return for the vouchers;
- allowing existing managers, workers and/or foreign companies to buy the SOE;
- handing over the SOE to managers and/or workers for free.

Private ownership, of whatever kind, is not enough on its own to guarantee success. There is also a need to improve management techniques, especially in the areas of stock and quality control, financial management and marketing. Existing managers, of course, lack such skills and it may take some time for them to be acquired, which has convinced some governments of the need to delay the privatisation process whilst the necessary 'restructuring' takes place. Others have 'imported' the required management techniques by selling (wholly or partially) SOEs to foreign multinational companies, such as the sale by the Czech government of Skoda to the German car giant Volkswagen and the sale of Hungary's largest supermarket chain to Tesco, the UK's biggest grocery retailer (see self-assessment task). In other words, the type of privatisation during transition is as, if not more, important than the scale of privatisation.

Self-assessment task

Read the material below and then answer the questions that follow.

Shopping ...Hungarian Style

It's barely 9 o'clock and like most Saturday mornings, the car park at Tesco's hypermarket on the outskirts of Györ is almost full. Situated midway between Vienna and Budapest, on the main rail and road axis, Györ is a town that has experienced a remarkable transformation since the last Russian troops left in 1989. After a difficult period of transition, the town is now benefiting enormously from foreign investment by the likes of United Biscuits, Audi and Phillips. Hungarian

Source: Tesco's at Györ.

salaries are well below those in neighbouring Austria but the influx of overseas capital has brought a new buzz to the town … and Hungarians like shopping!

It was this projected prosperity that attracted Tesco to Hungary in 1994 when it purchased Global, a regional grocery retailer in north-west Hungary. Tesco now runs 22 small grocery shops and five supermarkets in Györ and neighbouring Szombathely. Its main expansion though has been through the development of 23 hypermarkets, more geographically dispersed, and selling a wide range of food and non-food products.

Tesco learned very quickly what appeals to Hungarian customers. In the early years, it tended to pack its stores with much-handled but seriously overpriced branded imports of UK grocery products, such as Kellogg's cereals, Nescafé coffee and Heinz baked beans. Although these products are still on sale, the company later made its mark through its own-label products, including its value range 'Tesco Gazdasagos'. As in the UK, these products are keenly priced, often 20 per cent below their branded equivalent. Tesco has also learned what Hungarians like to buy, with most of its products coming from local rather than UK suppliers. Tesco's business is now so large in Hungary that it has recently

opened a new centralised distribution centre close to the Austrian border at Herceghalom. Close to a major international rail hub, this new facility is strategically placed to receive products from the UK as well as from all over Hungary and other parts of Central Europe.

Tesco may well have made its mark in Hungary, despite competition from Metro and Kaiser (Germany) and Jules Melni (Austria). Elsewhere though, particularly in the Czech Republic and Poland, it faces stiff competition from Carrefour and Auchan (France), Metro (Germany) and Billa (Austria).

A recent report from Budapest-based DTZ International has warned that too many investors are chasing too little money with the proliferation of new shopping centres. They predict that some developers will go bust due to market saturation.

Not all Hungarian's approve of the changes that are taking place. Sandor Lezsak, chairman of the right-wing Democratic Forum, has recently said, 'Today we are not threatened by tanks but, much more insidiously, by globalisation. Budapest is ringed just as it was in 1956, but now it is multinational companies of uncertain backgrounds that are preparing to occupy us.'

1 Suppose that you are Tesco's European Business Development Manager. Explain what economic data you might have used in advising the company to expand its hypermarkets in Hungary.
2 Comment upon the costs and benefit of foreign direct investment on:
 ◆ the Hungarian people,
 ◆ the Hungarian economy.

Trade liberalisation

Liberalising prices does not make much sense without trade liberalisation. Since a lot of industry is monopolised by SOEs, liberalising trade can create the competition which might otherwise not exist. However for trade to be liberalised it is necessary for the currency to be convertible into other currencies, at least for transactions involving goods and services (so-called current account convertibility). As we saw in section 12, international trade brings important static and dynamic benefits. By allowing resources to be allocated on the basis of comparative advantage, economic efficiency is improved and there is a spur to greater dynamism in the long run.

In theory, trade liberalisation can be achieved fairly quickly by removing the state monopoly on trade, all tariffs, quotas and non-tariff barriers to trade and by allowing the currency to be convertible. Some temporary protection of domestic industries might, however, be justified, given the inefficient state of many SOEs, the need for the government to raise revenue in the early phase of the transition process and the need to stop the 'monetary overhang' being translated into a big surge in the demand for imports and a consequent deficit on the current account of the balance of payments. But tariffs on imports will cause problems for those industries trying to export since it will increase the cost of their imported inputs.

The transition economies of Central Europe have been in a fortunate position with regard to trade. Geographically close to the European Union, they have been able to find alternative markets for their exports after the collapse of Comecon, unlike Eastern European states and the economies of the CIS. In addition, they have gained tariff-free access to the EU in the form of various Europe Agreements, which have, in some instances, paved the way for full membership. Consequently their pattern of trade has undergone a major change and they are becoming more closely integrated with the economies of Western Europe.

Currency convertibility means that the government has to take some view on what sort of exchange rate regime it is going to adopt. Freely floating exchange rates cause problems as the exchange rate will have a tendency to depreciate and this will add to the uncertainty already caused by the transition from one economic system to another. Fixed exchange rate regimes are likely to be difficult for transition economies to support, since they lack the necessary foreign exchange reserves. However, if the exchange rate is fixed at a low enough rate and against the 'right' currency, there is every chance that not much speculation will take place and this will minimise the amount of intervention needed to support the currency. For this reason, most transition economies have opted for a fixed exchange rate regime.

Reform of the financial sector

As we have seen, many of the reforms required as part of the transition process require a fully functioning financial sector. The elements of a typical reform package should include:
 ◆ establishing a Central Bank to control the money supply and interest rates independently of government and to act as a lender of last resort to the commercial banks;
 ◆ creating banking institutions for collecting savings and channelling these savings to former SOEs so that they can invest and re-structure themselves;
 ◆ setting up a framework to supervise and regulate the activities of the financial sector;
 ◆ creating a market in which governments can sell bonds to finance any excess of expenditure over taxation receipts.

Given the nature of the financial system inherited from the years of planning, these reforms are a major task for governments and likely to take many years to complete.

The diverse performance of transition economies

Despite their shared goal of building a market economy, the former command countries have shown diverse economic performance (see section 7). In general the economies of Central and Eastern Europe appear to have suffered a shorter transitional recession and a more sustained period of recovery. Why has the performance of transition economies been so diverse and why is there such a clear divide between the experiences of the CEE and CIS countries?

Some economists have attempted to explain this diversity in terms of the speed and comprehensiveness of the reform measures implemented. One crude measure of progress might be to look at the size of the new private sector as a proportion of GDP. Countries which have a large private sector might be thought of as making more headway in transforming a command economy into a market economy. However, there is a very weak relationship between the size of the private sector and the successfulness of the transition. For example, the private sector in Russia is larger than that in Poland, but this does not associate with strong economic performance over the period.

The European Bank for Reconstruction and Development (EBRD) uses various indices of reform progress in each of the areas we identified above. So countries are ranked on a scale of 1 (very little progress) to 4 (almost complete reform) in terms of large- and small-scale privatisation, price and trade liberalisation, bank reform, legal reforms and so on. There is a stronger relationship if these various indices are added together and then related to GDP growth, which has tended to lead some to argue that the shock therapy approach to transition is superior to the gradual approach. But there are still some important differences that need to be explained. For example, Albania and Georgia are very similar in terms of the amount of reform each has undertaken but their economic performance (in terms of GDP growth over the period) is markedly different.

Some economists have argued that an important lesson to learn from the experience of the transition economies is that it is the determination of governments to control inflation that is the key to success. Why should this be so? The market system works by sending signals about the relative scarcity of

goods, services and factors of production. These signals are sent via the price mechanism through changes in relative prices. When inflation exists there is confusion about whether rising prices are signalling something about the relative scarcity of particular goods and services. The result is that the price mechanism no longer allocates resources efficiently. In section 7 you learned that inflation erodes the international competitiveness of an economy. Both of these costs of inflation are likely to adversely affect economic growth. In countries such as Georgia, inflation averaged over 2000 per cent from 1991 to 1998 and consequently recovery from the initial recession has been difficult. This relationship between inflation and growth is very strong, suggesting that the key to a successful transition is very tight, anti-inflationary fiscal and monetary policies.

The ability to attract foreign direct investment (FDI) is a further important condition for successful transition in that it allows the transfer of technology and management techniques as well as capital from more advanced market economies. Japanese FDI into Britain, for example, has brought with it management techniques, such as Just-In-Time (JIT), which have spread widely amongst British businesses, improving efficiency. Volkswagen's involvement with Skoda in the Czech Republic may be thought of as important, not only for the dramatic improvements in technology, efficiency and design which have occurred at Skoda, but also because 80 per cent of Skoda's inputs are sourced locally. This has a multiplier effect on the Czech economy as a whole (see section 8). In Hungary, Ford, Suzuki and Audi have set up their own local component suppliers to source their vehicle production plants. However, the amount of FDI which transition economies have attracted is not significant. Hungary attracted the lion's share ($15 billion) in the period 1989–97, yet this is equivalent to only $1,519 on a per capita basis. Research indicates that there is only a very weak relationship between levels of FDI and success in transition in terms of GDP growth.

So, what other factors may have contributed to the relative success of some transition economies? In section 8 you learned that one of the major determinants of economic growth was improvement in the quality as well as the quantity of the factors of production. In particular, economists have tended to stress the role played by improvements in labour productivity. Productivity data tend to show that economies such as Poland and Slovenia have outperformed other transition economies and this is an important part of their success, with industrial productivity leading the rest of the economy. In Poland, this improvement in labour productivity has taken place alongside falling unemployment, which is a major achievement. In Russia, falling GDP has coincided with constant declines in the productivity of labour as economic theory would suggest. The key question is what has caused this superior productivity performance. FDI may have played a role, but, as we have suggested, the evidence is weak. It would appear that most of the productivity advances have come from small- and medium-sized firms. In economies where such firms were not swallowed up by the command economy and have survived, the record has been good. It would appear, then, that it is as much the legacy of planning as the actual reforms which matters in terms of a successful transition.

Another determinant of economic growth also introduced in section 8 was investment. Rates of investment have been higher in the CEE countries than in the CIS countries. In addition, these economies have also been much more open to international competition and they have probably benefited from their geographical closeness to, and their ability to integrate with, the EU. In preparation for EU membership economies such as Poland have introduced effective competition and monopoly policies, which have been important in improving levels of efficiency.

Explaining the diverse performance of transition economies is therefore very complex. Clearly, the extent of reforms and macroeconomic stabilisation are important but they do not account for all the variations amongst economies. It may be that a much more general explanation of success is needed in terms of the legacy of planning, political stability and the ability to attract aid and investment.

Integration with the EU

In 1993 the European Commission(EC) established three criteria for former command economies to gain full membership of the EU. These so-called Copenhagen criteria were:

People standing in a queue to buy milk at a lower price in central Moscow
Source: Popperfoto Reuters.

- ◆ stability and democracy, with particular protection of the rights of minorities;
- ◆ a fully functioning market economy which would be able to compete with the economies of the EU;
- ◆ the ability to meet the requirements of full membership, including effective competition and monopoly policy, the ability to adopt the rules of the Single European Market and, ultimately, to participate in monetary union.

Meeting these criteria has been a long and difficult task, full of false hopes and disappointment for the applicants. Almost a decade later, in December 2002, eight former command economies (Poland, Hungary, the Czech Republic, Slovenia, Slovakia, Estonia, Latvia and Lithuania) were invited at a summit in Copenhagen to join the European Union in May 2004. Together with Malta and Cyprus this brings the total membership of the EU to 25. Romania and Bulgaria may be invited to join in a second wave, possibly by 2008. Whilst there are substantial benefits to be gained from membership, there are short-term problems that should not be underestimated.

In the long run the countries of both the EU and the eight CEE economies have much to gain from closer integration. As we saw earlier, integration provides new markets for both goods and services and represents an increase in the investment opportunities for firms. The benefits of free trade within the Union are increased, leading to static and dynamic efficiency gains. For example, there will be trade creation and trade diversion effects (see section 12). Since the eight countries currently trade mostly with the EU potential trade creation effects should be maximised and trade diversion effects minimised. The larger market is likely to lead to:

- the ability to benefit from economies of scale;
- enhanced competition, driving down costs and prices;
- more product and process innovation;
- increasing levels of cross-border investment and the transfer of technology.

The result, at least according to economic theory, should be a higher GDP for all countries and an enhanced rate of economic growth.

The enlargement of the EU means a 'New Europe' of 465 million consumers – the biggest single market in the world. 'At the end of the day, there will be no borders, no tariffs, no obstacles to trade and investment, just one single Europe', Franz Fischler, European Commissioner for Agriculture, Rural Development and Fisheries told a conference of the semi-conductor industry in Austria in February 2003. The greater competition and mobility of capital is likely to raise productivity and push down costs. High-technology industries are already heavily involved in accession countries, attracted by low unit labour costs and the addition of 75 million people with increasing real incomes and a growing demand for consumer goods.

For example, the Czech National Bank has reported that the Czech Republic attracted a record $7 billion of foreign direct investment for the first three quarters of 2002. Unlike previous investments, the trend in the Czech Republic is towards high-technology operations by firms such as Honeywell, Matsushita, Logica and Rieter. CzechInvest, the government's agency for attracting foreign direct investment, is reported to be targeting investments in microelectronics, biotechnology, pharmaceuticals, electrical engineering, aerospace and medical technology. The benefits of FDI, through the multiplier process, spill over to local suppliers in these sectors and to the national economy. In addition there will be benefits in terms of quality control, financial and personnel management.

The impact on firms in accession countries will not be universally beneficial. Some will have to restructure themselves to gain competitiveness and this is unlikely to occur without bankruptcies, takeovers and mergers and further rationalisation. Highly labour intensive firms in the manufacturing sector are likely to face the least risk from EU integration, given the low unit labour costs in the accession countries (see table 13.1). For example, Slovakia's unit labour costs are just over 10 per cent of those in Ireland which has been the home of the lion's share of both extra and intra-EU FDI. Of course, low unit labour costs on their own are no guarantee of foreign investment. Countries such as Ireland will continue to benefit from high and growing labour

	Hungary	Czech Republic	Slovakia	Poland	Greece	Belgium	Ireland
GDP per head ($ at PPP)	9,470	14,586	9,060	9,280	18,460	26,946	31,593
GDP (% real change pa)	3.8	3.26	3.29	1.00	4.1	1.01	5.85
Government consumption (% of GDP)	11	19.23	19.97	16.59	15.5	21.56	12.4
Budget balance (% of GDP)	−2.52	−3.14	−4.4	−4.60	0	0.19	1.35
Consumer prices (% change pa; av)	9.16	4.68	7.12	5.50	3.36	2.47	4.88
Public debt (% of GDP)	50.9	22.97	41.8	39.90	101.6	107.72	36.47
Labour costs per hour (US$)	2.01	2.16	1.42	2.80	7.93	20.25	13.31
Recorded unemployment (%)	5.69	8.55	18.62	16.22	10.5	6.59	3.76
Current-account balance/GDP	−2.11	−4.65	−8.58	−4.05	−5.1	4.96	−1.01
Foreign-exchange reserves (m$)	10,727	14,342	4,140	25,648	5,154	11	5

Table 13.1 Statistical profile of selected accession and EU countries, 2001

Source: Economist.com

Self-assessment task

Study the information below and then answer the questions that follow.

Output performance of selected transition economies 1989-99			
	Decline in GDP to lowest level (%)	Year in which GDP was lowest	Annual average growth in GDP since lowest level (%)	Ratio of output in 1999 to output in year before transition began
Albania	39.9	1992	6.6	1.03
Armenia	65.1	1993	5.4	0.56
Azerbaijan	63.1	1995	5.9	0.53
Czech Republic	15.4	1992	1.7	0.95
Estonia	36.5	1994	3.2	0.87
Georgia	76.6	1994	5.8	0.46
Hungary	18.1	1993	3.1	0.99
Poland	13.7	1991	5.1	1.28
Russia	46.5	1998	3.2	0.59
Slovak Republic	24.7	1993	4.9	1.01
Slovenia	20.4	1992	3.8	1.05

Sources: International Monetary Fund, *International Financial Statistics, World Economic Outlook;* IMF staff estimates.

(a) Which country has apparently experienced the fastest transition since 1989? Use the information above to justify your answer.

(b) Use economic analysis to explain why the output performance of the transition economies has varied from 1989–99.

(c) Comment upon the likely consequences for transition economies of the trends in output shown in the above table.

productivity. Firms in the accession countries operating in business and financial services will be at risk from integration with the EU, given the EU's comparative advantage in this sector.

Whilst enlargement brings market opportunities for some EU firms, it also increases competition from low-cost producers as explained above. The EC argues, however, that for existing small firms in the EU this is little different from the competitive pressures experienced as a result of increasing global competition. It has urged existing EU governments to put in place policies that increase the knowledge and skills base of smaller firms, particularly in more labour-intensive industries as a way of preparing for the increased competition from Central and Eastern Europe.

Integration with the EU will without doubt bring economic change in the accession countries. In some, such as Slovakia, large and inefficient enterprises still

dominate the economy. The Economist reports in its Country Briefing on Slovakia that enterprises employing more than 250 employees account for over 50 per cent of the total value added of the economy and consistently record declining profits. Such productive inefficiencies are likely to require workers to switch between industries as free trade and competition within the new, enlarged EU leads to the decline of 'sunset' industries. There could be much structural and technological unemployment as a result of these changes, which may persist in the absence of labour mobility or reform of the labour market. A report on the labour market situation in the eight accession countries by the EC in early 2003 suggested that there was an urgent need for them to increase employment rates, to increase employment in services, to reduce the reliance on agriculture and traditional industrial sectors and to increase skill levels. In the light of the significant and rapid economic restructuring that will follow accession, the EC recommended that the countries set themselves four priorities to:

- increase labour supply and bring back major numbers of the working-age population into the labour market as a precondition for economic and social development;
- increase employment rates which, together with high productivity growth, are a key condition for strong economic growth and for real convergence of incomes;
- ensure that the functioning of the labour market supports the restructuring of the economy, and that the labour market enables people to manage economic change and to move from declining to modern industries;
- increase skill levels against the background of an ageing labour force, of restructuring and of future pressures linked to adjustment to the Single Market, and increase productivity to the levels required to be competitive in an enlarged EU.

Labour market concerns are not just confined to the accession countries. As table 13.1 shows, there is a marked difference between the GDP per capita of the eight CEE economies and the three members of the EU.

For example Slovakia's per capita income is 50 per cent of that in Greece, the EU's poorest country in 2001, and less than 30 per cent of that in Ireland. There is concern that the free movement of labour in the enlarged EU will lead to the migration of CEE workers west. But as the boxed article below suggests, fears of consequent unemployment in the current EU15 of such migration are often rooted in politics and emotion rather than sound economic analysis. Immigration may yield benefits for the EU15, as suggested, and reduce the strains on the EU's regional and structural funds caused by enlargement.

Differences between the accession economies and the EU15 also include stark contrasts in terms of economic structure. Poland, for example, has 27 per cent of its population engaged in agriculture as opposed to an average of 5.3 per cent in the EU15 in 2001. Since the eight CEE economies are much more dependent on agriculture, full membership is likely to significantly increase the financial and economic cost of the EU's Common Agricultural Policy (CAP). In 2001, agricultural expenditure by the EU totalled €40.5 billion, representing 45 per cent of the total EU budget. There are three main features of the CAP:

- price support, through guaranteed minimum

Self-assessment task

Consider the data in table 13.1 and the four bar charts below and then answer the questions that follow.

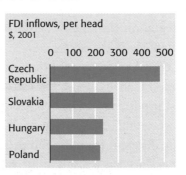

Sources: OECD; UNCTAD.

(a) Use the data in table 13.1 to make an economic comparison between the four accession countries and Greece, the weakest economy in the EU15.

(b) Comment upon the issues that this comparison raises for:
- the monetary policy of the ECB,
- fiscal policy in the accession countries,
- the EU's regional development strategy.

(c) Comment upon the relationship between labour costs, unemployment and FDI inflows in the four accession countries.

prices, intervention purchases and storage and subsidies to exporters totalling €10.6 billion (12 per cent of the total EU budget);

◆ direct payments to farmers in the form of subsidies per hectare or per animal, totalling €25.6 billion (30 per cent of the total EU budget); and

◆ rural development programmes designed to help diversify the rural economy, totalling €4.2 billion.

Extending the CAP to cover agriculture in the eight accession countries would be prohibitively expensive, so the EC has set limits on additional expenditure as a result of enlargement. In this sense, the eight accession countries will *not* receive the benefits of membership which existing members receive. Naturally, this has caused resentment in countries such as Poland (see box). Nevertheless, additional expenditure is planned to rise from €1.9 billion in 2004 to €4.2 billion by 2006. In addition, there will be increases in the cost of EU structural and cohesion funds totalling €6 billion in 2004 rising to €8.8 billion by 2006. The combined financial cost of enlargement of the EU to be borne by the EU budget is €9.9 billion in 2004 rising to €14.9 billion by 2006. These budgetary costs of enlargement need to be off-set against the economic benefits of enlargement. There is though a clear and substantial net cost to the EU in the short run.

The enlargement of the EU raises important economic and political issues. Increased market size will

The Economics of Immigration

Europe probably needs more immigration rather than less, contrary to popular opinion. Indeed the UK government's high growth forecasts are based on the assumption that the high growth of immigration will continue. Immigration causes a rightward shift of the AS curve raising the productive capacity of an economy and is, therefore, not something recipient countries should be unduly worried about from an economic perspective. Immigration can also help to compensate for demographic trends in an economy such as the growing old age dependency ratio. It can also help relieve skills shortages in the labour market, as exemplified by the proposed German 'green card' system to admit up to 20,000 computer experts.

'There are, however, losers in these countries. The increase in the supply of labour presses down on the wages of competing workers, at least in the first instance. Later, as the stock of capital grows in response, that effect may be partially reversed' (*Economist,* 10 May 2001).

As the wages of the unskilled in Europe continue to fall (in both absolute and relative terms), pressure mounts to restrict the immigration of unskilled workers and to give preference in immigration policy to skilled workers. But the result of such a policy (offical or unofficial) is that there is an increase in illegal immigration (the economic incentives

for migrants are still there despite the trend in unskilled wages). The result, perversely, may be that this illegal supply of low-skilled labour pushes wage rates down further at the bottom of the income distribution – restricting immigration by labour skills may bring more harm than good.

Not that this economic analysis of immigration cuts much sway with the politicians. The Germans have pushed for a seven-year transition period for the free movement of labour as the EU expands to Central and Eastern Europe.

French railways employees arrest illegal immigrants at a freight terminal in Frethun, near the entrance of the channel tunnel October 30, 2001
Source: Popperfoto.

clearly enhance the benefits of integration. Few would dispute this. Enlargement is not without its critics (see the boxed article by economist Patrick Minford) who raises the question as to whether it is better to deepen integration amongst existing members rather than to widen it by geographical enlargement. What is clear is that deepening integration is far more difficult in an enlarged EU. The outcome may well be a two-tier future structure, with those firmly committed and economically equipped for greater integration being in the first tier as is currently the case with the eurozone members. Just where this might leave the UK is a matter which will affect all UK citizens and have a profound effect upon their economic well-being in the first decades of the twenty-first century.

Small Polish farmers still alarmed

'Agriculture stands at the centre of negotiations, yet neither the Polish government nor Brussels have come up with any sort of constructive plan for the future of the Polish countryside', says the International Coalition to Protect the Polish Countryside (ICPPC). 'On the contrary, they seem intent on destroying the exceptional biodiversity and cultural wealth of its one and a half million small family farms, through a programme of "restructuring" agriculture to fit the standard, large-scale, monotonous, monocultural model which has already devastated farmland and farming communities across the continent of Europe. Neither has anything yet emerged out of the EU/CAP package that offers realistic support for Poland's struggling rural economy', says the coalition.

ICPPC says it is 'increasingly evident' that the 'health of the Polish countryside is inseparable from the future of its small family farms'. Sixty-eight per cent of the 2.1 million farms in Poland are small family farms (with less than 8 hectares of land), 'but most of these farmers are unaware of the dangers now facing them' – including, says ICPPC, 'the health and environmental consequences of using toxic chemicals and GMO seeds which are now being heavily promoted in Poland, and the ever-more oppressive food and hygiene regulations pouring out of Brussels'.

'How and why we need to protect the small family farms in Poland and how their survival can set a precedent for European small farms' is the theme of the special meeting being organised by ICPPC in London on 7 February. It is urging that the best way for these farms to survive is by 'maintaining their traditional roots, and moving towards organic agriculture, greater farmer to farmer and consumer co-operation, local processing, ecotourism and other ecological activities'. This will help keep people living in the countryside and prevent waves of unemployment and migration to 'already overcrowded' cities.

Source: *Enlargement Weekly*, Enlargement Directorate General of the European Commission, 28 January 2003.

Source: Jan Baks/Alamy.

Wherever is Europe going when the borders move east?

In Copenhagen recently, the European Union Council of Ministers agreed to admit virtually all of eastern Europe into the union over the next decade or so, making them a delightful New Year present.

It was a bold, historic move; I, for one, am delighted that my students from those parts will be able to stay on and get jobs without any bureaucratic hassle. The politics of establishing close relations, together with free movement of people, capital and goods within the widest possible borders, is surely of immense benefit.

Unfortunately the economics of the EU are in disarray. The EU's pioneering of an ever-wider 'economic space' has come with a deepening of regulation and of protection that is increasingly troublesome. This trouble is visible in the stalling of growth at the heart of Europe – in the big three, Germany, Italy and France.

The reason for this lies in their inability to allow their economies to adjust to the modern US-style structure based on services and high tech; instead, urged on by powerful trade unions, they protect manufacturing (maintaining an 'industrial museum', in the words of a friend), and penalise vital small businesses with worker rights, intrusive taxation and excessive regulation. Their unemployment rates are now rising through the symbolic 10 per cent mark, having dropped below it until about a year ago – and this 10 per cent figure conceals a far worse waste of human resources if we compare them, say, on the proportion of their population actually employed.

Such unemployment paralyses other policies. It is now impossible to reform the labour market in these countries (e.g. by removing job protection) because this usually raises unemployment in the short term. Hence the Luxembourg Process, aimed at creating 'labour market flexibility', is hopelessly bogged down.

In fact, Germany is even going backwards, Chancellor Schröder having introduced yet more powers for unions to prevent change in the run-up to the last election.

Matters do not end there. France, faced with potential social unrest, has sabotaged the planned reform of the Common Agricultural Policy. This was intended to reduce the huge cost of farm support to facilitate the entry of eastern European economies. Now, how will the sums add up and who will pay? Unfortunately the main payer will be us. Already the CAP costs us about 1.5 per cent of our GDP (some £15 billion a year), which we cheerfully hand over to French and Dutch peasants, or more accurately to their rich landowners.

The litany of protection goes on. Manufactured goods prices in the EU are kept up by the cleverly concealed 'anti-dumping' policing of imports from the Far East. To avoid anti-dumping duty, importers raise their prices in the EU well above world levels – effectively a CAP for manufacturers.

Again, as new entrants from Eastern Europe come inside the EU's protective customs union, their manufacturers too will receive this protected price. Who will pay the bill? You guessed. We will be the main contributors. It probably costs us about 0.5 per cent of our GDP (£5 billion a year) to pay the inflated prices of our large net manufactured imports. Because the big three of the EU do not like the idea of free competition in the labour market from a mass of Poles, Hungarians and Czechs with low wages and free access to the EU market, the price of entry is increasing regulation of their markets. The Social Dimension of the EU is an agenda to reduce labour market competition by embedding expensive workers' rights into all EU member countries' laws.

With our relatively unregulated markets, this is dangerous for us; but the regulation of the new entrants will also damage us, as they have so far been a source of competition through their free trade agreements with the EU.

If the economics of the EU are so bad, why can't we jettison them and keep the politics? That really has been the British idea all along. That was why Margaret Thatcher was so keen to sign the Single Market Act; she and her advisers, like Lord Young at the DTI, thought it would lead to economic liberalisation. But the Commission president, Jacques Delors, made sure it did no such thing but rather played to the French protectionist agenda. He did so partly by introducing the Social Dimension, and partly by ensuring the new single market regulations would by and large harmonise on the most expensive, permitting no competition between alternative regulative regimes.

The politics of being involved with the EU appeals to our Foreign Office as a modern extension of the old 'balance of power' game we historically pursued in Continental politics. But the economic cost is proving prohibitive – 2 per cent of GDP in payments up front (one third of the cost of our National Health Service) and much more damage from regulative interference mandated from Brussels. It will get worse: enlargement has added a new cost without any check to the old. EU politicians have resolved that as they cannot reform they should boldly expand, to distract attention from the current economic failure. It may well be time to think about ways in which we could achieve our political objectives without being taken endlessly to the cleaners. Why not, for a start, follow De Gaulle's example and maintain an 'empty chair' until CAP reform is reinstated?

If the French can ruthlessly protect their economic interests, why can't we?

Source: Patrick Minford, *Telegraph*, 30 December 2002.

Glossary

Key words have been identified **when they first occur** in each section of the text.

These key words consist of economic terms and concepts which students should know and which are likely to be used in OCR examination questions and stimulus material at AS and also at the A2 level. It is good practice for students to incorporate these terms, where appropriate, in examination answers.

This list does not include:

◆ institutions (for example, Bank of England, Competition Commission),

◆ organisations (for example, European Union, OECD),

◆ other specific examples used in the text (for example, Retail Prices Index, Labour Force Survey),

as some of these have changed over time and will change in the future.

It should also be emphasised that this glossary has been produced for guidance only and that some of the terms, particularly those introduced in the sections of units 2 and 3, may be subject to alternative definitions.

Section 1

capital consumption   also known as depreciation, this is the way in which capital is used up and loses value during the production process.

capital goods   man-made aids to production, such as industrial machinery and factories; one of the factors of production.

choice   a consequence of the economic problem, this is the process whereby consumers, producers and governments have to select from various possibilities which are available.

consumption   the process by which goods and services are used to satisfy wants.

developing economy   a country with low living standards compared with the advanced industrial economies of the world.

division of labour   the way in which the production

process can be broken down into a series of tasks; the outcome is to increase output when compared with a situation where individuals undertake all tasks.

economic growth   an increase in the productive potential of the economy in real terms and that can be represented by an outward shift of the production possibility curve.

economic problem   the fundamental underpinning of Economics whereby resources are scarce/limited in relation to unlimited wants.

enterprise   the willingness to take risks in order to achieve business success; the management or responsibility for this process is in the hands of an entrepreneur; one of the factors of production.

factor endowment   the underpinning quantity and quality of factors of production available in an economy.

factor mobility   the extent or otherwise that factors of production can be reorganised to produce different goods and services.

investment   the creation of capital goods in the process of production or adding to the stock of real productive assets in an economy.

labour   the human resources available in an economy; one of the factors of production.

land   the natural resources available in an economy; one of the factors of production.

medium of exchange   a function of money that facilitates the process of exchange between individuals, avoiding the need for barter.

money   anything that enables exchange to take place whilst retaining its value, for example coins, notes or physical assets such as gold.

opportunity cost   the amount or cost of any other good or service that could have been obtained instead of any particular good or service; often expressed in terms of the 'next best' alternative.

production   the process of making goods and services.

production frontier   it shows what an economy is capable of producing; it is normally shown in the context of the physical amounts of two particular goods.

production possibility curve   the maximum level of output an economy can achieve when using its existing resources; usually shows the maximum output of one good, given the output of another good.

production transformation curve   as production possibility curve.

resources   anything that contributes or can contribute to production.

reallocation of resources   the process by which resources are transferred from one activity to another.

risk   the uncertainty that entrepreneurs face in the production process.

scale of preference   the ordering of wants in priority order.

scarcity   central to the economic problem whereby there are limited resources and unlimited wants, necessitating choices to be made.

specialisation   the process by which some goods and services are produced rather than others.

wants   anything that anyone might wish to acquire.

Section 2

ceteris paribus   literally means 'other things being equal', it is used as an assumption when looking at how demand or supply changes with a change in the price of a good or service.

complements   pairs of goods for which a rise in the price of one decreases demand for the other.

consumer surplus   the difference between the value a consumer places on all units consumed and the payments needed to be made to actually purchase that commodity; it is represented by the area under the demand curve and above the price line.

cross elasticity of demand   a numerical measure of the responsiveness of demand for one product following a change in price of a related product; this measure is positive in the case of substitutes and negative for complements.

demand   the quantity of a good or service that purchasers want to buy at various prices.

demand curve   the relationship between the demand for a good or service and its price.

demand schedule   the numerical data which are needed to draw the demand curve for a good or service.

derived demand   a situation whereby the demand for something, for example labour, is dependent on the demand for another final good or service.

disequilibrium   a market situation where demand and supply are not equal.

effective demand   demand that is backed or supported by purchasing power.

elasticity   the responsiveness of demand/supply to a change in another influencing variable.

equilibrium   a situation where under present circumstances there is no tendency for change.

income elasticity of demand   a numerical measure of the responsiveness of demand following a change in income.

inferior goods   goods that have a negative income elasticity of demand, that is, are demanded less as income rises.

labour market   a market where workers and employers are brought together.

market   whenever buyers and sellers get together for the purpose of trade or exchange.

market demand   the total demand for a good or service.

money market   a market where the rate of interest is determined where the demand and supply of money are equated.

normal goods   goods that have a positive income elasticity of demand, that is, are demanded more as income rises.

notional demand   demand not necessarily backed by purchasing power.

perfectly elastic   where price elasticity of demand or supply is infinity, that is, if price rises above a particular price, nothing will be demanded or supplied.

Glossary

perfectly inelastic   where price elasticity of demand or supply is zero, that is, demand or supply is not at all responsive to a change in price.

price elasticity of demand   a numerical measure of the responsiveness of demand to a change in the price of a particular product.

price elasticity of supply   a numerical measure of the responsiveness of supply to a change in the price of a particular product.

producer surplus   the additional revenue gained by a producer over that represented in the area under the supply curve of a good or service.

rate of interest   the payment that has to be made in order to obtain money or the reward for parting with the money.

sub-market   a particular part or segment of a market.

substitutes   pairs of goods for which a rise in the price of one increases the demand for the other.

supply   the quantity of a good or service that producers are willing to sell at various prices.

supply curve   the relationship between the supply of a good or service in relation to its price.

supply schedule   the numerical data which are needed to draw the supply curve for a good or service.

unitary elasticity   where price elasticity of demand or supply is 1, that is, demand or supply responds exactly proportional to a change in price.

Section 3

abnormal profit   profits earned over normal profits; likely to attract other new firms into that industry; also known as supernormal profit, particularly in perfectly competitive markets.

average fixed costs   total fixed costs of production divided by the quantity produced; decreases as output increases.

average revenue   total revenue divided by the quantity that is sold.

average total costs   total costs (fixed costs and variable costs) divided by the quantity produced.

average variable costs   total variable costs of production divided by the quantity produced; decreases with output but only up to a certain point.

barriers to entry   anything that stops new firms entering a particular market; they tend to be more prevalent as the degree of competition in markets decreases.

collusion   informal action by firm's designed to refrain from competition in their own markets.

concentration ratio   a measure of the extent to which a market is in the hands of a given or particular number of firms.

contestable market   where there are few barriers to entry and where there are potential entrants waiting to join the market if say abnormal profits are being earned.

diminishing returns   as the variable factors used by a firm increase, there will come a point where the returns to the variable units begin to fall.

diseconomies of scale   when the output of the firm increases too rapidly, long-run unit costs start to rise.

economies of scale   the benefits in terms of falling long-run average costs as output expands.

firm   general term used in Economics to denote the basic unit of production and decision making.

fixed costs   costs that are independent of output in the short run.

increasing returns   a situation where a firm's output is rising proportionally faster than its inputs into the production process.

long run   the time period when the firm can alter all of its factor inputs; all factors of production are, therefore, variable in the long run.

managerial objectives   the explanation of the objectives of firms in terms of the specific motivations of their managers; in particular, this can apply where the objective is other than profit maximisation.

marginal cost   the addition to total cost when one more unit of output is produced.

marginal revenue the addition to total revenue when one more unit of output is sold.

monopolistic competition a market structure with a large number of competing sellers and few barriers to entry.

monopoly a market situation with one seller protected by barriers to entry.

non-price competition any methods by which firms compete, other than through price cutting; typical examples are advertising, quality of product and customer service.

normal profit included in the costs of production of a firm and just sufficient to keep that firm in operation in that industry.

oligopoly a market structure with only a few firms; each firm has a sufficiently large share of the market to consider the reaction of others to any price changes it may make.

optimum output the most efficient level of output represented at the minimum point of the average cost curve.

perfect competition a benchmark used by economists to compare real-world market structures in which there are a large number of buyers and sellers each acting as price-takers.

price-taker where a firm is able to sell whatever it produces at the ruling price and where its actions will not influence market prices.

private costs costs which are directly incurred by the owners of the firm; also used for costs incurred by an individual carrying out a particular activity.

profit the difference between revenue and costs in the production process.

profit maximisation the usual objective of the firm in economic theory; it occurs at the output where marginal revenue in all market structures.

sales maximisation an alternative objective of the firm where output is maximised.

sales revenue maximisation a situation where a firm is seeking to maximise its revenue from the production process.

satisficing where the firm's objective is to keep various groups, such as shareholders, happy by making sufficient profits; it may also be used as a means of not attracting attention to the firm's business activities.

semi-fixed costs costs to the firm which possess the characteristics of both fixed and variable costs; an example could be the heating costs of a hotel once it has decided to open its premises for business.

total revenue the total receipts of a firm from its sales.

variable costs costs which are directly related to the level of output of a firm.

Section 4

allocative efficiency this exists where the selling price of a product is equal to its marginal cost of production.

economic efficiency where an economy is using scarce resources in the most effective way in order to meet the highest level of wants.

Pareto optimality when it is not possible to make one person better off without making someone else worse off.

productive efficiency where production is at the lowest point on the lowest average cost curve.

Section 5

de-merit goods any good that has negative externalities associated with it; typical examples are passive smoking and drinking excessive alcohol.

equity fairness (say) in the distribution of income or wealth.

external benefit a situation where the social benefits exceed the private benefits; this benefit accrues to a third party.

external cost a situation where the social costs exceed the private costs; this cost is imposed on a third party.

externality this arises if a third party is affected by the decisions or actions of others.

fairness see equity.

free rider the advantage that some consumers receive from the purchase of a commodity by other consumers; it has particular application in the context of public goods.

geographical mobility the way in which workers are able to move easily and quickly in order to find employment.

information failure used in the context of merit goods, this refers to a situation where consumers do not have the relevant information or right information with which to make choices.

market failure any situation where a free market fails to produce the best use of scarce resources.

merit goods a good, such as health care or education, that has positive externalities associated with it.

negative externality a situation that occurs when an external cost exists.

non-excludable a characteristic of public goods whereby it is impossible to stop all from benefiting from the consumption of that good.

non-rival a characteristic of public goods whereby, as more people consume that good, the benefit to those already consuming it is not diminished.

occupational mobility the way in which workers are able to move quickly and easily from one type of job or occupation to another.

paternalism a situation where society knows best and has some right to make a value judgement.

positive externality a situation that occurs when an external benefit exists.

private benefits the benefits which accrue to an individual consumer or firm.

public good a good which possesses the characteristics of non-excludability and non-rivalry; they can be provided by the private sector as well as by the public sector – typical examples are a street light and national defence.

quasi-public goods goods, such as roads, that are public in nature but that do not fully possess the essential characteristics of public goods.

social benefits the total benefits arising from a particular action.

social costs the total costs associated with a particular action.

value judgement an opinion about the relative merits of a particular situation or set of circumstances that cannot be effectively investigated.

wealth the accumulated stock of assets.

x-inefficiency a situation where firms do not have to produce goods at the lowest possible cost.

Section 6

controls statutory forms of government intervention.

cost–benefit analysis a technique for assessing the desirability of a particular project, taking into account all of the respective costs and benefits.

financial intervention the use of taxes and subsidies by the government to influence market outcomes.

government failure problems of resource allocation that occur as a consequence of government intervention in markets, for example food shortages in a centrally planned economy.

income transfer a deliberate means of redistributing income by government, for example social security benefits.

in-kind transfer a free service provided by government but generally funded from tax revenue.

mixed goods a good or situation where negative externalities and information failure can be recognised.

nationalised industry a rather dated term for an activity wholly operated by the public sector.

net present value the outcome of discounting a stream of costs and benefits to a common base date. A positive value indicates that there are valid reasons for a project to go ahead.

privatisation the sale of a state owned or operated activity to the private sector.

progressive tax any tax where the revenue collected

rises more than proportionally to income, for example income tax.

regressive tax any tax where the ratio of tax paid in relation to income falls as income rises, for example poll tax, VAT.

regulation general term used to describe a wide range of measures used by governments to control a market.

shadow price a price imputed in situations where no market price is available, for example value of time.

social justice justification on the part of government for the redistribution of income or wealth.

social security benefit any handout which transfers income to low-income groups or to other disadvantaged groups.

spillover effects outcomes from market situations where there are external benefits or costs; the market mechanism is unable to take these into account.

subsidy a payment made by government to consumers or producers that reduces the market price of a good or service.

Section 7

aggregate demand the total spending on goods and services produced in an economy.

anticipated inflation a situation where the rate of inflation recorded is broadly in line with that which has been expected or forecast.

balance of payments a record or overall statement of a country's economic transactions with the rest of the world, usually over a year.

capital account part of the balance of payments showing transfers of capital between a country and the rest of the world.

circular flow of income a simple model of the process by which income flows around an economy.

cost-push inflation a situation where inflation is caused by increased costs of production.

current account the most important part of the balance of payment; it is a record of the trade in goods and services plus investment income and current transfers.

demand-plus inflation a situation where inflation is caused by an increase in total demand.

expenditure method a method of calculating the GDP of an economy by estimating the total value of what is spent in a year.

exports any goods or services sold to another country.

financial transactions an important part of the balance of payments relating to capital flows entering or leaving the economy.

fiscal drag a situation where, due to inflation, the proportion of income collected in taxes rises, and where tax thresholds remain unchanged.

fixed exchange rate where the price of one currency in terms of another is pre-determined.

floating exchange rate where the price of one currency in terms of another is determined by market forces.

government spending spending by central and local government on goods or the provision of services.

Gross Domestic Product a measure of total output produced in an economy by activities located in that country.

Gross National Product a measure of total output produced that takes into account the net income of residents from economic activities carried out abroad as well as at home.

hidden economy transactions of goods and services that are not declared and not included in GDP.

hyperinflation a very high rate of inflation, the outcome of which is that people lose confidence in money.

imports any good or service bought from another country.

income method a method of calculating the GDP of an economy by estimating the total incomes earned by the various factors of production.

inflation a persistent increase in the level of prices in an economy.

international competitiveness a measure of the relative ranking of an economy compared with the rest of the world.

living standard the amount of goods and services enjoyed by residents in an economy; often measured in terms of real GDP per head.

managed exchange rate where the price of one currency in terms of another moves within narrow pre-determined bands.

net errors and omissions formally known as the balancing item, this is a measure of any discrepancies in the balance of payments of an economy.

nominal GDP GDP measured in terms of current prices in a given year.

non-marketed goods and services items not included in GDP due to no financial transaction taking place.

output the amount which is produced by an industry or service in an economy.

output gap the shortfall between actual and potential output in an economy.

output method a method of calculating the GDP of any economy by estimating the total value of what is produced in a year.

potential growth an increase in the productive capacity in an economy; can be represented by an outward shift of the production possibility curve.

productivity a measure of the output produced per unit of a factor of production.

ratchet effect the tendency for import prices to rise as a consequence of a fall in the exchange rate, in turn prompting wage rises.

read GDP GDP measured in terms of the actual goods and services produced, taking into account any price fluctuations

recession where real GDP growth is negative or significantly less than in the previous year.

shoe leather costs of inflation the costs of moving money from one asset to another in search of the highest rate of interest at a time when the rate of inflation is rising.

stop–go policy a short-term tendency for the management of aggregate demand to produce periods of contraction and expansion in the economy.

sustainable economic growth a growth strategy whereby future needs are not compromised by current growth policies.

transfer payments any payment made from taxpayers to non-taxpayers, for example welfare payments.

unanticipated inflation a situation where the rate of inflation exceeds that which had been expected or forecasted.

unemployment a broad term to describe those willing and able to work but who are unable to obtain a job.

value added the difference between the final value of sales and the cost of inputs.

Section 8

aggregate supply the total output of an economy.

consumer spending the amount spent by individuals on goods and services.

disposable income personal income which is available to spend, usually total income less direct tax and social security contributions.

expectations what people expect to happen, for example outcome of external factors which can affect business well-being.

first-round effect the first stage of the multiplier process.

fiscal policies the use of taxation and government spending to influence the economy.

hot money money which is liable to rapid transfer from one country to another.

injection an autonomous addition to the circular flow of income.

investment expenditure the process of adding to the stock of productive assets in an economy by private and public sectors.

leakages an autonomous withdrawal from the circular flow of income.

marginal propensity to consume the proportion of any increase in income which is spent on consumption.

monetary policies   the use of interest rates or controls on the money supply to influence the economy.

multiplier effect   the process by which any change in spending produces a more extensive effect upon total economic activity.

net expenditure on exports and imports   total expenditure on exports less total expenditure on imports.

savings   the difference between income and consumption.

supply-side policies   any policy that affects the total output of an economy.

Section 9

broad money   money held in banks and building societies but which is not immediately accessible.

crowding out   where an increase in one form of spending leads to a fall in some other form of spending, for example an increase in aggregate demand through lower taxes could reduce expenditure on investment and exports due to an interest rate rise and a higher exchange rate.

deregulation   an aspect of privatisation whereby barriers to entry into a particular market are removed.

exchange rate   the rate at which one international currency is exchanged for another.

government bond   a security issued at a face value and that pays a fixed annual rate of interest.

money supply   the total amount of money in an economy.

narrow money   notes, coins and balance available for normal transactions.

unemployment trap   where individuals actually receive more in benefits than when they are actually in a job.

Section 10

deindustrialisation   a feature of many industrialised economies over the last 30 years or so whereby employment in the industrial sector is declining in importance relative to that in the service sector.

dumping   selling goods in an overseas market at below the cost of production.

exchange control   setting a legal limit on foreign exchange transactions.

expenditure-dampening policies   domestic policies that reduce aggregate demand in order to reduce expenditure on imports.

expenditure-switching policies   policies that seek to switch expenditure from imported to domestically produced goods.

free trade   a situation where international trade takes place unimpeded by any restrictions, that is, market forces operate to provide the best allocation of resources.

import penetration ratio   the proportion of the domestic sales of a product that is met by imports of that product.

infant industry   a newly established industry that is unable to compete in the market.

international trade   the buying and selling of goods and services across national frontiers.

mercantilism   the view that economies should aim to be self-sufficient and that there should be a balance of payments surplus for international transactions.

protection   any measures or devices that protect an economy or its industries from foreign competition.

quota   a physical restriction on imports into an economy.

self-sufficiency   a situation whereby all needs in an economy can be met or produced from within.

tariff   a tax on imported goods.

Answers to selected self-assessment tasks

Below are some suggested answers to a few of the self-assessment tasks contained in the book. These answers are for guidance – you should appreciate that in some cases other answers are possible. Please ask your teacher for guidance.

Section 1
Choices facing an economy (p.27)

If point p was chosen, then gross investment is less than capital consumption. Net investment is therefore negative. The capital stock in this economy will decline and the production possibilities will diminish. The PPC will therefore shift inwards. Although the present standard of living is high, the future standard of living will be less.

If point q was chosen, gross investment would equal capital consumption. Net investment is therefore zero. The capital stock and production possibilities are unchanged. The PPC maintains its current position. The future standard of living will remain at its present level.

If point r is chosen, gross investment would exceed capital consumption. Net investment is therefore positive and production possibilities will increase in the future. The PPC will shift outwards from the origin. This choice has reduced the standard of living at present as fewer consumer goods have been produced; the benefits will be seen in the future as future generations enjoy a higher standard of living with the increased capital stock accumulated in the present time period.

All the above assumes no other factors affect the position of the PPC.

Section 2
The demand curve (p.31)

1 5,500 PCs
2 £1,930
3 'Ceteris paribus', that is, all other factors, such as income, the price of related products and our attitudes towards PCs, remain the same.

The supply curve (p.36)

1 2,500 PCs
2 £860
3 'Ceteris paribus', that is, any other supply-influencing factors, such as the costs associated with supplying the product, the size, structure and nature of the industry or government policy, remain unchanged.
4 Advantages – a very simple representation
Disadvantages – not always easy to read off accurately

Price elasticity of demand (p.45)

1 Branded products in general, such as Coca Cola, are likely to have a relatively low or inelastic price elasticity of demand. Producers try to build up a brand image in order to protect the status of their products. To some though Coca Cola and Pepsi Cola may be seen as substitutes and therefore an increase in the price of one may cause consumers to switch to the other. The broader group of products will have a more elastic price elasticity of demand (soft drinks). Tobacco and fuel though have no close substitutes and are therefore likely to have an inelastic price elasticity of demand.
2 All PED estimates are negative, that is, an increase in price will lead to a fall in demand or vice versa. Mail order ties have the most elastic demand, whilst ties sold from fashion stores have a low inelastic price elasticity of demand. For independent retailers, any reduction in prices is met with an equal increase in demand or vice versa.

Section 3
Fish and Chips Case Study (pp. 68-69)

1 Low overheads is an alternative term for low fixed costs (for example, low property rental, low capital costs)
2 Price rises will not make a fish and chip shop owner better off because it is implied that there is a high price elasticity of demand for the product. A shop's

rivals may not immediately follow suit, compounding the loss of revenue.

3 In a monopoly, the price elasticity of demand would be much lower – the firm could increase prices in order to raise total revenue.

4 Local advertising could shift the demand curve to the right; as the article indicates, though, improving product quality is the most likely way of increasing revenue.

5 Barriers to entry are low because of:
   ◆ low set up costs,
   ◆ low overheads,
   ◆ no particular training required,
   ◆ no special license required.

   although a food hygiene certificate is now required for all staff handling uncooked food.

6 Marginal cost and marginal revenue may not be measurable; cost-plus pricing is therefore used. The owner may have alternative objectives, for example, satisficing as a consequence of limiting the number of openings of his business.

Section 5
Challenges facing the NHS (pp. 93–94)

(a) (i) A product that is better for people than they realise. Positive externalities are associated with its consumption.

  (ii) Health care provides greater benefits than people realise. A good instance is the case of a vaccination – recipients tend to under value its benefit to themselves and the community.

(b) (i) Many people would not be able to afford the treatment if it had to be purchased through the market, for example people on low incomes or those with chronic illnesses where the cost of treatment would be very expensive.

  (ii) People living in different parts of the country have access to different levels and qualities of health care as provided by the NHS.

(c) (i) Figure 1 shows that
   ◆ there was substantial year-by-year variation in the percentage real change,
   ◆ total spending consistently increased,
   ◆ real change was more pronounced at the end of the period.

  (ii) Market failures mean that state provision is

justified on the grounds of:
   ◆ distribution of income,
   ◆ health care would most likely be underprovided without government intervention,
   ◆ problems of administering a charging system,
   ◆ hospitals could abuse their monopoly power if charging.

(d) (i) Very little overall change over the period but with a peak around 1998.

  (ii) Resources for health care are limited. At a zero price the demand for health care is very high/unlimited. Not all patient demands can realistically be met. Decisions must therefore be taken as to what care can be provided free and what cannot be provided free of charge.

Section 6
Method of government intervention (p.101)

(a) Regulation: the government has used legislation to limit pollution from vehicles. In this case the government regulates the quantity of pollution produced by a vehicle's exhaust emissions. Regulation is used to correct for a market failure owing to negative externalities.

(b) Regulation: the government has used legislation to fix prices. In this case the government fixes the minimum price of labour or the wage rate. Minimum wage rates may be used to redistribute income or to overcome market failure caused by uneven power in the labour market (employers have more power than low-paid workers).

(c) Financial intervention: higher tax rates on petrol are used to discourage consumption of leaded petrol. In this case the government is keen to stop the production of leaded petrol which causes more pollution than unleaded petrol. Thus this type of financial intervention is used to reduce negative externalities.

(d) Financial intervention: free eye tests are the same as a total subsidy. They are used to encourage pensioners to have their eyes tested on a regular basis. This may be to correct a market failure: pensioners are unable to value the importance of frequent eye tests or they may be free for equity reasons.

(e) Regulation: the government uses legislation to impose a minimum standard of driving on the community. This is intended to ensure that all drivers show a minimum competence to drive a vehicle. It corrects for two potential market failures: external costs and imperfect information.

(f) Regulation: legislation is imposed to restrict the purchase of lottery tickets by age. Some people argue that young people are unable to correctly value the costs and benefits of addictive products, such as gambling, and thus need protecting against them. Thus the government is protecting young people against market failure due to imperfect information.

(g) Income transfers: job seekers' allowance is a form of transfer of income from tax payers to those seeking work. One reason for this intervention is to protect against loss of income due to unemployment. However, if the individual has large amounts of savings then it is argued that they do not require as much protection against loss of earnings as they have a source of income on which they can draw.

(h) State production: in this case the state is producing education by providing both the building and the staff to run the schools. Alternatively the government could have used financial intervention by providing the finance for the schools to be built privately and staffed by a private education 'company'. The reasons for intervention of this type in education are varied and will include market failure owing to external benefits from education not being valued by private markets. Market failure might also result from imperfect information as both parents and students are unable to correctly value the private costs and benefits of education. Finally government may intervene to produce education for reasons of fairness or equity, measuring that all children have an equal and fair access to education regardless of their parents' income.

Section 7
International comparisons of GDP (p.127)

(a) GDP is measured in terms of prices in a given base year It is calculated to show actual changes in the quantity of goods and services produced. Can be referred to as real GDP at it is adjusted for inflation.

(b) Germany (30.5 per cent)

(c) UK (15.6 per cent)

(d) A wider range of data including the inflation rate, the trade balance in goods and services, the level and type of investment, the exchange rate and research and development factors. A comparative analysis between the UK and its main trading partners, though, should be handled carefully, as differences in the compilation of statistics between countries might result in the wrong conclusions being drawn.

Section 8
Aggregate demand (pp. 144–145)

1 Various possibilities including:
- the relative decrease in government expenditure over the period;
- no change in the percentage from consumers expenditure from 1990 to 1997;
- an increase in the percentage derived from international trade, particularly imports;
- an increase in the percentage of investment over 1980 to 1990.

2 Again, various explanations of the above could include:
- the impact of privatisation;
- as consumers get richer their propensity to consume often falls;
- a consequence of the close integration of the UK with its EU partners, particularly through the realisation of the Single European Market;
- a period of lower interest rates.

3 For example, the government could:
- increase taxation;
- reduce its own spending;
- increase interest rates;
- cut back on government spending.

Problems include:
- inflationary effects of increasing indirect taxes;
- not always easy to cut back on government spending (central and local), usually unpopular with electors;
- problem of a 'time lag' due to the complex workings of the economy.

Section 9
Effects of policy changes on AD and AS (p.154)

(a) AD will decrease. In the short run consumers have less disposable income; in the long run workers may react by working harder or by choosing to work less and exist on social benefits. AS can move either way or remain stable.

(b) As (a), except that in the long run pensioners may receive higher pensions, which will then boost AD.

(c) Reduces real incomes and hence AD. May in long run act as a disincentive to work, so reducing AS.

(d) AD gets a direct boost; AS should expand slowly in the long run.

(e) Opposite to (a) above. AD increases in the short run but in the long run AS might decrease as some workers decide to leave the labour force and live off state benefits.

(f) Investment will fall, so in the short run AD decreases. In the long run AS could shift to the left.

Index